A VANQUISHED HOPE
The Movement for Church Renewal
in Russia, 1905-1906

<u>Book report</u>

1.) short discus. of author & his purpose

2.) 9-5 # scope of the book

3.) 2 or 3 major themes

4.) reaction

A VANQUISHED HOPE
The Movement for Church Renewal in Russia, 1905-1906

BY

JAMES W. CUNNINGHAM

ST. VLADIMIR'S SEMINARY PRESS
CRESTWOOD, NEW YORK
1981

Library of Congress Cataloging in Publication Data

Cunningham, James W.
    A vanquished hope, the movement for church renewal in
Russia, 1905-1906.
    Bibliography: p.
    Includes index.
    1. Russkaia pravoslavnaia tserkov'—History—20th century.
2. Church renewal—Russkaia pravoslavnaia tserkov'. 3. Soviet
Union—Church history. I. Title.
BX491.C78   281.9'47   81-9077
ISBN 0-913836-70-2   AACR2

© Copyright 1981

by

ST. VLADIMIR'S SEMINARY PRESS

ISBN 0-913836-70-2

PRINTED IN THE UNITED STATES OF AMERICA
BY
ATHENS PRINTING COMPANY
NEW YORK, N.Y.

To Godfrey Diekmann, O.S.B.,
Monk, Teacher, Scholar

Table of Contents

Preface

One of the common assumptions made by historians of pre-Bolshevik Russia is that the Russian Orthodox church was a moribund relic of the cultural past, content to serve as a quaint but sometimes oppressive instrument of the tsarist government. This traditional view of the church was established and fostered by anti-church intellectuals of the nineteenth and early twentieth centuries, prominent among whom was Pavel Miliukov, who gave a series of lectures in 1903 and 1904 in the United States, and whose bias was picked up by western scholars and continued down to the present day. Two of the more recent examples of this bias are the chapter titled "The Church as Servant of the State," in Richard Pipes' *Russia Under the Old Regime* (New York, 1974), and almost every reference to the church in Harrison Salisbury's *Black Night, White Snow* (New York, 1978).

When, however, the student of the Russian church makes even the most cursory investigation of the literature put out by both the religious and secular press on topics relating to the Orthodox church during the final years of the nineteenth century and the opening years of the twentieth, it becomes clear that the church was neither withdrawn, intolerant, quaint, nor as moribund as secular historians, Russian and western, Marxist and non-Marxist, would lead one to believe.

One of the purposes of this study is to examine the record as revealed in ecclesiastical publications like the annual report compiled by the staff of the Procurator of the Most Holy Synod (*Vsepoddaneishii Otchet Ober-Prokurora Sviateishago Sinoda po Vedomstvu Pravoslavnago Ispovedaniia*) which described the administration of the far-flung church from the vantage point of the central administration in St. Petersburg.

9

Two other fundamental documents that reveal the vitality of the church in the first years of the twentieth century are the collection of reports from the diocesan bishops on the problem of reform of the church (*Otzyvy Eparkhial'nykh Arkhiereev po voprosu o tserkovnoi reforme*), published in three volumes in 1905, and the minutes and protocols of a precouncil commission which met during much of 1906 to prepare the agenda for a national sobor of the Russian church which was expected to be summoned shortly after the commission finished its work (*Zhurnaly i Protokoly Zasedanii Vysochaishe Uchrezhdennago Predsobornago Prisutstviia*, 1906-1907, 4 vols.). The expected sobor would have been the first such convocation of the whole Russian church since the Great Sobor of 1666-1667, which approved a series of liturgical and administrative reforms, restricted some of the church's claims to authority in the political and proprietary realms, and deposed the famous Patriarch Nikon Minin (1605-1681). It was rather because the civil authority, under the decisive leadership of Prime Minister Peter Stolypin (1862-1911), feared the political consequences of an independent church, than any docility on the part of the ecclesiastical administration, that the national sobor was not held in 1906 or 1907. It was postponed for ten crucial years during which some reforms in administration were instituted by the Synod, while the substance of administrative autonomy and an independent role in the social and political spheres was entirely repressed. The sobor was finally held in 1917-1918, during the upheaval of revolution and civil war. It was abruptly terminated by the Soviet authorities who thereupon subjected the church to the most intense and vicious persecution it has ever experienced. The remarkable aspect of the persecution is not that the church collapsed administratively under its impact, but that it managed to endure so that the administration could be reconstituted in the 1940s—and continues to the present day, however closely controlled.

At the opening of the century there was growing pressure on the civil bureaucracy to abolish the Ecclesiastical Regulation imposed in 1721 by Peter the Great. Dissatisfaction with the Regulation had always persisted among the hierarchy and clergy in varying degrees, because the Regulation by its very nature was at variance with the canons of the Eastern church. The canons, deriving from Byzantine times, had guaranteed autonomy of administration to the church and conceded to the church a major voice in moral and social legislation. The effect of the Regulation had been to stifle the church and to paralyze its ability to react to and suggest solutions for social and moral dilemmas, especially in the nineteenth and twentieth centuries. Ecclesiastical intelligentsia—priests, prelates, and professors—were nearly unanimous in their belief that restoration of the church's autonomy was a *sine qua non* if the inner vitality of the church were to be effective in the social, economic, and political transformation occurring in Russia. Religious intellectuals understood that emancipation of the church would bring it into occasional conflict with the state. However, they were convinced that this tension and conflict could only be ultimately beneficial to the state. Few of them expected prolonged rivalry. An emancipated church would give the masses of the people a sympathetic voice in restructuring the social, moral and economic order. A revitalized church would provide friendly support for the civil authorities as they sought ways to adjust to the modern era. The church could help the state overcome tendencies towards political senility.

The drive for emancipation of the church did not produce unanimous agreement on how the subsequent governing of the church should be conducted, however. Should there be a patriarchate? Most of the personalities in the debate agreed there should be. However, there was considerable disagreement on what powers the Patriarch should possess. There was much disagreement on what powers the diocesan bishops should have. More disagreement centered on how to restructure and restore the vitality of the parish.

The documents reveal virulent exchanges among churchmen when they tried to find answers to these questions as they reacted to rapidly changing political conditions.

Originally, interest in this subject was sparked by lectures on the theology of the Russian church given by Dom Godfrey Diekmann of St. John's Abbey, who based himself upon the writings of Nikolai Berdyaev, Sergei Bulgakov, and G. P. Fedotov. Interest was fanned by Professor T. G. Stavrou of the University of Minnesota whose own academic interests and cultural background are Russian history on the one hand, and Orthodox Christianity on the other. A particularly lively debate with Professor Robert F. Byrnes of Indiana University during a lecture series at the University of Minnesota on whether or not there was significant vitality in the Russian church in the nineteenth and early twentieth centuries stimulated my interest even more, as did Professor Nicolas Zernov of Oxford University when he visited Minnesota.

Many persons made the collecting of documents possible. Professor Peter Weisensel of Macalester College introduced me to the intricacies of the Helsinki University Library in Finland and, when he subsequently returned on a Fulbright scholarship, had a number of necessary items microfilmed and sent to me. Later, as an exchange student in Leningrad and Moscow, he sent me other key documents on microfilm from the Saltykov-Shchedrin Public Library and the Lenin Library. The staff of the Lenin Library in Moscow were of gracious assistance to me while I was there in 1977. Ms. Elisabeth Tokoi of the Helsinki interlibrary loan service had several essential sources microfilmed or xeroxed and sent them to me. Ms. Albina Kuzetsuova of the Saltykov-Shchedrin Library in Leningrad spent many hours with me, showing me how to use the intricate cataloguing system permitting me to condense my search there to a relatively short time. Mrs. Gertrude Battell and her staff in the interlibrary loan division of the University of Minnesota Libraries have been most cooperative in securing a number of items. Her staff and the staff of Vice-President Walter Mondale's office in Washington made it possible for me to acquire a complete series of the annual reports of the Procurator of the Synod from 1888 to 1914 on microfilm. Stephen Beskid of the St. Vladimir's Seminary Library went far beyond the call of duty to get volumes of the Responses of the Diocesan Bishops microfilmed for me. In addition, Mrs. Margaret Conant and Sister Melissa Elliott of the interlibrary loan service of the St. Catherine College Library secured many essential monographs and microfilmed documents for me during various phases of research. Sister Alberta Huber, Grants Coordinator, secured financial assistance. Fr. John Meyendorff of the faculty of St. Vladimir's gave encouragement and advice on manuscript revision while at a symposium at the University of Minnesota in 1976 and again at a symposium at St. Catherine's College in 1980. Virginia Steinhagen, my student assistant, has aided with bibliographical and biographical materials, while last, but not least, my wife Mary has been of indispensable assistance in editing, transporting manuscripts, and keeping our active son Andrew out from under foot.

Feast of St. Catherine of Alexandria
November 25, 1980

CHAPTER I

The Russian Church Enters the Twentieth Century

At the beginning of the twentieth century, the Russian Orthodox church was a very complex institution undergoing change in response to the pressures that developed during the half century of social and economic change since the Emancipation Decree of 1861. Numbering more than 83,000,000 communicants, 63 percent of the population of the empire, it was the state church, established by law, supported by the State Treasury for a significant percentage of its financial needs, and defended against enemies and rivals, political and religious, by the laws of the state which were backed by the policing agencies of the Ministry of the Interior.[1]

Orthodox religious doctrine was taught in the various state school systems while at the same time the church operated its own, rapidly expanding, elementary system. For all practical purposes, the Orthodox school system was the primary system for the empire in the attempt to provide basic literacy and skills to future citizens wherever they lived. Improved education for the masses of people was the basic need in Russia if she were to remain among the ranks of great powers and partake of the benefits of modern technology. Parish schools were the avenue through which students made their way to higher education and at the same time were the means by which their loyalty to the church was strengthened. The Education Commission of the Holy Synod, headed by Bishop

Gurii Okhotin, understood that rote repetition of ritual would no longer suffice to maintain that loyalty, and that literacy would provide for a greater sophistication in appreciating the cultural and spiritual values of the Orthodox tradition.

The church was governed by the Most Holy Governing Synod, an invention of the state imposed in 1721 by the command of Peter the Great. Before that time the church had been headed by a Patriarch, who governed through a hierarchy of archbishops, bishops, archabbots, abbots and archpriests. Peter believed that the patriarchal organization of the administration was a stumbling block in the path of his ambitious reforms, especially his efforts to centralize control, and had created the Synod to prevent the church from ever becoming a rival for power in the empire. The Synod was composed of the three metropolitans of St. Petersburg, Moscow, site of the patriarchate, and Kiev, the mother city of Russian Christianity when ancient Rus' had been converted in 987 A.D.; and the exarch of Georgia, whose pre-Nicaean church had been subordinated to the Russian Synod in 1811. At the turn of the century the prelates who occupied those sees were Antonii Vadkovskii (1846-1912) in St. Petersburg, Vladimir Dogoiavlenskii (1040-1910) in Moscow, Feognost Lebedev (1847-1903) in Kiev and Flavian Gorodestskii (1840-1915) in Georgia. The metropolitans and the exarch were assisted by various bishops of other sees, depending upon the personal influence of the bishop or the importance of the diocese. The archbishop of Finland regularly served, as did one or another of the bishops from the Volga dioceses, the bishops of Volhynia, Novgorod, Kholm-Warsaw, Mogilev, Riga, and Vilna-Lithuania. The Synod met in two regular sessions, spring and fall, and frequently had interim summer sessions as well in order to handle the growing volume of work.[2]

The day-to-day administration of the church's central structure was under the Procurator of the Synod and his chancellory, a vast bureaucracy that occupied the Synod wing of the Senate-Synod building on the bank of the Neva River. The Procurator, whose office was established in 1722, was originally intended to have been a watchdog, sitting in on the Synod sessions, to make known the Emperor's views on various matters and to see to it that decisions taken by the Synod did not violate the sovereign's will or the laws of the land. In the nearly two hundred years of the Synod's existence, however, the Procurator had become the de facto ruler of the church, controlling it through a highly centralized bureaucracy whose personnel and directives came from him. Bishops on the Synod had found that their real authority was severely circumscribed, while bishops in their dioceses found that their consistorial secretaries really had more to say about policy and personnel than they did themselves. A hierarch who opposed this order of things often found himself demoted to lesser sees or retired to some distant monastery to contemplate the ways of God and the Procurator. One of the motives for undercutting the bishops in this manner and for transferring them rapidly from diocese to diocese was to ensure that they did not build up influences among their flocks that might hinder the sway of the civil authorities. A bishop who did not oppose the established order found himself moving up the ladder of promotions and honors, while the bishop who demonstrated too much independence usually found himself moving down the ladder.[3]

In 1900 the church was divided into sixty-six dioceses within the empire and one outside, the diocese of the Aleutians and Alaska which embraced the entire North American continent. There were also vigorous missionary efforts underway in Japan, Korea and Peking.[4]

Five new dioceses had been created during the 1890s—in Finland, Vladikavkaz, Blagoveshchensk, Vladivostok and Omsk—to cope with a growing and shifting population and for specific political ends. The larger dioceses—Kiev, Moscow and St. Petersburg—had three or four vicar bishops attached to them. Vicar bishops served as assistants to the incumbent and often ran the day-to-day business of the diocese while he was away. The vicar bishop had his own residence and cathedral in the town of his title, together with a miniature administration to deal with local needs. Moscow had vicar bishops in Dmitrov, Mozhaisk and Volokolamsk, while St. Petersburg had vicar bishops in Iamburg, Godovsk, Narva and Kronstadt. Vyborg, Finland, had been a vicar bishopric under

St. Petersburg until 1892, when a separate diocese of Finland had been created.[5]

The sixty-six dioceses were loosely grouped into ten regional districts to permit their administrations to cooperate in common ventures, such as missionary efforts to counteract sectarian influences, to coordinate religious festivals, to coordinate school building, and other common needs. All such activities were closely supervised by the Procurator's chancellory in St. Petersburg.

Each diocese was subdivided into *blagochiniia* (deaneries) headed by a *nastoiatel'*, a dean who was a white priest and pastor of some prominent parish. The *nastoiatel'* held the ecclesiastical title of *protoierei* (archpriest) and had reached the peak of his advancement with that title and position. He was an appointee of the secretary of the diocesan consistory and could operate quite independently of his bishop if he so chose, providing he and the consistory secretary were on good terms. The *blagochinie* deans were responsible for maintaining harmony among the clergy in their areas, for preventing discord between clergy and laity and between clergy and civilian authorities, for coordinating such common efforts as orphan care, church repair, clergy widows' benefits, and signalling the arrival of sectarian propagandists in their territories.[6]

Canonically the diocesan administration was the responsibility of bishops, but bishops had seen their real authority whittled away during the eighteenth and nineteenth centuries because they had at first resisted the absorption of the ecclesiastical administration by the state and then had not functioned as efficiently as state agents among their flocks as the government had expected. Diocesan administration was conducted by the consistory, presided over by the bishop and coordinated by the secretary, under whom worked several lay clerks depending upon the size of the diocese and the volume of work. The secretary drew up the agendas for meetings, kept the minutes, and transmitted reports and requests for permissions and monies to the Procurator's offices in St. Petersburg. Priests were appointed or reprimanded on the say of the secretary. Bishops frequently found that to clash with their secretaries meant that they were usually transferred to another diocese. The secretaries and their clerks were required to have academic and legal qualifications that were comparable to those of the personnel in civilian bureaucracies, were appointed from the Procurator's chancellory, and hoped to one day work in that chancellory or in one of the better paying state ministries. Often they were still students when appointed, and they finished their academic courses while drawing church salaries. Bishops were annoyed with their often half-hearted work in the consistories and with their eagerness to get away as rapidly as they could gain the influence necessary to effect their advancement. The Procurator, in turn, lamented the brain drain that siphoned off better talent into government agencies. The state would not authorize competitive salaries for church employees.[7]

Monastic tonsure was canonically required before a man could advance to the higher offices in the church. The brighter and more imaginative graduates from the seminaries were encouraged to qualify for one of the four theological academies, take tonsure, and become rectors in seminaries, inspectors or rectors in the academies, abbots of monasteries, archabbots of lavras, bishops, archbishops, or even one of the metropolitans of the church.

There were four great lavras in Russia—the Alexandro-Nevskii in St. Petersburg, the Sergei-Troitskii near Moscow, the Pecherskaia in Kiev and the Pochaev in Volhynia, near the borders of the Austrian Empire. The metropolitans of the three capitals were the heads of the lavras in or near their cities, but the lavras were actually under a lower ranking bishop, an *igumen*, who administered for them. The Pochaev, taken over from the Uniate church in 1839, was administered by the bishop of Volhynia, who was its *igumen*. Appointment to any office in one of the lavras was an indication that a career in the higher offices of the church was in the offing.[8]

At the bottom of the hierarchical order stood the parish and the parish priest. Originally the parish had been a defined territorial entity identified with the region and community of its locale. However, one of the purposes of the ecclesiastical reforms of the Petrine era and later was to break up the parish identity and loosen the bond between priest and parishioners. That way the community became more homogeneous and less likely to resist political changes, especially the steady imposition of serfdom and the legal closing of avenues of escape. By the end of the nineteenth century the parish had no legal identity or even a clear territorial definition. One of the means to ensure that priests would not become spokesmen for popular causes was to convert them into police agents who were required to report indications of political discontent in their flocks, even to violating the seal of confession. Priests who complied with the law often found their ties to their flock tenuous. Priests who did not were liable to serious criminal penalties.[9]

The pastors were drawn from the white clergy, who were excluded from promotion to the higher ranks of the church because they had not taken monastic tonsure. They were usually married and fathers of rather large families. Oftentimes they succeeded their fathers as pastors of their parishes, or they succeeded to the parishes of their fathers-in-law. They were usually married to daughters of priests who had been sent to diocesan women's schools and specifically prepared to be useful wives of priests. Since a man could not marry after his ordination, he often took a year or two off after his seminary training to court and marry his bride and to decide if he truly wanted to continue to ordination. Many times sons of priests opted to enter the civil service or to become doctors, lawyers or teachers in state and *zemstvo* organizations. Where the bishop personally knew the man seeking ordination, he sometimes aided him in finding his fiancée as well. At the turn of the twentieth century the caste-like nature of the priesthood was beginning to erode, and women from the middle classes or the lower ranks of the bureaucracy married seminarians.

Once a rural or small town priest was appointed to his parish, he usually remained there until he retired or died. In larger cities, priests enjoyed much more mobility, moving from parish to parish, to various chaplaincies, or from office to office in the ecclesiastical bureaucracy. Occasionally a prominent archpriest (*protoierei*) would be widowed, or his wife might voluntarily retire to a convent, and he would be tonsured and would move into the ranks of the hierarchy. Normally, however, attaining the rank of *protoierei* and being appointed to a large parish or some lower level office was as far as a white priest expected to go. A number of them found their way onto the faculties of the theological academies and diocesan seminaries.[10]

Parishes in large cities had several priests, deacons and psalmists on their staffs to take care of the many hours of liturgical ceremonies, counsel their parishioners, engage in missionary work among the population—many of whom had recently migrated from rural villages—and keep track of the mounds of paperwork demanded of them by the Procurator's office. Deacons and chanters (psalmists) were often students in the local seminary.

Rural parishes usually had one priest and one psalmist. The psalmist had obtained the minimal instruction necessary to function in his capacity and usually did not expect to advance further in the church. He was married and had a family. He and the priest often worked at other livelihoods as well—usually farming—because their salaries were too small to allow them to subsist entirely on them alone. Ecclesiastical salaries were improving at the turn of the century but still did not meet the needs of the average rural priest. Priests and psalmists sometimes earned supplementary salaries from the Ministries of Finance, Agriculture and State Domains by qualifying themselves to teach blacksmithing, lathe operating, hygiene, horticulture, or any one of a number of programs those ministries were trying to implement in the changing rural economy of Russia. These new avenues of employment provided the way to other professions than the priesthood for the priest's children if they did not feel especially attracted to the clergy. It was another sign that the clerical caste system was in flux.[11]

The opening of the twentieth century witnessed an increasing demand among the Russian clergy for greater autonomy in their pastoral work and for constituting the parish as a legal personality so that it could own property in its own right, set up cooperatives and credit unions, and so become a more integral part of the social and economic lives of parishioners.

Priests and the religious intelligentsia envisioned a parish *obshchina* (community), which would integrate the lives of parishioners on many levels, rather than exclusively for purposes of cult and sacraments. With the expanding emphasis upon parish schools as the means to literacy and acquisition of skills, it was logical that the total community would be immeasurably strengthened if the parish had the legal right to own and foster the structures that advanced the communal and economic lives of their constituents. Civil and synodal authorities were less than enamoured of the idea, however, because such local control would mean a loss of some authority over the lives of the people and because priests would become vocal champions of popular grievances.[12]

The church was experiencing the pains of adjusting to rapidly changing social and political realities in the empire in the aftermath of the Emancipation and in the quickening industrial revolution. These changes required a fundamental change in the relations between clergy and people. Formerly the local landlord had simply appointed the priest and had expected him to follow his command, an attitude that was carried over by government bureaucrats who treated priests with a measure of contempt, expecting them to be mindful of their inferior status. Now that priests were better educated, sometimes drawn from the new middle class, and felt the same pressures and demands as their flocks, their flocks looked to them for leadership and initiative. They readily supported pastors who demonstrated leadership. In turn that put pressure on the hierarchy to stand up and defend their clergy against the stifling controls imposed upon them by the civil authority or outright harassment. The tension created not a few conflicts in clergy-bishop relations and in church-state relations.

A major purpose was to improve seminary education to meet the intellectual and skill needs of the clergy. A whole series of courses, introduced during the late 1880s and 1890s, gave priests practical skills needed to teach their flocks. Foreign observers noted as the nineteenth century drew to a close that skills such as animal husbandry, market gardening and horticulture were being taught by the clergy to the economic advantage of their people. Gradually the elevation of the level of clerical education began to obviate some of the more virulent criticism from enemies of the priesthood. Clergy-taught skills enabled some peasants to break out of the poverty cycle and to improve their rural economy or to find employment in the towns and cities.

A field in which priests critically aided their flocks was in health and hygiene. After the famine of 1891-1892, the subsequent outbreak in 1892-1893 of cholera, and various epidemics of diphtheria and scarlet fever that followed, courses in the rudiments of medicine (*narodnaia meditsina*) were introduced to enable seminarians to counteract these diseases for themselves and also to teach their people how to avoid unsanitary conditions that fostered the spread of those diseases. Priests collaborated with doctors in the employ of the *zemstvo* to educate the public to prevent the spread of epidemics in the future.[13]

The church thus had mounted an attack upon the deficiencies of clerical education, had elevated the quality of the lives of the clergy, and was counteracting the scornful judgments that secular and atheistic intellectuals had habitually heaped upon its priesthood. The more the clergy were able to meet socialist and anti-religious propagandists with effective learning, and thereby undercut the attacks on the faith of their flocks, the more virulent anti-clerical and atheistic groups became. At the same time the church combatted these new types of adversaries, it continued to combat adversaries of an older, more traditional nature.[14]

*   *   *

A serious and consistent threat to the tranquility of the church came from three types of religious movements, two of which had their origins in the sixteenth and seventeenth centuries and one that had originated in the years since the Emancipation in 1861.

The Uniate church had been created in 1596 at the behest of the King and greater nobility of Poland-Lithuania. It was an eastern rite of the Catholic church and recognized the Pope as its head rather than the Patriarch of Constantinople. It came into existence directly as a result of the creation in 1589 of the Moscow patriarchate and was intended to prevent the Orthodox masses of the Ukraine and White Russia from gravitating politically into the sphere of the Tsars of Moscow. Because the patriarchate of Constantinople lay under the heavy yoke of the Ottoman Turks, it could do little but utter a feeble protest as millions of its adherents were separated from its jurisdiction. The separation was supported by most of the Orthodox bishops in Poland-Lithuania but was strongly opposed by the lower clergy and lay brotherhoods (*bratstva*) which had been formed to resist the campaign for Unia and which led the struggle to maintain a separate Orthodox identity once the union had been proclaimed.

Legally the Orthodox church ceased to exist in Poland-Lithuania, while the new Uniate church carried on the canonical regulations, liturgy and customs of the Eastern church. All properties of the Orthodox church passed into the hands of the Uniate church. The Uniate church remained separate from the Latin church in Poland-Lithuania and in theory was placed on an equal footing legally and politically.[15]

Practically speaking, the Uniate church and its Ukrainian and White Russian constituency never achieved political and social equality with its Latin counterpart despite their common recognition of the papacy. Besides, the Uniate church was not popular among the lesser princes and the peasantry. In the Ukraine the Cossacks opposed Unia because it meant not only abandoning their allegiance to Eastern Orthodoxy and the patriarchate of Constantinople but also the extension over them of the power of Polish landowners who sought to reduce them to serfdom. As the Cossacks struggled against the extension of serfdom, they struggled to maintain the Orthodox church and a unique Ukrainian identity. Liberty and Orthodoxy were the same cause.

Several times smoldering resentment flared into violence and was crushed, until a massive uprising, 1648-1654, led by Bohdan Khmelnitskii, tore the region east of the Dnieper River from Polish control. Khmelnitskii had originally been willing to collaborate with the Polish regime in return for autonomy for the Cossacks and for freedom for the Orthodox church, but after both guarantees had been reneged upon, he had led the revolt and asked Moscow to take the Ukraine under its jurisdiction. In return Moscow pledged to respect Cossack autonomy and the independence of the Kievite church, the metropolitan of Kiev to remain under the Patriarch of Constantinople.[16]

However, Russian landowners penetrated into the Ukraine three quarters of a century later seeking both new estates and former serfs who had escaped from the north. Not only did Moscow want the land and the people of the Ukraine, but also—to bind them more closely—the subordination of the see of Kiev as well. The campaign to subordinate the Kievite church obscured the reasons for rejecting the Uniate connection, especially since autonomy was forfeited in either case.[17]

From the point of view of Moscow it was necessary to subordinate the Kiev metropolitanate in order that the Ukraine would not again seek a political connection with Poland or an ecclesiastical connection with Rome. To make the patriarchate's jurisdiction coterminous with that of the Tsar, both of whom used the term "all-Russia" as part of their titles, would confirm Moscow's claim to rule all Eastern Slavic peoples.

Accordingly, Prince Afanasii Lavrentevich Ordin-Nashchokin was sent to the Ukraine to aid Moscowphile clergy and to warn independent-minded priests and prelates that there was danger that Unia, secure on the west bank of the Ukraine, would be reestablished in Kiev and on the east bank. On the west bank, the King of Poland appointed a Uniate-sympathizing bishop, Iosif Shumlianskii (†1708) of Lvov, as administrator of the Kiev metropolitanate with that very idea in mind.

The hetman of the East Ukraine, Ivan Samoilovich, worked with Patriarch Ioakim Savelov (1620-1690) of Moscow, an energetic and determined prelate, to smooth the way for the subordination of Kiev ecclesiastically. Savelov had been educated at the Kiev Theological Academy, had many friends there among the Moscowphile clergy, and found it incomprehensible that there should be any serious objection to the Moscow connection. Savelov urged the hetman to appoint his supporters to vacant church offices in Kiev and gradually those who wanted a Moscow connection came to dominate the Kievite church.[18]

Matters were facilitated when the incumbent metropolitan, Antonii Vinnitskii, died in 1679. Vinnitskii had been opposed to the Moscow union and wanted to keep Kiev in its ancient allegiance to Constantinople. He had worked with non-Uniate prelates on the west bank to maintain the unity of the Kiev church. With his death the backbone went out of the resistance. In 1683, Hetman Samoilovich appointed Varlaam Iasinskii as *igumen* of the Pecherskaia Lavra, giving him the authority of *locum tenens* in the metropolitanate. Iasinskii was a Moscowphile. Control of the Lavra was the final step toward determining who would succeed as metropolitan.

In 1685, Samoilovich and Patriarch Ioakim of Moscow announced that the vacant throne would be filled and summoned an electoral sobor. Meantime negotiations were conducted with the patriarchate in Constantinople to effect canonically the union of the Kiev church with Moscow. The negotiations were unsuccessful and their outcome remained unknown, but the sobor was held and Bishop Gedeon Sviatopolk Chetvertinskii, a Savelov supporter, was finally elected in 1686. There was considerable opposition from clergy and lay leaders who questioned the canonical validity of the sobor and who had themselves been excluded from its deliberations. They refused to recognize Gedeon and appealed to Moscow for another convocation. Patriarch Ioakim refused their request and affirmed that Gedeon had indeed been canonically elected. Thus, after seven hundred years, the tie to the Ecumenical Patriarchate was broken. Constantinople's response was muted. It was in no more a position to prevent loss of jurisdiction in Kiev in 1686 than it had been in 1596 when the Uniate church had been proclaimed.[19]

On the Polish-controlled west bank, the disappearance of Kiev's ecclesiastical autonomy meant that the resistance to the Uniate church died away rather swiftly. As vacancies occurred in the dioceses under the patronage of the King of Poland, they were filled with Uniate or Uniate-sympathizing prelates. In 1691, Innokentii Vinnitskii of Przemysl, a relative to the late metropolitan of Kiev, acknowledged Rome, as did Bishop Iosif Shumlianskii of Lvov in 1700. In 1705 the Lvov Stauropigial Brotherhood, founded originally to defend Orthodoxy against Unia, became Uniate, as did the Pochaev Monastery in Volhynia in 1721, the same year that the Ecclesiastical Regulation went into effect abolishing the Moscow patriarchate.[20]

The way was open then for the Uniate church to consolidate its position outside the territories controlled by the Tsar. Legal support from the Polish government strengthened the hand of the Uniate clergy while restrictions upon the Orthodox church saw the latter whittled away to less than half a million members in the territories under Poland. The Uniate church numbered more than four million members during the eighteenth century. Because Russia utilized the Orthodox minority in Poland to justify intervention in Polish political affairs, feelings against the Orthodox were strong among Uniates and Latin Catholics as well. The Uniate church came to be the repository of a separate Ukrainian identity.[21]

The situation was dramatically reversed, however, at the close of the eighteenth century when the West Ukraine and White Russia were incorporated into the Russian Empire. The Uniate population of the former Kingdom of Poland found itself a minority *vis-à-vis* the Orthodox majority in the Russian Empire. At the time of the third partition of Poland in 1795, the military commands of Kiev, Polotsk and Volhynia *guberniias* launched a vigorous campaign to coerce the Uniates into the Orthodox church. Uniate priests either fled, were imprisoned, or conformed, signifying the latter by growing beards and removing prayers for Pope Pius VI from the liturgy. Unreconstructed Uniates were comforted and supported by Latin rite leaders and many of them joined the Latin church outright, refusing to join what they considered to be the "schismatic" church.

Their situation was eased under Emperors Paul (1796-1801) and Alexander I (1801-1825), both of whom regarded Unia as a bridge between Orthodoxy and Catholicism. In 1797 Uniates were given imperial sanction to join either the Orthodox or Latin churches. The Uniate hierarchy was placed under the Roman Catholic department of government, while the chief Uniate bishop, Ignatii Lisovskii of Polotsk, a friend of the Emperor, was allowed considerable communication with the Uniate metropolitanate at Lvov in Austrian Galicia.

The reign of Nicholas I (1825-1855) abruptly altered the condition of Uniates in the empire, especially after the Polish uprising in 1830-1831. Uniates openly sided with Polish insurrectionists and Uniate clergy excoriated Russian rule. The Tsar could see little difference between Latinism and Unia, especially when the Pochaev Monastery had turned out to be an arsenal where the revolutionaries cached their weapons. His sense of outrage was deepened when upon the death of his mother, Dowager Empress Marie Fedorovna, the Uniate archbishop of Brest-Litovsk, Iosafat Bulgak, would not allow the *panikhida* for the dead to be sung in his churches. On Nicholas' orders, the Uniate metropolitan of Vilna, Iosif Semashko (1798-1868), prepared the ground for gradual separation of the Uniate church from Rome and unification with the Russian church. In 1839 all Uniate dioceses except Kholm in the government of Poland were suppressed. All properties were transferred to state control and all Uniates declared legally to be members of the Orthodox church.[22]

Secret societies and brotherhoods were formed to resist this. Police harassment and evictions from their homes only hardened Uniate resistance. Latin clergy secretly baptized their children and buried their dead. Banned Uniate clergy crossed the frontier from Austria to minister clandestinely. Laymen crossed the frontier to Galicia to worship, visit relatives and engage in smuggling.[23]

In the wake of the second Polish uprising, 1862-1863, the diocese of Kholm was also suppressed and formally incorporated into the state church in 1875. Unlike the gradual manner of Bishop Semashko's approach in the 1830s, the bishop of Kholm, Markel Poppel (1825-1903), rigidly and swiftly suppressed Uniate practices and dealt with resistance by summoning the Cossacks. Polish sympathizers supported the resistance while former Uniate churches stood empty of worshippers. The resistance reawakened sympathy among former Uniate families where the church had been suppressed earlier and created a general distrust of the Russian civilian admin-istration that caused concern. Uniate sympathies were sus-ceptible to Austrian political propaganda in the years before World War I and would welcome the separation of western regions from Russia afterwards.[24]

In those circumstances bishops in the western dioceses hoped that parish schools would be the means through which the next generation might be won for the Orthodox church and instilled with a loyalty to the Russian nation. Grants from the Treasury, gifts from Russian or Russophile landowners, military officers and merchants were beginning to overcome the lag in school building and staffing in the western areas. Priests still had to contend with shouting students who refused to be taught doctrine in the Orthodox manner and who in-sisted upon hearing Latin priests. It was discovered, however, that where Latin churches were distant, the population grad-ually became less hostile and by 1900 had begun to support Orthodox churches financially in some regions, notably in the diocese of Lithuania. Religious festivals were another means to de-Polonize former Uniate families. The Pochaev Lavra at the turn of the century had been thoroughly purged of its Uniate aspects and once again was being frequented by fam-ilies who had boycotted it. Instead of making the longer pilgrimage to the Catholic monastery at Czestochowa in Poland they were returning to the Pochaev.[25]

There remained, however, annoying outbursts of back-sliding of entire parishes that had been Orthodox for a gen-eration or more. During the coronation preparations in 1895 there was a rumor that Nicholas II (1894-1917) was going to restore the Uniate church and its former properties. As a result, certain Orthodox parishes expelled their priests and awaited the reappearance of the Uniate clergy.

Thus the confrontation with Catholicism, Latin and Uniate, seemed to be at a stalemate. Only prolonged pressure by the civilian authority in the defense of Orthodoxy was likely to achieve the desired elimination of Uniate sentiment and hos-tility to the state. In addition to that, the gradual transforma-tion of the economic and social structures of the western *guberniias* would dissolve the ties that bound Ukrainian and

White Russian peasants to Catholic and Polish interests. No one could foresee the imminent upheavals of 1905 or that those areas would be lost to Russia entirely after 1917.[26]

*   *   *

The Old Believer schism, the *Raskol*, originated in the early seventeenth century, growing out of the confusion and xenophobia of the harrowing Time of Troubles, 1598-1613. During the turmoil resulting from the end of the Rurikid line of rulers, 852-1598, the Kings of Poland and Sweden, both descendants of the house of Vasa, attempted to overrun Muscovite Russia and to impose their religious systems. For each of them, control of Moscow would have immensely enhanced his power *vis-à-vis* the other. Rejecting foreign creeds, the church summoned Russians to unite, eject the invaders and set an Orthodox prince on the throne. The Romanov family owed its position to the church—Michael (1613-1645) enthroned as Tsar and his father, Filaret, enthroned as Patriarch (1619-1633).

Moscow was allowed some measure of tranquility when both Poland and Sweden were drawn into the great religious conflict among Western Christians, the Thirty Years' War, 1618-1648. During that time, the Zealots of Piety, a group of priests and lay persons, eager to purge their own lives and the lives of their fellow Russians of spiritual slovenliness and alien influences, rose to champion true Orthodoxy. Besides the indifference of many clergy and lay leaders towards proper observances, churches stood in disrepair since the time of the civil war and foreign invasion. The Romanovs were preoccupied with restoring order, preventing a recurrence of civil war, and meeting the threat of another invasion from Poland or Sweden.[27]

Remarkable clergymen made up the nucleus of the Zealots, among them Archpriest Avvakum Petrovich (1620-1682), the man who ultimately led the Old Believers out of the church and who was to be burned at the stake.

Among their goals was liturgical reform and renewal, elimination of Latin and other alien cultic practices, and restoration of clerical and public morality so that the Muscovite church would reflect more truly its image as Third Rome, the inheritor of the tradition of the apostles.

By the middle 1630s the Zealots had the support of the patriarch and many clergy. By the next decade north Russia was caught up in the excitement of reform, some of which was reflected in those parts of the *Ulozhenie* of 1649 that dealt with the church.[28]

Not all Muscovites wished to be reformed, however, and many objected to the reformers' interference in their private lives, whether to root out pagan rituals or to destroy foreign art objects. Not infrequently Zealots found themselves bloodied and battered after they had intervened to stop public orgies or profanation of churches. Occasionally the authorities arrested more extreme Zealots and incarcerated them for causing public disorders. Their followers thereupon flocked to their cells to hail them as martyrs. Zealot spokesmen also enlisted themselves in the struggle against the extension of serfdom, even to the point of identifying the tsarist government as the source of the oppression of God's poor. Zealots thus earned the hostility of the landowning *dvoriane*, who did not hesitate to warn Tsar Alexei Mikhailovich (1645-1676) that Zealotry was leading to political anarchy.[29]

By 1650 the Zealots dominated the administration of the church and felt sufficiently strong to denounce by name any official who offended public propriety, who molested the clergy or who violated the canons of the church, and they went so far as to canonize several martyrs murdered by recent tsars and boyars. The most notable canonization was of Metropolitan Filipp, who had been murdered by agents of Ivan the Terrible in 1570 for refusing to countenance the depredations of the *oprichnina*.

At the moment of their ascendancy, however, the Zealots split into two factions. They could not agree on which texts and traditions were the authentic texts and traditions that conveyed the inheritance of the apostolic era to their time. Arguments arose between the Muscovite traditionalists who based their claims on the councils and fathers of the church of Moscow, especially those held since the formal break with the see of Constantinople in 1448, and the reforming Byzantinists who insisted that usages that did not conform to Greek models clouded Moscow's claim to be Third Rome. The church split and eventually allowed the state to intervene, expel the Patriarch, and severely curtail the autonomy of ecclesiastical administration.

The traditionalists believed that the very fact that certain customs were of Greek origin was reason enough for rejecting them. The Greeks after all had submitted to First Rome at the Council of Ferrara-Florence, 1438-1439, and had been punished in 1453 by loss of their independence to the infidel Turks. Traditionalists were further suspicious of using Kievite clergy, texts and usages because Kiev had submitted to Rome, 1596, and had been infected with Latin thinking and customs. The fate of both those churches was ample indication of the wrath of God upon them.[30]

Reforming Byzantinists, on the other hand, believed that Moscow had to reflect the same rituals and usages as Constantinople, because Moscow bore the burden of leading the Orthodox *oikoumene* now that the Greek church lay under the yoke of the Turk. Byzantinists were receptive to the overtures from the eastern patriarchates to aid in their struggle against total extinction. Byzantinists welcomed Ukrainian clergy and scholars to help them reform the Moscow church.

The arrival of Patriarch Paisios of Jerusalem in Moscow in 1649 greatly encouraged the Byzantinist faction. Paisios stressed the need for common forms of worship to reflect the unity of the Orthodox world. Among those won over to Paisios' point of view was the archabbot of the Novospasskii Monastery, Nikon Minin (1605-1681), one of the Zealotry's ablest spokesmen. Paisios, who had welcomed Bohdan Khmelnitskii to Kiev's St. Sophia cathedral for Christmas liturgy in 1648 and had impressed upon the Cossacks their responsibility to defend Orthodoxy, left one of his retinue at the Chudov Monastery in the Kremlin, and took Arsenii Sukhanov, a monk of the Sergei-Troitskii Lavra, with him. Sukhanov travelled at some length in the East, the Balkans and Venice to compare and acquire texts and copies of the canons that would aid the reform in Moscow.[31]

Within three years of Paisios' departure, Nikon had been

made archbishop of Novgorod and been recalled to Moscow as Patriarch (1652-1666). He furthered the moral reforms of Zealotry, banning among other things all foreigners from residing in the precincts of Moscow so that their western heresies and loose habits would not distract the natives. Thus came into existence the so-called German suburb, where the Tsar's son Peter (1672-1725) would soon be disporting himself. He also sought to modify sections of the *Ulozhenie* that subjected the incomes of the church and the discipline of the clergy to the authority of the state. These were contrary to the Byzantine mode of administration in which the Tsar and Patriarch functioned as a "symphony," the Patriarch deferring to the Tsar in matters of civil administration and the Tsar deferring to the Patriarch in matters of faith and discipline.[32]

Nikon ran into a storm of opposition, however, from his fellow Zealots when he instituted changes in a missal about to go to press in 1652. He ordered suspension of the two-fingered manner of the sign of the cross, the traditional Moscow way, and substitution of the Byzantine form of three fingers. A number of other modifications were inserted, all to the distress of the priest Ivan Nasedka, another Zealot, who was in charge of the patriarchal printing press. He refused to insert the changes and Nikon dismissed him. Just before Lent 1653 Nikon issued an encyclical commanding the changes and threw the Muscovite church into a turmoil.[33]

Clergy and laity in considerable numbers refused to accept the changes, especially when Nikon took steps to strengthen his hand in the administration of the church at the expense of some of the more freewheeling clergy. Nikon, in turn, used a complaint from the governor of Nizhni-Novgorod against a priest there whom he had jailed to demonstrate patriarchal authority over the clergy. The priest in question was a Zealot, and Nikon ordered him before a convocation of Moscow clergy which condemned him. Ivan Neronov, one of the original Zealots, protested to the Tsar that Nikon had violated canonical procedure because the priest had been tried outside his own diocese. Alexei ignored the protest, and Nikon had Neronov arrested as well. This time it was Avvakum Petrovich, pastor of St. Basil's cathedral on Red Square, who protested and warned the Tsar that violation of priests' rights would tear the church apart. Again Alexei did nothing, and Nikon had Avvakum arrested and banished to Siberia. To the traditionalists, Avvakum had become a martyr. Many of them accompanied him into exile, witnessing to the appearance of the sign of the Antichrist in Moscow.[34]

Nevertheless, Nikon, with the approval of the Eastern Patriarchs, convoked a series of local sobors in Moscow which decreed liturgical changes that brought Moscow into harmony with the eastern churches and the metropolitanate at Kiev. The imposition of these reforms further embittered the Old Believers, for whom the changes—in the spelling of the name of Jesus, in the number of times alleluia should be sung, and in the type of vestments to be worn at liturgy—mutilated the vehicle of their salvation.

Meantime, Nikon's elocutions on the proper relation of the Tsar and Patriarch came to be regarded in government circles as a form of papalism. Nikon's claims to intervene in civil authority and to use the title *gosudar* equally with the Tsar corresponded to the claims made by Pope Gregory VII (1073-1085) against the Holy Roman Emperor. Alexei and his boyars, especially the *dvorianstvo*, suspected the establishment of a state within the state, whose claims to exemption from taxation and conscription on its properties would endanger the very existence of Muscovy. Such a spectre was especially dangerous since 1654, when Moscow had annexed the Ukraine and plunged into an exhaustive thirteen-year war with Poland. The uproar led directly to the Great Sobor of 1666-1667, which was attended by the Patriarchs Paisios of Alexandria and Makarios of Antioch.[35]

Nikon was not allowed to present his own defense or to examine the credentials of his interrogators, particularly the signatures on the accusations against him by the Patriarchs of Constantinople and Jerusalem, which he knew to be forgeries; and he was not accorded any of the dignities that went with the office of Patriarch. A drumhead review of the evidence condemned Nikon for having strong-armed his way into the domain of the secular ruler, for abandoning his flock when he had retired in order to bring pressure upon the Tsar, for refusing to resign and allow the election of another Patriarch, for enriching himself from other people's properties in order to build monasteries to reflect glory upon himself, for having been cruel to his bishops and clergy, and for having offended the dignity of the Eastern Patriarchs. The latter two charges were true, but were not canonical grounds for dismissing a Patriarch. Nevertheless, presuming to speak for the absent Patriarchs as well as themselves, Paisios and Makarios anathematized Nikon, deposed him from his office, unfrocked him as a priest, and reduced him to the status of a simple monk. He was sentenced to solitude in a remote northern monastery, to remain there until the day he died. He was whisked away through secluded routes to avoid public demonstrations on his behalf that would embarass the Tsar, his boyars and the two Patriarchs. He became the rallying point for political dissidents during his lifetime and his fate was lamented in some ecclesiastical circles still in the twentieth century.[36]

The Old Believers found no comfort in all of this, Avvakum and his followers denouncing the irregular manner of Nikon's deposition. When the Sobor was reconvened in April 1667 to assess the validity of Nikon's reforms, Old Believers expected them to be rescinded. But their spokesmen were presented with questions about the reforms in such a way that they could answer only yes or no and were not allowed to remonstrate at length. The questions asked were whether the Eastern Patriarchs were Orthodox, whether Greek liturgical books were Orthodox, whether the Moscow sobors that had given Nikon approval for changes were valid, and others equally devoid of pertinence. To ensure that the reconvened sobor would run smoothly, only hand-picked prelates were invited to attend, together with those clergy who had accepted the new rituals. The majority of white priests, the spokesmen for the church among the people, were excluded. It was among them that the Old Belief had its strongest support, and they fell under the excommunication that was decreed for all who would not accept changes. The resulting schism in the church left it weakened in the face of the challenge of the Petrine Ecclesiastical Regulation in 1721 and continued to reverberate in the church at the time of the Bolshevik holocaust of the twentieth century.[37]

The Old Believer legacy was one of defiance and despair. Without bishops they had no access to a validly ordained clergy and thus faced the loss of the life-giving sacraments. Persecution by the state was proof that it was the agent of the Antichrist. They fled southward, eastward and northward to escape serfdom and persecution, carrying their devotion to the old liturgies with them. Many parish clergy accompanied them, driven out of their churches for adhering to traditional practices or voluntarily ministering to the needs of the refugees. Two immediate indicators of the depth of Old Believer resistance were the insurrection of the monks of the Solovetskii Monastery on the White Sea and the rising of the Don Cossacks under Stenka Razin, 1670-1671.[38]

The reign of Peter the Great was a time of most intense persecution for the Old Believers. Special taxes were imposed upon those who lived in permanent communities, while multitudes roamed afar trying to avoid arrest and persecution. Peter's subjection of the state church to a non-canonical regime only confirmed their belief that he was the Antichrist and that the state church had lost all vestige of being the transmitter of Christian life. Even within the state church there was a feeling that Peter was the Antichrist and that the Old Believers were right.[39]

As the pre-1667 clergy died off, and there was no way to replenish them, leaders decided that priests from the state church could be accepted providing they had been baptized before the schism and would minister in the old rites. With the death of Peter and the lessening of persecution, some Old Believers even found it acceptable to worship in official churches, but used their own forms under the benign eye of the authorized clergy. The reign of Catherine the Great (1762-1796) saw a further effort to conciliate them when the Edinoverie was created, an Old Believer rite under the jurisdiction of the Synod, a form of reverse Unia. Agreeing to recognize the canonical validity of the state church and to pray for the Tsarina, a significant minority of Old Believers accommodated themselves, but when a severe crackdown on dissident Old Believers was undertaken in the reign of Nicholas I (1825-1855), state authorities failed to distinguish carefully between them and the legitimate *Edinovertsy*, with the result that the latter shrank to fewer than half a million while the Old Believer population may have numbered 20,000,000 by 1900.[40]

The renewal of persecution forced Old Believers to resume their search for a "true" Orthodox bishop who could consecrate bishops and ordain priests for them. The search was rewarded when they found Metropolitan Amvrosii, formerly head of the church of Bosnia, then in retirement in Austrian Trieste. Amvrosii had been deprived of his see by the Patriarch of Constantinople at the command of the Sultan because he had been too openly sympathetic with anti-Turkish nationalists. The Austrian government lent a hand as a means to register its ire at the fate of Uniates in Russia, and permitted him to establish himself in 1846 at Bela Krinitsa in Galicia. There Amvrosii consecrated bishops and ordained priests who, like their Uniate counterparts, slipped across the frontier into the Russian Empire. Despite a "White Terror" launched to suppress them, the Old Believer movement enjoyed a rapid revival, now that the crisis of obtaining a valid priesthood was over. By 1900 there were twenty Old Believer bishops, a sufficient number of priests to ensure continuity, and, with sympathy from some prelates of the state church, they were pressing for an *ukaz* that would grant them religious toleration.[41]

*   *   *

Stundism, a development within a faction of priestless Old Believers, was the first appearance of a western Protestant type of sectarianism among Ukrainian and Russian peasants in the latter half of the nineteenth century. There had been communities of German Protestants within the borders of the Russian Empire ever since the close of the sixteenth century, when regions along the Baltic Sea had been annexed. The German suburb outside Moscow contained a population that was largely Protestant. But Protestantism had had no influence among the Russian and Ukrainian peoples because it was culturally and religiously alien to their traditions.

The way for Stundism was prepared by a variant of Old Believers known as the Molokane, the Milk Drinkers. Molokane had made their appearance at the end of the eighteenth century at the same time as other groups such as the Dukhobors and the Khlysts, in a complex subdividing of that branch of the Old Believers who had lost all hope of obtaining a validly ordained priesthood. Priestless sects (*bezpopovtsy*), which had broken from the mainstream of Old Believers, were characterized by strange rites and practices which they believed brought them into direct communication with the Holy Spirit or to direct access to Christ because he was reincarnated again and again in various personalities generation after generation.

The Molokane were more moderate than other priestless sects, distinguishing themselves by refusing to venerate icons, to attend official liturgies or to make pilgrimages to Orthodox shrines. At the same time they made a point of drinking milk on the days of the Orthodox fast. Their attitudes vaguely approximated those of certain Protestant evangelical sects in Western Europe when at the turn of the nineteenth century they fell under the influence of the quasi-mystical Russian Bible Society favored by Tsar Alexander I (1801-1825).

Under its influence Molokan leaders gave up their adherence to the Orthodox sacraments, the tradition of patristic writers like Cyril of Jerusalem, John Chrysostom and Athanasius of Alexandria, and espoused a more typically Protestant belief that the Bible alone was the vehicle to salvation. Molokane who did not accept this variation were generally absorbed into the Dukhobors, Khlysts or more typically Russian sects. (Rasputin was an example of Khlyst extremism.)

Stundism took its name from the German word "stunde," meaning hour, and placed emphasis on personal meditation of the scriptures and on gatherings for hymn singing and promptings of the Holy Spirit. It made its initial appearance among Russian and Ukrainian communities in Bessarabia and the Ekaterinoslav provinces, where German Mennonite communities had colonized during the reign of Catherine the Great.

The relative tolerance of the era of Great Reforms in the 1860s and 1870s permitted Stundism to spread from German communities to the Slavic communities around them. At the same time it came under the influence of Baptist missionaries from abroad, broke with its Mennonite source and became a distinct sect.

Social and commercial intercourse with Old Believer communities in the Kiev, Kherson and Poltava dioceses permitted Stundo-Baptist preachers to communicate with the Slavic population in their native tongue. The usually superior economic position of the Stundists was an additional attraction. Millers, landowners, blacksmiths and other German ethnic artisans actively recruited converts from among the people who patronized them or who economically depended upon them. Stundist emphasis upon literacy as the means to reading the scriptures paralleled the popular quest for literacy as the tool to social and economic advancement. Converts could trace both the divine plan and improve their material circumstances by becoming literate.[42]

Petersburg Stundo-Baptism at first showed no overt hostility to the established church. Most of its members were members of the Orthodox church or became active members when they experienced conversion. However, in 1884 Petersburg evangelicals invited delegates from Stundist, Baptist and Molokan communities in the south to seek unity. The delegates quarreled among themselves about the meaning and form of the sacraments of baptism and the eucharist. At the same time, state officials became suspicious of the anti-Orthodox nature of their activities. The delegates were arrested and dispatched back to their homes. The effort, however, had created a precedent and subsequent efforts were made towards unity.[43]

Stundist teachings were socially and politically inflammatory, especially when the gospel doctrine of personal freedom was transmuted into a doctrine of political freedom. In urban areas—Kharkov, Kiev and the towns along the Volga— Stundism fed upon filthy living conditions, outbreaks of epidemics, low wages and long working hours. The doctrine of religious democracy in which every man was his own priest

and interpreter of the scriptures appealed to the new converts, who were not long in questioning the rightness of an
order where a few were privileged and the masses were
servants.

On July 4, 1894, the government issued an *ukaz* forbidding
the preaching of Stundism. Stundist missionaries simply
reverted to their earlier method of working within legitimate
organizations, toned down their anti-Orthodox preaching, and
awaited a better day.[44]

To combat this eruption a major missionary effort was
launched in 1895 by Metropolitan Ioanniki (Rudnev (1826-
1900) of Kiev to coordinate anti-Stundist activities. The deans
of the numerous *blagochiniia* were given instruction in
Stundist teachings and techniques, a diocesan missionary network was created in which priests and lay persons were regularly instructed in Stundist activities, and travelling preachers
traversed the diocese to enlighten the faithful, to persuade
wavering Orthodox to stand firm, and to provide an early
warning system so that Stundist activities could be noted as
they occurred. The next year the bishops of Kherson, Kharkov,
Tambov and Ekaterinoslav followed suit, setting up programs
modelled after Kiev. A series of all-Russian missionary conferences grew out of these efforts in the years preceding World
War I.[45]

*   *   *

The Orthodox parish school system was the instrument
through which church authorities expected to be able to stem
the activities of Stundists, Old Believers and Uniates. An attractive educational system would provide the knowledge and
skills needed by the population to meet the challenge of rapid
social and economic change and consolidate the loyalty of the
Orthodox young in the tenets and culture of the church.

The parish school system had been revived and revitalized
in the wake of an imperial *ukaz* in June 1884, which had envisioned making the school system the bulwark against the
civil anarchy and spiritual disorientation that had swept the
empire in the 1860s and 1870s. In the two decades before the
ukaz the number of parish schools had declined from 21,420

in 1865 with an enrollment of 412,524, to only 4,064 schools with an enrollment of 105,317 in 1881. Control of the primary schools of the empire had been taken from the church and put into the hands of the Ministry of Public Education.

The task of reviving the parish primary schools had been put into the hands of Archbishop Leontii Lebedinskii (†1893) of Warsaw and Sergei A. Rachinskii (1833-1902), a well-known conservative educationist who had experimented in folk schools in the western provinces.[46]

Growth of the parish system in the next two decades was impressive, a challenge to the pervasive illiteracy and poverty of the people. In 1888 the Synod Education Commission had increased the number of schools to 17,715 with an enrollment of nearly half a million students, and in the fall term of 1890 there were 21,666 parish schools with 621,182 students. Five years later, at the beginning of the first full term in the reign of Nicholas II, there were 31,835 schools with an enrollment of 981,076. At the turn of the twentieth century there were 41,402 schools with 2,147,916 students in the parish system.[47]

The system continued to expand until 1906 when, because of internal disorders and a scarcity of funds, it went into a decline that lasted till 1910. Between 1910 and the outbreak of World War I the schools again increased in enrollment and facilities, but the beginning of the war sent them into a decline that became a total collapse once the Bolsheviks seized power.

During those years the schools underwent a transformation that was needed to keep pace with the changing demands placed upon them. Initially they had been simple schools of literacy that provided basic penmanship and grammar coupled with the rudest instruction in doctrine. Gradually they were expanded into three-, five- and seven-year schools, patterned after those of the Ministry of Public Education. Gradually, too, the ingrained suspicion and hostility between the agents of the Ministry and the *zemstvo* organizations on the one hand, and the clergy on the other, had begun to lessen and give way to cooperation. Initially *zemstvo* officials had opposed church schools because they deprived them of funds that they wished to use for their own schools and projects. In certain areas local landowners were especially obstinate because they resented

the taxation that went for the schools and they resented loss
of authority over the local priest that had come in the wake
of Emancipation. The close bonds that existed between priest
and peasant and the increase in peasant influence in the
zemstvo councils gradually obviated the hostilities, so that by
1900, zemstvos were contributing about 15 percent of the
total parish school operating expenses.[48]

The law of 1884 had envisioned a multiple economic support system for parish schools that would include parish trustee
organizations, town duma monies, zemstvo funds, private
donors, diocesan support, Synod financing, and grants from
the State Treasury. It was hoped that local organizations
would carry the main burden of school funding. It was gratify-
ing that, by 1900, out of a total parish school budget of
14,552,775 rubles, less than half, 6,814,250 rubles, came directly from the State Treasury.[49]

The Synod Education Commission was concerned not to
remain overly dependent upon direct aid from the Treasury,
because they feared the possibility of another decline if hostile
bureaucratic attitudes should cut off funds for church schools
again. Thus, non-Treasury funds were steadily developed in
the opening years of the century, so that they increasingly out-
weighed the support coming directly from the Treasury. Substantial contributions by wealthier peasants and small merchants during the 1890s and early 1900s indicated popular
support for the schools and offered hope that cuts in state
funds would not precipitate the decline of 1865-1884 again.
In 1902 half the primary education in the empire was in the
hands of the Synod Education Commission, which hoped that,
by the opening of school in the fall of 1907, every child who
wanted parish school education could have it, free of tuition.
Tuition charges were one of the main obstacles to enrollment
at the turn of the twentieth century. No one could have fore-
seen the upheavals of war and civil disorder that were to come
in the meantime.[50]

The parish clergy was the backbone of the school system,
providing both the majority of religious instructors and a significant portion of teachers of non-religious subjects. For example, in the 1889-1890 school year, 9,900 out of 12,000

religion teachers were priests, while in 1900, 26,383 out of 37,948 religion teachers were priests. Most of them received no compensation. They were assisted by a rapidly growing force of lay teachers—11,211 in 1896, 41,281 in 1898, and 49,078 in 1900. This rapidly growing number of lay teachers necessitated setting up special teachers' schools by the Synod Education Commission and adding special pedagogical courses to the curriculum of seminaries, diocesan men's and women's schools, and to the newly established second-form (*vtoro-klassnye*) schools. In 1900 there were eighteen teachers' schools and 349 second-form schools. The second-form schools themselves were the highest form of parish schools and could admit students only after they had completed five years in two-class (*dvukhklassnye*) parish schools. The teachers were woefully underpaid, the majority of them being paid one hundred rubles or less per annum. It was no wonder that they left the parish schools for better paying jobs as soon as they could. In 1900 only 23 percent of the teachers had been in the system five years or longer. Thus, besides having to wheedle and cajole funds and buildings to start new schools, the priests had to remain the backbone of the permanent teaching staff and at the same time scramble each year to find replacements for teachers who could not afford to stay.[51]

In keeping with the challenges the church faced, the concentration of schools was heaviest in areas with Uniate, Old Believer and sectarian populations. The Kiev diocese had the largest number of schools operating in their own facilities. The majority of parish schools in Russia in 1900 operated entirely or in part in churches, private homes or apartments, rented facilities, or donated space—anywhere room was available.[52]

Curriculum changed to keep pace with the changing economy and social demand. During the 1890s courses were added to the rudimentary instruction in religion and literacy in such areas as choral singing, Old Church Slavonic, ethics, history, literature—especially Pushkin—and arithmetic. In 1896 one-class schools which took three years to complete began to expand into two-class schools that took five years to complete. The expanded curriculum included more history, geography, more mathematics, and courses in such skills as bootmaking, woodworking, blacksmithing and cabinet making for boys and in weaving, sewing and spinning for girls. Besides new funds from the Treasury for this expansion, the Ministry of State Domains provided annual grants to underwrite courses in market gardening, agriculture, agricultural economics and horticulture, and guaranteed students who took those courses employment in its extension services. The increased load of courses often extended the time of graduation to six and even seven years. Thus, peasant students who would be remaining in the countryside and those who would be moving into the towns and cities were given the skills they needed, together with an appreciation of the music, art and doctrine of the Orthodox church.[53]

One of the more attractive features of Orthodox education was the rich musical heritage of the church. Thousands of parish choirs were formed in the 1890s with special funds from the Synod to enhance the worship and cultural life of the masses and to impress the non-Orthodox and non-Russian populations of the empire. Synod Education Commission authorities were gratified to see Old Believer populations in the Urals and along the Volga gradually ceasing to resist official liturgies connected with school affairs and to see thousands of Catholic and Lutheran children enroll in Orthodox schools in the western and Baltic provinces, attracted by the opportunities provided by choral singing societies.[54]

It goes without saying that the priests in the parish schools received their training in the diocesan seminaries. Other non-ordained male teachers and the women teachers received their education in diocesan men's and women's schools. The Synod issued regulations in 1889 that the curriculum for the seminaries and for the diocesan schools should be standardized as soon as possible, but there remained wide variation from diocese to diocese during all the years before World War I. In places like Moscow, St. Petersburg, Riga, Kholm, Vilna and Kiev, seminary education compared well to that of European and Russian gymnasia, thanks to their proximity to the theological academies or to seminaries of Lutheran or Catholic competitors, while in remoter areas the level of instruction was lower.[55]

Seminary curriculum covered a six-year span, the first two of which coincided with the last two years of course work in the diocesan men's schools. Included were four years of theology, philosophy, hagiography, general church history, Russian church history, history of the Raskol, Church Slavonic, liturgical music, Russian literature, calligraphy and public speaking. Public speaking was given special emphasis during the 1890s and early 1900s to compensate for its almost total neglect before that time and to utilize the preaching of the word as a means to enlighten the Orthodox public about atheistic and sectarian propaganda. The rising level of sophistication of the masses necessitated intelligent preaching.[56]

In areas where Great Russian was not the dominant language, seminaries were developing new liturgies in the languages of the native populations. Diocesan authorities experimented in liturgies in the Estonian, Latvian, Mongolian, Chuvash, Tartar and Mordvinian languages. A ritual in Finnish was developed in 1907. Most seminarians were expected to learn Greek and Latin, and, in some seminaries after 1887, Hebrew. In seminaries like Tobolsk and Irkutsk, students were exempted from the classical languages in order to study the native languages of the non-Russian population or, if they were not Russian, to study Russian.[57]

The brighter and more promising seminarians were encouraged to apply to the theological academies to further their learning. Four academies, graduate schools on a par with the state universities, existed in St. Petersburg, Moscow, Kiev and Kazan. The St. Petersburg Academy was located at the Alexandro-Nevskii Lavra founded by Peter the Great. The Moscow Academy had been founded in the 1670s by students from the Kiev Academy, which in turn had been founded in 1633 by Peter Moghila, the first metropolitan of the restored Orthodox hierarchy there. The Kazan Academy had been founded in 1842 by Nicholas I. The academies trained the faculties of the fifty-eight diocesan seminaries, the religion faculties in state schools, and were staffed by such eminent men as Vasilii V. Bolotov, Alexander I. Brilliantov, Alexei P. Lebedev, Evgenii E. Golubinskii, Ilia Berdnikov and Vasilii O. Kliuchevskii. Because of the prejudice against Rus-

sian ecclesiastical education existing before the Bolshevik upheaval, and, subsequently, because of that upheaval itself,
the reputations of these men and their peers are not yet fully
appreciated in the West.[58]

According to Synod regulations of November 1890, the
admission of applicants was to be stringently surveyed, with
only those having the best academic records and secret character references being admitted. Once admitted, students were
closely supervised. They lived in dormitories on academy
premises, signed in and out when coming and going from the
campuses, and were home in their rooms by midnight on days
when they were allowed out. The controls were designed to
ensure that students spent their time at the academy profitably
and to curb their penchant for joining with university students in political activities. Drunken and rowdy behavior was
cause for suspension or permanent dismissal. All literature
had to be cleared with the academy librarian before it could
be kept or read on the academy premises.

During their four years in the academies, students worked
out their own curriculum under the supervision of the rector.
They could choose one of two tracks, either to study the
church fathers and the theological and historical developments
of the eastern and western churches, or they could set up programs in pastoral social work or missionary work. At St.
Petersburg pastoral social work was emphasized, while at
Kiev and Kazan missionary work was stressed.

The St. Petersburg program was geared towards the rapidly
growing urban working class. Priests and students not yet
ordained worked under the supervision of Rector—later
Metropolitan—Antonii Vadkovskii in preaching stations set
up around the city. The program had been launched in 1888,
with the approval of Konstantin Pobedonostsev, Procurator
of the Synod, and was known as the Society for Religious and
Moral Propagation.[59]

With collaboration from professors at the academy,
libraries, reading rooms and counselling facilities were established near various factories and working class residential
areas. Gradually credit organizations and relief agencies became part of the Society's operation. Vadkovskii intended to

make known the presence of the church as an antidote to the anti-religious socialist agitators who operated their own circles and reading rooms in the city, albeit illegally.

As in the seminaries, most students in the academies were sons of priests, but at the turn of the century a growing number of students entered from the universities, the gymnasia, the real schools, the medical schools, artillery schools, technical schools, and branches of the imperial civil service. These students broadened the background of the ecclesiastical intelligentsia and were another sign that the clerical caste system was fading away.

The number of students never exceeded seven hundred in the four academies combined. More than half of them were on government stipends, a number paid their own way, and the remainder were on stipends provided by ecclesiastical educational brotherhoods or by the academies themselves.[60]

The four-tiered church school system was the main hope of the Orthodox administration to prepare the next generation of Russian youth for the society that had evolved in the wake of the Emancipation. It was hoped it would provide skills and cultural tools that would enable the church to remain involved in the life of the people, combat the propaganda of religious dissidents, and counter the claims of atheistic agitators. The state regarded the schools as the guarantee that the church would remain a pillar of the established political order. Government officials assumed that the interests of the church and the state were identical. Many churchmen, on the other hand, increasingly saw them as divergent.

CHAPTER II

Confrontation: The Procurator and the Two Antoniis

At the opening of the twentieth century, the head of the Russian church for all practical purposes was Konstantin Petrovich Pobedonostsev (1827-1907), Ober-Procurator of the Most Holy Synod. Appointed to that position in 1880, less than a year before the assassination of Tsar Alexander II (1855-1881), he guided the destinies of the Russian church for a quarter of a century (1880-1905). A Burkean conservative, Pobedonostsev believed that change had to be made slowly, within the context of existing traditions, so that social and governing apparatuses would not collapse and bring on anarchy.

Pobedonostsev entered Russian state service in 1846 in the Moscow division of the Imperial Senate, the Russian equivalent of a Supreme Court. One of the young liberals of the mid-nineteenth century, he saw the necessity of abolishing serfdom and instituting reforms to guarantee the continued existence of the Russian Empire. The goal of his life was the restoration of power and greatness in the aftermath of the Crimean War. In 1861, Pobedonostsev was appointed tutor to the Tsar's children. At the same time, he worked in a select committee of the Committee of Ministers—a law-drafting agency created to reform the judicial system.

However, between the promulgation of the new judiciary in 1864 and the creation of a new military service system in

1874, Pobedonostsev underwent a thorough disillusionment
with liberal legislation and institutions and became convinced
that those systems and structures would not civilize a society.
In those ten years Russia had reaped a whirlwind of anarchy
and civil violence, which gravely weakened the government
and added to its humiliation in the eyes of foreigners. Several
attempts had been made to assassinate the Tsar, and
Pobedonostsev had come to believe that Alexander himself
was leading Russia to destruction. He criticized Alexander
to the Tsar's own heir, and had the satisfaction of knowing
that the Tsarevich agreed with his tutor. When, in terrifying
fulfillment of his worst expectations, the Tsar was assassinated on March 1, 1881, the Procurator believed that the
Tsar had prepared his own destruction.

Alexander III (1881-1894) was a man from a different
mold. Gruff and stern, he wasted no time interdicting a series
of reforms his father had authorized and, at the Procurator's
urging, began to turn the clock backwards. Both men looked
to a religious revival as a vehicle to rehabilitate Russia, and
as head of the church, Pobedonostsev was determined to see
that the church was capable of that mission.[1]

Accordingly, reforms were instituted restoring order in
the seminaries, weeding out students who espoused liberal
political ideologies or who led other students into violence
and internal discord. Students were put under the surveillance
of administrators and the teaching staff. Staff members who
did not keep close records, regardless of whether the student's academic performance was satisfactory, were dismissed.
Students were deliberately walled off from the social and
political influences of their times. The Procurator noted with
satisfaction that most of the violence in the seminaries had
tapered off by the 1890s.

Together with efforts to expand the ecclesiastical education system in general, much effort was devoted to raising
the standards of instruction in the seminaries, establishing
trusteeships and endowments and attracting students of the
same calibre as those attending schools under the Ministry
of Public Education and other government agencies.
Pobedonostsev expected that a docile and patriotic clergy,

whose impact upon the believing masses would go far to stifle revolutionary currents, would be a mainstay of the tsardom.[2]

In the twenty years after his appointment to the procuracy, Pobedonostsev saw a whole new generation of priests and prelates into office. As they were all his appointees, he believed them to be men who shared his ideas about the proper role of the church as a bulwark of the state and the instiller of patriotism and loyalty to the Tsar. By 1900, however, the Procurator was disquieted. In 1894, his pupil and mainstay, Alexander III, had died, prematurely, leaving on the throne his son Nicholas II, a man whose character was, if anything, weaker than his grandfather's. The Procurator knew that unless the social ferment of the 1890s was contained, the disorders of the 1860s and 1870s would reappear and work the same destructive course on the tsardom. By the turn of the century, the erosion had already gone deep, alien ideological forces were sapping the strength of the regime, and the Procurator was tired, pessimistic and old—seventy-three years.

The church was feeling the strain of social ferment, with priests, bishops and articulate groups of laymen struggling against the straitjacket of the Procurator and the state bureaucracy. Arguments that questioned the very validity of the governing apparatus set up by Peter the Great had mushroomed into demands for the removal of the Procurator personally and the dismantling of the procuracy itself. Pobedonostsev felt alone, abandoned by the tsardom he had labored so hard to uphold. His heavy-handed administration had produced its own counterpressure within the church, from members of the hierarchy who refused to be simply place-fillers, from clergy, from professors in the church schools and from the religious intelligentsia. They reflected the concern of Fedor Dostoevskii, who, before his death, had forcefully lamented the paralysis of the church.[3]

*   *   *

Three main centers of pressure for reform were the Sergei-Troitskii Lavra near Moscow, the Alexandro-Nevskii Lavra in St. Petersburg, and the Kazan Theological Academy. Among the capable leaders who guided the destinies of those centers in the last decade of the nineteenth century, two stand out—Antonii Vadkovskii (1846-1912) and Antonii Khrapovitskii (1863-1936). Over the years their political views diverged radically, but they were united in the conviction that the crippling hand of the state had to be removed and the church had to be allowed to govern itself according to the canons of Eastern Orthodoxy.[4]

Born in August 1846, Vadkovskii came from a typical rural Russian clerical family. His father, Vasilii Iovlevich Vadkovskii, was pastor in the village of Shiringusha in the Spassk *volost'* of Tambov province. His mother, Olga Nikiforovna, was the daughter of Archpriest S. N. Kashmenskii of Viatka cathedral. The Vadkovskii family was poor. Antonii was one of seven boys. Two besides himself became priests, two became doctors and one remained a psalmist in Shiringusha. There is no information on the seventh child, who may have died at an early age. There were, besides, two sisters.[5]

The future metropolitan entered the Tambov Diocesan Men's School when he was ten years old and transferred when he was fourteen to the diocesan seminary. When he completed six years in the seminary, he entered Kazan Theological Academy on a government scholarship in 1866. Kazan Academy opened his eyes to the enduring timelessness of the traditions of the church. He began to view a renewed church as essential to the future renewal of Russian social and political order. Specializing in homiletics and pastoral theology, he prepared himself for the fray and excitement of a Russian pastorate. He finished the academy in 1870 and was invited to join the teaching staff.[6]

As docent he wanted to become a monk immediately, but his father, mindful of his active nature, cautioned him to wait, to remain a layman on the academy faculty till he could better judge his vocation.

Vadkovskii's popular lectures stirred his students to preaching and pastoral leadership. His own master's thesis was entitled "The History of Preaching in the Early Church." Vadkovskii stressed that effective preachers like

Ambrose of Milan, Cyril of Jerusalem and Basil the Great had had decisive influence in their times and that men of their stature were necessary to influence the course of modern events.

In 1872 he married Elizabeth Penkovskii, sister of one of his colleagues at the academy. It was to be a short marriage, as Elizabeth was ill with tuberculosis. She died in 1879, leaving two young children, Boris, aged six, and Lydia, aged two. A third son, Igor, had died earlier. Boris and Lydia in turn fell victim to diphtheria and died within a week of each other (November 1882).

Within a year, Vadkovskii took monastic tonsure, became a member of the community of the Ioannovskii Monastery and almost immediately was named its superior. He was ordained, became a hieromonk, rose to archimandrite, and was appointed Inspector of the Kazan Academy, all within two years. By then he was well known not only for his teaching, but also for his compassion as a monastic father. The Ioannovskii Monastery experienced a renewed vitality, which was reflected not only in the academy, but through its graduates in monasteries, dioceses and seminaries throughout the Russian church.[7]

In 1885 he was appointed Inspector of the St. Petersburg Theological Academy, and during the next seven years his influence spread via graduates from that prestigious academy. In 1887 he was consecrated bishop of Vyborg, a vicarate of St. Petersburg, and was made rector of the academy. He used his new position to break down the barriers between the cloistered life of academe and the turbulent social and political life outside its walls through preaching circles (*kruzhki*) organized among the students of the academy and patterned on study circles organized by anti-religious political agitators, among whom was the young law student Vladimir Lenin, just then launching his political career in Social Democratic study circles in St. Petersburg.[8]

At the end of 1892, Bishop Antonii was named the first archbishop of the newly autonomous diocese of Finland. Antonii was an expert on non-Orthodox sectarian teaching because of his past experience at Kazan. Lutherans interested

him, although to him Lutheranism was an odd, arid type
of Christianity that provided its faithful with only a partial
glimpse of the deep mysteries of the ecumenical church. If
exposed to a positive expression of Orthodoxy, he felt, Finns
would be attracted to Orthodoxy as had their ethnic brothers,
the Karelians.[9] But Vadkovskii's experience in Finland turned
out to be a bitter disappointment, his pastorate frustrated by
the preemptory demands of the civilian administration.
Finally, in 1898, he clashed violently with the governor-
general of Finland, Nikolai I. Bobrikov (1839-1904), so that
the Minister of the Interior, Viacheslav K. Plehve, prevailed
upon Pobedonostsev to remove him.

The Lutheran problem in the Russian Empire had puzzled
officials ever since large areas, predominantly Lutheran in
population, had been incorporated into the empire by Peter
the Great. Lutherans lived along the Baltic littoral and in
Finland. They were more concentrated than Old Believers,
Uniates, Latins or Moslems. Vigorous Russification was extended in the 1890s to Lutheran areas, even though Lutherans
had never mounted a proselytizing effort of any significance.
The Lutheran problem derived from the Uniate problem, because Uniate and Lutheran areas were contiguous to each
other. The argument that justified the suppression of Unia—
safeguarding the borders of the empire and the identity of
the Russian nation—was applied to the Lutheran regions,
particularly after the unification of Germany in 1871. The
new Germany, governed by a Lutheran regime, was considered a source of subversives akin to the Austrian Empire.

Two events in 1892 signalled the government's attack
upon Lutherans: the suppression of Dorpat University as a
German, Lutheran institution and the creation of the autonomous diocese of Finland. In Estonia and Latvia, Orthodox
convents, monasteries, parishes (up to fifteen annually from
1892 to 1900) and schools were opened. A law in 1894
forbade Lutheran clergy to perform marriages between Orthodox and Lutherans, to baptize the offspring of an Orthodox-
Lutheran mixed marriage, or to administer confirmation to
anyone born of an Orthodox-Lutheran marriage. Numerous
orphanages were opened, modelled after institutions opened

during the 1880s in Uniate areas, to house children of mixed marriages and ensure their being raised in the Orthodox faith and Russian nationality.

Missionary activities aimed at the Estonian and Latvian peasant populations exacerbated antagonism towards the German landowning nobility and the German-dominated administration. Orthodox tracts emphasized the antiquity of Orthodoxy as compared to the recentness of Lutheranism and pointed out the alterations in doctrines made by the Lutheran reformers. Experimental rites in both the Estonian and Latvian languages attracted a handful of native priests by the turn of the century to supplement Russian-born clergy.

By 1900 there were flourishing convents at Wesenburg in Estonia and Illukst in Courland and a promising monastery, the Alexeev, in Riga. These institutions ran schools, dispensaries and orphanages, which were staffed with zealous monks and nuns. Together with the newly established parishes, these foundations gave assurance that the offensive had been successfully launched. With enough time, sizable portions of the non-German population would cease to be Lutheran. In the diocese of Riga, approximately thirty Lutheran pastors had been brought to justice for violating the law of 1894 and were either imprisoned or deprived of their pulpits. The effect had been to reduce resistance from the Lutheran clergy significantly and to dampen the kind of underground activities carried on by the Uniate and Latin clergies to the south. At the same time, it alienated both the native and German populations, so that when the opportunity arose they opted to separate from the empire.[10]

In Finland the offensive was less successful. Two major reasons stood out: the Grand Duchy of Finland was a separate entity in the administration of the empire, and therefore the law of June 1894 did not operate there; and the Orthodox population was so small, barely fifty thousand persons in the whole of Finland, concentrated in the east and south. There was no possibility of developing an active Orthodox community, except in the extreme eastern portions, in places like Vyborg, where the diocesan cathedral was located on the border between Finland and Karelia.

Antonii was able to organize an effective diocesan consistory in 1897 and held his first convocation of clergy in 1898, the year of his departure. Since the Lutheran church monopolized primary and secondary education and since Orthodox schools barely numbered twenty in the whole of Finland, there was little hope that Orthodox education would have any attraction for the Finnish population. Furthermore, teachers of religion in Orthodox parish schools had to be trained at the teachers college in Serdobol, which was staffed by Lutherans who were indifferent, if not openly hostile, to Orthodoxy. Unless trained at Serdobol, the Finnish Senate refused to pay their salaries. In addition, the Finnish Inspector of Schools had authority over Orthodox parish schools and disapproved of the teaching of Orthodoxy, Russian language and literature, or cultural courses that were not Finnish and Lutheran in content.

Official policies created a backlash in Finland. Antonii's complaints to the Synod and the Procurator produced no relief. He was profoundly relieved to be recalled to St. Petersburg in December 1898. He had not liked being an agent of the government and returned to the capital convinced that the church had to avoid being the tool of the state if the Orthodox heritage were to have appeal among non-Orthodox.

Antonii's former bishop in Kazan, Palladii Raev, who was made metropolitan of St. Petersburg in 1892, had died in 1898, and Vadkovskii was named to succeed him.[11] His return to St. Petersburg was the occasion for considerable rejoicing among the city's clergy. His activities as rector of the academy had made him very popular, and now that he was back as metropolitan his clergy expected activism on a much wider scale. No other nineteenth-century Russian prelate, with the exception of Filaret Drozdov (1782-1867), metropolitan of Moscow, enjoyed such influence and esteem.

Soon after his return to St. Petersburg, Antonii created a stir by urging the government to grant amnesty to several political prisoners, among them Mikhail Novorusskii, who had conspired with Alexander Ulianov, brother of Lenin, to kill Tsar Alexander III in 1886. Novorusskii was incarcerated in the Schlüsselberg fortress, and Antonii's visits to him and other prisoners raised society eyebrows and irritated the security police.

Students, clergy and the public were impressed by Antonii's humility and simplicity. Guests at his table were surprised by the simple monastic fare and by a life-style unaffected by the grandeur that went with the office of metropolitan. When given gifts, sometimes amounting to thousands of rubles, he immediately passed them into the hands of needy students, priests and causes. One of his most ambitious undertakings was to open new parishes for the rapidly growing working masses of the city and parish schools to allow them to educate their children and consolidate their loyalty to the church.[12]

Antonii was especially disturbed by the alienation of the Russian intelligentsia from the church. He believed that their antagonism was directed more against the political structure and the practices of the state than against the teachings and traditions of the church. He viewed his metropolitan pastorate as the opportunity to demonstrate the renovative tradition of Christianity, and he was disturbed that practically none of the social reform movements during the past sixty years had had a religious orientation, though many revolutionaries, like himself, were from clerical families. Because the church appeared to be an arm of the state, social reformers had written it off as useless, a detriment to social progress.

By the turn of the century, single-minded atheistic monism was losing its luster. A younger generation of intellectuals had found materialism unsatisfactory. Deeper understanding of the psychology of the human person and its place in the universe was being sought, and Antonii was convinced that intellectuals would find satisfaction in the traditions of the Eastern church. The problem was to bring the intellectuals and traditions together. The metropolitan wanted students from the academy to develop an understanding of the moral and social ideologies of the secular world and to become aware of their challenge to the church. The church, he felt, had to abandon its esoteric language and begin to understand the vocabulary and mind of the secular world.[13]

Antonii's intentions were happily supplemented by a group of young artists who were weary of the positivist materialistic thinking of the past forty years. Several of them, including those connected with the literary magazine *Mir Isskustva*, which had begun publication in 1889 under the direction of ballet maestro Sergei Diaghilev (1827-1919), persuaded Antonii in 1901 to hold joint meetings between themselves and representatives of the church, faculty and students from the theological academy. With Antonii's support, they founded the Religious-Philosophical Society and held the first of twenty-one brainstorming sessions at the Imperial Geographical Society offices on October 29, 1901.

The personnel at these sessions were diverse, ranging from Archimandrite Sergei Stragorodskii, rector of the academy, Archimandrite Feofan Bystrov, inspector at the academy, and several professors, to popular poets like Dmitri Merezhkovskii (1865-1941) and his wife Zinaida Gippius (1869-1945), Dmitri Filosofov (1861-1907), Alexander Benois (1870-1960), and intellectuals like Sergei Bulgakov (1871-1944). It was a remarkably imaginative collection of individuals, religious and secular, who shared a common concern for the ideological and moral future of Russia.

To the dismay of more conservative churchmen like Archpriest Mikhail Semenov and Archimandrite Antonin Granovskii (1865-1928), censor at St. Petersburg Theological Academy, many of the instructors and students at the academy agreed with the secular intellectuals on issues like the place of women in society, changes in marriage contract relations, the corresponding need to alter religious and civil regulations governing marriage, religious freedom, freedom of conscience and outdated legislation concerning bastard children.

The participants focused on the clumsy church administration and its fawning subservience to the state as one of the reasons for the irrelevance of the church. Church intellectuals like Anton V. Kartashev (1875-1960), professor of church history at the academy, and Fr. Alexander Brilliantov, theologian who succeeded to the chair of the late V. V. Bolotov in 1900, voiced their conviction that the only solution to the church's malaise would be a church council.[14]

The debates of the Society created a sensation in the secular and religious press during their eighteen months and stirred public interest to an extent that displeased the Procurator, particularly when the debates focused upon church administration. Pobedonostsev's watchdog at the debates, V. M. Skvortsov (1869-1932), pressed him to suppress them, as did churchmen like Fr. Ioann Sergiev (1829-1908) of Kronstadt, a popular preacher and healer. Influential officials urged the suspension of the Society as well, and the Procurator ended the debates on April 5, 1903.

But the effort had not been wasted. Antonii wished to bring the voice of the church to the attention of the non-ecclesiastical public and had partially succeeded, if for no other reason than because people like Merezhkovskii and Gippius had confronted it and had rejected it. The exchange intrigued young Marxist intellectuals like Sergei Bulgakov and Nikolai Berdyaev (1874-1948), who, already disillusioned with the narrow materialism of the Marxist ethic, were looking for a broader context in which to lodge their concept of man. Their search led them and others like Peter B. Struve (1870-1944) and Simeon L. Frank (1877-1950) to reject materialism for a religious orientation to man's basic identity, a "deviation" from Marxian orthodoxy which disturbed Lenin not a little.[15]

* * *

Antonii Khrapovitskii's background was quite different from that of his namesake in St. Petersburg. Born in March 1863, more than sixteen years after Vadkovskii, in the village of Vatagino, Krestitskii *uezd*, Novgorod province, he was of the *dvorianstvo* who had entered Muscovite service in the seventeenth century. Antonii was the third of four sons born to Pavel and Nataliia Khrapovitskii. His father, a none-too-successful manager of the family estate, had moved to Petersburg in 1870 to work for the Volga-Kamskii Bank and subsequently for the Nobles' Land Bank.

In Petersburg, Antonii developed a keen interest in the church and frequently served as an acolyte at St. Isaac's and

Kazan cathedrals. Such an interest was looked upon with skepticism among fellow students of the Fifth Gymnasium, where loyalty to the church was viewed as passé.

His years at the gymnasium were troubled by the internal strife and stress of social and political upheavals that ended with the assassination of Alexander II. Khrapovitskii became convinced that far-reaching reforms were indispensable if Russia were to avert similar tragedies in the future and that the church would have to reform itself if the country were not to lose its moral bearing entirely. He believed that the abolition of the patriarchate by Peter had been a mistake and that a Patriarch would enable the church to restore its canonical bases and become the culturally and socially cohesive force so desperately needed in Russia. A Slavophile along with Ivan Aksakov (1823-1886), he believed the renovation of the church to be the keystone to moral revival, not only in Russia but among the Slavic peoples as a whole.[16] Another powerful impact on the young student was Fedor Dostoevskii (1821-1881) whose *Brothers Karamazov* pictured a moving description of the monastic life. Dostoevskii, following the unexpected death of his son, had visited the famous Optina Monastery in the company of Vladimir Solovicv (1855-1900). Dostoevskii found solace there in the company of Fr. Amvrosii Grenkov (1812-1891). Khrapovitskii himself made pilgrimages to Optina and found Amvrosii inspiring. Dostoevskii's death the same year as Alexander's assassination was a blow.

In 1881, that same spring, Antonii finished the gymnasium. Expected to enter the Petersburg Law Faculty or the Alexander Lycée in Tsarskoe Selo, the normal route for a graduate of the Fifth Petersburg Gymnasium, he opted instead for the Theological Academy of St. Petersburg, despite family pressure to dissuade him. In 1885, Khrapovitskii's last year, Antonii Vadkovskii was named inspector of the academy. The older man's inner dynamism had considerable influence among the students. To Khrapovitskii he was the very model of Dostoevskii's monk. One of Khrapovitskii's closest friends, Mikhail M. Gribanovskii (1862-1898), once a skeptic and agnostic, took monastic vows under the influence of Vadkovskii. Khrapovitskii, too, when he graduated from the academy in May 1885, decided to take monastic tonsure.[17]

As a hieromonk, he became an assistant to Vadkovskii. Together with Vadkovskii and Gribanovskii, he worked with a nucleus of students who went out to preach among the working classes of the capital. They were opposed by Bishop Arsenii Briantsev (1839-1914), rector of the academy, who threw up roadblocks in the path of the young monks, because he distrusted their enthusiasm and disapproved of their political and social activism. The rector resented student protests against regulations and rigid formalities, and looked upon the young monks as a kind of revolutionary *bunt* within the walls of the academy. Arsenii got Khrapovitskii exiled to the seminary in Kholm, while Gribanovskii was sent off to Athens as pastor of the Russian embassy church.

But Arsenii was made bishop of Riga within a year of Khrapovitskii's exile to Kholm, Vadkovskii was elevated to the rectorship, and Khrapovitskii returned to the academy as professor of Old Testament. Khrapovitskii used his position there to agitate for the restoration of the Russian patriarchate and for administrative independence for the church. Khrapovitskii was befriended by Vladimir Soloviev in his belief that the canonical structure of the Russian church since the time of the Petrine reform was questionable. Both men felt that Old Believers had a valid case when they questioned the legitimacy of the Russian church, particularly in their rejection of the Petrine reforms. Khrapovitskii criticized government persecution of Old Believers and opposed the offensive courses offered in the academies and seminaries designed to refute Old Belief. He further suggested that the authorities ponder the possibility that common oppression might one day drive Old Believers and Uniates together. His lectures on the Old Testament stressed how the prophets had withstood, cajoled, and defied the Kings of Israel in their concern for the religious welfare of their people. Modern churchmen should expect to do likewise in Russia. In articles appearing under the signature S.S.B. (*Sluzhitel' Slova Bozhii*) in *Russkoe Slovo*, the young monk lamented the passive role of the Russian clergy and made it clear that the reason for passivity was not lack of interest in social affairs, but the officialdom and the police who pounced upon any priest who defended the oppressed or protested injustices.[18]

Khrapovitskii's agitation in Petersburg was unwelcome to the Procurator. He was transferred to Moscow Theological Academy, thanks to an old friend, Leontii Lebedinskii (†1903), formerly bishop of Kholm and Warsaw and now metropolitan of Moscow, who in the Synod prevented Antonii's exile once again to a remote seminary.

Khrapovitskii's appointment as Rector of the Moscow Theological Academy came over the strenuous objections of the former rector, Sergei Liapidevskii (1828-1898). Sergei regarded Khrapovitskii as a crypto-papalist because of his agitation for restoration of the patriarchate and because of his friendship with Soloviev. Sergei's objections were seconded by such influential men as Professor Evgenii E. Golubinskii (1834-1912), the well-known church historian whose writings Khrapovitskii had denounced as crypto-Protestant, and the historian Vasilii Kliuchevskii (1834-1911), whose writings Khrapovitskii regarded as devoid of spiritual content, something especially regrettable in view of the fact that the author had once been a seminarian. Leontii put a great deal of pressure on Pobedonostsev to remove Sergei and make him archbishop of Kazan. Leontii had the support of Princes Sergei N. (1862-1905) and Evgenii N. (1863-1920) Trubetskoi. Sergei was duly removed and never forgave Khrapovitskii.

Archpriest Alexander Ivantsov-Platonov, professor of theology at Moscow Academy, welcomed Khrapovitskii. Ivantsov-Platonov had been active for church renewal and independence from civil control before the assassination of Alexander II. One of the casualties of the post-assassination crackdown, he had been content to teach theology and not to advocate his ideas about church government openly. Now that Antonii had come to the academy, however, Ivantsov-Platonov felt that the time had come to urge reform again and, with Antonii's encouragement, published an article exposing the non-canonical government of the church and recommending restoration of the patriarchate. Shortly thereafter, a much annoyed Procurator had the archpriest removed from his post, and Ivantsov wound up teaching religion at the Alexandrov Military School in Moscow, remaining there until his death in 1898.

Antonii was popular with the students of the academy, viewing them as fellow laborers in a common effort rather than military cadets to be ordered about as if they were in barracks. He frequently came to their rooms to discuss personal problems, studies, theology or any topic that might interest them—a radical departure from previous practice.

One of Khrapovitskii's favorite places was the New Jerusalem Monastery near Moscow, the pride of Patriarch Nikon in the seventeenth century, which still, at the end of the nineteenth century, breathed the presence of its founder. Nikon's effort to reform the Russian church in the seventeenth century was something Antonii believed had to be revived. He believed that Moscow's claim to be the Third Rome had been gravely compromised by the outcome of the Great Sobor of 1666-1667. With Rome itself revived under the papacy of Leo XIII (1878-1903) and making a serious claim once more to represent all Christendom, Nikon's vision was once again vital for the Russian church. Antonii also felt that if the emphasis upon biblical history upheld in the liturgical and monastic traditions of New Jerusalem were better known, neo-Protestant influences infecting Russia could be obviated—at New Jerusalem, the biblical roots of the church were everywhere in evidence. Western religious forms, both Catholic and Protestant, he believed, were too intellectualized and isolated the scholarly aspects of Christian learning from the daily living of the wholeness of Christianity. Orthodoxy did not compartmentalize and desiccate the deification and redemption of the person.

One of Khrapovitskii's early accomplishments was to make the theological journal *Bogoslovskii Vestnik* the official organ of the Moscow Theological Academy (November 1891). During the following quarter century it served as the vanguard of church reform.

When Antonii's friend Metropolitan Leontii died in

1893, he was succeeded by Sergei Liapidevskii, one of whose first moves was to reinstate the old barracks-like administration in the Moscow Theological Academy. Annoyed that his articles and pamphlets had been criticized by Antonii as formalistic, devoid of feeling and relevance and smelling of Catholic scholasticism, the two men collided in a confrontation of major proportions, which necessitated an official investigation by the Synod. Sergei, a ranking member of the Synod, had the ear and sympathies of the Procurator, who appointed A. P. Nechaev to conduct the inquiry. Nechaev had been a student at the Petersburg Academy at the same time as Khrapovitskii and had not liked him. Nechaev recommended that Antonii be transferred to the rectorship of the Kazan Academy for the fall semester of 1895. His replacement in Moscow was Archimandrite Lavrentii Nekrasov (1836-1908), formerly an officer in the Cadet Corps, who restored the old regulations forthwith, even calling his students "cadets." Only Lavrentii's early transfer prevented the complete destruction of Antonii's labors in Moscow.[19]

Antonii's career in Kazan was much the same as it had been in Petersburg and Moscow. Kazan Academy, founded in 1842 by Tsar Nicholas I, was not only a center of theological studies where such luminaries as Viktor Ivanovich Nesmelov (1863-1920) and Ilia S. Berdnikov (1841-1914) were on the faculty, but it was also the center of anti-Old Believer and Moslem missionary organization and studies in Russia. An entire network of missions directed at the non-Russian population of the Volga region and Siberia was headquartered at Kazan. Antonii's predecessor, Archpriest Alexander Polikarpovich Vladimirskii (1814-1897), had organized and nurtured this network, so that by the time Antonii took over there were several mission stations scattered from the banks of the Volga to the reaches of the Altai Mountains and to the far northeast in Kamchatka. While he sympathized with and appreciated the work among the non-Christian populations, Antonii thought the courses offered to "refute" the Old Believers were ridiculous and that they needlessly antagonized a whole section of the Russian people whom he thought should be conciliated. Again, he insisted that the only way to solve the Raskol problem was to restore the patriarchate and end the Petrine "heresy." As expected, Antonii's ill-concealed antagonism towards the anti-Raskol program antagonized the anti-Raskol faculty at Kazan and the synodal bureaucrats in St. Petersburg.[20]

Thus, in the summer of 1900, Antonii was removed from Kazan and installed as bishop of Ufa, a remote diocese in the Ural foothills where the majority of the population was Raskol and Moslem. It was a dismal place, and Antonii's detractors hoped that he would spend the rest of his days there, unable to create turmoil for the established interests in the ecclesiastical bureaucracy. Antonii was moved so hastily that he did not even have the funds saved to pay his fare to Ufa or to have his books transported there. Happily, a local millionaire, Ivan Grigorevich Strakheev, lent him the money to move to Ufa and to rent living quarters.

By this time, however, he had become somewhat of a hero to the supporters of reform in the church. A generation of students who had studied under him and had been counselled by him were outraged at his treatment. Groups of them made pilgrimages to Ufa for further encouragement and to protest what had happened.

An ecclesiastical event in the eastern Mediterranean gladdened Antonii's heart. In 1901, Joachim Devedgis (1834-1909) was reinstated as Patriarch of Constantinople. Elevated to the Ecumenical Patriarchate in 1878, in the wake of the Russo-Turkish War, Joachim had set out to revive the prestige and authority of the patriarchate in the Eastern church. This had not pleased the Ottoman, nor, as it turned out, the Russian government, so in 1884 Joachim was obliged to retire to Mount Athos. Joachim was a champion of Greek domination of the Orthodox hierarchy in the Middle East, a domination the Russian government was trying to end. Among those most delighted at Joachim's restoration was the bishop of Ufa, who congratulated Joachim for having been exonerated and expostulated upon the need for a vigorous patriarchate for the welfare of Orthodox Christendom. Antonii's views, in a letter, were published in the *Ufa Diocesan News.* They infuriated the Procurator, who stripped Antonii of his nomination to the Order of St. Anne and reprimanded him for agitating to restore the Russian patriarchate.

Less than two years later, however, he was transferred to Volhynia. Several reasons lay behind the termination of his exile, despite the Procurator's displeasure with him. His friend, Antonii Vadkovskii, had been made metropolitan of St. Petersburg and was designated first member of the Synod in 1901. He now spoke with more authority and was able to counter the influence of the Procurator. A more important reason lay in the growing animosity between Austria-Hungary and Russia. The Uniate church in the Austro-Hungarian Empire stirred Ukrainian nationalism in the western provinces of the Russian Empire. To counter the appeal of Metropolitan Andrei Sheptyskii from Lvov, a vigorous Russian prelate was needed. At the behest of political interests, the provocative bishop was transferred to Zhitomir. Khrapovitskii wasted no time engaging Sheptyskii in a polemical correspondence, which the latter declined to continue once Antonii began to accuse him of Latinism. As bishop of Volhynia, a crucial area for political interests, Khrapovitskii's influence in ecclesiastical affairs was greatly increased.

Khrapovitskii found himself in an area with a strong Roman Catholic minority led by a vigorous archbishop, Stanislas Niedzaglkowski of Zhitomir, who was passively assisted by the city governor (mayor) Roman Domanewski, also a Pole. Zhitomir had been a Uniate area, and the latent hostility of even the nominally Orthodox population towards the government was still strong. The town of Zhitomir itself was approximately 60 percent Jewish, out of a total population of about 100,000. The Austrian regime in nearby Galicia was a model in its treatment of Jews. Russian Jews longed to establish that kind of regime in their homeland too. Thus, the political sensitivity of the area, particularly after 1900, was considerable. Khrapovitskii's determination to reestablish the patriarchate was reinforced during his years in Volhynia, for he became convinced that the patriarchate could be effective both for religious and political objectives.[21]

* * *

Besides the pressure for reform exerted by the two

Antoniis, the Procurator was beginning to feel that of another force—the press. In the opening years of the twentieth century, the Russian press became more liberal than it had been in the twenty years since the assassination of Alexander II, and religious editors were as capable of utilizing the media for their purposes as were political editors. Pobedonostsev never did comprehend the influence of the religious press, particularly in forming the attitudes of priests and bishops who, imperceptibly but increasingly, became convinced that not only the Procurator himself but the whole apparatus of the procuracy had to be swept away.

One of the major works that sparked the new revival of interest in the church in the public press was the reprinting of a series of sixteen articles that had appeared in 1882 in the Slavophile journal *Rus'* the organ of Ivan Aksakov. Rarely had the interests of the Slavophiles and the state coincided. In church affairs, Procurator Pobedonostsev had found Aksakov, his one-time friend, a bit trying.

The sixteen articles reappeared in 1898, reprinted by the Porokhovshchikov Press in St. Petersburg. Their author was none other than Archpriest Alexander Ivantsov-Platonov. They dealt with a wide range of issues—restoration of the voice of the Orthodox laity; restoration of the Orthodox parish as a viable social and legal unit; granting to the clergy and laity a voice in the selection of bishops; the end of the practice of moving bishops frequently and rapidly from diocese to diocese; cessation of granting ecclesiastical dignities to unqualified candidates; ending contravention of the canons; reduction of the power of consistories in diocesan administration; abolition of most of the paperwork that forced bishops to neglect their flocks; establishment of collegiality (*sobornost'*) on all levels of church administration; reduction of the power of the Synod and decentralization of ecclesiastical administration; curbing the administrative authority of the Procurator; and, finally, granting the church autonomy and real control over its affairs in order to end its humiliating position as just a department of the civil administration.[22]

Ivantsov, like Khrapovitskii, believed that the Russian

church should restore a Patriarch at its head, as was the
custom in the Eastern church, because the canons of the Orthodox church presumed a Patriarch at the head of its metropolitans and bishops. Ivantsov felt that since the Patriarch
of Constantinople lay under the power of the alien and non-
Orthodox Turks and was thus unable to exercise his ecumenical prerogatives, and since other states like Serbia and
Rumania had Patriarchs, it was incumbent on the Russian
church not to remain headless. The prestige of a patriarchate
would also counter the attraction from Rome to bring Eastern
churches under papal jurisdiction. The archpriest expected
the Russian Patriarch to play a dominant role among the
Eastern churches.

Fr. Alexander expected the cathedral throne to be in the
Uspenskii Sobor in the Kremlin, but the Patriarch would
normally reside in Petersburg, the seat of the government.
A *locum-tenens* would be assigned to govern the patriarchal
diocese in his absence. Patriarchal revenues would come from
all Russia, not just the Moscow diocese alone, as had been
the case before 1700. The Patriarch would be named in a
sobor of bishops assembled from all over Russia, not by the
Tsar. The Tsar would have the right to suggest candidates
to the sobor but would not determine their choice. The Patriarch would deal directly with the Tsar on the church's behalf
and not through any intermediary like a Procurator or a
Synod.

To those who objected that the restoration of the patriarchate would again give rise to Nikonism and create conflict with the civil authorities, Ivantsov answered that the
original confrontation between the Tsar and the Patriarch
had been instigated by the boyars in Alexei's court to safeguard their privileges. There was never a direct attack by
the church on the Tsar's authority, either in fact or in theory.
Furthermore, the history of the Byzantine Empire gave no
evidence of serious conflict between church and Emperor
that ever resembled the battles between Popes and Emperors
in the West.[23]

Ivantsov-Platonov pointed to diocesan administration as
the place where the Orthodox pastorate broke down most

seriously. The frequency of transfer of bishops made them almost powerless, with the result that real authority in the diocese lay in the consistory, theoretically an administrative agency, but which in practice overawed the clergy and rivaled the bishop himself. The chairman of the consistory, appointed by the Procurator directly from among the personnel of his chancellory, received directives from the chancellory and turned to the chancellory for instruction. Unless the bishop was an especially willful man, he was ignored. When bishops tried to invade the bailiwick of the chairman, the latter complained to the Synod, and more often than not, the bishop was removed. Consistory chairmen, untrained in canon law, usually did not have the faintest personal concern for those beneath them. Marriage problems, divorces, mixed-marriage cases, annulments—all went through the consistory. Consistory clerks were every bit as venal and crude as their counterparts in the civil bureaucracy, oftentimes literally taking the widow's last mite. It was not surprising that many people took their cases to civil courts, where they were settled much more cheaply and humanely outside the influence of the church.

The consistory had to become the arm of the bishop, with the umbilical cord to the Synod cut. Persons appointed to consistorial offices would have to be trained in the canons of the church and in pastoral theology, not just in accounting and civil law.

Bishops should celebrate liturgies and preach in their cathedrals, in the monasteries and in the parishes frequently. Archpriests should be bishops' assistants, representing them in important parishes, and should be few in number. The Russian church had literally thousands of archpriests that it did not need. In places like Moscow and Petersburg, nearly half the clergy bore the title archpriest, sometimes three or four of them assigned to a single church.

When bishops came to be elected locally, they would remain in close contact with their pastors and flock. The haughty bishop who disdained his people and abused his clergy would disappear swiftly. The Russian diocese would have to be considerably reduced in size, with vicar bishops becoming heads of new dioceses and having their own assistant bishops.[24]

In this plan, Ivantsov-Platonov transferred the center of authority from the Procurator's bureaucracy to the semi-annual convocation of diocesan clergy. All priests in a given diocese would automatically belong to the convocation. Currently, the convocations were useless formalities. Decisions from the Synod or from the diocesan consistory were announced to the assembled clergy, who were not asked for their judgment but were expected simply to carry them out. In the future, all diocesan policies, programs and disciplinary matters would be determined at the convocation. The bishops would have only the right to confirm or veto decisions of the convocation. The convocation could override an episcopal veto. The transfer of the locus of power from the center to the diocese and the granting of near autonomy to the diocesan clergy was one of the most popular and controversial ideas debated in the Russian church before the Bolshevik Revolution.

Thus, the whole life of the church would ensure communication between the various levels in an open and free manner and would be liberated from the crippling interference of civilian authorities. Ecclesiastical administration would be cleansed of complacent bureaucrats, and the doors would be opened for new talent and vigor. *Sobornost'*, loosely translated as "conciliarity," was the term used to describe interchange and exchange among all levels of the church, from the lowest parish to the central administration. Autonomy for the church and decentralization of bureaucratic control would avoid the shortcomings of both the Protestant and Catholic systems. By reviving *symphonia* between ecclesiastical and civilian authorities, the church would allay the fears and animosities of civil bureaucrats.

The reissuing of Ivantsov-Platonov's writings spearheaded an upswell of pressure for reform of the church, both in ecclesiastical and secular circles. The demand rose from 1900-1901 to a crest in 1905-1906 and remained a continuing concern in the years before World War I.[25]

Moscow Academy's *Bogoslovskii Vestnik* led media coverage of the reform issue during those years, followed at a distance by the official journal of the St. Petersburg Academy, *Tserkovnyi Vestnik,* which labored under the shadow of the Procurator's bureaucracy. Other ecclesiastical publications such as *Trudy Kievskoi Dukhovnoi Akademii* (Kiev), *Missionerskoe Obozrenie* (Kazan), and *Pravoslavnyi Sobesednik* (Kazan) echoed that interest.

Coincidentally with the beginning of the Religious-Philosophical Society debates, *Bogoslovskii Vestnik* ran an article in February and March 1902 by Professor A. S. Pavlov, noted retired canon lawyer of Moscow University and a friend of Khrapovitskii, entitled "The Relation of the Church to the State." In this article Pavlov denounced the stranglehold by the state on the church and compared the current condition of the Russian church to that of the early church under the pagan Roman Emperors. He insisted that government was not competent to administer the church, which had its own mission and purpose outside the realm of the civil authority. The only time the Emperor had the canonical right to intervene in church affairs was to protect it from heresy and prevent it from dividing into schism. Emperors who went further than this protective role met with eventual disaster. Forced policies, or even teachings, which contradicted the church's inner nature, had inevitably been rejected and the memory of the Emperor disgraced. Although canons of the church were regularly incorporated into civil law, the state could not presume to legislate for the church. The proper relation between Emperor and Patriarch had been laid out in the *Sixth Novella* of Justinian (527-565): each guides and reproves the other, yet avoids interference in the separate jurisdiction of the other. Emperor Basil the Macedonian (867-886), in his *Epanagoge,* stated that while the Byzantine law had its roots in Roman law, it had to remain in conformity with the canons of the Orthodox church. The Emperor was bound to consult with the church through the Patriarch, who was Christ's representative on earth. Patriarch Photius in his *Nomocanon* declared that where there was a conflict between civil and canon law, the latter always takes precedence, because the canons represent the divine law, which is superior to human law.

Pavlov summed up the relations of church and state, Patriarch and Emperor, under three basic headings: (1) The Emperor was chief law-giver and ruler in the civil realm, the protector of the church, but under the regulations and laws of the church just like any other Christian. (2) The Emperor had no authority over the inner life of the church, over definition of doctrine, or over strictly ecclesiastical administration and discipline. He was bound to protect the church, prevent schism, guard it against heresy and uphold the definitions of the councils. (3) The Emperor could intervene to summon councils, supervise their proceedings, ratify their decisions and candidates for Patriarch, name leading hierarchs to their sees, supervise the public and moral lives of clergy to prevent scandal, and see that council guidelines were put into practice. Emperors guided the church, but did not contravene its autonomy or integrity.

Pavlov went on to state that in the West emperors had had great influence in the church prior to the collapse of imperial authority, when the bishops of Rome were left without protection. The transgressions of Leo the Isaurian (717-741) during the iconoclastic controversy were the direct cause of Rome's repudiation of imperial influence in the church. Pope Gregory II's resistance to Leo's attempt to coerce the Italian church and Leo's failure to capture Gregory broke the bond between the churches. The subsequent excesses of papal claims were the outcome of imperial transgressions against the church.

In both the Kievan and Muscovite eras the relations between the church and the civil authority had been correct. True, men like Ivan IV had oppressed the church and even murdered metropolitans and clergy, but they never claimed to head it. Ivan, like Emperors Michael Paleologos and Leo the Wise, had sinned against the church and had met suitable misfortunes, keenly aware of their sinfulness.

The Petrine reform had no precedents in the civil or canon law of Byzantium. The state simply absorbed the church, its administration, court system, and piece-by-piece its property. His *reglament* was based on the Protestant maxim "cujus regio, ejus religio." Peter had seen in Calvinist Holland the type of church administration he wanted. Therefore, under the pretext of terminating confusion about supreme authority, he made himself the supreme authority in both civil and ecclesiastical affairs. The Synod was his ecclesiastical cabinet, on a par with the Senate.

The result had been that all distinctions between civilian and religious loyalties disappeared. One could not be a loyal Orthodox without being loyal to Peter, who even violated the seal of confession. One of the main causes of the decline of the Russian clergy lay therein. Now the church was expected to anathematize anyone who disputed the claims of civilian authority automatically.

Another result was that churchmen defending the church were prosecuted by civilian authorities. Such was the case of the bishop of Tver, Feofilakt Lopatinskii, who wrote in defense of Orthodox doctrine and attacked Lutheran teachings. Ernest Biron, a Lutheran, the leader of German hegemony during the reign of Empress Anna, had him unfrocked and imprisoned in the Peter and Paul fortress. Thus, the church had lost the right to defend herself as well.

Pavlov went on to point out that during the reign of Elizabeth (1740-1762), the bishop of Rostov, Arsenii Matseevich, and the archbishop of Novgorod, Amvrosii Iushkevich, both demanded abolition of the Synod, restoration of the patriarchate, and independence for the church. Iushkevich demanded abolition of the oath to the Tsar as supreme authority of the Synod. Arsenii was appointed to the Synod and refused to take the oath of supremacy, but Elizabeth let the issue lie and died without resolving the dilemma. In 1763, when Catherine the Great secularized church properties, Arsenii denounced her. Arsenii was unfrocked, tried for treason, and imprisoned in the fortress of Revel, where he died in 1772. After him no prelate dared raise his voice. The church, shackled with a Lutheran administration, had only Old Believers to protest her imprisonment.

Pavlov ended with a vigorous assertion that in matters of administration and doctrine, only the church had authority, not the Tsar. It owed him allegiance as head of state and

protector, but was autonomous. The Tsar was as subject to
the church in matters of faith and morals as any other
Christian.[26] Thus, Pavlov's article left the Tsar in a very un-
comfortable position. By the structure of the law, he was an
oppressor of the church. It was something that gave the regime, seeking to secure public support and under severe
criticism from many quarters, pause to think.

Shortly thereafter, a pamphlet written by Alexander A.
Papkov, a noted legal expert, made the rounds. He advocated
that the parish be recognized under law as a legal person
with full rights to acquire and dispose of income and properties in its own name, to set up corporations and institutions
in its own name, and to have full autonomy in selecting its
officers and personnel. Summarizing much current thinking
on restoring the parish, it gravely disturbed the Procurator,
the Okhrana, and police agencies of the Ministry of the Interior. The autonomous parish had been deliberately destroyed
in the nineteenth century because it too often had been the
bulwark of local intransigence and a catalyst for rebellion.
Bureaucratic discomfort increased when another canon lawyer, this time of Moscow Theological Academy, Nikolai
Zauzerskii (1919) reviewed the pamphlet in *Bogoslovskii
Vestnik* and warned that if Orthodoxy were not to die the
ignominious death atheistic radicals predicted, the vitality of
the parish had to be revived forthwith. He pointedly noted
that parish life had become the deadest during the tenure of
the current Procurator.[27]

Two months later (December 13-15, 1902) another much
more significant article appeared in three installments in
Moskovskiia Vedomosti, and was read in high government
circles and by the Tsar. Its importance lay in two factors: it
was written by Lev A. Tikhomirov (1825-1923), the daily's
editor and publisher, who during the 1870s and 1880s had
been one of the leading anti-monarchist, anti-ecclesiastical
revolutionaries but who had been pardoned and converted
into an advocate of monarchism; and after reading it,
Nicholas II set in motion a series of conferences directed at
ways to reform the church.[28]

The articles were so much in demand that they were

issued early in 1903 as a separate pamphlet, *The Demands of Life and the Administration of Our Church.* Tikhomirov stated that the recasting of church administration by Peter and his right-hand man Feofan Prokopovich had been a mistake.[29] From that mistake flowed the weakness of the Russian church in the twentieth century. A Protestant type of hybrid church administration had been superimposed upon the decapitated Orthodox church. The Synod was, as it were, designed for weakness. The bishops who served on it met only twice or three times a year and had no continuing contact with the problems and issues placed before them for consideration and no direct administrative links with the lower levels of church administration. Instead, they depended upon the chancellory of the Procurator. Originally intended to be a kind of legal adviser to ensure that synodal decisions did not run counter to the civil law, he had become the administrator of the church, subordinating the bishops, the dioceses and every aspect of administration to his bureaucracy. The result was inefficiency and destruction of the parish. The first loyalty of the procuracy was to the civil bureaucracy. Its point of view, its starting point for every problem that arose in the church, was to consider the government's interest. Thus, the church had no independent voice of its own, and it was impossible for any kind of consensus to arise among churchmen under the existing circumstances.

The contrast with the papal administration of the Catholic church was striking, he went on. In it there was a concentration of ecclesiastical authority in one place, making for an effective and mobile administration. The hierarchy looked to Rome for direction, and almost every religious order and lay organization had its headquarters or a liaison officer in Rome. Thus, the Roman church could take strong stands, mobilize grassroots support, and resolve problems fairly quickly. The concentration of administration still permitted diversity in tasks and services. A myriad of religious orders existed within the Latin church, each having specific purposes in diverse places. There were hospital orders, teaching orders, missionary orders and contemplative orders.

That was not the case with Orthodoxy. Recently, beginning in September 1902, in the course of a three-way discussion of Russian monasticism between the journals *Dushepoleznoe Chtenie, Bogoslovskii Vestnik,* and *St. Petersburgskiia Vedomosti,* a certain Kruglov had stated that Russian monasteries were wasteful, that they utilized resources for too little public benefit, and that they should devote themselves more to public services. That was followed by a bitter exchange between various monks, professors and priests about Russian monasticism. Little mutual respect or love befitting members of the church was shown. The exchange resolved nothing. What was needed was an open church forum in which ideas could be considered and useful solutions arrived at about what public services Russian monasteries could and should perform. But the church had no such forum.

Another, more serious problem besetting the church was the problem of the ecclesiastical courts, especially in the field of annulment and divorce and their relation in these matters to the civil courts. Confusion had grown steadily worse during the thirty years since civil courts had been reformed and no solution, or even any serious consideration of one, had as yet come from the church. The Synod, as an administrative apparatus, had neither the canonical authority nor the qualified personnel to resolve the confusion.

There was no forum where the problem of divorce could be debated by the church. No ecclesiastical agency had authority to work out guidelines. Divorce proceedings were engulfed in the murky necessity of proving infidelity or non-consummation, took so much time to process, and were the object of such graft on the part of consistorial clerks that many Orthodox simply took their cases to district courts of the Ministry of Justice, where proceedings were shorter, less complicated and more humane. Ministry of Justice courts were taking over the problem and establishing precedents in marriage and divorce to the exclusion of the church. The idea of marriage as a sacrament, a union that transcended civil regulations, was simply lost. Lawyers and judges who disliked the church and were bent on eliminating her as a factor in these matters found the disorder in the church administration to be to their satisfaction.

Another area of confusion was Leo Tolstoi and his ridicule of the church. No voice had been raised in her defense for a long time. Recently, a prominent St. Petersburg priest had even publicly defended Tolstoi and criticized his excommunication. (Presumably that was Fr. Sollertinskii at the Religious-Philosophical Society.) The church spoke without clarity in his case. Furthermore, no alternative moral leadership had emerged that might have obviated the challenge from Tolstoi. Vladimir Soloviev had once demanded of Tikhomirov to define the authoritative voice of the church. He could not. Soloviev's solution was to advocate papalism.

What the proper relation of the Orthodox church to Old Catholics[30] and Protestants with episcopal organization like the Anglicans? Should they be included in Orthodox ceremonies and prayers? Should requiem liturgies be sung for Catholics in Orthodox churches? Recently, a general, Polish and Catholic, had died. In Vilna the (Orthodox) bishop had refused to allow the *panikhida*, the service for the dead, to be sung for him. In the Caucasus the church authorities had permitted it. Could Protestants have the *panikhida* in Orthodox churches? Some places allowed it while others did not. The faithful were confused. Old Catholics, cut off from their former center, were seeking communion with the Orthodox. For thirty years the issue had been stalemated. The Russian church offered no resolution because of its lack of leadership.

The church was in confusion as to the reform of parishes and the relation of parishes to their diocesan administrations and to the central bureaucracy. Non-ecclesiastical and anti-Orthodox principles governed those relationships. In 1721, the government established inadequate regulations out of fear of papalistic tendencies in the patriarchate. It created a Protestant invention which absorbed the church into the state. Peter did not understand the Orthodox tradition regarding a patriarchate.

The current situation had to be changed. The church needed a first bishop to speak for her. The Holy Synod was a liability to the church. The so-called collegial patriarch was a farce.

Tikhomirov urged a return to the ancient canons of Orthodoxy in order to enable the church to speak for itself and to function more effectively in social and political matters. He outlined five needs of the church: (1) regular national sobors, both to make policy and to see that policy was carried out; (2) a chief bishop with administrative authority and reduction of the Synod to the status of a consultative body, the chief bishop residing in the capital and holding the title Patriarch of All Russia; (3) members of the Synod to be consultative and rotated regularly; (4) the Procurator to be a legal consultant, the liaison to keep the civilian authorities abreast of ecclesiastical affairs; (5) the head of the church to deal with the head of state directly, in person, and to enhance the prestige of the Russian church *vis-à-vis* the other Eastern churches and the papacy in Rome.

Tikhomirov concluded by saying that none of his suggestions signified a radical change in the constitution of the church. Rather, they signified the restoration of traditional Orthodox governing principles which still subsisted beneath the alien, imposed superstructure.[31]

* * *

Tikhomirov could not be ignored. He made church reform a public issue. The Procurator realized too late that Pandora's box had been opened. Suspending the Religious-Philosophical Society a few weeks later only demonstrated his estrangement from the deep-running currents in the church. The church was striving for a legitimate structure in conformity with the canonical tradition of Eastern Orthodoxy. He and the apparatus he controlled were alien to that tradition.

Tikhomirov's articles quickly found their way into the hands of Nicholas II, who was so disturbed by the problems they raised that he gave copies to Metropolitan Antonii at ceremonies opening a home for the handicapped in Petersburg, March 6, 1903, and asked the metropolitan to read them and give him an outline of problems facing the church and suggestions as to how they could be resolved. A few days earlier, February 26, the Tsar had ordered the Commit-

tee of Ministers to formulate suggestions about easing restrictions on Old Believers and other non-Orthodox in the
empire. The two issues became one. Liberating the non-
Orthodox vitally affected the Orthodox. Antonii and his advisers soon were consulting members of the Committee of
Ministers.[32]

Pobedonostsev began to lose his grip on events as early
as 1903. The Committee of Ministers debated a whole range
of problems related to the non-Orthodox populations and
concluded that it was counter-productive to discriminate between non-Orthodox religions on the basis of their historical
or theological origins. If Roman Catholics and Lutherans
were granted large-scale autonomy to govern their church
bodies, then why not extend the same autonomy to Old Believers and sectarians like Stundists? Only sects that undermined civil order or the state itself should be restricted.

The Committee was disquieted by growing animosity in
the southwestern and western provinces towards the government. Religious repression was the key to that animosity. The
same was true in the Baltic provinces and in Finland among
Lutherans. There was concern that the Austrian sect of Old
Believers and the Uniates would make common cause unless
one or both groups were conciliated. Harassment of non-
Orthodox sectarians sometimes took especially ridiculous
forms, like closing their chapels because the shutters on the
windows were different from those of houses around them.
If Catholics and Lutherans could build churches that were
distinguishable by their architecture, why not Old Believers
and Stundists? Religious oppression was creating, not suppressing, civil unrest.

When the war with Japan began in January 1904, the
problem of religious persecution and civil unrest was inten-
sified. Metropolitan Antonii was invited to brief the Committee on how a manifesto of religious toleration would affect the church. He supported Sergei Witte, Chairman of the
Committee, in his view that the treatment meted out to the
Lutheran population was counter-productive, and he presumed
that similar treatment of other non-Orthodox would be equally
counter-productive.[33] From the point of view of the Ortho-

dox church, nothing was more frustrating than to have the
church harnessed as the agency through which the state oppressed minority populations. It would be better to have substantial defections from the nominally Orthodox population
to other sects and allow the church the freedom to minister
to its own faithful than to continue existing policies, which
alienated minorities and disgusted the church's own constituency.

Furthermore, the metropolitan argued, laws against mixed
marriages and the enforced registration of all children of
mixed marriages as Orthodox and legal sanctions to enforce
such registration violated every principle of respect for individual conscience. The church should determine regulations governing mixed marriages and problems that arose
from them, not the state. The church was not inclined to
violate a person's conscience. Likewise, the legitimacy or
illegitimacy of the Old Believers and their traditions would
have to be settled outside the arena of legal sanctions and
political oppression.

Antonii warned the Committee, however, that toleration
and organizational freedom for Old Believers and sectarians
would have to be accompanied by the unshackling of the
state church. It already had one hand tied behind its back
because of existing administrative controls. To free its enemies
while leaving it fettered would be to tie both hands and
threaten its destruction.

Vladimir K. Sabler (1847-1923), the Assistant Procurator,
defended Pobedonostsev and the Petrine system. He warned
against freeing non-Orthodox populations from restrictions,
because they would turn their new-found liberties against
the Russian state. This was particularly true of Uniates, who
were nothing more than Latins in Greek clothing and Polish
in culture and loyalties. Hundreds of thousands of Orthodox
would defect if Unia were restored or if restrictions against
Latin proselytizing were lifted. If Old Believers were given
equality with Orthodox, whole areas would immediately
abandon official Orthodoxy. Thousands of newly won converts in the Volga area would revert to Islam if sanctions
against Islam were removed and they could hold office,

possess property and enjoy the same advantages as the Orthodox. The Lutheran population was so aroused by the past
decade's Russification that all inroads would be lost immediately if they were given full freedom. Sabler was
vigorously supported by Count Alexei Ignatiev (1842-1906),
whose pan-Slavic attitudes were deeply offended by the
projected religious toleration, and by Peter Durnovo (1844-
1915), a conservative nationalist who believed that toleration would mark the beginning of the dismemberment of the
Russian state. Pobedonostsev, infirm and personally miffed
at the Witte-Antonii collaboration, absented himself from
the Committee's deliberations.

The dismal Japanese War weighed heavily upon the Committee and helped turn the tide toward the inescapable conclusion that to continue repression of non-Orthodox minorities
would be to exacerbate civil violence in Russia. Early in December 1904, the Committee recommended religious toleration for minority populations, and the Tsar issued an *ukaz*
on December 12 promising toleration as soon as suitable legislation could be drawn up.[34]

The Pobedonostsevian regime was coming to an end,
thanks to able churchmen like Vadkovskii and Khrapovitskii
and religious publicists who articulated the problems facing
the Russian Orthodox church and Orthodox society at the
beginning of the century. They continued the struggle during
the next two years in the hope that, by restoring the Byzantine symphony of relations between church and state, the
church could be effective as a renewing and healing influence
upon the Russian people and empire.

CHAPTER III

Towards a Sobor: The Church in 1905

Ten days after the promise of toleration, on December 22, 1904, Russia suffered defeat by the Japanese at Port Arthur on the Liaotung Peninsula in China. The defeat recalled the humiliation of Crimea fifty years earlier, and filled churchmen with a foreboding that the eleventh hour had come.[1] The Christmas season of 1904 was joyless in Russia. It was ironic that Witte, who had worked hard to alert the Tsar to the folly of war in the East, and Vadkovskii, who had worked to alleviate the social miseries that caused disorders, were both held responsible for the holocaust that now swept Russia.

But the churchman who dominated the scene during the explosive year of 1905 was Fr. Georgii Gapon (1870-1906), one of the members of the Society for Religious and Moral Propagation. The invective and opprobrium heaped upon this hapless priest—by all parties, left and right—was also to be directed shortly upon the metropolitan himself.

Georgii Gapon's early life showed a number of similarities to that of Antonii.[2] Born in the village of Beliaki, Poltava province, the Ukraine, he was of peasant parentage. His parents were liberated from serfdom in 1861. Of modest means, his father, Apollon Grigorevich, born about 1835, had received rudimentary education in a parish Sunday school and had grown up a respected man in the Beliaki community.

Apollon held the position of secretary of the *volost'*, a governmental unit created in 1865 to replace the landlord as intermediary between the peasant commune (*mir*) and the county (*uezd*) administration. Through endless dealing with local landlords and officials during the 1870s, 1880s and 1890s, Apollon was fully aware of the double-dealing to which peasants were subjected and took a detached, bemused perspective. His sons, born during the tumultuous 1870s and better educated than their father, could not maintain his attitude. They were filled with humiliation and anger towards the lords who treated peasants with hauteur in the *volost'* *zemstvo* meetings and never hesitated to take advantage of them.

Georgii learned from his father the history of the Ukraine, of the Cossacks, and the struggle of the peasants against serfdom. He recoiled at the thought that peasants were still subjected to being flogged, naked, in public. From his maternal grandfather, he learned the lives of the saints and heard about the heroes of the Russian church. Thanks to his grandfather, he was able to see through the superstitions of his mother and how they varied from the essentials of Orthodoxy. He was not intimidated when she tried to scare him by calling down the displeasure of the devil. By the time he was twelve, he had finished the parish school and was enrolled, in 1882, at the diocesan men's school in Poltava.[3]

The diocesan men's school was a prelude to enrollment in the seminary and ordination to the priesthood. Both his parents revered the priesthood and understood that the priest alone commanded respect from peasants and attention from officials. Gapon skipped preparatory classes, finished the men's school when he was only fifteen years old, and entered Poltava Seminary in the fall of 1885 on a government scholarship. He was already an independent-thinking young man, fond of Tolstoi's writings and rather critical of the slovenly spiritual life he found pervasive among the clergy of the ecclesiastical bureaucracy. His reading proclivities, together with criticism of the clergy, brought him a warning that he could lose his government scholarship. He replied by renouncing the scholarship and earned his way tutoring the children of local merchants and priests.

In the seminary he began to doubt whether he should be a priest. A university degree would allow him to devote his life to the people as a doctor, teacher, or some kind of agricultural expert. He finished the seminary convinced that the latter course was where he could be of the most service, but found to his dismay that he had acquired an unfavorable character reference—the sinister *donos* which the Procurator of the Synod required all seminary rectors to keep. Even though he finished high in seminary examinations, the university was closed to him. So he faced a boring career as a clerk in a local *zemstvo* office. Disillusioned, he avidly read the clandestine literature of *narodnik* authors. Stories of heroes of the previous decade thrilled him, and he might have become one of thousands of crypto-revolutionaries lodged in the *zemstvo* administration if he had not met and fallen in love with the daughter of a Poltava merchant in whose home he had given lessons. She persuaded him that his future lay in the priesthood. The bishop of Poltava, Ilarion Iushenov (1823-1904), persuaded his fiancée's mother, who objected to a peasant's son, to give in and approve the marriage. Gapon was ordained a priest. Though he was assigned to a cemetery church without a defined parish, he soon had it overcrowded every time he celebrated the liturgy. His devotion at the eucharist and his sermons caused his reputation to spread far beyond the confines of the town of Poltava.

Like Vadkovskii's, Gapon's marriage was short. His wife's health steadily deteriorated, and she died after only four years of marriage, leaving behind a son and a daughter. Her death was a stunning blow to Gapon. He gave up his priestly functions and went through a prolonged period of depression.

Through direct appeal to Pobedonostsev from Bishop Ilarion, plus the influence of a local aristocratic family upon the Assistant Procurator, Vladimir Sabler, Gapon got an appointment to the Petersburg Theological Academy despite his unfavorable *donos*. Leaving his children in the care of his parents, Gapon entered the academy in the fall semester 1898. Because he was older than most of the students, he was somewhat of a novelty. He was attracted to three out-standing personalities at the academy—Professor V. V. Bolotov (1853-1900), a renowned church historian who gave selflessly of himself for his students; Archimandrite Feofan Bystrov, who became his spiritual adviser;[4] and Vicar-Bishop Veniamin Bornukov, who was in charge of the Society for Religious and Moral Propagation. Bishop Veniamin recognized Gapon as a leader and asked him to work with him. So did Fr. Filosof Ornatskii, who succeeded Bishop Veniamin as Chairman of the Society in 1901 when the latter became bishop of Kaluga. Gapon found the Society's work much more in keeping with the gospels and his active nature than the academic life.

Illness forced Gapon to suspend studies during the school year of 1899-1900 and take a leave of absence in the Crimea. Like Vadkovskii, he contemplated entering monastic life, but friends like Anton Chekhov (1860-1904) and Vasilii Vereshchagin (1842-1904), noted author and painter respectively, persuaded him that monastic life would be a form of escapism. Besides, he was scandalized by the wealth of monasteries in the Crimea and the indolence of the monks. He returned to Petersburg to complete his work at the academy and to devote himself to the working proletariate.

Through the influence of Sabler, Gapon was appointed to the Church of the Sorrowful Mother, a dockyards parish located on Vasilevskii Island. Sabler was an elder in the parish. Gapon's background and sympathies appealed to the parishioners, most of whom were recent arrivals from rural villages. Though the law required priests to report political dissent when they learned of it in confession, his penitents were surprised to find that Gapon did not consider political activities a matter for confession. At Sorrowful Mother, Gapon conceived the idea to broaden the Society for Religious and Moral Propagation into a workmen's compensation organization. There was much more to comforting the Petersburg proletariate than preaching temperance and sexual abstinence to men whose wives and fiancées were in villages thousands of miles away. He approached Veniamin and Sabler with the idea.

Gapon was appointed pastor of the church at the Blue Cross Refuge Center, and, with the help of several high-placed personages, went forward devising schemes to organize workers. He was denounced to the Okhrana, and only the timely intervention of Metropolitan Antonii prevented his being expelled from the academy and banished from the city.[5]

At the suggestion of Princess Lobanov-Rostovskii, Antonii transferred Gapon from the Blue Cross Refuge Center to the chaplaincy at the Petersburg Red Cross (autumn 1902). It was his last term at the academy, the turning point in his career. At the meetings of the Religious-Philosophical Society, he was struck by the intellectual and mental chasm between secular intellectuals and the churchmen. Coupled with his own experience among the workmen, his awareness that the church was losing touch made him suspicious of government-sponsored labor organizations. He wrote to the metropolitan pleading that the church withdraw priests from government-sponsored labor activities. Antonii had already denied government labor organizers use of Society for Religious and Moral Propagation facilities. He, Bishop Sergei Stragorodskii, rector of the academy, Fr. Filosof Ornatskii (1863-1918), Chairman of the Society for Religious and Moral Propagation, and other religious leaders did not want the church's efforts for the workers to be subverted by the police and political interest groups, whether government or radical. Nevertheless, Gapon was invited to collaborate with Sergei V. Zubatov (1869-1917), chief of the special section of the department of police in the Ministry of the Interior.[6]

The Zubatov invitation left the priest in a painful predicament. To accept the invitation would be to risk his credibility with the men and women who already had come to look to him for leadership and guidance. He would appear to have become a police agent, an identification that he had strenuously sought to avoid. Not to accept the invitation, on the other hand, would be to lose the support of such government figures as Sergei Witte, Minister of Finance, who already knew of Gapon and was favorably inclined towards him. Gapon had to walk a very thin line to avoid being undermined on either side.

Zubatov had already set up a police-run workers' organization in Moscow that had had mixed success. Both leftist intellectuals and churchmen viewed it with misgiving. Zubatov's bid, with the full support of Viacheslav K. Plehve, Minister of the Interior, to involve the Society for Religious and Moral Propagation and, through it, the authority of the Orthodox church in his scheme did not engender great joy among Petersburg churchmen either. Gapon, for one, clearly saw that the embrace of the Ministry of the Interior could lead to the suffocation of his ministry among the proletariate of the capital.

Nevertheless, he travelled to Moscow during Christmas time, 1902, in the company of Ilia Sokolov, one of Zubatov's organizers there. He was disquieted by what he saw and returned to Petersburg to sound out his metropolitan about transforming the Society into some sort of workers' organization instead. Antonii did not think the church should go directly into labor organization, because it was illegal and in direct competition with the schemes of the Minister of the Interior. He did, however, authorize Gapon to accompany Fr. Ornatskii to perform liturgies for meetings arranged by Zubatov. Both the metropolitan and his priests tried to walk a line that increasingly snapped in the tension between political and police activities and their own pastoral efforts for the workers.

Pressure was stepped up early in 1903 when Zubatov went ahead with his organization in the capital. With misgivings, Gapon sent several of his worker associates to Zubatovite meetings to see if there were some way cooperation with it could be arranged. Men like Ivan Vasiliev and Semen Kladovnikov reported back that they, like the priest, were suspicious of the Zubatovite ballyhoo. They faced, however, the need for some sort of collaboration, or risked seeing their efforts superseded.

Reluctantly, they decided to work with Zubatov. Gapon personally liked Zubatov, but felt that he was naive and easily manipulated. He was also aware that the working masses of the capital shied away from the Social Democratic and Socialist Revolutionary agitation and that he was more apt to have worker support if they felt that he and his men worked under the benign eye of the law. He and his men decided to collaborate at arms length, maintaining their own inner network of trusted men and women who would not be under Zubatov's control.[7]

By summer 1903, Gapon was well beyond the police labor organization concept, though temporarily forced to remain within its confines. His way was made easier by four changes of officialdom: the firing of Witte in July, arranged by Plehve, Pobedonostsev and others who had personal grievances against him or who disapproved of his views on worker control; the firing of Zubatov himself in August for utterly mismanaging a police-inspired strike in Odessa; the appointment of Ivan Foulon (1844-1918) as city-manager (*gradonachalnik*) of St. Petersburg; and then, the fortuitous assassination of Plehve (July 1904) when he was about to move against Gapon and his men because they had been organizing in Moscow and wooing members from the stagnant Zubatovite organization there.[8]

Meanwhile, while Gapon prepared for and defended his dissertation at the academy, he and his organizers went forward with their union in Petersburg. Bishop Sergei Stragorodskii (1867-1944), rector of the academy, encouraged Gapon to be tonsured so he could be consecrated a bishop and work within the hierarchy. He refused, however, mindful of his wife's counsels and those of Vereshchagin, so that he could work more closely with the Petersburg common people. He was able to bring his children to Petersburg to live at the house of a local merchant, while he himself had a room nearby at the Pokrovskii Obshchina on Vasilevskii Island. Christmas 1903 was his first with them since he had left Beliaki. His nearly non-existent income was supplemented by a gift of a hundred rubles from Metropolitan Antonii.

April, 1904, saw the Association of Russian Factory and Plant Workers formally come into existence and grow so rapidly that by the end of the year it became the first mass workers' union in Russia. Bishop Sergei agreed to officiate at the opening ceremonies but was forbidden to do so by the Procurator. Though the Association moved decidedly out from under the umbrella of the Society for Religious and Moral Propagation, Gapon remained a respected colleague of Ornatskii and Bishop Sergei. They, together with Ivan Foulon, were Gapon's best supporters in high places. It is one of the ironies of history that the network of cells and tea-rooms set up by Gapon became the framework for the development of the Petersburg Soviet the very next year—after its founder had been driven from his country.[9]

The Association's membership reached more than five thousand dues-paying members at the end of August 1904, after a gala variety show performed in the Pavlovskii Hall by workers and prominent Petersburg artists, and by the end of October there were more than ten thousand members, organized in eleven locals, each headed by one of Gapon's inner circle of men and women. Besides the Putilov Works, the capital's largest employer, the Association had organized the Franco-Russian Steamship Yards, the Semiannikov Ship-building Works and the Kronwerke near the Peter and Paul fortress, to name only the larger concentrations of workers. He expected to have nearly all working men and women in the city unionized by the end of the Christmas-Epiphany holidays of 1905.[10]

But the brightness of worker organization was overshadowed by the clouds of the Russo-Japanese War. By the end of October, Russia had suffered many defeats, and the public mood about the war had become exasperated and ugly. Gapon, Peter Rutenberg, Ivan Vasiliev, Dmitri Kuzin, Alexei and Vera Karelin, Nikolai Varnashev and the rest of the Association leadership found it difficult to resist anti-government and anti-factory owner agitation from Social Democratic and Socialist Revolutionary propagandists. The declining living standards of the Petersburg proletariate made them more and more receptive to criticism of the authorities. However, an attempt to effect a meeting of minds with such moderate Social Democrats as Sergei Prokopovich (1871-1955), Ekaterina D. Kuskova (1869-1958), and V. Ia. Bogucharskii (1861-1915), at a meeting arranged by

Maxim Gorkii (1868-1936), was unsuccessful. Gapon, Rutenberg, Varnashev, the Karelins and other Association leaders had been heartened at the successful outcome of a series of *zemstvo* conferences during the autumn of 1904, the most successful being that held in the Petersburg apartments of Korsakov and Vladimir Nabokov (1869-1922), prominent liberals. The Association leadership conceived the idea of likewise holding political consciousness sessions, drawing up their conclusions, and forwarding them to the Tsar. The unpropitious coincidence of those three situations—the war, the success of the *zemstvo* conferences and the aspirations of the Workmen's Association—led to the upheaval known to posterity as Bloody Sunday, January 9, 1905.[11]

The immediate cause of the confrontation was the decision of the employers of the major Petersburg factories to destroy the Workmen's Association. Early in December, Anatolii Tetiavkin, a foreman in one of the railroad car factories at the Putilov Works, fired four workers—Semen Subbotin, Ilia Sergunin, a man named Ukolov, and another named Fedorov—all of them members of the Association. The four were summarily fired without following normal notification procedures established by the government, temporary suspension for minor infractions, or permitting allegedly offending workers to explain their side of the story. When Putilov workers remonstrated with Tetiavkin, he taunted them with "go tell your Association." The challenge was unmistakable. It came at a time when news had reached the public that the Russian garrison at Port Arthur had finally fallen after nearly a year of bitter resistance to the Japanese. Negotiations via proper channels having failed, Gapon was drawn into the dispute. He tried to make headway by working through Metropolitan Antonii, Ivan Foulon, Sergei Witte, and Maxim Gorkii, among others. None of them were able to effect a change in the intransigence of the Putilov management, especially when it became increasingly clear that they had the backing of the other major employers of the capital.[12]

A tense Christmas followed, with the Association sponsoring a series of parties and festivals for its members in the various locals and at the same time consolidating its deter-

mination not to back down in the face of the Putilov arrogance. Belated and half-hearted efforts to placate the Association only strengthened their resolve. On January 2, with
Gapon's blessing, the Putilov Works was struck, followed
during the next five days by strikes at the other major industrial establishments. The capital was paralyzed.

The authorities were stunned, Foulon panicked, and Metropolitan Antonii tried to intervene with Gapon. Gapon tried
to impress upon various officials—including Witte, Chairman
of the Committee of Ministers, and Pavel Sviatopolk-Mirskii,
Minister of the Interior—that the movement now had to be
reckoned with or a clash was unavoidable. Gapon never lost
his belief that the clash between workers' demands and employers' intransigence could be peacefully ironed out—until
the Cossacks began to kill his workers in the streets.

A way out suggested itself through the medium of the
Prison Administration. Gapon had been appointed chaplain
of the Main Transfer Prison in Petersburg in 1903 by Metropolitan Antonii. As one of the more active ministers in the
mission to prisoners, Gapon had become known to several
leading figures around the court who also had an interest
in the prison mission. The Empress Alexandra was the general patroness of the mission. Because of their common interest in prisoners and prison reform, Fr. Gapon had been
invited to celebrate a liturgy at Tsarskoe Selo the evening of
January 7, at the opening of a new model prison there. Attending would be Nicholas and Alexandra themselves. Gapon
would appeal to the Tsar directly. However, it was known
at Tsarskoe Selo that Gapon was the leader and organizer of
the Workmen's Association, which had now shut down the
industry of the capital during a critical phase in the Japanese
War, and the court had been alarmed during the Epiphany
ceremony of the blessing of the waters when a cannonade
from the Peter and Paul battery in the Neva had showered
the metropolitan and the imperial retinue with live shot. It
was not certain whether it had been an accident or whether
there might have been some connection with the spreading
strike. The liturgy at the new Tsarskoe Selo prison was can-
celled and Gapon disinvited. The approach to Nicholas had

been blocked and the Association had to try another avenue.[13]

Only then did they decide that they would try a massive, traditional procession of the cross (*krestnyi khod*) from the various headquarters of the Association to the Winter Palace to beseech their Tsar to hear their petitions and right the wrongs that had been done to them. During the frantic night of Friday, January 7, and during the day of Saturday, January 8, the petition was put into final form, incorporating some of the demands aired by the *zemstvo* conferences and some themes of Social Democratic origin into their own long-thought-out Association grievances against their employers. Basically, their demands were their own, worked out in long discussions in their tearooms and among the Association leadership since October 1904.

Their pleas included better working conditions in the factories, established rates for men and women laborers, standard rates for piecework, permanent arbitration boards at each plant and factory on which the workers would have trusted members, no penalties for strikers or Association organizers, convocation of a constituent assembly based on universal, equal, secret and direct suffrage, and separation of church and state. The latter two petitions came from their newly acquired political fellow travellers, though some church reformers had suggested separation of church and state as a means to achieve restoration of canonical *symphonia* between the government and the administration of the Orthodox church.[14]

The rest is history. Gapon's faith in the open-heartedness of the court and the higher bureaucracy was not reciprocated. The *krestnyi khod* was met by gunfire, and several tens of people were killed and several hundreds wounded. The imperial structure was shaken so badly that it nearly collapsed. It was so weakened that it could not bear the weight of World War I when it came nine years later. Now, in the latter quarter of the twentieth century, it is idle to speculate what might have been if wiser heads had prevailed and listened to this voice from the people and their church. It is one of the crueler ironies of twentieth-century Russian history that it was to be a charlatan named Grigorii Rasputin

who would soon be embraced by the court as a genuine spokesman for the Russian *narod* and the Orthodox faith, rather
than Gapon, who now had to flee from his country and within
a year was to be murdered by Socialist Revolutionaries to
prevent his regaining his leadership with the working masses.

Metropolitan Antonii, working at the time of the upheaval with the Committee of Ministers to formulate laws
to restore autonomy of the church and toleration to sectarians,
fell under a cloud that was to overshadow him for the remainder of his life for not having moved faster to short-
circuit the Workmen's Association and its leader. It was left
to the metropolitan to go to the Putilov Works and com-
miserate with the workers. Bishop Sergei Stragorodskii published a bitter denunciation of the bloodletting in *Tserkovnyi
Vestnik*, the organ of the Petersburg Academy, which was
picked up and broadcast by the secular press.[15]

*   *   *

Russia dissolved into three years of anarchy, disaster and
insurrection. It was her eleventh hour. A public outcry of
"where was the church" made reform a more critical need
than ever before. A priest had been for the working masses
the prophet they sought to lead them out of economic and
social bondage. Relaxation of restrictions on sectarians, Old
Believers and other non-Orthodox religions which the Tsar
had promised left the church open to every kind of hostile
propaganda and proselytizing, from both non-Orthodox
Christians and anti-Christian revolutionaries. Church leaders
believed the church had been abandoned by the politicians
after having been constrained to serve as the mainstay of the
autocracy. Its enfeebled position left it defenseless. Reform
and liberation from the crippling wardship of the state were
essential to its future existence.

In the wake of the Bloody Sunday catastrophe, Metropolitan Antonii bore down upon the members of the Committee of Ministers in Special Sessions and urged them to
consider ways and means that would lead to the convocation
of a national church council, the first since the Great Sobor
of 1666-1667, which would be just as crucial to the future

of the Russian church. Seizing the opportunity of Pobedonostsev's illness, Antonii pressed for an unequivocal statement that the restoration of autonomous administration would
be an integral part of the reform and that the procuracy would
be terminated.

The Gaponovshchina and the news from the war front
caused Sergei Witte to waver from forthright championing
of the church for its own sake to the traditional viewpoint
of the church as a support of the state, pacifying the masses
and reaffirming the authority of the Tsar. Antonii deter-
minedly continued to emphasize that the only way the church
would regain her credibility in the public eye was to convoke a general sobor and proceed at once with general
reformation. The church was the guardian of public morality
and Orthodox tradition, whether or not they happened to
coincide with the needs of the government. But a church
free from government ties and with a restored patriarchate
on its own terms was viewed with unease in government
circles. Deaf ears met entreaties by churchmen to waste no
time in summoning a sobor.[16]

The Procurator's chancellory busied itself trying to restrict the business of any possible sobor to the election of a
Patriarch who would be a docile servant of the politicians.
If he were elected by bishops alone, appointees of the Procurator, his subservience to political purposes would be un-
questioned. The government and the procuracy were determined to exclude any significant representation of the white
clergy and laity, who were closely in touch with the social
and political developments of the electric months of 1905.
Their representation in any sobor would radicalize the
somnolent church and endanger the already tottering tsardom.
Both the liberal and the reactionary press found common
cause in opposing liberalization in the church, which would
allow it to become an autonomous influence in the Russian
Empire. The former looked upon the church as a decayed
relic of the past which could only confuse things if allowed
to express itself freely, and the latter saw a docile church
as necessary for the restoration of traditional political hegem-

ony. Reactionaries feared that an autonomous church might
swing into the camp of political reform.[17]

The deliberations of the Special Sessions of the Committee
of Ministers were soon common knowledge among the professors of the universities, academies and seminaries and clergy
concerned about church reform. In February, a group of
twenty-five prominent Petersburg priests of the Diocesan
Pastoral Council called upon Antonii to press for the earliest
convocation of an all-Russian sobor that would be open, representative of all elements of the church and not just the
monopoly of the hierarchy or of the black clergy. Most of
these priests had participated in various sessions of the
Religious-Philosophical Society in 1901-1903. They had met
often in the two years since the Society meetings were suspended and had grown more determined to break out of the
strictures, the narrow regulations which the Synod and diocesan consistory placed upon them. They stressed that the
principle of *sobornost'* necessitated inclusion of the widest
possible representation of clergy and laity in the church and
that the agenda for the council should not be controlled by
the Procurator's bureaucrats. They left Antonii a memorandum
entitled "The Urgency of Restoring Canonical Liberty to the
Orthodox Church in Russia," a document that closely echoed
the ideas he had stressed before at the Special Sessions.
Antonii urged the pastors to continue meeting and enlarged
the Pastoral Council to involve other Petersburg priests. The
pastors in turn warned Antonii that unless parishioners were
speedily involved in parish planning and management, there
would be large-scale defections to the Old Believers, especially Old Believers maintaining a close resemblance to Orthodoxy, and serious inroads by atheistic political propaganda.

In the Committee of Ministers, the metropolitan warned
that the state had failed in its mission to protect and foster
the interests of the church and that serious questions were
being raised by churchmen now as to whether the church
was bound any longer to remain a supporter of the state.
Needless to say, he surprised the ministers in the Committee
and was rebuked by Witte. Antonii further noted that, contrary to western theories of caesaropapism in the Eastern

church, the canonical relation of the church to the state should be one of symphony, not one of subordination. The suffocating control of the Russian church and the blithe indifference of the civil bureaucracy to the real interests of the church placed the church in a position of de facto antagonism to the state. The metropolitan's words sounded ominous to the ears of government men, perturbed by violence and breakdown in civil order. Meanwhile, news from the eastern front became more alarming with the fall of Mukden in February 1905.

Antonii further warned that if autonomy were granted to non-Orthodox bodies and their pastors and ministers were given legal status as heads of their communities, the state would build into the framework of the empire potentially antagonistic, not to say revolutionary, societies. Therefore, the Orthodox parish must acquire the rights of a legal entity or corporation. Cohesion of the parish would give authority and prestige to Orthodox priests so they could compete with sectarian, Old Believer and denominational clergy as equals. Anything less than that would gravely impair whatever support the church might offer to the tottering state. The Tsar indicated on June 26, 1904, that the Orthodox clergy should become active in local affairs. Now was the time to take legal steps to effect their participation.

Vadkovskii further demanded that the church have a voice in the inner councils of government. Church spokesmen should be in the Council of Ministers and in the State Council to defend the church from oppression by the civil bureaucracy and to advise them on social and moral aspects of government policy. The patriarchate had played such a role in the Byzantine Empire, and should in Russia.

The metropolitan demanded that the church recover the management and disposition of real property, bequests and gifts. Presently, monasteries were erected, foundations established and churches constructed which in no way benefited the public worship of the people or the corporate interests of the Orthodox church. Too often foundations were deliberately placed among non-Orthodox populations, to whom they were an affront. Ecclesiastical funds were exhausted in their main-

tenance and charged off to the church budget without benefit
to the church.

Witte was convinced by Antonii and his experts that the
two-century-old control of the church by the Synod and the
Procurator's chancellory had to end. As presently constituted,
the synodal structure worked to the advantage of sectarians
and schismatics. Witte was in perfect accord with Bishop
Sergei Stragorodskii in the belief that as long as Nicholas
had proclaimed the goal of religious toleration in December
and it was to be embodied in legislation, it was necessary to
go the whole way and grant freedom to the Orthodox church
as well. Any delay would be serious, because non-Orthodox
bodies would seize the disparate moment in publicity and
propaganda. Witte was persuaded that a Russian patriarchate
was essential and made an impassioned appeal to the Committee to petition Nicholas to restore it.[18]

Early in March, the arguments for reform were summarized by professors from the Petersburg and Moscow Theological Academies, prominent among them canon lawyers
Nikolai Zaozerskii of Moscow and P. V. Tikhomirov of
Petersburg. The summary, entitled *Questions on Needed
Reforms in the Constitution of the Orthodox Church*, dealt
with the need to grant equality of status to the state church,
together with a plea for autonomy of administration, legal
incorporation and self-government of parishes, and a guaranteed right of pastors and members of the hierarchy to be
involved in and members of political and public organizations. It concluded with the demand that exclusive control
of ecclesiastical properties, impounded by the state since the
reign of Catherine II, be restored to the church. Only then
could the beleaguered regime expect to get any meaningful
support from the church.[19]

Witte took the *Questions* to Professor Nikolai Suvorov
of Moscow State University, an old friend, and canonist
A. S. Pavlov, who put them into historical context, explaining how the Russian state had, over the past two hundred
years, slowly suffocated the Orthodox church. Their combined efforts resulted in Witte's *Memorandum on the Contemporary Situation of the Orthodox Church*, which pointed

out that the Petrine reform of the eighteenth century had been motivated in part by the need to kill the independent spirit of the Orthodox parish so that the expansion of serfdom could go ahead with a minimum of hindrance. One of the most violent things done to the integrity of the Russian clergy was to force them to become police agents, spying on their flocks and reporting political matters up the chain of command to the Ministry of the Interior and the Okhrana, a most serious violation of the canons and spirit of Orthodoxy. The titles and exterior forms of diocesan administration and central administration had been artfully preserved, but they had been deliberately drained of all substance and subordinated to political agencies.

Witte denounced the manner in which the ecclesiastical school system had been "sanitized" during the past twenty-five years so that most of the current political and social literature read by the public was completely unknown to the average priest. Under the circumstances, priests could hardly be expected to provide any intelligent leadership against political agitation and sectarian propagandists.

The Russian state had systematically bled the life out of the church and now, when the state needed a loyal and vibrant church, there was none. Witte urged the Tsar to proclaim immediate autonomy for the Orthodox administration and to summon a general sobor to reconstitute the governance of the church along the lines of *sobornost'*, in full conformity with the canons of the early church, particularly of the councils of First Nicaea, Chalcedon, Second Nicaea, and Fourth Constantinople. Witte's memorandum was forwarded to Nicholas in late February and appeared in the press on March 28, after circulating among the ministers of the government.[20]

Witte and Antonii both had audiences with Nicholas at Tsarskoe Selo on the topic of church reform. Antonii had taken the other bishops of the Synod along, and they had pressed the Tsar to order the convocation of a sobor immediately. Nicholas promised to convoke a sobor, possibly by the end of May or early June 1905. Nicholas reaffirmed that Orthodox priests and hierarchs ought to have permanent positions in government bodies at all levels, from the *volost'* all the way to the State Council and the Council of Ministers, and that ecclesiastical administration had to be separated from civil bureaucratic control.

Pobedonostsev regarded all this as impertinent, a violation of the proper legal order of things. He, after all, was the Procurator of the Synod, the one man whom the law empowered to deal with the Tsar on matters affecting the church. He had been bypassed by Witte, whom he regarded as an uncultured bureaucrat with no real knowledge of the church and its relation to the autocracy in any case. He was offended by Antonii, too. Though he was designated first hierarch of the Synod, he was not the primate of the Russian church and therefore had no business dealing with the Tsar directly. Pobedonostsev believed that Peter the Great had had great wisdom when he decapitated the church and brought it under government control. Furthermore, the tone of the discussions in the Special Sessions of the Committee of Ministers was insulting. Year after year Pobedonostsev had reported on the state of the church. Year after year he had pleaded for more funds to improve the church school system and to elevate the level of education among the clergy. Year after year these funds had been inadequate because the government had to channel its resources elsewhere. The war with the Japanese was only the latest drain on funds that were better spent elsewhere. And now these experts of the church were quite directly holding him and his chancellory responsible for the mess they thought the church was in and recommended that, if he were not completely abolished, he should at least have his authority curtailed. After twenty-five years of loyal service, that hurt.

The Procurator went on the offensive and wrote his own assessment of the situation of the church. His ghost writer, Stepan G. Runkevich, Ober-Secretary to the Chancellor and a minor church historian, had written a volume on the history of the Minsk diocese in 1893 and a survey of Russian church history in the nineteenth century, which was published in 1901. Runkevich had warned the Procurator about the danger of allowing the meetings of the Religious-Philosophical Society in 1901-1903. Runkevich had been refused the doctorate in church history by the *sovet* of professors of Petersburg Theological Academy, but through the intervention of Pobedonostsev had received it anyway.[21]

Entitled *Considerations on the Question of Changing the Existing Situation in the Orthodox Church*,[22] Pobedonostsev's rejoinder was spirited and sarcastic, but it missed the point. He accused Witte of wishing to separate the church and the state and thereby bring about their mutual destruction. He asserted that the Russian church in the seventeenth century was known for its corruption and that the patriarchate had been the chief cause of its disgrace. He even ventured to say that the Petrine reform had come at the request of the clergy themselves and the synodal structure of the administration embodied the very principle of *sobornost'*, so ardently desired by the reformers. The weakening of the church in the eighteenth century had come about by accident, thanks to the German regime that followed Peter's death, and not through any deliberate design. Furthermore, the only reason the church had had any life in the nineteenth century was because the state had stood it up on its feet and had been its crutch. The church was incapable of running its own affairs and would have to create an entire bureaucracy duplicating the civil bureaucracy if it were given autonomy. If it was really paralyzed, as Dostoevskii had said and as had been repeated *ad nauseam* by would-be reformers, then that was because it had already been paralyzed before the state took it over, not as a result of the takeover. The existing arrangement made it possible for priests and bishops to devote themselves exclusively to their proper religious functions and not involve themselves in the details of administration and areas outside their lawful concern. As far as the claim that there were never any sobors was concerned, he himself had authorized three regional sobors over the past twenty-five years.

If the diocesan administrations were lifeless, that was because the bishops did not bestir themselves enough to breathe life into them. The parishes were as alive as could be expected, and Pobedonostsev doubted that the ideal parish, so lamented in the press nowadays, had in fact ever existed. If the clergy really wanted to imagine what misery was, let them consider what their livelihoods would be like if they did not receive state subsidies for their salaries, their education and the education of their children. The Procurator deeply resented the criticism of the ecclesiastical schools and wondered what kind of disorder would sweep them if the Synod administration did not keep a close watch on them and their personnel. Who would pay their professors and teachers if the church were separated from the state? If the clergy were relieved of their obligations to keep local records and tax ledgers and did not have to report politically subversive activities, the state would have to create another whole category of bureaucrats to handle those responsibilities. The population would be burdened with even more taxation to support them.

Pobedonostsev wound up his tirade by noting darkly that those who were questioning the Petrine administration were the same people who nowadays were working against the whole monarchical system of government in the empire. That was treasonous. Finally, the Witte memorandum was vague and full of generalities, something that he did not have time to concern himself about.[23]

The Procurator had chosen to overlook the crucial charge that the church had in effect been swallowed by the state. His argument that the church needed the advice and counsel of state administrators was one that no one had gainsaid, and he ignored the fact that the synodal system as constituted by Peter the Great was uncanonical in the Eastern church. He tried to pass off a strictly regional convocation of bishops, called to coordinate missionary efforts against Raskol and sectarianism, as some kind of *pomestnyi sobor*. Too confined by the viewpoint of the church as an apparatus, Pobedonostsev could not envision it as a dynamic vehicle for spiritual revival that could transform men and sociopolitical institutions. Such a transformation could be politically destabilizing.

The Procurator went straight to the Tsar. Pobedonostsev pointed out that the whole legal structure of church-state relations was being violated, that the proper place for discussions on the reform of the Russian church was in the Synod, not in the Council of Ministers, and much less in the press.

Unless the Tsar moved now, the whole church business could become a political liability, one more cause espoused by anti-tsarist groups.

Needless to say, Nicholas was impressed. On March 13, he issued an *ukaz* removing the discussion of church reform from the Committee of Ministers and placing it entirely in the hands of the Synod. That meant that Antonii and his episcopal cohorts could be much more closely controlled, and if the Procurator chose not to report anything to the Tsar on the matter of reform, the reform movement could be stopped dead in its tracks.

Witte, Antonii and the professors were not to be stopped, however. Pobedonostsev's *Considerations* had angered them, and now this blatant attempt to out-maneuver them fired their determination that takeover by the Synod would not smother the momentum they had engendered.

Bishop Sergei, Anton Kartashev and others who had been present at Runkevich's defense recognized that Runkevich lay behind Pobedonostsev's arguments. Runkevich's ill-fated dissertation had been rejected in 1902 because it had been poorly researched and bent its sources so badly to support its arguments that it violated even the most casual interpretation of academic standards. They helped Witte draft a point-by-point refutation of Pobedonostsev's statements, beginning with the fact that the Petrine reform had created an ecclesiastical administration that had no sanction in the canons of the Orthodox church. Canons can be changed in an ecumenical council, not by the fiat of some civil ruler or bureaucrat. When Patriarchs in the Orthodox church step out of line or try to usurp too much power, they are tried by a sobor and curbed or deposed. The cure of excesses does not lie in abolishing the patriarchate itself.

Witte was astounded that the Procurator would equate vital pastoral activity with shuffling papers and filling out forms. That was not the kind of "vital link" he and the academicians had been talking about. That very misconception, however, was telling and proved that Pobedonostsev had no idea what pastoral leadership was. Witte continued that it was absurd to equate an occasional congress of missionaries, restricted in area and concerned with narrow agendas, with a sobor or to imagine that it evidenced any sign of the ideal of *sobornost'*.

On the question of the education of the clergy, Witte noted that it was true that they were better educated in the twentieth century than in the seventeenth. But so were all the other classes of society, and the balance had tilted heavily against the clergy. Clergy should be drawn from all classes of society and reflect the education and interests of all classes. They would be better pastors as a result. The situation of the clergy was simply not adequate. The social antagonism between clergy and intellectuals was one of the more painful aspects of modern life in Russia.

When it came to the question of whose sources were more dependable, Witte acidly noted that one of his sources was the respected Professor Alexander Papkov, whom Pobedonostsev in 1903 had singled out for an award for academic and journalistic excellence. Then he listed a number of the most prominent members of the faculties of the theological academies and indicated exactly from which of them he had drawn the ideas in his memorandum. Where else, he asked, than in the theological academies would one expect to find the most up-to-date and well-researched thinking on the nature and canons of the church? Then he bore down on Pobedonostsev's single source, the hapless Runkevich, a bureaucratic flunky who owed his doctorate entirely to Pobedonostsev's overriding of the professors of the Petersburg Academy and granting one in the name of the Synod Education Commission. Runkevich did not know anything about the canons of the church, so Witte was not surprised that Pobedonostsev's *Considerations* did not reveal any sophistication on the subject either. Witte dismissed Pobedonostsev as a pseudo-intellectual, more concerned with obfuscating the issue of reform rather than really getting to the root of the problem.

Pobedonostsev was devastated. Nicholas was angry at the Procurator for having dragged him into the affair prematurely and having appeared foolish, together with Pobedonostsev, when the Witte rejoinder was circulated, and he was angry at the Chairman for having so thoroughly discredited the synodal chancellory when he had already committed himself on their side. Needless to say, Nicholas' intervention, without first consulting him or the metropolitan, did not favorably dispose Witte towards the Tsar either.

Antonii and Witte were able to have the *ukaz* transferring the reform question from the Committee to the Synod recapitulate point by point the arguments made in the religious press, in the Religious-Philosophical Society and in the Special Sessions of the Committee of Ministers. Nicholas noted that the canonical bases of the Russian church were questionable, that parish life in the Russian church had fallen into paralysis, that the church's schools (particularly those responsible for educating the clergy) were inadequate, that the relationship of the church to the state was incorrect and that the principle of *sobornost'* had not been exercised since some time in the fifteenth century and had to be revived.

The Procurator's attempts to squelch the idea of reforming the church failed. Nicholas had shown interest in rehabilitating the church as early as 1903, and was still interested, despite the terrible war with Japan.

*   *   *

The *ukaz* of March 13, 1905, produced an uproar of many dimensions. Two issues caused particular discord: (1) Would a sobor of bishops alone adequately represent the church, or should the clergy and laity be broadly represented? And (2) where should the sobor sit? On the latter issue, Pobedonostsev presumed that Petersburg would be the site of the sobor. The chancellory offices were headquartered there, and the sessions of the Synod were held there. Furthermore, the government was located in Petersburg, and it would be easier to have recourse to government influence when necessary to guide the sobor.

For that very reason, many churchmen opposed convening the sobor in Petersburg, especially those from Moscow. Petersburg was the creation of Peter the Great; it was western-oriented, out of touch with the traditions of the Muscovite church. Moscow was the site of the most influential and

prestigious of the Russian theological academies and was sufficiently distant from Petersburg to enable the sobor to have
some measure of autonomy from bureaucratic interference.
Besides, Moscow was the site of the Uspenskii cathedral, the
traditional patriarchal cathedral, and the site of the last Great
Sobor (1666-1667).

Some questioned whether a patriarchate was really necessary, because a Patriarch might again try to rival the Tsar,
particularly in times as turbulent as 1905, as Nikon had done
in the seventeenth century. A more serious concern was that
the Patriarch might simply replace the Procurator as a docile
servant of the interests of the state and become a worse burden upon the metropolitans, bishops and clergy than the patriarchate had been in the seventeenth century. Opponents of
restoration pointed out that Peter's abolition of the patriarchate was at least in part a response to members of the
hierarchy who resented the attempts of certain Patriarchs,
chiefly Nikon (1652-1666) and Adrian (1690-1700), the last
Patriarch, to dictate to them. A Patriarch might endanger the
ideal of *sobornost'* in the church. Whether or not they wanted
restoration of the patriarchate, all agreed that the head of
the church would have to have limitations placed upon him
to ensure that he would remain *primus inter pares* and not
try to assume autocratic powers within the church.

The white clergy were particularly concerned about a
possible restoration of the patriarchate. Their position in the
church was already that of second-class citizens, excluded
from the hierarchy by the fact that they had not taken monastic tonsure and were married. White clergy had not fared
well in the seventeenth century under the patriarchate, and
there was no certainty that they would fare any better under
one in the twentieth century. Some suggested—after the Duma
was promised—that the white clergy, the clergy with the most
immediate contact with the people, might gain more and be
able to have a more direct impact upon the process of church
reform through the Duma rather than through a patriarchate.
Some white clergy wished to have canonical prohibitions
against elevation of white clergy to the episcopate removed.
They ran into determined opposition from the monastic clergy.

This conflict was particularly acute early in 1905, when the bishop of Perm, Ioann Alexeev (1861-1905), died and left in his testament the suggestion that a local archpriest be elevated to the episcopate there. The Procurator refused.

On the day after the *ukaz* was issued, the Petersburg Pastoral Council, prominent among whose number was Fr. Filosof Ornatskii, Gapon's friend, met to formulate plans to put pressure upon the Synod not to curb the momentum that had been generated for church reform. They published the main points of the discussion they had had with Metropolitan Antonii in February in the journal of the Petersburg Academy, *Tserkovnyi Vestnik*.[24]

This group, which came to be known as the Petersburg Thirty-Two, entitled their article "The Inevitability of Change in the Administration of the Russian Church." In it they appealed for an immediate return to the canonical forms of Orthodox administration and liberation of the state church from the crippling restrictions imposed upon it by the government. They pleaded with the Orthodox clergy to avoid taking one side in the current disorders and not simply to repeat platitudes put out by the authorities. They asked for an autonomous episcopate, the end to bishops revolving from diocese to diocese every year, and measures that would bind bishops closely to their flocks. They recommended increasing the number of dioceses in the Russian church greatly and creating a metropolitanate in virtually every province. The Thirty-Two asked for immediate convocation of an all-Russian sobor, unfettered by any legal restrictions, that would be free to embark on a complete renovation of the administration and inner life of the state church. Such a reform would appeal to the masses and to the Old Believers to end their two-hundred-year schism.[25]

Together with Witte's memorandum, the letter of the Thirty-Two stirred considerable discussion in both the religious and secular press. In the middle of March 1905, the reading public became aware that reform of the church and the possibility of restoring the patriarchate were under serious consideration. This information, together with the electric news from the Japanese front, profoundly stirred the Russian public.

The Synod began debate on March 18 and finished on March 22. The somnolent chambers had not seen such animation in a quarter of a century. The Procurator blundered by not attending the meetings, entrusting obstruction to Vladimir Sabler, Assistant Procurator, who was sympathetic to Antonii. Pobedonostsev thought Sabler had his signals straight, but he and several key bureaucrats sided with the reformers, skillfully led by the metropolitan. The bishops opened a wide breach in the Procurator's apparatus, and his bureaucrats became confused about where authority really lay. The Synod truly functioned as the voice of the church during those days, albeit belatedly.

By the time the exhausted participants left the Synod building late on March 22, it was clear that there would be a reform, that it was the will of the clergy that a sobor be called, and that all the various issues raised in the past few months at the meetings of the Special Sessions would be on the agenda. Antonii lobbied during nocturnal sessions with the other bishops between the regular Synod sessions. The bishops remained united in their pressure on the bureaucrats and forced them ultimately to capitulate.[26]

Removal of the reform issue from the jurisdiction of the Committee of Ministers thus actually allowed the metropolitan more freedom of action. Witte was interested in a reformed church that would conciliate the masses of Old Believers, reunite them to the state church, and provide a new source of stability for the tsarist regime. Old Believers, despite their long-standing feud with the tsardom, were quite conservative socially and politically. For that reason Witte championed Antonii's efforts for reform and for liberating the church from the suffocating embrace of the government. Witte, more than Antonii or the academy professors, aimed for complete restoration of the patriarchate. A patriarchate based on the principle of *sobornost'* and free of the neopapalism of Nikon would give the state church the prestige and credibility needed to counter the objections of the Old Believers.

Antonii was walking a tightrope between a Procurator who was determined that no change at all should be made in church-state relations and a Chairman who, cooperative though he was, tended to see church-state relations largely from the point of view of state interest. Extracting as much maneuverability as was possible in that situation required delicate politicking and maximum persuasiveness. But having gotten Witte to deflate the credibility of Pobedonostsev with his rejoinder, Antonii found the going much easier in the Synod. The Procurator's men were unprepared for the onslaught they experienced in March 1905.

The Synod placed the various problems facing the church under two main headings: church structure, when made to conform to canonical norms; and the details of governing and financing the new church establishment once canonical norms were reestablished.

There was no question in the minds of the bishops on the Synod that the synodal structure should be completely dismantled. If there was to be any remnant of the Synod, it would only be to function as the chancellory for the administration of the church. Dismantling the synodal authority would shift much administrative detail from St. Petersburg to the dioceses. Only functions which could not be handled at the diocesan level would remain concentrated in the central administration. The bishops only peripherally touched on what form the central administration should take, and avoided, for the time being, a bitter wrangle over how much authority the Patriarch should have and how his administration should be structured.

The Synod's bishops agreed that the Russian church should be subdivided into several metropolias (*tserkovnye okruga*), each of which would be headed by a metropolitan. The new metropolitans would hold positions of honor—*primi inter pares*—among the bishops of their metropolias. The metropolitan would govern his own archdiocese and would have the right to convoke annual or semi-annual convocations of fellow bishops. Bishops in a metropolia would deal with special local problems, such as the resurgence of Uniate and Raskol activities or the outbreak of atheistic propaganda.

Areas once outside the jurisdiction of the Moscow Tsars constituted special problems. There was reason for concern about the degree of local autonomy to grant metropolias and dioceses in those areas in view of the threat from non-Orthodox bodies. Other regions of special concern were the Caucasus and the Volga. In both places there was either a long tradition of ecclesiastical independence or a large population in schism or not even Christian. The debate over these regions revolved around the concern that granting large-scale local autonomy to the Orthodox administration might open the door to separatism of a political nature. The problem was especially acute in Georgia, where demands for restoration of autocephaly were strident during the years 1905-1909, and where a Russian bishop was murdered in his cathedral at Tiflis in 1908. The Procurator's men argued that ecclesiastical decentralization meant de facto a weakening of the church and its political mission to bolster the state. The reformers responded that not to reform the administration of the church, not to decentralize, meant in the long run that the church would simply collapse in those areas anyway together with the church in the rest of the empire.

Chancellory bureaucrats were forced to agree to the idea of decentralization and to the loss of status they would suffer in consequence. Then, discussion moved item by item to consideration of what a decentralized administration would be like.

Ecclesiastical courts would be separated from the consistory. On November 20, 1864, civil courts had been separated from the civil administration; such separation was thirty years overdue in the church. The workload of church administration was so heavy that neither the administration nor the legal aspects of diocesan government were handled adequately. Orthodox canon law postulated separate church court systems.

Consistories would be stripped of control of schools, missionary activities, brotherhoods, diocesan convocations of clergy, retirement homes and funds for clergy, candle factories and the whole host of responsibilities that needlessly tied up central diocesan administration.

The bishop's chancellory, a reformed consistory, would

came under the scrutiny of the diocesan convocation of clergy. All diocesan activities, particularly those involving financial commitment and expenditure, would be controlled by the convocation. The convocation would become an autonomous and implementing body, not just an advisory body. Its authority would be limited only by the canonical prerogatives of the bishop, which would be spelled out by the national sobor.[27] The revitalized parish, reconstituted as a juridical person, would take over much day-to-day administration from the consistory. Much paperwork would simply vanish when the need to keep track of every minute transaction, from the purchase of altar wines to renovating a church, was handled locally.

The Orthodox parish would have primary jurisdiction over its own finances and how funds would be utilized, subject in major cases to approval of the diocese. The parish would have the major voice in selecting its own clergy and arranging their maintenance. All almsgiving and charitable institutions on the local level would be controlled by the parish. The village community and the parish organization would blend into one strong, self-sustaining unit.

The ecclesiastical school system came in for severe criticism. The closed, caste-like nature of church schools would be rapidly done away with. Children of all classes would be encouraged to avail themselves of the facilities of the church schools. Students in diocesan schools and seminaries would be exposed to the broad currents of contemporary culture. Students would learn by developing their own intellectual sophistication as to what to accept and what to reject. The reformers noted that the students in church schools often took the lead in rioting and either infected their fellows in the state schools or followed them into the streets. It was obvious that they had not been insulated from the influences that agitated students in state schools. Rote emphasis upon discipline and the artificially maintained distance between teacher and student, student and administrator, would disappear.

Financial maintenance of clergy and ecclesiastical institutions would be alleviated by granting clergymen the right to acquire and dispose of property in their own name, rescinding a law of 1900 which specifically excluded priests from the right to acquire and dispose of real and movable property. Nevertheless, much of the support of the clergy would still have to come from government sources—the Imperial Treasury, local *zemstvo* organizations, the town administration or from various ministries. Local sources were preferred, in keeping with the decentralization of the administration of the church, because they were more easily influenced without strings being attached, unlike the case with funds coming from the center. Church lands and properties would be released from the wardship of civil authorities and left to church management. Local church organizations would manage properties that pertained to their functions. Only properties of major importance would be managed by the patriarchate.

The question of the relationship of the church to the state, a topic hotly debated in the press and seriously considered in the Special Sessions of the Committee of Ministers, never came up.

Pobedonostsev was determined that the agenda of items to be considered should be drawn up and edited by his men before the sobor was ever summoned. He countenanced no suggestion of spontaneously summoning a sobor and letting it work out its own agenda. He was determined that the Synod should remain an integral and powerful part of any new church organization. The reformist ferment penetrating to the grassroots of the church would have to be curbed before a sobor was summoned. The only way to cool the excitement was through the state's agencies of control.

The Synod retired for the Lenten observances and Easter holidays during the remainder of March and April 1905—churchmen in the expectation that the Russian church was at the dawn of a new resurrection, and the Procurator's men in a state of perplexity, worried that the religious intoxication of the moment would fuel the political confusion. The whole religious and political foundation of the Russian tsardom could come tumbling down. It was a disquieting spring for Pobedonostsev, Runkevich and their lieutenants. The Procurator issued a communication on March 23 briefly outlining the subjects debated, stressing that when the sobor was held, the Synod—meaning his bureaucracy—would be in charge.[28]

On Thursday, April 24, *Tserkovnyi Vestnik*, organ of the Petersburg Academy, ran an editorial which reviewed the articles appearing in the secular press and warned the Procurator against obstructing reform. *Tserkovnyi Vestnik* noted that most of the press favored a thoroughgoing reform, and stressed that now, when Russia was experiencing a humiliating loss of face in Manchuria, one of the few consolations her people had left was their faith in the Orthodox church. The editorial observed that many who otherwise could have cared less about the church were nevertheless aware that it was the one institution that could keep the Russian nation together. The editorial expressed the hope that the Tsar, upon whom everything depended for reform, would speedily give his attention to the matter and give the command to begin. The clergy was aroused. The hierarchy was aroused. The laity was aroused. Now, if ever, was the time to restore autonomy to the church and allow it to restructure itself along sobornal lines so it could bind the wounds afflicting the Russian people.

The same day, *Slovo*, backgrounded by someone immediately involved in the Special Sessions of the Committee of Ministers, recounted point by point the clash between Pobedonostsev and the chancellory bureaucrats on the one hand, and Witte, Antonii and the academicians on the other. *Slovo* noted the excellent impression the metropolitan and his academic advisers had made upon the ministers and department heads, while the chancellory men had been badly prepared and arrogant in their presentations. The article dwelt in detail upon the *Questions* and the *Memorandum* and how well they had been thought out and what a farce Pobedonostsev's and Runkevich's *Considerations* had been. *Slovo* noted that Pobedonostsev had the church reform discussions transferred to the Synod with the intention of strangling them there, but that the bishops had bulldozed the chancellorymen over and pushed through the petition to call a sobor and elect a Patriarch. The lines of battle had been drawn between the Procurator, in his last-ditch effort to sustain the two-hundred-year-old administration of the church, and the reformers who had wrestled the initiative from his hands and now struggled to restore an authentic canonical Orthodox administration.

In his *ukaz* of March 13, Nicholas used the phrase "at a suitable time" when announcing that a sobor would sit. Pobedonostsev had used the same phrase in his report after the March session. The questions of who would control the destinies of the sobor and when it would actually convene were left unanswered. There remained a danger that the Procurator would so emasculate the sobor that it would be useless—or worse, that there might never be a sobor at all. The Procurator's office might engineer the establishment of a patriarchate in such a form as to leave the Synod very little altered, in control of the church at any rate. In that way, the appearance of reform would be had without any of its substance. The reformers, for the most part, wanted the organizing of the sobor out of the hands of the Procurator altogether and far removed from the influence of government bureaucrats. They expected the "suitable time" to be that spring, to coincide with the feast of Pentecost.

Another unresolved issue was whether it would be a sobor of bishops only. No mention was made of representing the white clergy or of any formal representation of the laity. The problem of white clergy versus monastic clergy and the exclusive right of the latter to enter the episcopate was a bitter problem, and was not resolved in the years before the collapse of the tsardom, thus giving rise to the so-called Living Church during the early years of the Bolshevik regime.[29]

All that had been settled was that the sobor would be summoned and that the church administration would be decentralized. In the hectic months that followed the March Synod meetings, pressure groups formed to try to affect the outcome of church reform. Antonii Vadkovskii and liberal professors from Petersburg and Moscow Academies, together with the Petersburg Pastoral Council and the parallel organizations of parish clergy and academy professors in Moscow, pressed for a sort of democratization of Russian church organization. They wished to see canonical norms restored and the Petrine straitjacket removed, but they wished to see those norms applied in an innovative fashion, not just by grafting onto the already unwieldly structure new components that would complicate church administration more. They wished to implement a broadened administration in which the white clergy, the standard bearers of Orthodoxy among the masses, and the laity, organized into various auxiliaries, brotherhoods and other bodies, would have real input in the future of the church. The "liberals," if they may be so called, were not of one mind when it came to structuring the future government of the church, however, nor were they of one mind about how close the ties of the church should be to the state. Some wanted a patriarchate, some did not. Some supporters of the patriarchate wanted it to be a strong executive, while others wanted the Patriarch to be little more than a figurehead. Some thought that ties between church and state should be abolished, even to the point of making the Orthodox church nothing more than the major religious denomination of the empire. Others felt that the church would become too discordantly involved in political and social turmoil if it became too independent, and therefore advocated strong government influence in church administration.

Among the "conservatives," there were many who wished the restored patriarchate to be a Russian version of the papacy, independent of civilian authority, which would wield much internal authority in the Russian church. Others would not grant it so much authority. But they all agreed that the church should be autonomous. To those in their own camp and in the "liberal" camp who warned of "Nikonism" in the Russian church, conservatives replied that Nikon had been maligned and that most of what he had accomplished had been good.

Conservatives rallied around Antonii Khrapovitskii, who during 1905-1906 moved steadily to the right in political matters and consorted with such groups as the Union of Russian People and the Black Hundreds, proto-fascist supporters of the tsardom. Very little common political ground was left between him and the metropolitan of St. Petersburg, who spurned the Hundreds and the Union. Khrapovitskii's ideal "liberated" church was to be stripped of the Procurator and Synod system. Diocesan bishops would be unfettered rulers in their dioceses, the monastic clergy would hold unconditional sway over the church, and the patriarchate would be the capstone of an episcopal oligarchy.[30]

The fortunes of the reformers in the church waxed and waned, parallel to the fate of the reformers in the political arena. Some of the same personalities were active in both spheres. The overriding weakness of the church reform movement was that the reformers were divided among themselves and never gained the cohesion necessary to assure them any sustained political pressure. As reaction set in in Russian political life, it inevitably had a corresponding paralyzing effect upon the church.

The spring months of 1905 were quickened by the excitement of reform in the Orthodox church and the granting of full religious toleration to non-Orthodox bodies. Until the humiliation of Tsushima and the subsequent worsening of disorders in the empire drove discussion of church reform to the inside pages, the Russian press of every persuasion and color discussed the church. During spring and summer 1905, the ecclesiastical press found itself distinctly outclassed by the secular press on the issue of reform and the excitement it generated.[31]

Press response swelled during March, after the appearance in *Tserkovnyi Vestnik* of the article by the Petersburg clergy. Regardless of its political proclivities, virtually every paper agreed that the church needed reforming. Two of the most effective publicizers were Dmitri Merezhkovskii, who bypassed the censors and published the proceedings of the Religious-Philosophical Society, heretofore forbidden literature, and Lev Tikhomirov, who had a long-standing interest in reforming the administration of the church. One of the most consistent supporters of reform was the neo-Slavophile and conservative journal *Novoe Vremia* (*New Time*). On the day the Synod debates began, *Novoe Vremia* ran a short article[32] noting that the Synod had taken up discussion of fundamental reform in the church, and in a subsequent article

it welcomed the Petersburg priests and supported their demand for liberation of the Russian pastorate from ignorance
and from the restrictions of the monastic character of the
hierarchy and the legal burdens of the Petrine reform. The
article went on to note that liberation of the Russian church
had been a driving concern of Alexei Khomiakov, Ivan
Aksakov, Metropolitan Filaret Drozdov, Vladimir Soloviev
and Leo Tolstoi, all of whom advocated lifting the heavy
hand of the government and diminishing the power of the
Synod. Now was the time to accomplish this, and *Novoe
Vremia* warned against again stifling reform.

Novoe Vremia followed up with two articles on church
reform directed at the Synod debates. One was by Bishop
Antonin Granovskii of Narva, and the other was by Vasilii
V. Rozanov (1865-1919), a neo-Slavophile champion of the
church as the mystical embodiment of Russian culture and
national identity and one-time debater in the Philosophical
Society.[33] Bishop Antonin's article, entitled "Dawn," sounded
the theme that church reform promised the dawn of a new
Russia, a renaissance of the Russian church that would heal
the deep fissures of society. Rozanov warned that church
reform had to reflect the aspirations of the Russian people.
The Eastern Patriarchs had told Pope Pius IX in 1848 that
the believing people, not a hierarchy or Patriarch, were the
conservers of true faith. Any reform or alteration of ecclesiastical administration that did not give ample opportunity to
the Russian people, the believing nation, to express themselves was null and void. The voice of the people had to be
heard—by the Synod, by the hierarchy, and by the Tsar himself. He warned the Procurator and his men not to attempt
some sleight-of-hand face-lifting and supported the Petersburg priests in their plea for a broad input of sentiment and
opinion at the coming sobor.

Rus' and the liberal Jewish *Bourse Gazette* (*Birzheviia
Vedomosti*) joined *Novoe Vremia* (March 21-23)[34] as news
leaked out of the Synod that church reform might be effected solely by a sobor of bishops. *Novoe Vremia* wanted to
know why. Who was the guardian of Orthodox belief?
Patriarchs? Hierarchs? "No," the paper said. A Patriarch

elected by members of the hierarchy would merely reflect the interests of those who elected him. Since the imposition of the Ecclesiastical Regulation the hierarchy had not been conspicuous in their defense of the church. Feofan Prokopovich was just the first of a long line of self-seekers and glorified bureaucrats. Metropolitan Filaret Drozdov was no better. In 1862, when the Minister of the Interior, Count P. A. Valuev, had suggested improving the education and social standing of the clergy as a class, Drozdov had not supported him, and the Procurator, Count D. A. Tolstoi, had opposed him. Furthermore, when it was suggested that members of the hierarchy become permanent members of the State Council and the Council of Ministers, Filaret was against it because he felt that they would not have the background to make intelligent decisions. The whole thrust of the Petrine reform had been to isolate the clergy, the white clergy in particular, because they were a disruptive element. Now was the time to harken to the plea of the Petersburg priests and remove the handicaps on the white clergy. The black clergy, by their very mode of life, were remote from the mass of the Russian people and from their aspirations and needs.

The *Bourse Gazette* pointed out that since the Petrine structures in other areas of administration had been phased out in the course of the nineteenth century, beginning with the reign of Alexander I, it was absurd to have a crippling, inefficient collegium still operating in the church. Promotions and administrative functions in the church were carried on in isolation. No rector, seminary inspector, archbishop or metropolitan ever came in regular touch with the mass of Orthodox believers. Reform must not be a means to enhance the hauteur and power of the episcopacy. The real leaders of the Russian people were the white clergy, yet their education and advancement was given last place in the priorities of the church. The lowly *batiushka* serving his parish was the real shepherd of the Orthodox. Therefore, if the upcoming sobor were to reflect the real interests and aspirations of the Russian nation, the white clergy would have to have a major voice in its proceedings. Selection of bishops by a small chapter of monks was not acceptable if one considered the manner of the election of Ambrose, bishop of Milan, as a true example of selection of a shepherd by his flock. Election of bishops by select personages was a later development. Peter's was only the most recent perversion of ecclesiastical norms. After the Synod debates were over, on Thursday, March 24, the *Gazette* interviewed Antonii Vadkovskii, who stated that the coming sobor would be made up of the sixty-six diocesan bishops of the church, plus their advisers. The sobor would begin by electing a Patriarch and then proceed to a restructuring of church administration. He emphasized that the procedure in both events would have to follow the canons, not any other method that might be contrived. Canonical norms guaranteed the legitimacy of procedure, not the other way around.[35]

Rus', on March 24, carried an article by Nikolai Simbirskii entitled "Towards Church Reform,"[36] which warned that the chief threat to the Orthodox church in March 1905 was the imminent granting of religious toleration to the Old Believers and the sectarians. Simbirskii claimed that without immediate wholesale reform of the church, many nominal Orthodox would abandon the state church shortly and affiliate with the Old Believers, particularly with the Austrian sect, which so closely resembled the state church and was looked upon by many in the state church with a large measure of sympathy. Once removal of political liabilities against joining the Old Belief had been accomplished, defection would be serious. If the state church were to make good its claim to be the legitimate form of Orthodoxy, it had to restore the patriarchate. The new Patriarch should be controlled by a Synod, whose membership would rotate in order to keep all bishops in touch with the problems of governing the church. The Patriarch should have limited authority. Diocesan administration should be given larger latitude, and the deadening consistories should be abolished. Frequent transfer of bishops from one diocese to another would have to stop. No bishop should be in a diocese for less than four years and should not transfer except for good reason. Salaries of bishops, which now ranged from fifteen hundred to twenty thousand rubles per annum, would have to be equalized to obviate the seeking of transfers for better income.

Simultaneously, there appeared in *Vestnik Iuga* (*Southern Messenger*) and *Zapadnyi Golos* (*Western Voice*)[37] an interview with a popular Petersburg priest, Archimandrite Mikhail Semenov, one of the Thirty-Two. Fr. Mikhail was a docent at the academy, a convert from Judaism and a popular writer of books and articles. He was impatient for church reform and feared real reform in the state church would be frustrated. He warned that now that the Synod had decided upon a sobor, it should be held soon. The sensation the announcement had caused roused so much interest that not to follow through would cause grave disillusionment with the church and mass defections. Those turned off by the anti-churchism of the old intelligentsia and who valued Christian moral teaching for renewing the social and political life of Russia especially looked to a sobor for direction. The Synod was killing the church and had to be abolished immediately and completely. The bureaucratic apparatus was devouring the church like a terminal disease. Peter I and Paul I brutally repressed the church and its clergy and cowed them, but in the twentieth century the church had to cease being a tool of the state for the sake of its own credibility. The blessing of wars and of unpopular political causes had to cease, lest the church appear to be the servant of mammon and not the witness of the gospel. Though the metropolitan was a loyal supporter of the autocracy, he was a foe of bureaucratic cancer and a most active promoter of the sobor. Those who doubted his political loyalty or questioned his dedication to reform were engaged in slander for their own destructive ends, Mikhail warned.

Another article appeared the same day in *Russkoe Slovo* by Fr. Georgii Petrov, another of the Thirty-Two. It was entitled "A Question of Misunderstanding," and expressed concern that reform of the church had been transferred to the Synod, which was less capable of handling such a delicate matter than the Committee of Ministers. Historically, the Synod had committed nothing but blunders.[38]

However, almost simultaneously, on Friday, March 25,

the strident notes of the right began to be heard, inspired by Pobedonostsev and like-minded reactionaries. *Moskovskiia Vedomosti* led the way, followed closely by such provincial sheets as *Kievskie Otkliki,* in accusing those spearheading church reform of seeking their own ends and treacherously working to undermine the tsardom. Church reformers, Slavophiles, political liberals and Jews all came under the baleful glance of these papers in a manner foreshadowing fascist smear campaigns of three and four decades later.

Moskovskiia Vedomosti denounced both Antonii and Witte for having sprung upon the Russian nation a "revolt" in the church and accused Antonii of striving for the title of Patriarch, a charge that was to be levelled at him again and again over the next several years. *Moskovskiia Vedomosti*[39] asserted on March 26 that Antonii was Witte's candidate for the patriarchate and that the two of them were plotting together to effect far-reaching changes in Russian public life and politics. The editors suspected that the meeting of Petersburg priests held on March 15, only three days before the Synod began to discuss reform, might have been another facet of that plotting. The fact that only five days later the Synod decided to call a sobor to elect a Patriarch was very suspicious.

The article demanded to know who had the right to summon a sobor anyway? A handful of bishops? What about the rumors that Pobedonostsev was about to be fired? *Moskovskiia Vedomosti*'s suspicions were heightened by the fact that the Jewish newspaper *Novosti* had been among the first to break the news about a sobor. In a time of internal and external danger to the throne and nation, it was premature to undertake such an important revolution in the church. To disrupt ties between the church and the state at this time was foolhardy. *Moskovskiia Vedomosti* warned that reform was a Petersburg invention and a snub to the Muscovite clergy, who were the real voice of Russia. The fact that the Synod had called for a sobor of bishops only revealed its intention to ignore the white clergy and laity. *Moskovskiia Vedomostii* played into Pobedonostsev's hands, helping him and his aides delay and sidetrack reform for several crucial months.

In dismay, Archimandrite Dionisii Valendinskii, former student of Antonii Khrapovitskii and pastor of the Orthodox cathedral in Warsaw, retorted in *Varshavskii Dnevnik*, "Surely *Moskovskiia Vedomosti* knows that the question of the patriarchate and the sobor did not just arise in the March 1905, doesn't it?"[40] But attempts like Dionisii's to moderate the discussion and keep to the real issues became increasingly difficult.

Novosti,[41] whose liberal Jewishness offended the editors of *Moskovskiia Vedomosti*, responded on Monday, March 27, that the separation of the church from the state would benefit the Russian clergy. In no country was the clergy as hamstrung by regulations as in Russia. There were those, of course, who were convinced that separation meant the downfall of both church and state. However, Russia could well consider a separation of church from state along the lines just introduced in France, where a total separation had just occurred and the state had ceased to support the church altogether. The principle of religion, vital to anyone, did not depend upon any given interdependence of government and religion. *Novosti* went on to say that it was regrettable that with all the discussion and planning for toleration of Old Believers, sectarians and other non-Orthodox, no thought was given to improving the status of Jews.

Den', a Jew-bating, anti-Witte sheet, asserted in an article the same day that the "Russian traitors and Jews" were utilizing the church-reform issue as just another way to weaken the lawful government of Russia.[42] *Den'* was extremely scornful of Witte's role as champion of the church, believing it was just a ploy to get his oar into some government ministry again. *Den'* warned that those who derided every achievement of Russia and who applauded the Japanese were undermining the church, and that all talk about reform was just a ruse to weaken the faith of the people.

On March 31, a vitriolic article in *Zaria*, entitled "Apropos the Presumed Reform of the Higher Church Administration,"[43] carried this genre of thinking several steps further, asserting that anti-church liberals and radicals, grouped around Witte, had made a sneak attack on the church and its stalwart defender, Pobedonostsev. Their "hooligan frame of mind" was particularly exemplified by such men as Vasilii V. Rozanov and Dmitri Merezhkovskii, who were leading "an open attack upon historical Christianity." Worse, the anti-church party had its agents dug in in the courts of the Eastern Patriarchs and had designs upon the Russian church. The worst aspect was that the hierarchy and the clergy were already infected with "liberal," "enlightened," "cultured," "progressive" thinking, and that was a threat to Russia at the very moment that she was on her knees in a grave war. The Thirty-Two priests, inexperienced products of the insidious Religious-Philosophical Society, creatures of Metropolitan Antonii, were working hand in glove with Witte. It was symptomatic that the whole business was conducted secretly. The country was in danger of being infected by St. Witte's dance.[44]

Unhappily, one of the better-known professors of St. Petersburg Theological Academy lent his name to this attitude in an article entitled "Why Thirty-Two?"[45] which appeared on Wednesday, March 29, in *Novoe Vremia*. In it he asserted that the Thirty-Two were a group of uninformed self-seekers who met in secret and decided to strike when they thought their opportunity best. They had stampeded the metropolitan into introducing the reform agenda in the Synod and rushing it through prematurely.

This professor, Nikolai Nikolskii, denounced the suddenness with which church reform was announced and denounced the priests, whom he described as obscure and sneaky (because they did not sign their names to their article). He asserted that they did not know anything about the history and structure of the Russian church anyway. Thirty-Two were hardly representative of the whole church, in which there were more than seventy thousand active white priests. Why had no one heard from them? The manner in which the reform discussions were conducted in the Synod was uncanonical, and therefore the call for a sobor and the restoration of the patriarchate was invalid. Nikolskii alleged that there was a

clandestine plot in Petersburg to undermine Pobedonostsev
and to blacken his name. That was why Runkevich had been
attacked by Witte.

The Thirty-Two Petersburg priests were advocating papal
absolutism in the church. Nikolskii reminded his readers that
the last papal Patriarch the Russian church had experienced
was Nikon, and everyone knew what kind of disaster he had
been. Nikolskii was leery of the cry of the Thirty-Two for
the "freedom" of the church, asserting that if that meant a
papal kind of freedom from political supervision, Russia did
not need it. They had raised the issue of reform at the wrong
time, when the civil authority found itself facing domestic
turmoil and foreign humiliation.

Men like Nikolskii were ignorant of the fact that the
Synod discussions had been aired in the Special Sessions and
had been rehearsed before that between the metropolitan, the
professors of the academy and the priests. They also were
ignorant of the fact that the initial momentum for reform
had been given by the Tsar himself in 1903. Nikolskii, a professor of theology at the Petersburg Academy, was closely
associated with the men who had worked with Antonii, so
his ignorance, if such it was, was surprising. An erudite man,
he was well versed in the history of the Russian church. During 1903 and 1904, he had had a falling-out with the monastic
clergy who dominated the academy and had asked for a
leave of absence. Nikolskii rejected the canons that excluded
white clergy from the episcopate and higher church offices
as inapplicable, arguing that black clergy by their very vocation were cut off from the needs and demands of the every-
day church. He argued that white clergy should really be the
men promoted and that laymen should have a guaranteed
voice in church affairs from the parish level upwards. His
views were looked upon as un-Orthodox and Protestant by
the academic establishment. Nikolskii's views were championed
by docent Alexander Vvedenskii, who in years to come would
be a vigorous supporter of white clergy rights, even to the
point of collaborating with the Bolsheviks after 1917 to
settle scores with enemies of previous years.

Fr. Georgii Petrov responded in an article in *Russkoe*

Slovo,[46] March 31, explaining that the reason that the Thirty-Two wanted a sobor as soon as possible was so the church could begin its reform without undue government pressure. Nikolskii's demand that guarantees for white clergy and lay interests be safeguarded before a sobor could even meet meant only a delay, which played right into the Procurator's hands. Nikolskii's charge that the Thirty-Two were edvocating a form of papalism delibeerately caused confusion. Petrov regretted that Nikolskii, because of his position, had access to a wide audience and thereby hurt the very cause he purported to champion.

Nikolskii's article also generated a response from Vasilii V. Rozanov in *Novoe Vremia,*[47] to the effect that the reason the seventy thousand white clergy of the empire had not been heard from was precisely because they did not dare speak out—they would have been penalized by the Procurator's flunkies. That had been the story for obstreperous clergymen under Pobedonostsev. Some had already been penalized. Furthermore, most of the Thirty-Two were active pastors, the very white clergy for whom Nikolskii had expressed concern. Rozanov ended by saying that for all his learnedness in canon law, Nikolskii did not know what he was talking about.

*   *   *

Unfortunately, it was the Nikoliskiis and not the Rozanovs who had the greatest impact during the next three years. As the political atmosphere turned murky, so did the discussion of church reform.

When the Tsar endorsed the request of the Synod on Friday, March 31, he reviewed the various points made in the Synod report and concluded:

> I recognize that it is impossible to carry out such an important undertaking, requiring quietude and deliberation, as the convocation of a national [*pomestnago*] sobor during such troubled times as these. I leave it to myself, in keeping with the ancient example of the Orthodox Emperors, when we enter once more upon times favorable for such an under-

taking, to put it into effect and to summon a national
sobor of the all-Russian church for the canonical consideration of problems of faith and ecclesiastical
government.[48]

A suitable time did not seem far off. The *ukaz* on toleration was being prepared and would come out in seventeen
days. In seventeen days more it would be the first week of
May. There was no reason to expect that the sobor could not
be called as soon as that, or in the autumn at the latest. It
was everywhere expected in church circles that the sobor and
the restructuring of the administration of the Russian church
would be part and parcel of the social and political changes
flowing from the *ukaz* on toleration. Among the Orthodox
the hope for reform, for rejuvenating the church, aroused
great expectation and optimism as they approached Easter,
while those who saw political gains to be had from a
strengthened church believed that the Tsar could not forfeit
the opportunity. The Procurator was still in office, however,
and was still the legal spokesman for the church.

CHAPTER IV

Deliberations and Debates: The Upper Administration

The Manifesto on Toleration, issued on Easter Sunday, April 17, 1905, gave non-Orthodox bodies the legal right to incorporate, to have their religious leaders speak on their behalf, to receive converts from each other's societies and from the Orthodox church itself together with children under fourteen years, the right of military exemptions for their clergy and the right to use official ecclesiastical titles hitherto limited to Orthodox, Latin and Lutheran clergy. The *ukaz* removed political liabilities associated with belonging to proscribed religious bodies and allowed officials and employees of the government to make formal change of religion. It permitted former Moslems to renounce expedient affiliation to Orthodoxy, former Uniates or their descendants to abandon Orthodoxy for Latin Catholicism, former Lutherans who for political, economic or social reasons had affiliated with the state church to revert to their former religion, and thousands of sectarians and Old Believers who had officially professed no religion or who had only nominally adhered to Orthodoxy to profess their religions openly. Accurate figures about how many took the opportunity to change their religious affiliation are not available, but it appears that anywhere from half a million to a million former Uniates alone took the opportunity to defect to Latin Catholicism. Figures proportional to denominational size can be estimated for other bodies as well.[1]

The government hoped that the announcement of the *ukaz* would bring a measure of civil peace. At the same time, it would not fully permit its implementation because of the conviction that a majority of non-Orthodox subjects were potentially subversive. Restrictions against non-Orthodox were never completely removed, because rank and file bureaucrats and administrators were antagonistic to the *ukaz*. Complaints and civil actions to gain promised liberties never fully received redress.[2]

Less than a month later, however, a serious humiliation in the war with Japan occurred when the Baltic fleet was destroyed in the Tsushima Straits off Japan on May 14 and 15. Negotiations for peace took place in the United States and resulted in the Treaty of Portsmouth. They fully occupied Witte until the middle of September, and the hope of convening the sobor in May 1905 vanished with the fleet. The Tsar, his ministers and his whole bureaucracy were preoccupied with ending the war and dealing with the public disorder that followed. In the meantime, Pobedonostsev and his bureaucrats seized the opportunity provided by the preoccupation of the bureaucrats and the public confusion caused by the outbreak of violence to insist upon exhaustive preliminary preparations designed to push the date for convocation off again and again. He now was supported by Filosof Ornatskii who, shaken by the February 4 assassination of Grand Prince Sergei Alexandrovich, uncle of the Tsar and governor-general of Moscow, and the debacle of the war with Japan, believed that reform of the church had to await a more favorable time. Ornatskii published an article in *Svet* which stated that granting toleration to the Old Believers and sectarians at this juncture of events was a mistake. To compound that mistake by weakening church-state interdependence would be a blunder.[3]

Ornatskii's concern was shared by the Orthodox Society of Moscow, a group of some sixty persons, lay and clerical, who included in their number such persons as Lev A. Tikhomirov, Fedor D. and Alexander D. Samarin, Dr. Alexei

Kornilov, physician to the grand princesses, and Fr. Serafim I. Ostroumov, who would soon be elected to the State Duma. They agreed that the church needed to be free from state control and the clergy liberated, but when the Synod took over the issue of reform they became suspicious that the Synod would frustrate true reform by substituting cosmetic changes for far-reaching reform and renovation. They expressed deep suspicion about the "Petersburg way of doing things" and suggested that Witte and Metropolitan Antonii were in collusion, trying to create a patriarchate with papal powers which would only worsen the lot of the common priest.

Within the Moscow Society itself, a split developed between the white clergy on the one side and their lay colleagues on the other. The laymen generally approved of the restoration of a patriarchate, while as time went on more and more of the clergy did not. The lay members felt that the fear of an autocratic Patriarch was exaggerated, that a Patriarch could be controlled effectively by regular sobors and a permanent Synod answerable to the sobors. In this regard they were of one mind with the majority of the Petersburg Thirty-Two, particularly Frs. Georgii Petrov and Mikhail Gorchakov, neither of whom saw a threat to the interests of the white clergy in a reformed church ruled by the principles of *sobornost'*.

The Moscow clergy reiterated the demand that all bishops be elected by the clergy and laity and that the parish, not the diocese, become the primary organizational unit. Authority of the bishops should be greatly curtailed. Restrictions limiting the episcopate to monastic clergy should be terminated and white clergy should be given equal status, as in the Western church. Until those principles were safeguarded, the Moscow group would not agree to the convocation of a sobor.[4]

In response came a series of documents from the pen of the bishop of Volhynia, denouncing both the Petersburg Thirty-Two and the group of Moscow clergy and asserting that if the Orthodox church were to make good its claim to being the true inheritor of apostolic tradition, then it would have to be organized strictly upon the canons transmitted from ecumenical times. Strict interpretation of the canons of ecumenical and local or national councils left no room for delegates from the laity or formal representation of the clergy. The canons made it very clear that only bishops had decision-making authority in the ecumenical councils.[5] Clergy and laity could have considerable influence upon the sobor, but in conformity with the canons their influence would have to be indirect. A lobby organized by the clergy and laity to bring issues to the attention of the bishops might be a solution, since the bishops themselves would need all the academic and practical information they could obtain from experts. Antonii rejected the notion that bishops were not sensitive to the needs of white clergy or society at large. Monks, too, he insisted, come from the ranks of the people and could hardly be regarded as alien to them. Bishops, taken from the ranks of monks, were truly of the people. If anyone could rise above the bureaucratic system it was the monk, who by his calling was detached from special interest pressures. Khrapovitskii denounced the artificial dichotomy being created between the white and the black clergy, a dichotomy he blamed upon the press.

In the twentieth century the titles abbot, archabbot and others of monastic origin were nothing more than civil service ranks anyway. The authority of the modern bishops was no greater than that of an archpriest or the secretary of a consistory. Both of these positions were filled by white clergy, so who could say that white clergy were not influential? Both the white priest and the hierarch were victims of the same system—bureaucracy. A conflict between them would only sidetrack the Russian sobor. It was useless to argue that the hierarchy had been appointed by irregular means, because if they were, so were the white clergy.

Khrapovitskii went on to repeat that the scriptures and canons nowhere envisioned parliamentarianism, nor did apostolic succession permit it. The bishops were responsible to God as successors of the apostles. The apostles and fathers of the church, together with the Russian fathers, held that bishops alone were responsible for the church. That tradition was embodied in the regulations of ecumenical and local councils. Liberate the bishops from bureaucratic and secular controls and they would liberate the whole church.[6]

The bishop of Volhynia was vigorously supported by former students and followers in Moscow and Kazan. Calling themselves the "New School," they preached, published and were interviewed by the press in support of a Russian Patriarch, a strong episcopate and the continuance of monastic monopoly of episcopal appointments. The "New School" made a considerable impact upon the idea of church reform and widened the breach between white and black clergy, meanwhile taking comfort in the political discomfiture of some of the more outspoken white priests.[7]

The Moscow clergy and lay experts responded to Khrapovitskii and the New School with loud and vigorous dissent, asserting that a close analysis of the various ecumenical councils, but more particularly of local councils like the ones held in Sardica, Rome, Carthage and Bostra-in-Arabia even before the Council of Nicaea in 325, would indicate that laymen and clergy below the rank of bishop had participated fully and had had a decisive voice in the final position taken by those councils. Furthermore, the organization of the church in apostolic times was not as complicated as it later became in the Roman Empire, and to insist on norms now only vaguely understood as having apostolic sanction was not realistic. The thing to do was to try to gain a feeling for the spirit of council regulations and an imaginative application to twentieth-century Russian conditions. A closed sobor of bishops who owed their appointments to the discredited synodal collegium would not gain acceptance from the mass of Russian believers. Citing a host of canon lawyers, eastern and western, dating from Byzantine and Roman times to the twentieth century, the Moscow experts argued that lay participation had been a regular phenomenon. In modern times, the reorganization of the Orthodox administration in the Ottoman Empire in 1856, part of a much larger reorganization of the Ottoman regime, had given laymen a regular, legal responsibility in the affairs of the Ecumenical Patriarchate. Furthermore, in the independent Kingdom of Greece, in the ecclesiastical administration in the Kingdom of Serbia, in the newly established patriarchate of Bulgaria, and in Rumania, laymen had regular positions in the synodal administrations of those national churches. Even in the Austro-Hungarian Empire, the recent convocation of Orthodox hierarchs at Karlowitz had incorporated laymen in the administration of the Orthodox church. Therefore, practical application of the norms of canon law of the Eastern Orthodox church in modern times regularly included laymen. To revert to rigid interpretations of the past would be a blunder. In the letter of the Orthodox Patriarchs to Pope Pius IX in 1848, the Patriarchs insisted that the believing faithful were the true conservers of the Orthodox faith. To exclude them would mean to lose the trust of the Orthodox faithful.

In support of this viewpoint came a carefully reasoned document from the archbishop of Finland, Sergei Stragorodskii, a man who suffered much for the Orthodox church later, first as *locum tenens* and then as Patriarch under Stalin. Sergei saw no difficulty in adhering to the canons and at the same time involving laymen and white clergy in active decision- and policy-making at the Russian sobor. Without this participation the credibility of any undertaking by the sobor would be questioned. The main participants in the future sobor would be the sixty-three diocesan bishops of the Russian national (*pomestnago*) church, but besides them there should be other participants who would have decision-making and policy-making authority, including vicar bishops of important sees invited by their diocesan bishops. Besides that, every diocese should send two representatives from its white clergy, archpriests from major parishes, and four representatives of lay organizations, together with professors of canon law and church history from the theological academies, the diocesan seminaries and the major Russian universities. All of these should have regular policy- and decision-making authority at the sobor. Sergei concurred with the Moscow Society that evidence from earlier Russian sobors, notably that of 1666-1667, showed that laymen had participated with full authority in all deliberations, as had white clergy. At the time, high-handedness and episcopal exclusivism led to the tragic Old Believer schism. To repeat the mistake would be foolhardy.[8]

In a thoughtful article entitled "The Restoration of *Sobornost'* in the Russian Church," Professor Vladimir Zavitnevich of the Kiev Theological Academy, one of the foremost Russian church historians of the early twentieth century, elaborated on *sobornost'* as a continual exchange among clergy and laity as two groups within the Christian community, and between the different levels of the ecclesiastical and civil hierarchy. The Russian church was dying, stated Zavitnevich. A sobor was desperately needed. Only a sobor could restore *sobornost'* as an active principle. Once its leavening effects were felt, the hostility of the Old Believer community would lessen and the antagonism of the intelligentsia would soften. The church would emerge from its skeleton of anachronistic forms and act as a reconciling force both in the religious and civil spheres. Zavitnevich detailed several specific areas, such as education, to show how the process would work.[9]

The divergence between the various schools on the sobor was not unbridgeable, and had the sobor been convened in May it would have had little difficulty ironing out the various differences that were in the process of developing. Delay meant the expansion of differences of emphasis into schools of irreconcilable positions, which became more divergent as political pressure and public violence caused them to take on political coloration as well. In the spring, the concern of the Petersburg white clergy, for example, was simply to get a sobor called. By autumn many of them were having second thoughts, suspecting that a sobor that reestablished a Russian patriarchate would be against their interests. The patriarchate came to symbolize the creation of a conservative ecclesiastical power structure to bolster a reactionary tsardom. The various schools of thinking gradually became embroiled in the political tides that swept the empire, especially after events forced the reluctant Tsar to issue the October Manifesto and promise to summon a Duma.

* * *

On July 27, while Witte was in America and the Synod

not in session, the Procurator ordered a poll of all diocesan bishops of the Russian church to gain their responses to a series of questions in the belief that they, his own appointees and conservative, would bolster his intention to reform existing administration as little as possible. With the bishops to back him up, the Procurator would take the wind out of the sails of those who insisted that the whole existing church administration needed overhauling. He would honor the arguments of the canonists without yielding to the substance of their criticism.

An *ukaz* in the Emperor's name ordered the bishops to make detailed responses to the various problems outlined in March, consulting with trustworthy individuals as they did so, and to forward all their documents to him by December 1. That ended the hope for a sobor in 1905. Prince V. P. Meshcherskii (1839-1914), editor of the conservative journal *Grazhdanin* and a major influence on the thinking of the Tsar, bitterly denounced Pobedonostsev for fostering a new cult of fanaticism as debilitating as the "Jesuitism" of Count Alexei Arakcheev, key counsellor to Alexander I, and a cult of rationalism as arid as the "deism" of Count Dmitri Tolstoi, Procurator of the Synod and Minister of Public Education under Alexander II. Under both men, the Orthodox church, bursting with vitality, had been ridden to the ground. Now, Prince Meshcherskii accused Pobedonostsev of trying it again, instead of opening up the church and freeing the pent up energy within.[10]

During September, October and November the cumbersome bureaucracies of the diocesan administrations were cranked into action, and sixty dioceses either incorporated the questions into the agendas of their diocesan convocations—something which made them really function for the first time in twenty-five years—or held special consultations of clergy and lay advisers.

The questions sent out by the Procurator's office covered the following topics: (1) composition of the sobor—who should be invited to participate and on what basis; (2) type and number of ecclesiastical divisions and whether or not they should correspond to the metropolias of the Byzantine and

Roman eras; (3) centralization or decentralization in church administration; (4) clergy roles in the deliberation and administration of imperial, provincial, county (*uezd*), township (*volost'*) and community governments; (5) the ecclesiastical court system, its relation to civil administration and its role in legislation on marriage as it affected Orthodox Russians or marriage between Orthodox and members of other religious denominations; (6) restructuring of diocesan administration; (7) restoration of the parish community; (8) acquisition and administration of ecclesiastical properties, their separation from civilian control and restoration to genuinely ecclesiastical purposes; and (9) problems of faith affecting relations with other bodies sharing the same faith, such as Russian *Edinovertsy* and other Orthodox churches, or with Latins, Old Believers, sectarians and Protestants, together with fasting, liturgical and disciplinary problems.[11]

The bishops surprised and dismayed the Procurator. Few agreed that the existing administration was adequate and the church needed no reform. Most believed that radical reform was necessary, even to the point of total separation of church from state if current political developments should result in a totally secularized state of the sort that had just been established in France.[12]

To the question of how the Russian sobor should be constituted, the bishop of Volhynia, Antonii Khrapovitskii, together with the bishop of Riga, Agafangel Preobrazhenskii (1854-1928), Germogen Dolganev (†1918) of Saratov, and the bishops of Stavropol, Orenburg and Ekaterinburg, answered that bishops should be the only members of the sobor because evidence from the canons of the First, Fourth, Sixth and Seventh Ecumenical Councils decreeing that there should be meetings of bishops annually or semi-annually in every metropolia did not mention presbyters or deacons. It seemed that if non-bishops were in attendance, they functioned only as advisers or clerks and did not have any decision-making authority. Furthermore, such regional councils as Carthage, Laodicea and Antioch had not mentioned the presence or participation of non-bishops.

Germogen Dolganev of Saratov was of the opinion that

the voices of white clergy and laymen should be heard as advisers to the bishops, not as separate interest groups. Laymen and selected representatives of clerical organizations would be part of the entourage of every bishop at the sobor. Separate representation would be uncanonical, in violation of the protocols of ecumenical and regional councils. Agafangel of Riga believed that separate interest groups would result in head-on clashes and irreconcilable differences. Bishop Mikhail Temnorussov (1854-1912) of Minsk added that the bishops should make the final decisions because they would be the ones who would have to carry them out. Furthermore, he argued, bishops were not representatives of lay or clerical clerks, but the direct successors of the apostles, to whom Christ had given his commission to bind and loose upon earth.[13]

The thinking of Khrapovitskii, Preobrazhenskii, Dolganev and Temnorussov was not dominant among the bishops, however. Twenty-three of the prelates, including the metropolitan of Petersburg, Antonii Vadkovskii, the metropolitan of Moscow, Vladimir Bogoiavlenskii, and the metropolitan of Kiev, Flavian Gorodestskii, together with Archbishops Anastasii Dobradin (1828-1913) of Voronezh, Gurii Okhotin (1829-1912) of Novgorod, Arsenii Briantsev of Kharkov, Sergei Stragorodskii of Finland, Nikandr Molchanov (1852-1910) of Lithuania, plus Bishops Tikhon Troitskii (1831-1911) of Irkutsk, Nikon Sofiiskii (1861-1908) of Vladimir, Evlogii Georgievskii (1868-1946) of Kholm, Alexei Molchanov (1853-1914) of Taurida, Kirion of Orel, Konstantin Bulichev of Samara, Mikhail Ermakhov (1863-1929) of Smolensk, Kristofor of Ufa, Stefan Arkhangelskii (1861-1914) of Mogilev, Arsenii Stadnitskii (1862-1936) of Pskov, Veniamin Bornukov of Kaluga, Ioanniki of Arkhangelsk and Antonii Korzhavin (1856-1914) of Tobolsk felt that laymen and white clergy should be present with the full right to participate and deliberate.

Arsenii Stadnitskii of Pskov quoted Bishop Nikodim of Austrian Dalmatia, a leader in the reorganization of the Orthodox church in Austria-Hungary, who had written that close ties between the laity and their clergy and between the clergy and their bishops allowed the Orthodox church to thrive there. The believing faithful must be the conservers of belief and religious discipline. Without them the clergy and the hierarchy would have no church. Nikodim of Dalmatia had noted, and Bishop Arsenii reiterated, that popular conservation of true belief had been the essence of the reply by the Eastern Patriarchs to Pope Pius IX in 1848.[14] Bishop Nikon Sofiiskii referred to the Acts of the Apostles (15:4-35) and noted that when Paul and Barnabas had come from Antioch to settle a dispute over whether new Christians had to be circumcised and follow the provisions of the Mosaic law, recourse was had to the Christian leaders in Jerusalem, and the apostles and presbyters deliberated together and decided together against requiring circumcision and certain provisions of the Mosaic law for gentiles. The Jerusalem presbyters were the equivalent of white clergy in Russia, and they had participated with no restrictions. Therefore, from the evidence of the scriptures, it was clear that the apostles (bishops) had not deliberated alone, nor had they decided the outcome alone. Nikon and Bishop Konstantin Bulichev cited post-apostolic instances both in the East and the West where clergy, and even laity, were involved in early council decisions.[15]

Metropolitan Antonii Vadkovskii appended an opinion by Professor Ioann Sokolov of Petersburg Theological Academy to his response. Sokolov examined a period of Byzantine church history from the opening of the tenth century to the close of the twelfth century and discovered that on several occasions clergy had participated with full authority in patriarchal councils. This practice was followed in the Russian church itself during its pre-synodal period, according to Bishop Evlogii Georgievskii.[16]

Since it was clear that the tradition of the Roman, Byzantine and Russian churches allowed clergy and laity to participate in a sobor, Nikon of Vladimir felt that in the twentieth century all factions had to be heard from or the cancer of decay that had been allowed to fester for so long would be fatal. The parish must be revived; ecclesiastical courts had to become effective; a true community among the members of the church, lay and clerical, high and low, had to be effected, with the broadest lay and clerical participation in the Russian sobor so that the whole church would be drawn once again together in a living union. Bishop Arsenii Stadnitskii of Pskov and others cited Professor Nikolai Zaozerskii of Petersburg, who advocated not only attendance of bishops and high-ranking churchmen, but of clergy and monks of every description—particularly elders from such monasteries as the Optina Pustyn—secular and religious publishers, theologians, men of letters, economists, lawyers and professionals from every field. It would be a gathering of the whole people to regenerate the church as a spiritual and civil force in the empire.

Bishop Stefan Arkhangelskii of Mogilev warned that a too-rigid application of the regulations of the seven ecumenical councils or the various regional councils of the early church would be self-defeating. He showed, by comparing the regulations of one council with another, that from time to time they were changed when circumstances warranted. The final determiner of who should or should not attend the Russian council, and with what authority, would have to be the council itself. It was so long since the last ecumenical council had been held—more than 1100 years—that it would not be possible to apply rules from times that had been long forgotten. The canons did not explicitly exclude anyone. Vladimir Bogoiavlenskii, metropolitan of Moscow, would include even those who were opposed to the Orthodox church or who fought against it, providing they wanted to come and did not try to use the sobor as a forum for anti-ecclesiastical purposes.

However, many of the same archbishops and bishops who thought the laity and clergy should be represented at the sobor and be allowed to participate in the discussions and deliberations did not think lay and clerical representatives should have the right to cast deciding votes in final resolutions at the sobor. They noted that regulations handed down from the First, Fourth, Sixth and Seventh Ecumenical Councils stated that decisions could be made by bishops only because they alone were the successors of the apostles. Antonii

Khrapovitskii, the most conservative interpreter, cited precedents from local councils at Antioch, Laodicea and Carthage to support the contention that only bishops made decisions at councils, whether or not laymen and clergy were present and took part.

Flavian Gorodestskii, metropolitan of Kiev, noted that Ignatius of Antioch witnessed the tradition of episcopal preeminence in the early church. When the Council of Chalcedon erupted in an uproar, imperial officials commanded the bishops to restore order, which they did. They also made the final pronouncements, over the protests of the clergy. Flavian believed that bishops alone were summoned to the ecumenical councils, even though clergy and laity came along as observers and advisers. The testimony of scripture and of the canons was of one accord when it came to ascribing the final decision-making to the bishops in the early church. The Gospel of Matthew (18:15-19) demonstrated that when Jesus admonished his disciples, the first bishops, to correct each other in a brotherly fashion, he authorized that whatever they bound on earth would be bound in heaven and whatever they loosed on earth would also be loosed in heaven. That was the essence of the doctrine of apostolic succession. Arsenii Stadnitskii of Pskov and Evlogii Georgievskii of Kholm advanced the same argument.

Presbyters were admitted to the councils, ecumenical and regional, with decision-making authority, only when they came as deputies of their local bishop or metropolitan. That preserved the principle of apostolic succession in the councils. But even then, the deputizing of a presbyter to represent a bishop was for a serious reason and not just because the bishop was too lazy to attend. Nikandr Molchanov, Mikhail Ermakhov and Stefan Arkhangelskii would deputize laymen, so long as it was clear that their authorization came from their bishops and the principle of the canons was maintained. Deputized laymen would participate in deliberations alongside their bishops.

A more conservative opinion was given by Professor Alexander Brilliantov of the St. Petersburg Academy, in an appendix to the response of Metropolitan Antonii Vadkovskii.

He stated that if laymen were to influence decrees of the sobor, it should be through the counsel they gave their bishops, not directly. Brilliantov emphasized that the bishops had to be in close contact with their clerics and lay advisers because it was Orthodox tradition that acceptance by the believing church guaranteed the validity of the proceedings of any council, but bishops alone had the authority to make binding statements.[17]

Four prelates thought that the laity could be given full rights of participation along with the clergy and the hierarchy. Bishop Ioann of Poltava, successor to Fr. Gapon's friend, believed that as a regional (*pomestnyi*) sobor rather than an ecumenical council, the Russian sobor would not define dogma, but would be an implementing and restructuring council and thus could permit full lay and clerical participation without violating the canons or apostolic succession.[18] Archbishop Sergei Stragorodskii of Finland suggested that diocesan bishops bring with them four experts—two clergy and two professors from the seminaries, universities and theological academies in their jurisdictions—who would have the right to cast votes as their deputies and sharers, for the time being, in their authority. Unassigned bishops, vicar bishops, experts who attended out of their own interest and representatives of the other autocephalous Orthodox churches would debate, but when the sobor voted, only those thus authorized would have the right to vote. If questions arose that touched upon canonical norms or dogma, such as the relation of the Old Catholic movement to the Russian church, relations with the Austrian hierarchy of Old Believers or the Anglican church, or a separate bishop or bishops for the *Edinovertsy* in Russia, then the sobor should decide on the spot whether to require a decision exclusively by the bishops.

Most bishops recommended that Tsar Nicholas II convoke the sobor and occupy a position of honor as the chief protector of the Russian church, as had Byzantine Emperors previously. Some believed the Eastern Patriarchs, Joachim III of Constantinople, Damian of Jerusalem and Photios of Alexandria, should be invited. Menander Sozontev (1857-

1907), bishop of Balta, thought that one of the Eastern Patriarchs should actually preside over the Russian sobor, since no one in the Russian hierarchy had the rank that entitled him to do so.[19] Some bishops recommended that Nicholas appoint the opening presider, while others felt that the Procurator should or that the oldest prelate in attendance should automatically be the opener of the sobor. Vladimir Filantropov, bishop of Ekaterinburg, felt that the presider should be some venerable starets from a prominent monastery like the Optina and that invitations should be sent to various abbots, retired bishops and vicar bishops in the most important sees.

Nikon Sofiiskii of Vladimir suggested that the synod immediately establish a Pre-Sobor Commission, which would report weekly on its progress, so that preparations would not get bogged down and the sobor never be called. Archbishop Sergei of Finland, a member of the Synod and well aware of how the Synod could stifle reform, felt that any preparatory commission should be independent of the Synod and that at a specified date it should be determined when the Synod would cease to have authority over the church. Authority would then pass to the sobor, which would be convened on that date. Nikandr Molchanov of Lithuania added that the preparatory sessions should be open, so that suggestions could be fed in all along the way, with the press and public keeping the proceedings under constant scrutiny. Sergei suggested that the sobor either hold several sessions or only outline the basic issues, set up commissions to work them out and set a definite date for the convocation of a second sobor. The commissions would be responsible to the next sobor, working out the details of proposals and problems without Synod interference.[20]

*   *   *

The bishops were practically unanimous that the Russian church should be divided into ecclesiastical districts or metropolias, in accord with the division of the church in Byzantine times and as was still the case in the West. Only three bishops—Paisii Vinogradov (1837-1908) of Turkestan,

Ioakim Levitskii (1853-1918) of Orenburg and Lavrentii Nekrasov of Tula—disagreed.

Vinogradov believed that all the bishops of the Russian church should be equal and that no distinctions should be made either in personal titles or in importance by sees. He resented the puffed-up importance of incumbents of larger sees like Moscow, Kiev and Petersburg, or the ill-concealed ambitions of others whose names he did not reveal. He did not think anyone should have permanent positions in the Holy Synod, but rather that the entire Synod should have a rotating membership, determined strictly by order of consecration, and all the bishops should serve in the Synod. Decisions of the Synod should be arrived at strictly by a majority vote, with no prelate or secretary having the right to cast a veto once a majority vote had been taken. Egalitarianism in the episcopate was Paisii's recommendation.[21]

As far as metropolias were concerned, he did not think they were needed in Russia. Metropolias had been useful in earlier days when communications were not easy, but now, in the twentieth century, with the lacing of the empire together with railroads, telegraph and telephone, there was no problem communicating with the Synod from any part of the empire. Hence, the key argument for metropolias fell before the technological advance of communications. The Russian church needed streamlining, not new offices, new bureaucrats and new titles to inflate the egos of its bishops.[22]

Ioakim believed that a restored Patriarch was the first business of the coming sobor, and once the patriarchate was restored, it should take over the centralized administration of the Synod and be absolutely independent of the civil bureaucracy. A patriarchal synod should function as the government of the church between sobors. Sobors, called regularly, should be the supreme authority in the Russian church, with the Patriarch answerable to them. Ioakim noted that metropolias in the early church existed for reasons of geography and ethnic enclaves. No such need existed in Russia, where the Russian population, Orthodox for the most part, was spread throughout the borders of the realm. Even the non-Orthodox populations had a heavy intermingling of Russians, so there was no reason for establishing separate metropolias in their areas. Administration of the Russian church needed to be centralized to carry on the struggle with the Raskol, Latinism and Lutheranism, to mention only a few. To divide the administration into metropolias would introduce bureaucratic confusion and slowness. Regional headquarters and staff would require a high financial outlay, which the church could not afford.[23]

Likewise, Lavrentii Nekrasov felt that another level of administration between the center and the diocese would make things worse. A replica of the civil bureaucracy in the church would be the despair of the Russian believer. The sluggish state of the ecclesiastical courts was just one example. If a poor believer would have to pass the hurdle of a diocesan consistory, a metropolitan court and finally a patriarchal or synodal court to get a case heard, he could well be dead before the process was ever completed.[24]

Most bishops, however, found the division of the Russian Empire into metropolitan districts both desirable and necessary.

Bishop Nikanor of Perm believed that to conform to the principle of *sobornost'*, which is the ninth point of the Nicene Creed in the Slavonic translation—"I believe in one holy, sobornal, and apostolic church"—metropolias were essential. With bishops gathered around a metropolitan, conscious of the mood and aspirations of their flocks, the ideal of the ancient ecumenical church could be realized. Large centralized administrations by their very nature stifled *sobornost'*— or the religious intimacy among the hierarchy, between the hierarchy and their priests and between priests and their flocks. The introduction of *bona fide* metropolias would be a step towards restoring it. Metropolias would coincide with the provincial division of the empire, facilitating exchange between the ecclesiastical administration and the civil bureaucracy, whose coordination was necessary for the welfare of the Orthodox faithful.[25]

Kirion of Orel believed that metropolias would assure the church greater freedom in internal life and administration. The vastness of the empire necessitated an administrative level between the center and the local diocese. Metropolias would reflect at a higher level the operation of *sobornost'*, which was expected to manifest itself at the diocesan level once restrictions had been removed. And, furthermore, the ancient canons demanded metropolias.

Bishop Nazarii of Nizhni-Novgorod cited Apostolic Canon 37, which decreed that regional bishops assemble twice a year, once in the fourth week after Pentecost and again on the twelfth day of October. The same stipulation was made by the fifth canon of the First Ecumenical Council, and could be inferred from the ninth and nineteenth canons of the Fourth Ecumenical Council, the latter stating: "It has come to our ears that in some metropolias the regulations of councils of bishops have not been observed, and that church affairs needing direction remain in carelessness. Therefore . . . we command that twice a year, bishops gather together . . ." The same point was made again at the Sixth Ecumenical Council at Constantinople (canon 8) and at the Seventh Ecumenical Council at Nicaea (canon 6). In each case, there was direct or indirect indication that these twice-yearly convocations of bishops were not being regularly held, and the ecumenical councils ordered that they be held. Thus, the Russian church, in order to renew itself and reclaim its authenticity, had no choice but to create metropolias and to be sure that bishops assemble regularly in council.

Bishop Pitirim Oknov (1858-1920) of Kursk, citing regulations of the First, Second, Third and Fourth Ecumenical Councils and various regional councils (Antioch, Carthage, Sardica), answered at length that the spirit and letter of the canons of the ecumenical councils made metropolias the true focus of ecclesiastical administration. Metropolitans were responsible for supervising administration of dioceses within their jurisdictions, admonishing bishops and supporting them. Bishops in turn were responsible for praying for their metropolitans in all their liturgies, consulting with them before making major decisions and deferring to their judgment when it differed from their own. Metropolitans had the main burden of dealing with civilian officials on behalf of the church.

It was clear that if the Russian church really intended to function according to the spirit of the ecumenical church, it would have to be divided into metropolias, and these units would have to take over the greater part of administration from the Synod.

Konstantin Bulichev of Samara added that proper ecclesiastical administration should subordinate every diocese to a metropolitan. Selection of diocesan bishops should be made by fellow bishops in the metropolia, under the supervision of their metropolitan. Administrative decisions and local interpretations of doctrinal statements of the ecumenical councils were to be made by the bishops in a metropolia together with their metropolitan. The Council of Laodicea had decreed that bishops who were appointed to secular positions should be deposed and excommunicated from the church, a process that fell within the jurisdiction of a metropolitan sobor. Civil bureaucrats who violated the autonomy of the church were supposed to be excommunicated as well. Konstantin quoted at length from the regulations of ecumenical and regional councils that made it clear that the metropolia was the locus of effective self-administration in the church. Restoration of those canonical norms would restore credibility to the Russian church in the eyes of Old Believers and Uniates, among others, and bolster its claim to the uninterrupted tradition that reached back to the era of the apostles.[26]

Cohesion and unity were the main reasons adduced by Flavian Gorodestskii for reestablishing metropolias in the twentieth century. The church, overburdened by centralized administration on the one hand and atomized by the dispersal of diocesan administration on the other, was left with neither strength nor flexibility to deal with regional problems adequately. Metropolias had appeared in the first centuries after Christian churches had ceased to be small, isolated communities. That type of local administration was needed in the Russian church. The synodal structure deliberately weakened the diocese. Flavian felt that the metropolia was the ideal level at which the principle of *sobornost'* could work. It was useless to mouth phrases about *sobornost'* un-

less there was a practical way to put it into operation.
Canonical regulations spelled out the way in detail. The
church had not been allowed to speak and function on its
own behalf for two hundred years because of the over-
centralized Synod system.

As an antidote to overromanticizing the Byzantine and
Roman past, however, Sergei of Finland and Professor
Brilliantov of St. Petersburg cautioned against the application of ancient canonical norms too rigidly. The Russian
church did not exist in the time or the geographical circumstances that gave rise to the Roman and Byzantine structures, and should therefore resist efforts to force it into an
archaic mold that would not correspond to the times.[27]

Antonii of Volhynia insisted, however, that practical necessity in administration demanded restoration of Byzantine-
style metropolias. Concentration of administration in St.
Petersburg had created an inordinate backlog of paperwork
and paralyzed administration. In the present situation, bureaucrats with absolutely no acquaintance with local conditions made decisions that vitally affected the lives of laymen, clergy and bishops everywhere in Russia. To the bureaucrats, these people were simply statistics. Gurii
Burstasovskii (1845-1907) of Simbirsk felt that, along the
Volga at least, bishops understood the temperament and needs
of their people better than bureaucrats in Petersburg did.
Furthermore, it was infuriating to have pledges of fiscal
support made by local communities, only to have paperwork
between the diocese and Petersburg take up so much time
and the matter handled in such a clumsy manner that donors
got fed up long before a promise of a donation could be
brought to completion. Many times this had happened to
him, while prelates and clerics with personal access to Synod
personnel got their requests handled with dispatch.

Evlogii of Kholm and Ioanniki of Arkhangelsk also expressed resentment that they were not permitted to inaugurate
programs or make decisions that took into account the local
conditions and needs of their formerly Uniate or Karelian
areas. Standardized policies were handed down from Petersburg, more often than not motivated by political considera-

tions, and they, the men in the field, could not implement them. Wrong direction from Petersburg aided anti-Orthodox missionary activities by Lutherans and Latins.[28]

The exarch of Georgia warned that the creation of metropolias in itself would not be sufficient, because the new structure might simply turn into a Russian form of papal administration, with the Patriarch appointing metropolitans and they in turn appointing and dictating to their bishops. He wanted guarantees that the new metropolias would not be the means of introducing papalism into Russia. On the other hand, safeguards had to be established so that metropolias would not separate the Russian church into loosely affiliated jurisdictions. Some kind of strong central administration had to exist. In Georgia, for example, there was great demand for complete autocephaly and severing of ties with the Russian church. It was a great political liability as well.[29]

Archbishop Stefan Arkhangelskii of Mogilev, former rector of the Tiflis Seminary in Georgia, envisioned a metropolia handling the bulk of regional church business in a metropolitan sobor made up of delegates from the clergy of every diocese in the metropolia, elected at diocesan convocations. Every parish priest and head of a monastery would be represented at diocesan convocations. Every metropolia would be headed by a metropolitan with some authority over its bishops, but limited by a metropolitan sobor.[30]

Khristofor of Ufa wanted more democratic assurances that vested interest groups would not permanently entrench themselves in the ecclesiastical administration, and believed that *sobornost'*, brotherly love and mutual deference was best protected by introducing elections at all levels of church administration. Parishes should elect elders, pastors, financial administrators and personnel to oversee parish institutions. Parishes, represented by pastors and lay delegates in diocesan convocations, should choose bishops. The metropolitan sobor in turn would be made up of elected delegates from all the diocesan convocations and should elect metropolitans. The same pattern should prevail at all-Russian sobors and for the election of a Patriarch.[31]

Bishop Vladimir Blagorazumov of Ekaterinburg, on the other hand, advocated that metropolitan sobors should have the right to nullify diocesan elections and to reject anyone it did not deem fit for the episcopacy. Bishops had a corporate responsibility to see that no unworthy or scandalous candidate was ever confirmed as bishop, whether or not he was locally popular. Free elections without review did not appeal to him, or to most of the other prelates.

Most bishops objected to the transfer of bishops from one diocese to another as uncanonical and denounced the practice in the Russian church of often leaving a bishop in his see less than a year. Only within the jurisdiction of metropolias should bishops be moved in the future. Only higher church authorities—Synod or Patriarch—should determine whether or not to move metropolitans. The canons required, however, that once elevated to a see, a bishop or metropolitan normally remains there till he dies.[32]

Bishops of lesser sees—Ioakim Levitskii of Orenburg, Alexei Molchanov of Taurida, Pitirim Oknov of Kursk, Nikon Sofiiskii of Vladimir, Afanasii Parkhomovich (1828-1910) of the Don, Filaret of Viatka, Nikanor of Perm, Tikhon of Kostroma, Khristofor of Ufa—were concerned that metropolitans not have authority to interfere in dioceses outside their own. They should be there to advise, to summon metropolitan sobors and to set the dates for election of bishops of vacant sees, but should not interfere in the independent administration of the dioceses of the metropolia. He would be *primus inter pares* in the metropolia, not an executive. He would have authority to solve disputes between bishops, but only in consultation with other bishops.[33]

There were many ideas about the location and number of metropolias. With regard to the latter, suggestions ranged from seven to twenty-two, the former being a suggestion of Fr. Alexander Ivantsov-Platonov.[34] He had suggested metropolitan cathedrals at Petersburg, Moscow and Kiev—because of their historical and political importance—and at Vilna, Kazan, Siberia and Caucasus-Georgia. Most prelates advocated his scheme and wanted Moscow to be the site of the all-Russian patriarchate. The metropolitan of St. Petersburg, however, envisioned eight metropolias, with an all-Russian Patriarch in St. Petersburg instead of Moscow. He added Voronezh to the number of metropolias.[35] Vadkovskii's scheme grouped the metropolias in such a way that areas with problems unique to the region would have their own local administration within a single metropolia. The problem of dealing with Latin Catholicism—a special threat since former Uniates now had the right to freely embrace it—and the resurgent Unia itself, threatening from across the frontier in Austrian Galicia, would mainly be confined to the Vilna metropolitanate, for example. The problem of dealing with resurgent Islam and newly enfranchised Old Believers in the Volga and Urals area would fall within the boundaries of the Kazan metropolitanate. Lutheranism would be confined to the Petersburg metropolitanate, while growing sectarianism would be mainly within the confines of the Kiev and Voronezh metropolitanates.

Several of the bishops thought that metropolias should coincide directly with the boundaries of the various political provinces and that every provincial capital should have a metropolitan cathedral, even such remote places as Rostov-on-Don.

Archbishop Tikhon Belavin (1865-1925) of the Aleutians and North America suggested a plan to provide a comprehensive administration for the growing Orthodox population of the United States and Canada. Taking note of the desires of various national groups of Orthodox—Serbians, Syrians and Greeks, besides Russians—he noted that in 1904 the Syrians had received their own bishop, Raphael Hawaweeny of Brooklyn, formerly an instructor in the Petersburg Academy, and that the Serbs were being currently administered by an archimandrite who might soon be elevated to the rank of bishop. Tikhon urged that the Russian church administration in the United States be elevated to the rank of an exarchate and that other Orthodox national groups be encouraged to subordinate themselves to it. The leading Orthodox bishop would be headquartered in New York and be Russian, with the Syrian bishop in Brooklyn and a Serbian bishop in Chicago, together with other national bishops in various sees as the need arose. Eventually, through sobors on the exarchate level, these churches would be blended into one administration, subordinate to the Russian patriarchate. He assumed that since the Russian mission began in Alaska, there would remain a diocese of Alaska under a Russian bishop.[36]

The bishop of Tomsk stressed that in a troubled year such as 1905 it was important not to confuse political and religious interests. Many non-Russian national groups in the empire sought some ethnic autonomy, and it was not the business of the church to become involved in these national aspirations. Rather, it was in the interest of the church to remain aloof in diocesan convocations and metropolitan sobors—if such should be held in the immediate future—from the political strivings of non-Russian populations. Only by refusing to espouse political goals would the church gain the credibility it needed to satisfy the purely religious needs of all the populations of the empire. At the same time, the church had to reassure the government, with which it was so closely connected, that it would not become a forum for anti-government movements and ideologies. It was a particularly difficult time the church was facing, and it had to tread very cautiously so as not to alienate either the people, whatever their ethnic background, or the government, which would reinforce the restrictions it was just about to lift. Convocation of regional metropolitan sobors to deal with the fragile situation was the one hope that the church had that it could thread its way through the maze of 1905. Similarly, Alexei Molchanov of the Taurida warned that the church must not become so agitated with change that it threatened to pull the supports from under the government. From ancient times, the church had been the bulwark of the government. The government especially depended upon it in 1905 in the western regions and in the Caucasus, to say nothing of maintaining the tenuous links that had been made to the Czech people, who in their religious roots were Orthodox.[37]

Metropolitan Flavian Gorodestskii of Kiev declared, to the contrary, that even if there were political separatist movements in 1905, the church had no reason to fear for its ultimate unity. For example, the separation of the Western and Eastern Roman Empires had come in the year 395, but it took six and one-half centuries (1054) before there was an official separation between the Eastern and Western churches. The causes of the political and the ecclesiastical separations were remote from each other and were nearly seven hundred years apart. Furthermore, he noted, even though West and South Russia went through a long period of political separation, the tendencies in the Muscovite and West Russian churches were towards unity with one another, and that was accomplished once political restraints had been removed. Therefore, the church had no reason to fear that political dissension would have a divisive effect upon the church. The church should not succumb to fears that those who wanted to subject her to political ends would succeed. Political bureaucratic centralism and religious unity had little to do with one another. They were different phenomena, and the church had no reason to fear that subdivision into metropolias would weaken it. The archbishop of Lithuania, in fact, felt that the present challenge from Catholicism in the western and southwestern dioceses would strengthen the unity of the Russian church, not weaken it, while two bishops from Georgia noted that thirteen centuries of separate administration in the Georgian church had not weakened its allegiance to the teachings and discipline of Eastern Orthodoxy. Thus, there was little reason to fear that separate metropolitanates in 1905 would endanger the church.[38]

* * *

In regard to reform of the higher ecclesiastical administration, most bishops considered it indispensable, though they did not agree on the profile of the reformed administration.

Opposition came from several sources. For example, Bishop Parfenii Levitskii of Podolia believed that talk about reforming the Russian church and summoning a sobor now would be poorly timed, because Russia was in the throes of upheaval and it could do serious damage to the civilian administration, which needed the church as an unwavering

support. Parfenii was afraid that wild-eyed reformers wanted
to saddle the Russian church with a neo-Protestant administration which would further emasculate its dignity and influence in the Russian Empire. The Orthodox church had
been weighed down with a Protestant regime in the years
after Peter the Great's death and had barely survived. It did
not need another persecution now.

Furthermore, he wondered, who needed a Patriarch? Was
not the ecumenical church much better off in the era that
preceded the development of the Byzantine patriarchate?
Were not John Chrysostom and Cyril and Athanasius of
Alexandria just as valuable and holy without the patriarchal
title? And did the seven ecumenical councils really stamp out
the heresies they were supposed to? The Christian world was
still riven with the Arian heresy, despite the condemnation
of Arius at Nicaea. The iconoclast heresy still persisted in
various forms, despite the Second Council of Nicaea in 787.
In the history of the Russian church, had the patriarchate
elevated religious life, settled dogma and disciplinary problems or otherwise made the Russian church more tranquil?
The patriarchate had led to a conflict with the civil authority,
something not experienced in Russia before or since, and had
given rise to the Old Believer schism, which still plagued
the church and particularly threatened it now since the unfortunate Toleration Law of April.[39]

More sarcastically, Lavrentii Nekrasov, a man of the old
Drozdovian school and a former antagonist of Khrapovitskii,
pointed out that if the church were in such a bad way that
it needed a Patriarch, it would be quite simple to reform it
and restore the patriarchate by a decree from the Tsar. The
Tsar had done away with the patriarchate in 1721; he could
restore it the same way in 1905. Convince the Tsar and the
deed was as good as done.[40]

Paisii Vinogradov rejected the idea that the patriarchate
would be more beneficial to the church than the Synod, because the Patriarch would just as easily elevate his authority
and abuse the rights and traditions of the bishops as the
Procurator had done. The Russian church historically had
been at its worst when it was ruled by a Patriarch. A power-

ful Patriarch had been bad for the Greek church and had led to different peoples seeking their own patriarchates to escape Greek control. The Roman papacy had led the Western church into heresy, while the patriarchate in the Russian church had led to the rise of the Old Believer schism. Out of the ten Patriarchs who had ruled the Russian church, not one had ever been canonized as a saint. If the Synod found itself constrained by the Procurator, it was the fault of the bishops in the Synod. Had they performed their duties responsibly, the Procurator would not have acquired the power he had. Not even the Tsar would be able to override the Synod if the bishops were responsible. As to the argument that the size and numbers of the Russian church demanded a patriarchate so that it could occupy a proper position of honor and dignity among the other Orthodox churches, Paisii thought that the size and numbers spoke for themselves and no Patriarch would enhance the prestige of the church further. The church needed the experience and wisdom of all its bishops, and they should all be involved in running the church. The Synod, with the Procurator stripped of office, should continue to govern. Twelve bishops at a time should sit, and they should rotate according to the date of their elevation to the episcopacy, with none of them having authority or honor that placed them over any of the others.

Most of the bishops, however, including the three metropolitans, believed that the existing governing apparatus and the whole concept of a Petrine-style collegium had to be swept away because the church was not currently governed according to the canons of the Eastern Orthodox church. The attempt to bend Orthodoxy to Protestant forms had to cease, and an administration formed along the lines of *sobornost'* had to be built. Bishops had to have real authority, not just the appearance thereof, both in their dioceses and in the central apparatus. The secular stranglehold had to be terminated, and immune civil bureaucrats had to be deprived of their distant and powerful control of ecclesiastical affairs. Persons responsible and answerable to the bishops and the needs of the church, for its own sake, had to replace the existing bureaucracy. Only then, when bishops were assured

that supports could not be pulled out from under them by
the merest whim of the Procurator or one of his lieutenants,
would they become a forthright body of men who fearlessly
and responsibly stood for moral and social integrity in the
empire, a force that could really tilt the balance in favor of
those human resources and principles that constituted the
solid fiber of society.[41]

The only way, many bishops thought, that the church
could adjust to the social demands being made upon it,
ameliorate the enduring hostility of the educated classes and
defend itself against other religious societies now that the
Toleration Law had been published, was to restore a powerful patriarchate to speak and act for the interests of the
church. When that meant clashing with established vested
interests—or even with the government itself—the risk had
to be taken. There was no question that the Russian church
would defend the autocracy, but there were times when the
church had to withstand even that autocracy. There was very
little point going into school reform, pastoral reform, or the
nature of central church government until the matter of reestablishing the patriarchate had been settled. To those who
objected that a patriarchate would jeopardize the prerogatives
of a sobor, or of a sobornal administration, the bishops
responded with the question: "Had not the whole sobornal
framework of church government fallen when the patriarchate fell?" The two—patriarchate and sobor—went together. Antonii Khrapovitskii, Evlogii Georgievskii, Arsenii
Stadnitskii and Tikhon Belavin were particularly adamant on
that issue. All were to play major roles in the future of the
Russian church in the twentieth century.[42]

Bishop Leonid Okropiridze of Imeretinsk, Georgia, emphasized that a patriarchate was the natural, historical and
canonical form of church government in Eastern Orthodoxy.
It was distinguished from the Catholic papal administration
in not being highly centralized but in leaving much local
initiative in the hands of diocesan bishops and their coun-
sellors, and it avoided the extreme subservience to the state
that was characteristic of the Protestant churches of the West.
The ultimate authority in the Russian church should be a

national sobor, periodically assembled. The sobor should determine canon law as it applied in Russia, questions of belief, reform of liturgy, selection of the Patriarch, the first prelate of the church, unfrocking and deposing prelates, restructuring ecclesiastical administration and the establishment of metropolias, establishment of new dioceses, regulation of relations between the Russian church and other Orthodox national churches, and relations with the Russian government. The sobor would also serve as a court of appeal from the ecclesiastical courts of the various metropolias and as the court of first instance at the patriarchal or central administrative level. The Patriarch or central administration would be entirely accountable to periodic national sobors and would render detailed written accounts to the sobors.

The frequency of sobors depended on what the bishops saw as the main function of the sobor. Some bishops thought the sobor should meet twice or at least once a year to conform to the regulations of the ecumenical councils, especially the Sixth Ecumenical Council. Others believed that the annual or semi-annual convocations of metropolitan sobors would satisfy the demands of canon law and that an all-Russian sobor should not be summoned more than once every four or five years. Special needs, like the election of a Patriarch, would require a sobor whenever they arose. Metropolitan Antonii of St. Petersburg did not believe that the question of how often to summon an all-Russian sobor should be decided before the first sobor itself had the opportunity to consider the question.

On one issue they all agreed. The future Patriarch would not have papal powers. He would be first among equals. His title would denote a primacy of responsibilities, not of personal ascendancy over other bishops. The Patriarch would be the first member of the Synod, over which he would preside. He would also be the spokesman for the Russian church in its relations with the Tsar and with the other Orthodox churches. He would be bound by the regulations and stipulations of the Synod, just as the other bishops were. His authority as a bishop would extend only in his own diocese. His relations to the other bishops would be as if he were the metropolitan over the whole church. He would only advise and counsel, not command. He would in turn be subject to the advice and counsel of the other bishops, either as members of the Synod, or, when it was sitting, the national sobor.[43]

His duties as first bishop of the Synod would differ from the duties of the other bishops in that he would convene the Synod and announce the dates for and convene national sobors. The Synod itself would be an instrument of the national sobors. Most of the bishops responding to the Synod's circular felt that the first prelate should have the title All-Russian Patriarch. Some thought it should be Patriarch of Moscow and All Russia, just as it had been before Peter the Great. The metropolitan of St. Petersburg and the Olonets Diocesan Commission thought the first prelate should have the title Metropolitan of St. Petersburg and Patriarch of All Russia and that he should reside in Petersburg. Some of the bishops noted that the Austrian sect of Old Believers were toying with the idea of selecting their own Patriarch of All Russia and felt that the state church should hasten to reestablish that office before the Old Believers preempted it. If the state church did so, it would become a drawing card for Old Believers towards some kind of unity with the state church.[44]

Sergei Stragorodskii suggested a way to select the Patriarch that would avoid the turmoil of party-inspired competition that so many of the bishops feared would ensue, particularly in 1905. For the purpose of election, the sobor should be divided into two chambers, one of bishops and one of clergy and lay delegates. Each chamber would draw up a list of possible candidates, debate their merits, and exclude those who did not fit canonical requirements. Then the list from the chamber of clergy and laymen would be passed to the chamber of bishops, which would delete those whom they could not accept for canonical or other reasons and combine the two lists of suggested candidates into one. This list would then be forwarded to Tsar Nicholas II, who would reduce the list to three names. If Nicholas felt that a significant name had been left out by the sobor, he would reduce their list to two and add the name he thought was needed. Then, the list with three candidates would be returned to the sobor. The three names would be placed on separate ballots, placed in a chalice on the patriarchal throne and, after a general prayer invoking the Holy Spirit, a respected starets would reach into the chalice and draw a name. He would read the name to the sobor, which would then acclaim the new Patriarch. Secretaries would certify that he had read the name properly, so that no question of who was Patriarch would arise. The selection would take place in the Uspenskii cathedral in the Moscow Kremlin, the traditional cathedral of the Russian Patriarchs. Many years later, under very different conditions, Sergei himself would be elected Patriarch by a similar procedure.[45]

Another interesting variation on the theme of electing the Patriarch came from Professor Ioann Sokolov of the Petersburg Theological Academy, one of Metropolitan Antonii's closest advisers since 1903. Sokolov suggested that the Synod name a *locum tenens* (*mestobliustitel'*) for the patriarchal throne and that a date for the election of a Patriarch, not more than forty-one days after the death of the incumbent (in the case of the restoration, not more than forty-one days after the decree of restoration), be set by the *locum tenens*. In the meantime, the Synod would draw up its suggestions of candidates for the patriarchal throne, while each diocesan bishop would forward his suggestion of a candidate and each diocese would hold a convocation of clergy and laity so that they could name a candidate. Five days before the electing sobor, a convocation of Synod members, bishops and delegates from the diocesan convocations would meet in the capital and compile a protocol, which would include the names of all the candidates suggested. Those candidates from the clergy and laity convocations would have to have the approval of at least a third of the bishops in order to go onto the list. The minutes of the conclave would be kept in full and published immediately after it ended. Then, two days before the electing sobor was held, another conclave would be held, and all the delegates—episcopal, clerical and lay—would vote in secret ballot for their candidates. The three candidates with the most votes would then become eligible for election. On the day of the electing sobor, all the delegates would again gather for liturgical services. After the services the bishops would proceed to cast their ballots in a chalice on the cathedral altar—much like the Roman Pope is elected—and the candidate with the most votes would be the new Patriarch. The *locum tenens* would then notify the Tsar, who would ratify the choice, and the ceremonies of enthronement would take place.[46]

Both suggestions, which were similar to those that came from various other dioceses, were careful to include lay and clerical participation in the selecting process, but adhered to the canonical dictum that the election be finally carried out by the bishops alone.

The bishops were also in agreement that the Synod had to be completely removed from the control of civil bureaucrats. All that would be left of the existing Synod apparatus would be the name and the building on the Neva River. The new Synod would be the governing apparatus of the church, strictly subject to the authority of regularly convened national sobors. Lay bureaucrats employed by the Synod would have no responsibility to the civil government and would in no way be answerable to it.

Most of the bishops agreed that the new Synod should consist of twelve bishops, including the Patriarch, but there was considerable difference as to how these twelve should be chosen. Many believed that, other than the Patriarch, there should be no permanent members. Some bishops believed that all the bishops of the Russian church should participate over a period of six to seven years. Some of the respondents, like the Olonets Diocesan Commission, believed that the Synod should have permanent seats for representatives of the clergy and the laity. These would be chosen in diocesan convocations and rotate as members of the Synod. The Olonets Commission and Professor Nikolai Zaozerskii of St. Petersburg Academy believed that the Synod should be at once a canonical ecclesiastical administrative agency and a *soviet* of believers' spokesmen. Zaozerskii had in mind the patriarchal Synod in Constantinople, which was both the administrative agency for the patriarchate of Constantinople and the council of representatives of the Greek peoples living in the Ottoman Empire. The majority of respondents believed that the Synod should have six permanent members and six rotating members. The six permanent members would be the metropolitans of Moscow, St. Petersburg, Kiev, Georgia, Novgorod, Kazan and one other major metropolitanate that might be established. The other six would be made up of other metropolitans and archbishops in rotation by seniority in consecration. Permanent members were necessary to give the Synod continuity and order. Some thought that the rotating members should not be exclusively metropolitans, but rather bishops from each of the metropolitanates chosen in metropolitan sobors in order to avoid prolonged absences from their cathedrals. Another variant suggested that the Synod be made up of four bishops, four white clergy and four laymen, chosen by a very complicated process that would combine rotation and permanent membership.[47]

Most bishops agreed that the departments of the Synodal chancellory should be rebuilt from the ground up. These departments—the School Commission, which oversaw the various seminaries, diocesan men's and women's schools and other special schools under the direct government of the Synod chancellory; the School Council, which rather loosely oversaw the various organizations involved in raising funds for the schools, like brotherhoods and trusteeships, and which included under its survey candle factories, which contributed to the maintenance of schools and of local churches; the Missionary Council, which oversaw such organizations as the Orthodox Missionary Society and the myriad of missionary endeavors against Old Believers, sectarians, Catholics and Lutherans, as well as the faltering effort against Moslems; the Committee for Brotherhoods, which tried to coordinate and direct their efforts, particularly against sectarians, Catholics and Lutherans in the western and southwestern provinces; the Committee for Trusteeships, which coordinated activities and which had expanded since the late 1860s from simply raising funds for school support to a host of public religious education programs, funding for parishes, monas-

teries and special religious centers—should be entirely restructured. Civil bureaucrats who had no training in church
programs, dogma and policies should be dismissed. The
bishops envisioned a paring down of much of the clumsy
bureaucratic apparatus, decentralizing it and placing it under
diocesan or metropolitan control and restaffing it with monks
and white clergy who had a more intimate knowledge and
concern for the problems and programs that these departments were serving. Naturally, the close control exercised by
the Procurator, whose own functionaries actually ran these
departments, and did so more in his interests than in the
interests of the Synod itself, would be terminated.[48]

The bishops were virtually unanimous in their condemnation of the subservience of the Russian Orthodox church to
the Russian state. For two hundred years the crippling influence of the state had bent the church to political interests
and forced it to anathematize political enemies of the state
when those people had done little inimical to the church or
to the religious welfare of the Russian people. The system
was Protestant caesaropapism. When the church regained full
autonomy in its internal affairs, it would release the religious
fervor of the Russian people and become a more powerful
moral influence in civil society. The church's negative image,
and its refusal to concern itself with the burning problems
of Russian society in the twentieth century, only condemned
it to ridicule and hatred on the part of the intelligentsia.
The bishops were well aware that in 1905 the intelligentsia
was being heard by the Russian masses as it had never
been listened to before. The church could not stand silently
by.[49]

Furthermore, the Manifesto on Toleration gravely
threatened the Orthodox church. The effective restraints upon her enemies that the state had maintained were being
dismantled. The church was being condemned along with
the state for these repressions, and yet this same state denied
it the freedom necessary to meet new challenges.

That did not mean that hostilities would immediately
arise between the church and the state. The Tsar, as the first
believer in the church, would naturally have the Orthodox

church's interests at heart before the interests of other religious bodies in the empire, and the church would continue
to pray for the interests of the Tsar and his realm. But the
ideal of "symphony" between state and church, mutually
beneficial to both, as enunciated by the great statesmen and
Patriarchs of the Byzantine church and incorporated into the
canons, would have to be the governing motif between them.
The State Council and the projected State Duma, as organs
of civil power, should stand parallel to the Synod and the
national sobor, the organs of religious authority. They should
reflect each other's concerns, but be very careful not to over-
step each other's prerogatives.

Rapid shuffling of bishops from see to see, oftentimes
for purely political reasons, had to be stopped. No bishop
should be moved at the behest of a provincial governor or
imperial bureaucrat unless the diocese from which he was
being transferred agreed to release him. The bishop himself
would have to be agreeable to such a move. Even a Patriarch should never be deprived of his office or deposed unless a sobor, free from duress by the state, agreed and ordered
it. No Tsar had the right to depose a Patriarch. The church
should be her own conscience and utilize her own discretion
in such matters.

Most of the bishops and diocesan commissions believed
that the office of Procurator should be abolished altogether.
The proper way for the church to consult with the state was
to have conferences between Patriarch and Tsar, or, if the
matters were not so serious, between their delegates at a lower
level. Most of the bishops believed that in order to avoid
another office like that of the Procurator, those delegates
should be chosen on an *ad hoc* basis each time an issue
arose.

There were some who envisioned the retention of the
Procurator but disagreed on his future. Some thought he
should be strictly the agent of the Patriarch and the Synod,
an intermediary with civil authorities. He would be appointed
by the Patriarch and Synod, receive his instructions from them,
and be answerable to them with no prior obligation to the
state. Others, like Archbishop Sergei of Finland and Archi-

mandrite Faddei Uspenskii of Olonets, envisioned the Procurator remaining as the representative of the Tsar in the Synod, but only in an advisory capacity. The Synod and Patriarch, however, would be under no obligation to conform to his advice. They would simply consider it. For all practical purposes, the Procurator figured dimly in the minds of the reformers.[50]

The overwhelming sentiment of the bishops was to decentralize the administration of the Orthodox church and to do away with the Procurator's powers and bureaucracy. They had searched the canons of the Byzantine era at length and had found the *reglament* of Peter the Great to have violated them in virtually every detail. They favored, in the majority, the immediate restoration of the patriarchate and the restoration of administrative autonomy to the state church.

The bishops were conscious of the need to involve the laity and lower clergy in the renovation of the church, but were baffled as to how this involvement was to be achieved without violating the very clear canons of the early church, which did not foresee any kind of church parliamentarianism. Still, if the crises besetting the church were to be solved, the vast numbers of the faithful would have to be involved.

It was with these factors in mind that the bishops and their advisers turned to the problem of restructuring the diocesan and lower levels of church administration. There the problem of gaining the support and the experience of the masses had to be resolved.

CHAPTER V

Deliberations and Debates: The Lower Administration

The concern of Russian hierarchs with injustice and inefficiency, discernible by every sensitive observer and experienced by the majority of Orthodox believers, drove them and their advisers to strive to effect reforms which would put them in a more competitive position to influence discontented sections of Russian society. Their concern accounts for the acrimonious and cynical exchanges between them and those who either discounted their efforts entirely or who were determined to prevent any serious reform, lest it do harm to vested interests.[1]

In discussion related to reform and restructuring of diocesan administration, they revealed deep resentment that they were required by civil authorities to do paperwork they regarded as simply unnecessary. They believed that required bureaucratic duties demoralized their flocks and separated them from the pastoral duties that their ecclesiastical position required of them. Much of the paperwork should simply be abolished, so that diocesan administration could operate more smoothly. Many of them thought that in the twentieth century, with the extension of the telegraph and telephone, much of the form-filling was no longer necessary. Indeed, it may never have been.

Bishops resented the fact that bureaucrats in their diocesan administrations were not really subordinate to them.

Consistorial secretaries were appointed by the Procurator, were responsible to him, and sat in the consistories like spies, ready to undermine their bishops whenever there was a disagreement. They particularly lamented the lack of closeness to their flocks, because they were rotated so rapidly and were burdened with too much office work. They so closely re-resembled their counterparts in the civil bureaucracy that any function other than conducting ceremonies at public events was denied them. The very size of their dioceses precluded their ever engaging their people effectively in truly pastoral work. Legal demands kept them apart from their clergy and caused them to be deeply resented by the latter.

Konstantin Bulichev expressed the sentiments of the majority of his colleagues when he emphasized that the desire of bishops to exclude bureaucrats and their insensitive manner from ecclesiastical administration in no way meant a desire to exclude laymen from influence in the administration of dioceses. On the contrary, he desired to involve laymen at every level, so that the clergy could devote themselves more closely to pastoral service to their flocks and so ecclesiastical administration would perceive and respond to the needs of the Russian masses more attentively. Bishop Konstantin was pained that the church was despised and ridiculed for being distant and irrelevant in the modern day. By involving laymen and heeding their counsel, the church could overcome that irrelevance. Reform of the ecclesiastical courts was a very concrete example of how laymen would have to give their advice and counsel in such delicate areas as mixed marriages and divorce. Konstantin emphasized that the Russian people were no longer a docile, uneducated, dumb mass. Educated servants of the people would show the church how to respond to their needs and aspirations while leading them to their eternal destiny. Bishop Ioann of Poltava envisioned that diocesan sobors would be the locus of true dialogue among the bishops, the clergy and the laity. Such sobors would be held annually or semi-annually, in keeping with canon law, and would combine convocation of clergy with representation from the laity and lay organizations. Problems discussed and decisions reached at diocesan sobors would establish guidelines for pastoral action and administrative policies. A true *sobornost'*, a fraternal responsiveness among all the elements of the church, would flow from such exchanges.

Metropolitan Vladimir Bogoiavlenskii expressed the sentiments of his confreres when he demanded the shifting of most of the work done in the Procurator's chancellory to the dioceses. Faster resolution would be possible and a great deal of useless paperwork avoided. Marriage counselling, for example, could be done at the parish and diocesan level, not left to mindless bureaucrats in Petersburg.

Only Gurii Okhotin of Novgorod and Lavrentii Nekrasov of Tula thought the Synod should have a voice in appointing members to the diocesan consistories. All the others disagreed, believing that the consistory should be under the chairmanship of the local bishop or his deputy, with all major decisions made at the diocesan level with the bishop himself supervising. Lesser matters, like approving the construction of chapels, the renovation of churches or the location of candle factories, could be left to the consistory without the sanction of the bishop. Most bishops agreed that the secretary of the consistory would be elected by the consistory members themselves, either from among their own number or from qualified personnel known to them. Appointment of secretaries from St. Petersburg and employment of students who neither knew nor cared anything about diocesan particulars would cease.

There were various suggestions as to how to include representatives of the laity and lay organizations in the consistory. Some thought they should be regular members, chosen by various lay organizations or through parish elections or diocesan sobors. Others saw the consistory (called in this case a *soviet* of presbyters) exclusively made up of white and monastic clergy, with lay experts as advisers.

Many bishops suggested that consistory proceedings be reviewed by annual or semi-annual diocesan sobors and that the consistory be merely the governing agent between sobors and entirely responsible to them. Most bishops thought that the consistory should be strictly an administrative organ and that all legal matters be removed from its competence and turned over to a separate ecclesiastical court system that would parallel the legal system introduced into the civil courts in 1864.

Antonii Khrapovitskii, Stefan Arkhangelskii and Ioakim Levitskii of Orenburg saw no reason for continuing the consistory at all, because the consistory was and would continue to be a barrier between the bishop and his clergy. Rather, the bishop should have his own chancellory, with personnel appointed by him, who could directly consult with him on matters that needed his consideration. His chosen aides would be mainly of the clerical class rather than laymen, and would enjoy his complete trust.[2]

*   *   *

Russian bishops uniformly condemned the existing structure of ecclesiastical courts because of their archaic form and their distance from the realities of the twentieth century. It was a problem of public concern, noted by Fedor Dostoevskii in *Brothers Karamazov*.[3] Chief among the types of cases that glutted the courts, especially during the closing two decades of the nineteenth century, were cases of consanguinity, marriage with persons of other denominations and divorce, which, in some cases, Orthodox canons allowed.

One of the repeated criticisms of ecclesiastical courts was that the primary reason they had been established by Peter the Great was apparently to punish clergymen who were regarded as subversive. They had not been designed to care for moral and religious problems that demanded ecclesiastical solutions. The *Ustav Dukhovnoi Konsistorii* failed to make distinctions. Clergy were considered as a class, rather than distinguished as individuals. Furthermore, the *Ustav* made no distinction between a crime committed by a clergyman, and therefore punishable, and a crime that had only been attempted. Often, if a priest was caught committing a crime, the other priests in the area or parish were also presumed guilty, not only of the attempt, but of actually committing the crime. The hand of the law fell upon their class, rather than upon them as individuals. Guilt by association had been eradicated from civil law since the reforms of 1864. Ecclesiastical courts had been controversial ever since. Civil courts were separated from administrative agencies in 1864. Ecclesiastical courts had remained a division of diocesan consistories. Administrative detail weighed down the consistories and inevitably forced judicial activities into a secondary place. This handicap had been overcome in the civil courts. Since the state had absorbed the church through the Ecclesiastical Regulation of Peter the Great, the ecclesiastical courts should have been reformed along the same lines as the civil reform. But forty years had passed and no effort to reorganize the church had been made.[4]

The subordination of the Synod to the government and the control of the Synod through the Procurator meant that no clergyman ever got impartial consideration when government interests were involved. Separation of administration and litigation needed to be introduced during the process of church reform. Pitirim Oknov demonstrated at length that it was impossible to arrive at objectivity and unbias when bureaucrats had to deal simultaneously with matters of administrative, legal and judicial nature. Even where a consistorial bureaucrat was not directly involved in a case against church personnel, he was obliged to read the transcripts of every proceeding and sign them before they were legally completed. If he should have to deal with the priest, monk or nun under question later on in another context, it was natural that what he had read would affect his dealings with them. A special committee had studied the whole problem of ecclesiastical courts in 1870 and had made extensive recommendations, but nothing had come of it. The uproar during the civil violence of the 1870s caused curbs to be imposed in the civil court system, while ecclesiastical court reforms fell into limbo and were never again considered.[5]

Pitirim scorned over-centralization in the ecclesiastical court system. Petty little affairs that should be settled at the diocesan level were transcribed in triplicate, sent to the Synod in Petersburg and often languished for years before the bureaucracy processed them. Meantime, the issues that had given rise to the cases had either vanished or the people involved had died, or else the cases had been transferred to efficient *zemstvo* courts, where petitioners knew they would receive rapid adjudication. Pitirim spoke for all prelates except Lavrentii of Tula and Paisii of Turkestan in lamenting the slowness of the court system in the Russian church.

The Novgorod Diocesan Commission noted that cases were usually introduced into ecclesiastical courts by persons not familiar with them or the parties involved. Advocates were untutored in civil law, to say nothing of Orthodox canon law, and were too often students whose main interest was to be paid while they pursued their schooling, rather than persons trained and paid for the job they were performing. Issues that could be argued and settled at the diocesan level were committed to paper and transmitted to Petersburg without any accuracy in the details or essence of the cases. In numerous cases, consistorial secretaries enlarged upon relatively minor cases with the sole aim of impressing the bureaucrats in Petersburg who read them.[6]

Konstantin Bulichev complained that without established procedures for investigating cases, no persons can be trained to handle specialized cases. Often the investigator was the *blagochinie* dean, a man who knew the parties involved beforehand and already was prejudiced for or against them. Usually, the diocesan consistory decided the case the way the *blagochinie* dean recommended, without thorough or dispassionate investigation. The Novgorod Commission noted that many a time a priest was hailed before the court by his *blagochinie* dean, tried and condemned for offenses that were really minor or even trumped up, solely because the dean did not like the priest and knew that once he was caught up in the court system he was finished. The alleged offense could be anything from rape to failing to excise Uniate practices from his liturgies. Once he had a record with the Synod, a man's life could be quite miserable. However, if he left the priesthood he was legally and socially a pariah the rest of his life. The practice of allowing the accused to face his accuser before an impartial judge or jurors simply had not been heard of. Sometimes, judgment was handed down like a thunderbolt upon a priest who was not even aware that he had been accused.[7]

Dmitri Kovalnitskii of Kherson cautioned against making a radical break in the existing court system, suggesting rather that through amending it and restructuring it piecemeal it could be improved upon. Metropolitan Flavian Gorodestskii of Kiev agreed that the existing system was a far cry from what Orthodox canons envisioned and from the principles of *sobornost'*, but suggested that past experience showed it was easier to achieve alteration in the system than to scrap it altogether and start afresh. Flavian cautioned that reform of the church court system could no longer be postponed. The civil government was about to effect a wholesale restructuring of its legal system. If the church did not act immediately it would find its prerogatives overlooked when civil codes were reworked. The church could not wait till civil restructuring was completed. In whole areas of moral and religious legislation the church had primary discretion. To wait would be to forfeit primary jurisdiction. If civil authorities transgressed areas where canon law gave the church priority, the church would have to resist. Bishop Nikon Sofiiskii of Vladimir noted that it was absurd for civil authorities to arrest, try and fine parish psalmists who had committed a crime against a church institution—like disrupting services—when they should be bound over to an ecclesiastical court and tried there.

Bishop Anastasii Dobradin of Voronezh urged that a complete codification of canon law, with cross references to civil law, be made so that church courts would have their own compendia of law. The Novgorod Diocesan Commission recommended that the church prepare a codex resembling the *Svod Zakonov* used by civil courts and officials.[8]

Gurii Burstasovskii of Simbirsk warned that the primary function of a separate church court system should be to safeguard ecclesiastical autonomy. Matters of religious and moral significance that affected the Orthodox and matters affecting discipline among the clergy were the responsibility of ecclesiastical courts. The church would have to resist attempts by civil authorities to take them over.

Antonii Khrapovitskii reminded the Synod that there had been several attempts to separate the ecclesiastical courts from civil jurisdiction since 1870, but to no avail. Since a State Duma was to be convened in 1906, it was crucial that the church gain independence in the matter of ecclesiastical jurisprudence. He recommended restoration of "Monday courts," along Byzantine lines, which would supplement civil courts in moral and religious matters. He did not think the civil system needed to be duplicated section by section, because much of the litigation that civil courts dealt with had no religious or moral significance. The formal adversary style of the civil courts need not be carried over into church courts. The principle of *sobornost'* and charity did not allow that. Civil courts did not consider charity a legal principle of procedure. Church courts would be more concerned with rehabilitating a person, making him see the error of his ways, than punishing him for the sake of punishment or of restitution to the civil community. Restitution was not the primary concern of a church court—rehabilitation was. In the end, civil courts had recourse to capital punishment. The ultimate punishment of the church courts was excommunication, depriving a recalcitrant of intercourse with the Christian community.

The bishop would be the only person in both the ecclesiastical administration and the ecclesiastical court. Participation in both was necessitated by the nature of the pastoral office. Bishops had to give overall guidance to the government of their dioceses and at the same time be fathers, reproving and cajoling their flocks along the path of salvation. They would be protectors of the ecclesiastical court system, because without their authority and prestige on the line, ecclesiastical courts would easily be overrun by the minions of the civil court system. In all other respects the ecclesiastical court system would be entirely separated from ecclesiastical administrative functions.

Several bishops believed that the courts at the diocesan level could be decentralized, too, not just separated from diocesan administration. *Blagochiniia* should have their own courts to take care of the less important cases, such as disputes over ecclesiastical incomes and properties, for example. *Blagochinie* courts could have specific kinds of cases to handle for the diocese. Only when situations became too difficult would they be passed up to the diocesan court. Even parish courts, *ad hoc* organizations elected in the parish assembly, could handle problems among parishioners or between parishioners and their pastor. They would be informal courts and could recommend transfer of cases to *blagochinie* or diocesan courts if necessary. *Blagochinie* and parish courts might even permit the parties involved to avoid more formal civil courts to escape publicity, scandals and unnecessary expense.

Bishop Tikhon Troitskii, who had been a parish priest in his youth, advocated a permanent parish court whose members would be elected for four-year periods, half of whom would be replaced every two years. Parish members twenty-five years or older would be eligible to be elected to the parish court. Parish courts could handle cases that might otherwise fall to civil courts—such as adultery, drunkenness, marital infidelity and other local problems—in an attempt to solve them before they became subject to more serious litigation. Laymen and clergy would be represented equally on these courts.

Led by Metropolitan Vladimir of Moscow, many of the bishops insisted that if church courts were to have public trust, open sessions were required, but would be limited to the Orthodox public. Metropolitan Vladimir believed that ecclesiastical courts would be controversial, not just rubber-stamp institutions. Many bishops envisioned that the Orthodox community, working out relevant definitions and applications of canon law, would be controversial. No man or woman would come into court prejudged, but would stand on an equal footing with his or her accuser. Cases would be judged impartially upon their merits. Rank and privilege would have no place.[9] No priest, monk, nun or lay person would be hailed before ecclesiastical courts without very serious charges being preferred against them. Persons charged would know exactly what they were charged with and would have ample opportunity and counsel to defend themselves. No secret reports against anyone would be accepted, and no hearsay evidence or secret witness would be tolerated. False accusations would be rejected and their perpetrators themselves prosecuted. No case should be appealed more than once. The second instance of a case would be the last one, so that cases would not drag out for years. Poor priests, monks, nuns and laymen would have free legal defense in the church courts, as provided for by the Council of Carthage of 401. Swift justice would be the operating motif of the ecclesiastical courts. Court decisions would be rendered immediately upon the conclusion of proceedings. If a jury were used, the time of decision would be longer. The bishops generally preferred three persons: judge, advocate and defense counsel, who could render decisions at once. Final written and published decisions would be handed down in not more than ten days after cases were concluded.[10]

The general outline of the court system that emerged from the writings of the bishops in 1905 described a five-level system. At the bottom was the parish, *uezd* or monastic court. Parish courts were favored by most of the bishops. However, they recognized that in areas of numerous parishes, on the one hand, or of relatively thin population density on the other, the *uezd* court would be more feasible, with members elected at the assemblies of the parishes of the *uezd*. Clergy and lay members would sit on these courts in equal numbers, six of each.

Many bishops believed that monastic courts should be separate from parish or *uezd* courts and be composed of twelve monks. Large monasteries would have their own courts, while smaller units would combine to share a court among them. The types of problems that would come before monastic courts—violation of monastic discipline, scandalous conduct and problems pertaining exclusively to the nature of a monastic establishment—were so unique that there was no point in trying to combine monastic and parish or *uezd* courts.

Above the parish, *uezd* or monastic court would be the *blagochinie* court. Members of the *blagochinie* court would be selected by the various parishes and monasteries. The *blagochinie* dean would preside over the court, composed of an equal number of clergy and laymen.

Diocesan courts would handle divorce cases, mixed marriage cases not resolved at lower levels, defrocking of priests and monks, and excommunication from the church, in addition to problems passed up from the lower courts. Cases currently handled by the Synod and Procurator's chancellory would be decided at the diocesan level. There was considerable diversity over how members would be elected or selected, whether they would include equal portions of laymen or clergy, and whether simple election from various *blagochiniia* and monasteries in the diocese would be the best way to choose the court members. Some bishops did not think election would be the best way to choose the personnel of the diocesan courts because elected members were not always the best qualified. They believed that at the diocesan level, court personnel would have to be full-time, paid living wages, be experts in canon and civil law and have law degrees or certificates.

Above the diocesan court would stand the metropolitan regional court. It would receive cases not resolved at the diocesan level, entertain complaints against diocesan bishops, and investigate charges of uncanonical procedure in choosing bishops, archimandrites and *igumeni* or other church dignitaries. Normally, the metropolitan court would be the court of last resort.

The highest court would be the patriarchal court. Complaints or charges against metropolitans, the members of the Synod, or even the Patriarch himself would be made there. The patriarchal court would be comprised of bishops and archbishops chosen by metropolitan sobors. Members of the patriarchal court would have to have the highest degrees in canon law and Orthodox history. The patriarchal court would receive cases from metropolitan courts only for the gravest reasons. Konstantin Bulichev envisioned it as a parallel to the Imperial Senate, a religious Supreme Court. Cases not determined in the patriarchal court would automatically go before the next national sobor or could be the reason for calling a national sobor.[11]

*   *   *

Among the more serious problems the bishops faced was

that of mixed marriages, now that the Toleration Law of April 17 was taking effect. Formerly, no one of sectarian, Old Believer, Catholic, Lutheran or non-Christian belief could marry an Orthodox unless he or she were married before an Orthodox priest and agreed to rear the children of the union in the Orthodox faith. Besides that, spouses of sectarian and Old Believer faith had to formally enter the Orthodox church.

Now, with the Toleration Law, no formal action had been taken by the Synod or the hierarchy to deal with mixed marriages or anti-Orthodox proselytism, with the result that widespread confusion and consternation was spreading among the Orthodox faithful. The Toleration Law permitted mixed marriages without forcing the non-Orthodox partner either to accept the Orthodox church or even to promise to rear the offspring in Orthodoxy. Mixed marriages with Old Believers were particularly difficult because of Old Believer insistence that the state church was not truly Orthodox. There were no statistics available, but the bishops were convinced that large inroads into the Orthodox flock were being made by the Old Believers, particularly the Austrian sect. Konstantin Bulichev was particularly incensed at Old Believer denunciation of the state church as heretical, as the "whore of Babylon." In the turmoil of 1905, anti-church propaganda was taking a toll. Not in control of its own affairs, the state church could not effectively respond. It did very little good to point out that the Sobor of 1666-1667 had anathematized the Old Believers, because as far as the Old Believers were concerned it was the state church that had deviated from the path of Orthodoxy. Common folk listened. Because of its close identification with the state, *any* criticism of the church was given respectful consideration in 1905.

Most of the bishops felt that the state had no right to force toleration upon the church. According to early fathers such as Tertullian, Cyprian, Jerome, Ambrose and Theodore, to say nothing of the Fourth and Sixth Ecumenical Councils and the Councils of Laodicea and Carthage, the church had the sole right to determine whether or not to permit mixed marriages. The weight of tradition was definitely opposed to such accommodation. Mixed marriages clearly put the faith of the Orthodox in jeopardy. The church needed the freedom to impose its own sanctions, especially since the protection of the state was being removed. It was a delusion to imagine that the Orthodox church was no different from any other religious body. Not only did the canons of the Byzantine church not permit mixed marriages, but neither did the traditions of the Muscovite church. The marriage of Elena, daughter of Ivan III, to Alexander of Lithuania, was a case in point. Despite considerable pressure from the Lithuanians to have her convert to Catholicism and assurances by Catholic canonists that their religion was just a variant of Eastern Orthodoxy, Elena held fast at the insistence of her father and the Muscovite hierarchy.

Not even the *reglament*[12] of Peter the Great had forced the church to accept mixed marriages, even though Peter himself had wanted to do so. The bishops in the new Synod had stoutly refused to violate the canons. It did not matter to the church if the government chose in 1905 to refer to the Raskol as Old Believers and not schismatics. They were still schismatics as far as the church was concerned, and until they recognized their errors they could not enter into marriages with the Orthodox. The bishops in dioceses with large Old Believer populations were particularly adamant on that point.[13]

Metropolitan Flavian of Kiev, in whose diocese sectarians were very busy, was equally adamant about not permitting mixed marriages with sectarians. Stundo-Baptists, for example, sought Orthodox partners with the sole purpose of tearing them away from the womb of the church. The canons of the church absolutely forbade this activity, and the Tsar did not have the right to impose toleration. The church had no choice but to make point eleven of the *ukaz* permitting mixed marriages a dead letter, because the councils and church fathers had forbidden them and the scriptures themselves had scathing words about casting pearls before swine. Flavian was further disturbed by the number of Orthodox, more than a thousand in just a few months, who had been married before Catholic priests in western and southwestern

Russia since the Toleration Law had been published.[14]

Vladimir Sinkovskii of Kishinev was disturbed at the lapse of the law requiring all children of Orthodox who had gone over to other religions to be raised in Orthodoxy till their fourteenth year. Statistics kept since 1889 indicated that those children amounted to several tens of thousands annually. Now their parents were ceasing to instruct them in Orthodoxy and were raising them outside the church. Newly born children of former Orthodox were not even being baptized according to Orthodox rites. The church would have to take energetic measures to halt this defection. Flavian of Kiev suggested that parishes construct orphanages, so that those children could be instructed in Orthodoxy and live in an atmosphere favorable to the church. The state would have to aid in freeing these children from hostile religious environments.[15]

*   *   *

Diocesan convocations caused the bishops substantial disagreement. Many felt that the very idea of diocesan convocations was a danger to their authority as pastors and would permit all sorts of divisiveness and ill will to manifest themselves. Others felt that diocesan convocations should be the very central focus of ecclesiastical government. Convocations should include all aspects of life in the dioceses and should set policy and supervise its execution. Laymen and clergy alike should participate in convocations and exchange ideas and expertise essential for the church in modern times.

But Lavrentii Nekrasov of Tula was unalterably opposed to diocesan convocations, because already they had been turned into forums for agitation against bishops. Young priests and deacons proclaimed that they were suffering under episcopal oppression and advocated a complete democratization of the convocations. Lavrentii warned that bishops would lose the right even to preside over the gatherings and in so doing lose the last vestige of authority over their clergy. Priests were agitating to undermine the consistories, to be allowed to go about in lay dress and fashionable clothing, to be liberated from teaching in schools, to be permitted to enter into second and even third marriages when widowed and to abolish inner missions aimed at the Raskol, sectarians and revolutionaries. All this was a scandal to the simple Russian *narod* and destroyed the very canonical basis of a bishop's authority. A bishop's responsibility was to keep young priests in check and guide them in their pastoral and patriotic responsibilities. If diocesan convocations robbed him of authority, he would be some kind of Protestant-style figurehead and nothing more. The Greek church did not permit that; the pre-Petrine Russian church had not permitted that; to do so in 1905 or in the future would ruin the discipline of the Russian church.

Lavrentii recalled that the convocation had originally been designed to devise means and ways to raise funds for diocesan programs, missions, schools and parishes that needed special aid. But who actually carried out these responsibilities? The bishops and their assistants. What good, then, was the convocation? The convocations were dominated by a few seminary rectors, inspectors, assistant inspectors and *blagochinie* deans who were usually bent upon impressing each other with the luxuriousness of their palaces and apartments instead of taking up the business of advancing an effective pastorate. They boasted to one another about the schools in which they placed their children—usually not ecclesiastical schools. They were a scandal to the poor sons of country pastors placed in their charge. It was no wonder that seminaries, under the supervision of men like these, erupted into violence and that their students were in the vanguard of the revolutionaries. Stundists and sectarians made much of these schools and their worldly administrators. It was not surprising that the simple Orthodox often fell into the hands of heretics when one considered the characters who ran Orthodox institutions. A good reform would be to abolish convocations.[16]

Lavrentii was rather alone in his outlook because most bishops saw a reformed convocation, allowing for fuller dialogue between bishops and clergy, to be the road to broader involvement and commitment to the church and its goals, keeping with the ideal of *sobornost'* which they were striv-

ing to restore to the Russian church. They would rename
the convocation a diocesan sobor and would model it upon
the metropolitan and national sobors that would soon be
the ruling agencies of the church.

Bishops would chair the sobors. Sobors would be composed of diocesan clergy and a large number of laity. All
diocesan institutions—education, missionary, philanthropic
and charitable, administrative, retirement and insurance—
would come under the supervision of diocesan sobors. The
sobor would name the personnel to run these institutions and
would demand annual accounting from them. The ways and
means for securing funds for these institutions would remain
a major concern of the sobors, but they would also provide
a forum for free and constructive exchange among all groups
in the diocese concerned with effective pastoral action.
Priests, laymen and administrators would all have the opportunity to exchange ideas and experiences with each other,
reprove and correct each other and work toward solutions
and new programs, acceptable to all and supported by all.[17]

The *Ustav* on Diocesan Seminaries of 1867[18] had limited
the activities of the diocesan convocations simply to money
raising and reviewing activities. Since then, convocations had
broadened their activities to building orphanages, churches,
schools, retirement homes for aged priests and their families, the support of widows, the establishment of insurance
and burial societies, libraries, candle factories and other
money-generating foundations as well as organizing various
information disseminating societies, brotherhoods, trusteeships and other infrastructures upon which the day-to-day
functioning of the church depended. During the past five
years activities had been further broadened to include pastoral counselling and agitation for the revival of the parish
as a moral and social unit, the bettering of relationships between priests and flocks, the standardizing of fees for services and the improving of the education and moral life of
the Orthodox priest. In a word, they had come of age, and
it was time to give them legal status and terminate the repres-
sive restrictions set down by civil law.

Some bishops noted that they had more recently become

forums for anti-episcopal agitation, for movements to make clergy and bishops elective, for converting monasteries and convents into schools and other activities which were contrary to Orthodox practice and dangerous to the future of the church. They could weaken the church, and priests advocating them would have to be curbed before their agitation became more troublesome. Some prelates had experienced particularly hostile convocations in 1905.[19]

In contrast, Metropolitan Vladimir Bogoiavlenskii of Moscow, Bishop Evlogii Georgievskii of Kholm, Archbishop Sergei Stragorodskii of Finland and Archbishop Nikandr Molchanov of Lithuania insisted that the future convocation would deepen and strengthen ties between the clergy and their bishops. The day of the silent, long-suffering priest was over. Now they spoke out on moral, social and political issues. Too often the hierarchy had been Judases who aided civil authorities in stifling and oppressing their clergy. Any priest who spoke out against suffering and injustice to the people was immediately slapped with both civil and ecclesiastical penalties. Bishops would have to stand between the authorities and their priests. Convocations would be forums of exchange, immune to government and vested-interest pressures. No doubt there would be sharp exchanges and bitter words in these convocations, but the priest had to know that whatever passed in the walls of a convocation would never be used against him. The convocation would be the vehicle through which the bishop would learn about his diocese and hear solutions to problems. From his priests the bishop would learn of the sufferings of his people, the oppression of the factory workers, the misery of the peasants, the conniving of the officials and monied interests against the commoner, and would be able to confront responsible authorities and create the moral pressure necessary for change and reform. In this manner, the common masses would regain their respect for the church and know that the church was their defender in this life as well as their teacher for the after-life. Innokentii Beliaev (1862-1913) of Tambov, once a white priest himself, expressed the wide-felt hope that antagonisms between the clergy and the laity would gradually vanish and the well-founded criticisms of the church by the intelligentsia would lessen.

Tikhon Troitskii of Irkutsk and Ieronimyi Ekzempliarskii (1863-1905) of Warsaw felt that the convocation should elect the diocesan consistory. The very fact of selecting administrators in the convocation would go a long way toward lessening the antagonism between clergy and laity on the one hand and the administration and the diocesan bishop on the other. Ieronimyi and Nikon Sofiiskii also felt that the convocation should be part of the diocesan court system. Serious complaints against priests, administrators or even the bishop should come before the convocation. They believed that a brotherly exchange there would lessen antagonism and reduce the margins of misunderstanding.

Many bishops felt that convocations should draw up lists of candidates for bishops to present to their metropolitan both for the diocese and for the vicarates within the diocese. Convocations should be able to determine whether to open new parishes and to define their boundaries. Convocations should choose rectors, inspectors and assistant inspectors for diocesan seminaries and men's and women's schools, seminaries, orphanages and parishes to see that administrators and clergy were doing their jobs properly. The visitors should report annually to the convocation and recommend changes and dismissals when they thought they were needed. Convocations should supervise the diocesan press, appointing editors and officers, suppressing superfluous journals and papers and/or establishing new media when they were necessary. Convocations would have the power to commit funds to needful projects and to rescind funds being wasted. Convocations would supervise homes for migrant workers, retired clergy, widows and orphans, to see that they sufficiently met living requirements. All in all, the bishops generally regarded the future convocation as the motivating organ of the diocesan administration, taking over many functions now handled by the Synod.

Many of the same bishops who hoped convocations would be the medium of fruitful mutual exchange among the clergy and the laity and between them and their bishops stated that the final disposition of the resolutions of convocations would be in the hands of the bishop of the diocese. If he approved, recommendations from the convocations would become operational. If he did not, they would not. No opportunity should arise for the convocation to override the final disposition of the bishop. If an unresolvable clash developed between a diocesan convocation and its bishop, then it would seem wise for the metropolitan and his synod to retire the bishop and appoint a new one.

Most bishops conceded that diocesan convocations, like ecclesiastical courts, should be open to the Orthodox public. It would be necessary to limit the coverage these sessions would receive in the secular press, but each convocation would have to work out those limitations on an individual basis. Secrecy was not a good rule, because leakage to the press would occur anyway and leakages generally led to distortion. The full protocol of diocesan convocations, noting speakers as they occurred by name, should be available to the public within fourteen days after the conclusion of any convocation.[20]

Most of the bishops believed that the clergy should have a powerful voice in civil organs of government in the Russian Empire. The church had a historical mission as a bulwark of the Russian state. In times of trouble, it had usually been the church which had pulled civil authorities out of their lethargy and propelled them to the defense of the Russian people and the safeguarding of their church. Now was such a time. The history of the Greek church, both in the Byzantine era and under the infidel Turks, also witnessed that the church was a bulwark of faith and civilization. The canons of the Seventh Ecumenical Council and the regional councils of Carthage (251) and Constantinople (861) as well as the scriptures themselves indicated that the clergy should have a significant voice in civil affairs. Bishops and clergy were pastors over the same flocks that the civil authorities governed and could not help but become involved in their social and political aspirations, too.

Some bishops, like Evlogii of Kholm and Dmitri of Kazan, were cautious about involving the clergy in civil government. Evlogii and Dmitri thought it best to limit the activities of the clergy to those circumstances directly affecting the church as an institution—such as church construction, schools and charitable institutions. Bishops Mikhail Ermakhov of Smolensk and Vladimir Blagorazumov of Ekaterinburg also had serious misgivings about clergy in politics, fearing that a French-style anticlericalism would result. A backlash might secure the separation of church and state.

Bishop Mikhail Temnorussov of Minsk noted that the Council of Constantinople of 861 had specifically forbidden clergy and prelates from taking government titles and dignities. They could be involved as churchmen, but not as civil functionaries. Peter the Great's placing the clergy on the civil service rolls was contrary to the canons of that council. The bishop of Kostroma noted that various church fathers— such as Sts. Gregory the Great, Basil the Great and Ambrose of Milan—had cautioned churchmen involved in civil affairs to tread lightly, to "render to Caesar the things that are Caesar's and to God the things that are God's." Mikhail Temnorussov went on to say that it was unfortunate that Constantine the Great, after Christianizing his government, had appointed bishops and clergymen to positions of secular responsibility and subordinated civil bureaucrats to their command. That not only distracted the churchmen from their rightful occupations but also opened the road for the secular authorities to intervene in church affairs.[21]

More recent examples of participation in the affairs of the civil authorities by the Russian clergy came from the Time of Troubles, particularly the years 1612-1618, when priests, bishops and deacons were present at the various *zemskie sobory* that elected the Romanov dynasty and brought together the warring factions of Russia to expel foreigners and unite the divided land. The political regime of the eighteenth century deliberately excluded the clergy from all government organs because the clergy, elected out of the local community, often sided with the interests of the common people against the government and the depredations of the landowners and *nouveaux riches*. The clergy antagonized the power structure and so they, together with their peasant followers, were depoliticized. During the 1860s the question of involving the clergy had arisen again and, because of the attitude of Filaret Drozdov, metropolitan of Moscow, got nowhere. Still, Orthodox bishops were automatically members of the upper houses of parliament in Rumania and Austria-Hungary.[22]

The laws of June 12, 1890, and June 11, 1892, governing membership of *zemstvo* and city governments specifically forbade the Orthodox clergy to either stand for election to those bodies or even to vote for the members.[23] The excuse reportedly given by the Procurator to the State Council was that such participation was contrary to the canons of the church and that the stature of the priest in his community would be damaged if he became involved in partisan politics. The directives of the 1890s ran directly counter to the laws of January 1, 1864, and June 16, 1870, promulgated by Alexander II, which specifically included the Orthodox clergy among those who were both eligible to stand for election and eligible to vote. All of this was peculiar if one bore in mind Pobedonostsev's repeated protestations that he had advanced the influence of the clergy.

Antonii Sokolov of Chernigov and Arsenii Briantsev of Kharkov found it especially strange that the State Council would issue restrictive *ukazy* at a time when there was mounting public criticism of the clergy for their aloofness from social and political interests. Members of *zemstvo* institutions and the civil bureaucracy did not hesitate to subject the clergy to belittling and scathing attacks, both in their public offices and in the secular press. Furthermore, in his manifesto of February 26, 1903, the Tsar had urged the clergy to play an active role in public social affairs. It was absurd to have them legally forbidden to participate in times of change and turmoil, to exclude them from active participation in the social and cultural developments of the people. The church had been the mainstay of civilization, both in the East and the West, over the past nineteen hundred years. That civilization was undergoing severe strain and attack. To exclude the church from participation in public events was a form of cultural suicide. To study the history of Graeco-Roman law as it filtered down into the Christian societies that succeeded classical times is to discover the humanizing influences of the Christian tradition on history. It was strange to hear both government bureaucrats, who regarded themselves as the mainstay of order in the empire, and the radical intelligentsia joining to exclude the church.

The clergy were the people to whom the masses turned for comfort and leadership in times of trouble. One heard regularly of child abandonment, murder of children and wives and rising rates of crime among the masses. If the authorities ever expected to restore civil tranquility based upon respect for the human person, they could not exclude priests from public life. Remove the healing influence of the church and the humble Russian masses become a raging mob. The year 1905 was a sufficient lesson.[24]

The public was crying out for the establishment of some durable community at the lowest level of Russian life to replace decaying social forms left over from pre-Emancipation days. The Orthodox parish was the natural nucleus around which these new communities could form. To leave priests out of *zemstvo* and city organizations was to strip them of constructive influence. If the new legal and social structures envisioned in government manifestos—from the Toleration Manifesto of April to the October Manifesto—had the remotest hope of succeeding, the government needed the fullest cooperation of the clergy.

Furthermore, it was unthinkable that while all other elements in Russian society were attaining freedom the church would remain excluded and shackled. Public disorder became serious in the very years when the clergy had been restricted. They would be far more influential and respected when openly participating in public life than when carrying out police-spying functions. If authorities wished strong peasant participation in the new political structures, then the clergy, their natural leaders, would have to be allowed to participate. The socialist parties, standing for election to the State Duma, were antagonistic towards the church and would do their utmost to weaken it and lessen its influence. Priests had to have the right to stand for election and to urge their parishioners to vote. The church was about to be left as just the first denomination of the empire and would no longer be defended by law from the depredations of other denominations and political forces. It was in mortal danger. If it were destroyed, the whole fabric of Russian civilization would come tumbling down. Likewise, the hierarchy must be represented in the highest councils of government—the State Council, the Council and Committee of Ministers—where they could speak freely, without reprisals from the Procurator or other government officials.[25] In every independent state in the Balkan peninsula the Orthodox clergy and hierarchy had the right to participate in public affairs without restraint, even in the Austro-Hungarian Empire, where the Orthodox church was distinctly the minority religion. It was ridiculous to distrust the Orthodox church in the largest Orthodox state in the world.

The canons of the church specifically charged the clergy with the primary responsibility for educating children. Canon 10 of the Seventh Ecumenical Council was explicit that no priest or hierarch could renege on that responsibility without seriously violating his priesthood and teaching duty. No state, therefore, had the right to deprive the priest of that function. It followed that all educational undertakings by the Senate must have due regard for the influence and right of the church to teach. It was inescapable that clergy be involved in state education. Furthermore, in relations between the Orthodox administration and the Ministry of Public Education—not always harmonious—participation of clergy and bishops in the government would help overcome hostility and suspicion.

The bishops of Kholm and Volhynia pointed out that in certain areas of the empire, if public education were taken away from the church the very Russian nationality of the citizens would be in jeopardy. In their areas in particular, Polish and latent Uniate sympathies would turn large numbers of people into Poles or Ruthenians culturally, and they would not only be lost to the Orthodox church but to the Russian nation as well. Therefore, it was essential that education be under the strictest supervision of the church.[26]

The bishops of Ekaterinburg and Smolensk did not agree.

Starting from the position that the church was about to be
fully liberated from secular controls, they felt that clergy
should reciprocate by staying out of partisan political strife.
When actions of civil authorities touched on the interests
of the church, then the church, through its representatives,
could negotiate acceptable solutions. Otherwise, it would be
demeaning for the church and its servants to be involved in
the hassle of politics. The two bishops were very much alone
in that line of thought.[27]

*   *   *

Reform of the Orthodox parish was the most important
reform the church had to attend to. Virtually every bishop
noted in his remarks that the parish was dead, reduced to a
mere caricature of itself, which explained the indifference
and antagonism to religion that was so widespread in Russia.
The fearful danger was that the newly aroused masses, listen-
ing for the first time to the blandishments of the revolutionary, socialist and atheistic intelligentsia, would abandon
the church in large numbers. Only a vital parish, in the communities where the Russian masses lived, would prevent mass
defection and assure that the new order would be imbued
with the humanizing principles of religion.[28]

The parish could become the democratizing unit in the
community. Here, like in no other place, the mighty and the
humble met on an equal footing. God, in his majesty, recognized no earthly titles, positions or distinctions. No person
knew what order of priorities God had. The gospels clearly
indicated that divine prejudice was in favor of the little
people, the poor and the lowly. If there ever was a levelling
and equalizing ideology it was the gospel of the brotherhood
of all people. One need not read far into the proclamations
and formulations of modern radical socialist parties to recognize that they had plagiarized most of their inspiration directly from Christian tradition. However, they had beggared
it by removing the eschatological content of the gospels and
injecting violence and hatred as the means to attain their
utopias. By contrast, the truth of the gospels could have an
electrifying effect on the Russian masses, if the parish could

be revived as an all-embracing unit at the most basic level of society.

The first order was to grant the Orthodox parish legal status as a juridical entity entitled to incorporate and become a property-owning institution. The parish would manage its own finances and the support of its clergy. Substantial subsidies would be required from the government to support the church establishment, and salaries of pastors would have to be supplemented from outside the newly incorporated parishes for a long time to come. Several bishops recalled, however, that large tracts of church property were "administered" by the state and that the state, drawing vast sums from those properties, had an obligation to continue to subsidize the church.[29]

Once liberated, the parish would have the right to inaugurate programs like building schools, orphanages and charitable institutions, on its own or together with other parishes in its region. Bishop Georgii Orlov (1839?-1912) of Astrakhan, who himself served as a parish priest in the 1860s, envisioned the parish as becoming a type of commune (*obshchina*), responsible for the material welfare of its members as well as their spiritual edification. Various credit organizations would emerge under parish sponsorship to allow peasants and town dwellers to borrow funds necessary to establish small workshops and businesses and to buy or improve their farms. The parish, and whatever property it could acquire, would be the collateral for credit unions. Parishioner ingenuity would then seek out untapped sources of revenue with which to expand the parish capital and their own wealth. Gradually, the net worth of entire parish communes would appreciate and allow them to undertake more ambitious projects. In the course of time, the parish would become a self-sustaining unit and no longer need outside subsidies.

Metropolitan Antonii of Petersburg, Bishop Evlogii of Kholm and Archbishop Arsenii of Kharkov were among those, however, who warned against the parish's becoming too much of a financial organization at the risk of losing sight of its spiritual goals. Too great an emphasis upon property management and aggrandizement might easily lead it into transactions that were detrimental to the spiritual welfare of its members. They agreed that the parish could be the catalyst that sponsored and encouraged such developments, but community properties and investments should be separated from strictly church properties and investments. To avert the diversion of proper parish focus, the diocesan administration should supervise parish undertakings. Abuses could be headed off or corrected before the parish was harmed.

Bishop Vladimir Sokolovskii (1852-1916?) of Ekaterinburg suggested that the actual title to the parish properties—the church building, school, pastor's residence and other properties directly related to the performance of the cult and propagation of the gospel—be vested in the name of the diocesan bishop. That way the danger of factionalism in a parish or attempts by hostile parties to seize control of the essential properties of a parish would be avoided. Vladimir noted that in North America and Canada that was the way the Catholic administration handled the problem and was thus able to avoid losing essential church properties. He suggested that if this had been the case in France before the traumatic separation finalized in 1905, the bitterness and litigation going on about which properties belonged to the church and which did not could have been avoided. If such a day should come in Russia, Vladimir implied, it would be better to be prepared for it.[30]

There was also the danger, with the issuing of the Law of Toleration and the subsequent step-up in proselytizing activities by Old Believers, sectarians and Catholics, that parishes, or the majority therein, could be misled into joining one or another of those denominations. Unless the essential property of the parish was safely in the hands of the bishop, there was the immediate prospect that church buildings and other essential properties could be transferred to those denominations. It was a well-known fact that Catholics in the western and southwestern provinces were agitating for the restoration of churches that had been Uniate or Latin before the confiscations of 1839 and 1875. With the prospect of the election of an Old Believer Patriarch and Raskol insistence that they were the true Orthodox, they could easily mislead unsophisticated parishioners. Metropolitan Vladimir Bogoiavlenskii believed that full autonomy in disposing of parish income and property was contrary to the canons of the church. Properties once invested in the church ceased to be ordinary commodities to be bought and sold on the open market—they became dedicated to God and the permanent property of the church community. They had too much significance to be under the simple jurisdiction of an individual parish and should be administered under the strict supervision of the diocese. Nikandr Molchanov of Lithuania, Dmitri Sambikin of Kazan and Afanasii Parkhomovich of the Don concurred that the parish should have only partial autonomy in disposal of its income and properties.

But Leonid Okropiridze (1865-1919?), exarch of Georgia, did not agree. He believed that undue control from the diocese left the parish without initiative and with every cause for the development of animosities between parish officials and diocesan administrators. He believed that parishes should have exclusive control over incomes and properties that pertained to them alone, while the diocese would administer and acquire properties on a larger scale for its needs.[31]

Bishop Filaret Lintchevskii of Viatka pointed out that when the Synod forbade parish trustees (October 12, 1868) to determine how parish funds were to be utilized, it violated canon law. The term *ekklesia* in the canons meant a community, not a building. Canon law intended that outside interests not interfere in the community's disposition of its affairs, including its funds. The canons said nothing about forbidding chosen members of the community to dispose of funds in the community's name. By misconstruing the meaning of the canons, the Synod, through its local consistory and *blagochinie* appointees, had robbed the parish of its right to manage income and properties.[32]

Bishop Arsenii Stadnitskii of Pskov wondered how anyone could expect the parishioners to become vitally interested in the welfare of their parishes if they were allowed merely to provide money and not have a word in how it was going to be put to use. Archbishop Stefan Arkhangelskii of Mogilev was of the same conviction, and warned that if the parishioners were left out of that vitally important part of parish administration they might as well be left out altogether, because they would not be interested anyway.

Sergei Stragorodskii of Finland, Tikhon Belavin of North America and Gurii Burstasovskii of Simbirsk saw no conflict between diocesan and parish administrations over the matter of income and properties. Clashes over those matters would be resolved in the diocesan convocation, a center of brotherly and trusting exchange. If parishes were really heard and respected in the convocation, they would see that it was to their own interest to coordinate efforts and undertakings with broader diocesan efforts. As far as canonical interdiction of parish control of parish finances, it simply didn't exist if the meaning of *ekklesia* as community were properly understood. Bishop Evfimii Shchastnev (1839-1913) of the Enisei diocese noted that as long as the church depended upon civil authorities for a large part of its revenue, it would be a fiction to presume to exclude laymen from making decisions in church finances.[33]

When it came to the thorny problem of who would appoint parish priests, most bishops, particularly Antonii Khrapovitskii and Sergei Stragorodskii, insisted that they alone had the canonical authority to appoint them. Many granted that parish elders and/or the parish assembly could have the right to veto candidates they did not feel met parish requirements, but the authority to name pastors belonged to the bishop. It was his responsibility to ensure the good government of parishes and to see that priests were capable men of moral integrity. Allowing parishes to select their own pastors risked choosing men who pandered to the vested interests of powerful personalities. The weak and ineffectual Protestant pastor was an example the reformed Orthodox parish should avoid. Parishes ought to have the right to request certain candidates to be their pastors or to suggest candidates when the pastorate became vacant, but the final disposition remained with the bishop. The energy with which the Catholic church operated in west and southwest

Russia was the result of a dedicated pastorate under the direct control of its bishops. The contrast with the weakness of Lutheran pastors in Finland, who were under obligation to those who appointed them, was striking. The First, Fourth and Seventh Ecumenical Councils, as well as the councils of Antioch, Carthage and Laodicea, all forbade election of priests because elections were all too easily manipulated from the outside by secular interests that did not have spiritual matters as their primary concern.

Khrapovitskii noted that election to *zemstvo* offices and the elections currently being conducted for the new State Duma were usually accomplished through the use of bribes and the consumption of much vodka. He shuddered to think that that procedure would be used to select pastors. Metropolitan Vladimir of Moscow opposed elected clergy because he felt parishioners would be inclined to vote for popular local men—perhaps not even literate or schooled in the traditions of the church—who would not have genuine religious vocations.

Alexei Molchanov of Stavropol noted that the elective principle among Old Believers was common but not very successful. Oftentimes the Old Believer communities were embarrassed by their own choices because of the public life of their chosen pastors, and oftentimes their pastors were so unlettered that they led their congregations into such sects as the Khlysts, Dukhobors or Stundists.[74]

A minority of bishops, however, felt that parishes should have the right to choose their own pastors. They noted that such church fathers as Sts. Basil the Great and Cyprian of Carthage urged the closest involvement of the people in the selection of their pastors. The Fourth Council of Carthage in 436 sanctioned the selection of pastors by their flocks, and the bishop was even forbidden to depose a pastor or prevent the ordination of a candidate without the approval of the people. The archbishops of Novgorod and Pskov pointed out that the elective principle had been common in the pre-Petrine church in Russia and had survived in some areas till the beginning of the nineteenth century.

Metropolitan Flavian of Kiev noted that there were

various ways to avoid having men who were not qualified elected to the pastorate. Diocesan authorities could simply insist that candidates for city pastorates have theological training in the higher ecclesiastical institutions, while those for rural pastorates would have to have at least seminary training. As the need for better-educated clergy arose, the diocese could impose higher educational standards. The archbishop of Kazan, together with the bishops of Podolia and Perm, urged recruitment of candidates for the priesthood from secular institutions in order to broaden the experience and perspective of the priesthood. They would have to pass examinations in theology and church law before being ordained, but would be a welcome infusion of new influences. The process of electing a pastor would come under the supervision of the bishops, just as the selection of a diocesan bishop would come under the supervision of the metropolitan. The bishop would be able to ensure that all canonical regulations were met before the man was officially installed as pastor of a parish.

The Olonets Commission, under Archimandrite Faddei Uspenskii, suggested that in case a parish did not have any candidate in mind, the diocese would present dossiers of candidates that they thought qualified to the parish council or parish assembly. Then, after a decision was made, the bishop would confirm their choice. In that way, with the parish selecting and the bishop confirming, all canonical requirements would be met.

Archbishops Agafangel Preobrazhenskii of Riga, Tikhon Troitskii of Irkutsk and Bishop Evlogii Georgievskii of Kholm believed that at least one-half of the parishioners should be involved in the election of their pastor to make his election acceptable. Women who were heads of households would have equal electoral rights with men. The protocol of an election assembly would be made available to the bishop for perusal before final moving of a pastor into a parish. Electing a pastor should take place in the church itself, not in a school or some secular hall.[35]

Flavian of Kiev suggested that if a parish could not agree on a priest within two months after a vacancy, then the bishop should have the right to appoint a pastor. If there arose serious complaints about a pastor, they would be brought to the bishop. He would admonish the pastor to rectify the causes of the complaints—such as fees for services and administration of sacraments, one of the loudest complaints the Russian peasants had against their pastors—and if no improvement occurred, the bishop would remove the pastor from his parish. Then the parish would elect another pastor. If more complaints came to the bishop and they could not be arbitrated, then the bishop would not only remove the second pastor, but would appoint his successor forthwith and the parish would lose its right to elect. The parish could not simply dismiss a pastor. That was a Protestant procedure which did not conform to Orthodox canons.

If the pastor of a parish, duly elected and duly confirmed, turned out to be a scandal because of alcoholism or whoring or any other type of conduct not becoming to a priest, the bishop would remove him from the parish whether or not the parishioners wanted him to go. In that case also, the bishop would name the successor and the parish would again forfeit its right to elect.

The parish would have the right to establish the salary and living arrangements of its priest, with the cooperation and supervision of the bishop. The priest would not be forced to accept starvation wages and humiliating conditions that would cripple an effective pastorate.

If a parish elected a man who was carrying out his pastoral functions properly and creditably, but the parish nevertheless insisted upon his removal, the bishop would remove him if the pastor himself was willing to go. If he was not, he stayed. If, however, he was willing to go, the bishop would name his successor and the parish would lose the right to elect. In fact, if a parish proved to be simply cantankerous and would not cooperate with their priests, complaining against them and having them removed, the bishop would strip them of their right to elect for five-, ten- or fifteen-year periods.

A priest, elected by a parish and confirmed by the bishop, who refused to go to the parish would be brought before the proper ecclesiastical court. If he refused to comply then, he would be defrocked.[36]

Most bishops felt that the Finnish parish system should be extended to the rest of the empire. Three bishops—Antonii Sokolov (1850-1911) of Chernigov, Serafim Meshcheriakov (1837?-1932) of Polotsk and Antonii Khrapovitskii of Volhynia—had reservations. All three felt that it was too close to the Lutheran parish organization and, therefore, undesirable as a model in Russia proper. However, Antonii of Volhynia thought it could be adopted with some changes to make it more truly Russian. The Finnish parish was made up of both a parish assembly and a parish council, the latter elected by the former from among eligible parishioners. The council, presided over by the priest (in the Lutheran parish by a lay administrator), was the day-to-day governing board. The council was responsible to the assembly and had to present annual accountings of its activities. The council was made up of ten to twelve members, including the priests, parish elders and elected parish members.

The parish assembly met twice a year, in keeping with the norms of the ecumenical church for meetings of regional sobors. Meetings occurred during the Easter season and in October. Women had equal rights in the assembly as men, providing they were of age and headed households or were independently employed.

In Finland the local civil, *uezd* officials were expected to participate in parish assemblies and to ensure that the parish did not intrude in areas that civil authorities believed were properly theirs. Bishops disliked that because it allowed too much political interference and because it was a typically Protestant form of caesaropapism.

All parish trusteeships, brotherhoods and special organizations predating the establishment of legal parishes would be subordinated to the parish assembly. Where brotherhoods and trusteeships included several parishes, negotiations between the diocese, the *blagochinie* and the parishes would work out the details of whether these organizations should be subordinated to one parish alone or to one of the other two levels of administration.[37]

The key to overall improvement of parish life, however, lay in improving educational standards in the seminaries and the social standards of the Orthodox clergy. The Kostroma Commission noted that there had been piecemeal attempts made by the Synod under Pobedonostsev to improve parishes in the past few years, but they had remained largely ineffective because the status of the clergy had not kept pace with social and cultural developments of the times. One of the most immediate needs was to end the mercenary relationship between priest and parishioners over the administration of sacraments and liturgies. This was where the mass of Orthodox people dealt primarily with their pastors, and it left an acrimonious atmosphere that affected all the rest of their relationships. Konstantin Bulichev noted that despite the often heroic labors of his clergy, this single problem poisoned relationships so badly that pastors were looked upon as exploiters of the poor, just like bankers, creditors and tax collectors.[38]

Metropolitan Vladimir of Moscow and many others felt that the salary scale of the clergy should be fixed at a prorated basis, just like the salaries of various city and *zemstvo* officials. They proposed that collection of those salaries be part of the regular city and *zemstvo* tax system, just as with the salaries of other officials. Veniamin of Kaluga believed that the country pastor should receive a salary of 1,200 rubles a year, while a city pastor should receive 1,500 rubles. Salaries of deacons would be 500 rubles per annum for country deacons and 800 rubles per annum for those in the city. Corresponding salaries would be apportioned for psalmists and other servants of the church.

Many of the bishops, including Sergei Stragorodskii of Finland and Dmitri Sambikin of Kazan, felt that salaries should come entirely from parishes. The bishop of Stavropol felt that Orthodox parishes should function in the matter of salaries just as Lutheran congregations. Annually, at the parish assembly, the salary of the clergy would be established, and the members of the parish would obligate themselves by tithe to meet the salary. The parish would be obligated to its priest in this vital matter, and wrangling with civil authorities over clerical salaries would be avoided. Konstantin of Samara believed that if a parish did not wish to support a pastor adequately, then he should be free to transfer to another parish where he would be supported. Parishes who lost pastors that way might find themselves more interested in supporting their clergy in the future. In Konstantin's diocese, beginning September 1905, peasants in many villages seized parish lands and forced their priests to pay land taxes like everyone else.[39] Evlogii Georgievskii felt that the self-sustaining parish was a goal to work towards, but in areas where the people were poor and the Orthodox population thin, an attempt to impose such a regime in 1905 would alienate parishioners. The Kholm area was one where Latin pastors and clandestine Uniate pastors from Galicia were only too happy to take advantage of unpleasantries between Orthodox priests and their people.[40]

Virtually every bishop insisted that it was essential to relieve the clergy of the onerous obligation to maintain records and tax rolls in their parishes. Those uncanonical civil requirements did enormous harm to the relationship of the pastor to his flock. The priest not only aided monied interests and civil tax collectors, but was often the cause of arrests and imprisonments of his parishioners. By law they were obligated to report anti-state activities to the police when they came to their attention. If they did not they were themselves subject to penalties. Too many Orthodox priests had seen the inside of a prison in that way. In 1905, it was a real agony for the conscientious priest to know what to do. These requirements, and their attendant penalties, seriously compromised a priest in his pastoral duties. There were times when the priest should support his parishioners in defiance of civil authorities. In the future, records kept by priests should be strictly for ecclesiastical purposes and not open to the civil authorities. Parish record books should be kept only for parish and diocesan archives, and be confidential.[41]

*   *   *

Various other problems concerned the bishops, among them the necessity to improve preaching among the Orthodox clergy. Too many were content to perform ritual in the most mechanical fashion, without trying to enliven it with the word. Ioann Sergiev of Kronstadt was an effective preacher they could all learn from. Another problem was drunkenness among the Orthodox clergy—a scandal not only to the people who were too much given to that evil themselves, but positively embarrassing in areas where Catholic, Lutheran and Old Believer clergy were models of abstinence by comparison. One bad priest who drank and caroused ruined the reputation of all his fellow priests, even though they might be models of sobriety.[42]

Konstantin of Samara wished to restore the practice of public confession to the parish. A priest should have the right to banish unrepentant parishioners from church services unless they mended their ways. No need to secure approval from the bishop should be attached to this local form of excommunication.

The exarch of Georgia and the archbishop of Mogilev, reflecting a growing sentiment, suggested that pastoral activities could be increased and made more effective if deaconesses were restored to the Orthodox church. A deaconess could function as a sort of lay nun, uncloistered, who would aid priests in parish visitations, attend to the sick, teach in the parish schools and otherwise relieve the clergy of burdensome details of pastoral work and bring to their attention situations the priest himself would not readily know about. Deaconesses, functioning in a sisterly manner towards their fellow parishioners, would do much to create close ties of *sobornost'* between the parish and its clergy and the church.[43]

Acquisition of church properties was one of the thorniest problems the Orthodox church had to deal with. Since Peter, the church could not acquire properties without the express consent of the Tsar. The church could not purchase properties on the open market or receive bequests on its own authority. Originally, this restriction had applied to virtually all classes and organizations in the empire, but during the nineteenth century various reforms made the passing of real estate and movable properties from one party to another easier as the Russian economy moved into the capitalist phase. But the church had been paralyzed in all of its activities by the government and was one of the few organizations left which could not act in its own name or to its own advantage in the matter of property.

Every parish or diocese to whom someone wished to give property had to appeal to the Synod to intercede with the Emperor before the exchange could be made legal. The process was incredibly complicated and took an extraordinary long time to complete. Often donations desperately needed were never finalized because the donors became frustrated with the red tape involved and gave up. This, in turn, forced churchmen and church organizations to rely upon direct monetary collections from their faithful for that part of their revenue that did not come from the State Treasury. It was a vicious circle which reinforced itself at every turn. With the promise of a Duma, it was virtually certain that the matter of church properties would be examined, with the prospect that the non-Orthodox among its membership would make the problem more, not less, difficult.

In theory, limitations upon the church's right to acquire property were imposed to prevent dioceses and monasteries from acquiring properties that would entail more expense than profit. That was the explanation that came out of the Senate on September 19, 1877, and was refined in an explanation that came out of the Synod in June the following year.[44]

Some bishops believed that if the acquisition of church properties had to be cleared with civil authorities at all, it should be done at the local level, rather than with the Tsar via the medium of the Synod. Diocesan authorities could clear prospective purchases or bequests with local provincial officials and, once parishes received legal status, they could negotiate with local *zemstvo* officials for clearance for their acquisitions. Pitirim Oknov suggested that the practice of clearing with the authorities be observed only if the acquisition exceeded 10,000 rubles in value. Most of the bishops, however, including the metropolitans of St. Petersburg and Kiev, thought that the whole entangled business of clearing acquisitions with civil authorities should be abolished.[45]

Many bishops pointed out that, whatever the explanation for the laws against the church, the real reason was that the civil authorities did not wish to have properties become tax exempt once they passed into the hands of the church. Most bishops declared that that fear was begging the issue, because most of the funds and properties the church raised were spent upon schools, orphanages, workers' dormitories, cemeteries, dispensaries and hostels—besides, of course, what was spent for the upkeep of church buildings, clergy residences, monasteries and convents—so there was little property held merely for profit. If it would make the authorities happier, those properties held simply for profit could be exempted from *mort main* and could be taxed just as any other non-exempt properties. Properties used for the maintenance of charitable and educational activities were generally exempted from taxation anyway, whether they belonged to the church or some other organization. Brotherhoods and trusteeships already could buy and sell properties at will. Thus, there were loopholes in the tax system anyway.

The bishops found it peculiar that when the October Manifesto guaranteed to all citizens of the empire the right to exchange properties according to their own interests, the same privilege was not extended to the Orthodox church. Other religious groups now possessed those rights. Over the past thirty years, *zemstvo* institutions that had set up public institutions such as schools, hospitals and homes of various sorts and had properties directly devoted to their support had been given tax-exempt status. Those organizations had no legal restrictions upon them when it came to acquiring and disposing of properties. Why then was the church shackled with restrictions when it operated institutions for similar purposes? Donors preferred to give to those organizations because donating them to the church involved too much time-consuming red tape. Whether a peasant wanted to give a cottage for the housing of a parish school or a merchant wanted to give some land or building, upon discovering the complications involved, they usually decided not to.

Not only should the church as an institution be relieved
of restrictions upon its acquiring and disposing of properties,
but so should the clergy. Orthodox priests, since the Law on
Toleration and the October Manifesto, were the sole religious servants in the empire who still did not possess the
right to acquire and dispose of properties in their own
names. Not only should they have the individual right to
acquire and dispose of property, but they should be allowed
to incorporate as a body, diocese by diocese, so that they
could collectively dispose of properties for the mutual welfare of their entire social caste. Various insurance societies,
credit societies, retirement funds, retirement homes and other
socially necessary organizations could be collectively operated
for the benefit of the clergy, without interference from diocesan administrators or from the Synod. Personal and col-
lective rights had now been granted to the clergy of other
denominations and sects. Not to do so for the Orthodox was
a strange kind of discrimination.[46]

*   *   *

Archbishop Arsenii Briantsev and Bishop Antonii
Khrapovitskii felt that the strictures laid upon the Old Believers in the great Moscow Sobor of 1666-1667 were much
too harsh and that at the opening of the twentieth century
they should be greatly softened or even abolished. Many Old
Believers were basically Orthodox in their beliefs. To continue to anathematize them and malign them was counter-
productive, as the course of the past two and a half centuries had shown. Leniency and conciliation would draw them
to the state church instead of driving them into the arms of
sectarians.

The Old Believers had been anathematized for the benefit
of the civil authority. Their recalcitrance, both to the state
and the state church, stemmed from genuine religious persecution. The state church should go more than half-way to
hold out the olive branch to them and try to effect a fraternal
conciliation. It would be necessary, however, to distinguish
between the various groups of Old Believers. The Popovtsy
were Orthodox, but the Bezpopovtsy were not. Permission to

utilize their own rites could easily be granted to the Popovtsy
along the line of concessions initiated by Catherine the Great
and the establishment of the *Edinoverie* rite in 1800. Since
the reunion of the Uniates with the state church, many Uniate
usages were still quietly tolerated. The Old Believers themselves made much more of an issue of rites than the state
church needed to. A reconciliation would end two and a half
centuries of religious fratricide and begin to bring a measure
of civil tranquility. Much anti-government rioting and revolutionary propaganda had its origins among Old Believers.

Mikhail Temnorussov of Minsk noted that the liturgy
was closely bound with the problem of the Old Believers.
The Russian church, the offspring of the church of Byzantium, had never used the language of the Byzantine church—
Greek. Liturgies had been translated nearly a thousand years
ago into Slavonic. Slavonic itself had undergone many evolu-
tions in the past millennium, and now it was time to consider seriously translating the liturgy into modern spoken
Russian. To many of the Orthodox the sacredness of the
unchanged liturgy was a symbol of the authenticity of the
church. They had support from the Popovtsy. Reuniting with
the Old Believers and modernizing the language of the liturgies at the same time would be very difficult.[47]

Another problem of liturgical reform was the length of
the liturgies, particularly on feasts like Easter, the Protection of the Mother of God and the Assumption. Of the fifty
thousand churches of the empire, perhaps only a thousand
attempted to celebrate the liturgies fully. *Ad hoc* abbreviations prevailed elsewhere. Some kind of uniform approach
to shortening the number of hours would have to be made
to coincide with the faster pace of modern times and yet
preserve the essence and beauty of the Slavonic liturgy.

Serafim Meshcheriakov of Polotsk and Konstantin
Bulichev of Samara hoped that the coming sobor would not
only soften the strictures against the Old Believers but would
also find ways to facilitate the union of Old Catholics with
the Russian church. Old Catholics were without a head since
their split with the papacy in the 1870s and resembled the
Orthodox so closely in their teachings that union should come

rather easily.[48] Serafim hoped that Orthodox churchmen would not make an insurmountable issue of the *filioque*, because there was room in the Orthodox tradition for both versions of the procession of the Holy Spirit. The only reason Eastern churchmen had made an issue of it was because the Western church had insisted upon inserting it in the Creed. To expect Old Catholics to renounce that part of their tradition was asking a bit much, Serafim thought. The same was true of relations with the Anglican church. They could not be asked to renounce the *filioque* either. There was some question about the validity of Anglican orders, but Serafim hoped that Orthodox churchmen would take a more open view of the problem than the papacy had.[49]

In discussing liturgical reforms, Serafim hoped that the church would not insist upon narrow interpretation of texts and precedents, but would instead concentrate on making the liturgy meaningful to the simple worshipper. He noted that too often debates on liturgy centered upon conflicts with other churches. Each side insisted that its form of liturgical interpretation was correct and altered their usages to prove that the other side was wrong. Such pettiness, Serafim thought, should give way before the larger issue of how to involve the worshipper more fully in the liturgical drama and make the act of worshipping a more truly communal affair. Now, the clergy usually did the praying while the people watched or visited. Serafim noted that Stundists characterized the Orthodox liturgy as "boring" and "doing nothing."

On the other hand, the attitude of the missionary clergy of the Kishenev diocese was directly the opposite of Serafim's. The Kishenev missionaries felt that the Law of Toleration of April had no real significance for the church. Old Believers were schismatics, condemned in the great Moscow Sobor in the seventeenth century, and that was that. Whether the state wanted now to begin easing up on them was the state's business, but as far as the church was concerned nothing had changed. The schismatics had not changed their attitudes, they had not recognized themselves in error and they were still mortal enemies of the church. Reconciliation with sectarians was also impossible. The only difference between

April and autumn was that heretics and schismatics had become more dangerous to the church.

The coming all-Russian sobor would be obliged to reaffirm that Anglican orders were invalid, just as the orders of the Old Catholics. It would be obliged to uphold the Ecumenical Patriarchate's refusal to recognize the Bulgarian exarchate of 1870.[50] It would have to condemn and anathematize the former Greek Bishop Amvrosii and the Austrian hierarchy of Old Believers. Among other things, it would have to reaffirm the strictest condemnation of sectarians and rigidly prohibit religious and social intercourse among Orthodox and other Christian denominations. Not to do so would bring its own Orthodoxy into question. And finally, it would have to reaffirm that no one but a cleric who had taken monastic tonsure could be elevated to the episcopacy. No white clergyman, and certainly no married priest, could ever be considered for the rank of bishop.[51]

Thus, between September 1, 1905, and January 6, 1906, the Russian dioceses held special meetings and convocations. Bishops, clergy and academic experts drew up observations about the coming sobor. The overwhelming majority believed that the church was being strangled by state control and that speedy return to autonomy guaranteed by Byzantine canon law was vital. Only a few believed it unwise to call a sobor when the civil order was so turbulent. Most believed that if the church were to survive the national crisis, it could not wait for a suitable time. If the church were to contribute to reestablishing order, it would first have to have a sobor, reform itself and regain the public trust.

As a result of the publication of the October Manifesto, Konstantin Pobedonostsev retired as Procurator after twenty-five years of controlling the church. A final plea to the Tsar to veto a patriarchate and curtail Vadkovskii and his fellow bishops was ignored. The new Procurator was Prince Alexei Obolenskii (1856-1933), one of Witte's protégés in the Ministry of Finance, an assistant in the Committee of Ministers and a member of the State Council. Obolenskii had participated in the special conferences among Antonii and the Petersburg professors and had helped give the Committee of

Ministers background on the problems the church faced since Toleration. He was firmly convinced that a sobor at the earliest opportunity was crucial. The appointment of Witte as Prime Minister on October 17 and Obolenskii's appointment as Procurator on October 20, 1905, gave optimists hope that a new era was beginning for the Russian Orthodox church in particular and tsarist Russia in general.[52]

CHAPTER VI

The Pre-Sobor Commission (1906): For Sobor and Patriarch

The resignation of Pobedonostsev led to joy on the one hand and paralysis on the other. Obolenskii's appointment gave encouragement to expectations that the sobor would be summoned for the end of 1905 or simultaneously with the Duma in 1906. At the same time, the Synod and Procurator's bureaucracy was swept with confusion and indecision, because no one knew what authority they retained or whether their positions would even continue to exist. The thrust for reform gained momentum as individual prelates urged the Tsar to convene a sobor immediately. Antonii Vadkovskii was able, in December, to get from Nicholas a commitment to convene a sobor in 1906 when all the reports from the bishops were in and the Synod had had a chance to correlate and study them. Vadkovskii utilized Obolenskii's sympathy and concern as he had used Witte's a year earlier. Obolenskii, like Lev Tikhomirov, had flirted with radicalism and then settled down as an aristocratic liberal in the 1880s. A constant supporter of the *zemstvos* in the 1890s, he became well known to the Tsar as a member of the Finance Ministry and later as a member of the Committee of Ministers.

In the latter he became alert to the need to reform the state church, both for its own effectiveness and for the role it could play in stabilizing the political order. With Witte in the new office of Prime Minister and Obolenskii in the

Procurator's office, the imminent summoning of the all-Russian sobor seemed assured.

However, Obolenskii, Vadkovskii and various bishops and clergy—particularly Frs. Ioann Ianyshev (1826-1910), chaplain to the imperial family, and Alexander Zhelobovskii (1834-1910), chief chaplain of the army and navy, both appointed to membership in the Synod in 1905—were impressed by the loud public outcry which insisted that the reform question needed further study and that segments of the church not officially consulted should be consulted before the sobor was convened. White clergy and academy professors felt that further input was needed. Obolenskii, pushing simultaneously in the Council of Ministers for broader franchise in the Duma, agreed and ordered invitations to go out to a larger group of priests and laymen than Pobedonostsev had wished to involve.

There was broad consensus that the final step towards the sobor should be taken by a Pre-Sobor Commission, which would review the topics outlined in March 1905 in the Synod and enlarged upon in the reports from the bishops and the overall situation as it had changed during the past year. The Commission would bring experts and the various contending factors into one place in a face-to-face confrontation.

While these delicate adjustments were being made, Russia was degenerating into a political and social backlash resulting from violence and political disorder. Among the uglier expressions of this backlash was the rise of organizations like the Black Hundreds and the Union of Russian People. Pogroms against Jews in particular, against minorities in general and against the Russian peasants themselves became a regular feature of Russian public life as 1905 ended. These organizations, and others of similar stripe, operated with the knowledge and secret support of the Tsar and the political old guard and, in a number of cases, were spurred on by the active cooperation of the police.

Among those whom the Union of Russian People harassed and the Black Hundreds openly attacked were Orthodox priests who were known for their support of legal, social and political reforms or who had in any way criticized or befriended critics of the regime. Priests joined their flocks in demonstrations demanding land, better working conditions, reductions in land payments and taxes and an end to brutality by the authorities. After the Gaponovshchina, priests led their people in violence in other areas in 1905 and 1906, were arrested, invariably defrocked and imprisoned. A number of the Petersburg Thirty-Two were personally intimidated and placed under political penalties at the instigation of members of the Union or the Hundreds.[1]

Bishop Antonin Granovskii was one of the victims. Deposed as bishop of Narva in 1906 for preaching against the police and eventually even refusing to commemorate Nicholas II and the imperial family when he celebrated the liturgy, he was retired to Voskresenskii Monastery outside Petersburg but persuaded Metropolitan Antonii to allow him to live at the Alexandro-Nevskii Lavra instead. At the lavra he wrote pamphlets denouncing the conservative bishops, Khrapovitskii in the forefront, and set out on barefoot preaching tours in the capital that caused such notoriety that the metropolitan ordered him to cease. He was relatively silent in the years of reaction, at the personal insistence of Nicholas II.[2]

In the countryside, priests were put on notice that if they did not condemn revolutionaries and collaborate in rooting them out, they would be harassed and hounded right out of their churches. However, there were many fanatical monarchists among the clergy themselves to whom any criticism or action hostile to the dynasty was a sacrilege and an expression of deep "evil forces." They believed that even such extreme measures as lynchings and the Stolypin field courts were justified if the fabric of Russian Orthodox civilization was to be preserved. Among these were Antonii Khrapovitskii, bishop of Volhynia; Fr. Ioann Sergiev of Kronstadt, popular healer and preacher; Pitirim Oknov of Kursk, who armed monks in Putivl to fight peasant revolutionaries; and Archimandrite Vitalii Maksimenko (1873-1960) of the Pochaev Lavra. These men, and others like them, spoke out against revolutionaries, rioters and their sympathizers with enormous venom and urged the Hundreds on to larger and more bloody

ventures. Naturally, they approved the persecution and elimination of priests who sympathized with the revolution. When
Metropolitan Antonii flatly refused to bless or endorse the
actions of the Union, the Union launched bitter personal attacks upon him, besmirched his name in pamphlets and patriotic rallies that affected people from the Tsarina down to
the lowest peasant, and slowly wore him down so that the
last four or five years of his life were a kind of martyrdom
without blood. Fellow prelates, Flavian of Kiev and Antonii
of Volhynia, allowed the Hundreds to use the great
Pecherskaia and Pochaev Monasteries as headquarters and
the monastery presses to run off their muckraking sheets.

At the time, during 1905 and 1906, serious peasant disorders spread from province to province while elections were
going on for the convocation of the State Duma. Peasants,
hungry for land, seized the fields and forests of monasteries,
cathedrals and churches, and even the small parcels of land
set aside for the support of their priests. In the Duma, they
demanded that the church be stripped of its properties for
distribution among peasants. They resented the thousands
of acres held in the name of the church when they were
charged fees for sacraments and liturgies. They believed that
priests should pay the same land fees they did. In St. Petersburg, the collapse of Gapon's Workmen's Society left the
workers without organization, and they gravitated towards
the sway of the Petersburg Soviet. Churchmen struggled to
turn the clock back and sent out students from the academy
to preach against violence, drunkenness and whoring, but it
was a losing battle. The average priest was caught between
the rage of his own flock and the intimidation of the Black
Hundreds and their sympathizers and supporters among the
hierarchy, while the simple Russian peasant became one of
the most radical anticlericals in the land.[3]

In those darkening circumstances, the Pre-Sobor Commission formally opened in the Alexander Nevskii Monastery
in St. Petersburg, 8:00 p.m., Monday, March 6, 1906. The
metropolitan of St. Petersburg delivered the opening address,
noting the propriety of their gathering in the Nevskii Monastery, the site near where Prince Alexander had withstood

the onslaught of alien foes, inspired by the pretensions of the papacy to attack Russia during the dark days when she was succumbing to Mongol hordes pouring out of the east. He warned that menacing forces were again afoot, poised to destroy Russia, her Tsar and her holy Orthodox faith, and that was what underscored the importance of their gathering. From them would come the suggestions and an agenda to present to the general sobor, which would be the catalyst of a new outpouring of spiritual life in Russia and a strengthening of the Orthodox faith in her people.[4]

On Wednesday, the same assembly of experts gathered in the Church of the Seven Councils for the solemn liturgy inaugurating the Commission, celebrated by Arsenii Stadnitskii, bishop of Pskov. At the end, Bishop Stefan Arkhangelskii of Mogilev delivered at lengthy address, emphasizing that while the substance of the Orthodox faith never changes, a glance at the history of the church and of Russia indicated how the church had adapted itself to changing external situations through the centuries: first, as a suffragan see under Constantinople, when Russia's faith was the faith of a child, then maturing through the intervening centuries till the reign of Peter, who endangered the church by opening his window to the West and letting in a host of alien intellectual and spiritual influence but at the same time equipped the church with the means to withstand those influences by establishing theological academies, elevating the educational level of the clergy and grounding his reforms in the institution of the Holy Synod. The church, Stefan declared, had been abundantly productive in spiritual life during the intervening two centuries, producing such illuminating individuals as Dmitri of Rostov, Innokentii of Irkutsk, Mitrofan and Tikhon of Voronezh, Feodosii of Uglich, Amvrosii of Optina and Serafim of Sarov, but now the synodal structure was a restraint which crippled the growth of the Russian church and clouded her light before the peoples of the world. There were positive developments that a reform of the Russian church would accentuate: the growth of the church in the Far East, for instance, and the desire on the part of foreign believers, especially Anglicans and Old Catholics, to profit from closer ties with the light of Eastern Christianity. Now the church was faced with the problem of restructuring itself along lines consistent with the principle of *sobornost'* so that all elements in the Russian church would be able to join in fruitful, fraternal labor to free the church from the Petrine restrictions and allow it to cope with the threats and problems that beset it.

After a hymn, the metropolitan of St. Petersburg again addressed the assembly, telling them that the Tsar was solidly behind them in their deliberations and that his interest in the problem of church reform was not recent. He outlined the course of events since 1903 and went on to say that not since 1714, when a council met in Moscow to condemn Calvinism, had the conciliar (*sobornyi*) voice of the church been heard and that now the time had come to relate the church's inner stirrings to the public fervor. In the Tsar's name he had issued a rescript on December 27, 1905, saying that as soon as this body had finished deliberating the sobor would be summoned.[5]

When he concluded, Alexei Obolenskii cautioned the assembly that they were there to reassure the simple believers. The Russian people remained basically true to the faith and teachings of the Orthodox church. It was the responsibility of the men assembled to rediscover and highlight the basic principles of Orthodoxy. He cautioned those who had conflicting interpretations of Orthodoxy not to press their interpretations to the extreme, lest they lead to divisions within the church and bring confusion to the simple believers.

> Religious thought and religious controversy are not without their impact on the general life of the fatherland and its troubled times. Elements of discontent, protest, and ill will have penetrated little by little, sometimes unwittingly into the airing of questions of faith. Conflicting social currents, reflecting various facets of truth in the principles of renewal, enunciated nowadays even from the heights of the altar, affect questions raised about the nature of the church. Influences from the troubled seas of political life that

flow directly from egotistical interests exert an impact on the understanding of religious truth. Though they have nothing naturally in common with faith, they strive to infect religious consciousness.[6]

He went on to say that it was the responsibility of the Pre-Sobor Commission to find ways to quiet the turbulence, to smooth out the divergent viewpoints and attitudes, to persuade the young to give up their animosities and learn to value the experience and wisdom of their elders. The Orthodox consciousness, relying on the scriptures and tradition of the church, should be illuminated by the labors and searchings of all, united in a single profession of faith.

When Obolenskii concluded, a telegram from Nicholas II was read wishing them God's grace and reminding them of the heavy responsibility they bore. Then followed a few words from Prince Evgenii Trubetskoi, professor at Kiev University and soon to be a member of Duma, suggesting to the Commission members that they have local synods in the various dioceses before proceeding to the general sobor, in order to have a better sampling of the voice of the church. Metropolitan Antonii replied that this had already been done in 1905 after the Synod asked the diocesan bishops to draw up reports and suggestions concerning the needs of the Russian church.[7] Obolenskii remarked that while that was true, the Commission members needed to be open to the broadest possible input from the Russian people, who were torn by confusing influences and could not be overlooked.

Nikolai Aksakov, administrator of the Synod chancellory, warned that the assembly would have to be guided by the ancient canons of the Eastern church and that it would not be easy to find solutions for the current ecclesiastical and social crisis in those ancient canons. Still, if they wished to have any assurance of validity for their labors, they would have to weigh the canons carefully. He listed the problems that the Synod and the bishop's responses had indicated as most pressing, dividing them into seven categories and noting that the Pre-Sobor Commission would be divided into seven sub-commissions. Members were free to sign up for the sub-commission of their choice.

The first sub-commission, chaired by Archbishop Dmitri Kovalnitskii (1839-1913), considered the makeup of the national all-Russian sobor, the order for presenting the agenda of the sobor and ways to restructure the central administration of the church. Twenty-eight members signed up for this important sub-commission, but its meetings were attended by virtually all the members of the other sub-commissions.

The second sub-commission, chaired by Archbishop Nikandr Molchanov of Lithuania, studied ecclesiastical subdivisions, metropolias, the government of metropolias, and restructuring the dioceses. The Nikandr sub-commission, composed of fourteen members, synchronized its meetings with those of the Dmitri sub-commission.

The third sub-commission was concerned with restructuring ecclesiastical courts and regulations governing marriages and mixed marriages. Following the bishop's recommendations of 1905, it proposed a four-level ecclesiastical court system—parish, *blagochinie*, diocesan and synodal—with appeals possible from the lowest to the highest and major issues to be appealed to an all-Russian sobor. Administration and church courts would be completely separate on every level.

The fourth sub-commission, headed by Archbishop Stefan Arkhangelskii of Mogilev, dealt with reorganizing the Orthodox parish, parish schools and parish properties, together with diocesan convocations and involvement of clergy in public and social institutions. It juxtaposed sessions with the first and second sub-commissions to allow members to attend each other's sessions.

The fifth sub-commission dealt with the reorganization of ecclesiastical institutions above the parish level. Bishop Arsenii Stadnitskii chaired.

The sixth sub-commission, dealing with questions of faith, the *Edinovertsy*, Old Believers and other related questions such as Uniates, Latins and Lutherans, was chaired by Antonii Khrapovitskii of Volhynia, recently elevated to the rank of archbishop.

The last sub-commission dealt with the defense of Orthodox teaching and worship from the attacks of sectarians and other groups, which had been particularly hostile since the extension of religious toleration. It was headed by Archbishop Sergei Stragorodskii of Finland.[8]

The meetings of the Pre-Sobor Commission and the sessions of its sub-commissions permitted the experts of the various theological academies and priests in positions of responsibility who had worked on the *Otzyvy* in their dioceses now to meet face to face for a prolonged span of time. In a prophetic statement, Lieutenant-General Alexander Kireev (1832-1910) warned the delegations to deliberate swiftly and present their recommendations so the sobor could begin soon. Delay would put the church in grave jeopardy, and the momentum for reform would be lost.

Antonii Khrapovitskii ended the session by warning that the issue of clerical and lay representation in the sobor could be a major stumbling block preventing harmony. The canons of the church forbade formal delegations from clerical and lay organizations and pressure groups. Councils were made up of bishops, the pastors of the church and successors of the apostles. The expertise of lay and priest representatives had to be utilized by the sobor, but the bishops would have to make the decisions. This problem was particularly acute now, he noted, because there were disturbing cleavages developing between the peasantry and their clergy on the one hand, and between the clergy and their bishops on the other. Healing those cleavages would be one of the main concerns of the sobor.[9]

*   *   *

Archbishop Dmitri Kovalnitskii's sub-commission on the makeup of the sobor and reform of the central church administration met for the first time on Tuesday, March 14, 1906. He noted that there was an unusually large representation of laymen in the group and only three priests present, but saw no problem. He noted that he himself had been a lay bureaucrat for thirty-five years and for only ten a servant of the church,[10] but that did not make him any less concerned for the welfare of the church. Consideration of the central church administration had been transferred to them, Dmitri said, because it was too complicated a problem to be handled in general sessions.

The archbishop reiterated Byzantine canons by declaring that it was the nature of the Orthodox church to be governed by bishops. Any movement to replace that tradition by some presbyterian organization would violate the canons and destroy the church. Without bishops there is no church—it was as simple as that. Within that context, the general government of the Russian church should be supervised by national sobors which would provide programs and policies for the church. A national synod of bishops could be the executive of the church in the interim between sobors.

Nikolai Aksakov responded that no one really quarreled with the concept of the church as being essentially episcopal in its administration and structure, but there was another dimension that had to be safeguarded: that of the believing people. Cyprian of Carthage had described the relationship between those two elements when he called the church *plebs episcopo suo adunata*, the people united around their bishops. From Cyprian's description came the other side of the question: without the people there is no church.

Nikolai Suvorov, canon lawyer at Moscow University, responded that if the archbishop was arguing the canonicity of the state church, he was on rather shaky ground. There was a serious question whether the existing church structure, bishops or no bishops, was canonical. The existing structure derived from Peter's *reglament* of 1721, which itself was uncanonical. As Professor P. V. Tikhomirov had pointed out in *Bogoslovskii Vestnik*, the *reglament* would have to have been accepted by the bishops of the church without coercion. Not all the bishops had agreed to it; Stefan Iavorskii, for one, had vigorously protested it. Furthermore, those who claimed that it was legitimate because the Eastern Patriarchs had approved it were mistaken, because only two of the Patriarchs had approved it and Constantinople had emphatically rejected it. So the presence of bishops alone did not make the organization of the church canonical.[11]

Dmitri responded that that was only partially true. There was no disputing the uncanonical nature of Peter's *reglament*, but the bishops were successors of the apostles, and that in itself was a mark of canonical legitimacy. The church had deviated from Orthodox norms, but to throw out the bishops now or to reduce them to mere figureheads would be to deviate even further.

Professor Nikolai Zaozerskii of Moscow Theological Academy pointed out that the question of canonicity was the most pressing problem the church faced. The first sobor would have to determine the structure and function of subsequent sobors, but how could it be guaranteed that the first sobor would be canonical? Who had the authority to summon a sobor? There was possibly a nearly two-hundred-year lapse in canonical administration in the Russian church. Zaozerskii and the archbishop believed that, whatever the canonical status of the church now, the sobor would have to be summoned by the Tsar. The Tsar's summoning it would give it legal status in the empire, and that would simply have to do as far as a canonical basis was concerned. The present church administration had been imposed at a Tsar's behest. Its removal would have to come in the same manner.

Nikolai Aksakov retorted that it did not matter who summoned the sobor—Tsar, Synod or anyone else. What mattered was that the decisions of the sobor be accepted by all Orthodox Christians and not cause division among them. Therefore, the main concern was that the sobor, when sitting, had to represent all the elements in the church.

General Kireev brought Aksakov up short by stating that the canons required only that bishops attend a sobor, no one else, and touched off a heated debate on whether or not bishops alone could attend and, if so, which bishops—diocesan bishops only or all bishops whether they actually governed dioceses or not.

Professors from St. Petersburg—Alexander Brilliantov and Alexander Rozhdestvenskii—joined professors from Kazan—Ilia Berdnikov, Nikolai Ivanovskii and Mikhail Mashanov—to support Kireev, while Professors Nikolai Suvorov and Nikolai Zaozerskii joined Archpriest Pavel

Svetlov of Kiev University in support of Aksakov. Thus was drawn the line between strict canonists, or Byzantinists, and those who would interpolate broader Slavophilic considerations.

Professor Suvorov, a Slavophile, argued that the data on council proceedings transmitted through the centuries since the ecumenical councils was incomplete. Though the names of laymen and clergy at those councils had been rarely recorded, they had been there. They must have participated in the deliberations. Both Cyprian of Carthage and Eusebius, in his *Ecclesiastical History*, indicated that there had been laymen and priests present at councils in their day. Origen of Alexandria, for example, had attended the Council of Bostra, in Arabia, as an expert and had actually dominated that council, but he was not a bishop at the time. Malchion had dominated the council that condemned the teachings of Paul of Samosata, but was not a bishop. Thus, others besides bishops had been active participants. St. Athanasius had been a vigorous participant in the Council of Nicaea in 325, but was not a bishop at the time. The records of the ecumenical councils indicated the presence of laymen and priests at virtually every one of them. However, it was true that there was no firm indication that they had attended as official delegates.

Suvorov's observations brought forth a lengthy statement from Professor Ilia Berdnikov, canon lawyer from Kazan, on Thursday, March 16, arguing that new scientific methods of philology and textual comparison made it possible to arrive at a fairly exact idea of how the early councils, ecumenical and local, had been conducted. The evidence was overwhelming that the only authorized participants in these councils had been bishops. Furthermore, the Byzantine *Nomocanon* laid out the proper way to constitute a council very explicitly. In the absence of any evidence to contradict these sources, they should be the norm for constituting the Russian sobor. Experts and spectators could be present, but decisions could be made by bishops alone. Arguments that the records from past councils were merely fragmentary and that councils had been constituted in any other way simply did not stand up to scrutiny. The argument advanced by men like Zaozerskii, based upon their interpretation of what went on at the Council of Carthage in 256, implying that deacons and priests must have had a part in the decisions, failed to mention that the final decisions at that council were made exclusively by bishops and that when St. Cyprian reported the actions of the council to Pope Stephen, he reported only the bishops' decisions, nothing else. The only time that priests and laymen are recorded as taking part in councils is when there is an election of a bishop, and even then there is no evidence that they acted in anything but an advisory capacity. Confirmation of the choice of a bishop came from the other bishops in his metropolia, not from election by priests and laymen.

Berdnikov pictured a typical council as having bishops seated in the positions of honor, with clerical advisers close at hand and lay experts and participants standing about observing. He went through several examples, pointing out that when decisions had been reached in councils, bishops made them, whoever else might have been present or might have expressed themselves. It was obvious, therefore, that the Russian sobor, too, would have to leave decision-making to the bishops alone, even though lay and priest experts would be present.[15]

Professor Nikolai Zaozerskii of the Moscow Academy, a member of the Orthodox Society and a leading champion of white priest and lay influence in the church, disagreed vigorously. He charged that Berdnikov had conveniently overlooked one very important council: the gathering of apostles, presbyters and brethren in Jerusalem to consider the problems laid before them by Paul and Barnabas when they came from Antioch, as recorded in the Acts of the Apostles. On the question whether or not gentile converts should adhere to the whole of the Mosaic law, all those present, including presbyters and brothers—in other words, priests and laymen—had had a hand in the decision. Did not the evidence of scripture and theological teaching take precedence over canons that had been compiled later? Did not such a fraternal gathering and consultation conform better with Orthodox teaching on the church as the body of Christ? Surely, the canons could not be construed to contradict the scriptures themselves.

Fr. Pavel Svetlov, scripture scholar from Kiev University, took up Zaozerskii's argument and cited Paul's letters to the Romans, Corinthians and Ephesians, where the members of the church were compared to parts of the body and it was noted that none of them could function without the others. Furthermore, the gathering of apostles in Jerusalem could properly be called the real First Ecumenical Council. The councils that were held between then and the Council of Nicaea very likely followed the pattern of Jerusalem. The church is an institution of morality and love among men and cannot be bound by legalities. Love, intimate exchange among brothers, should be the motivating force in the church, not nitpicking laws.

Berdnikov shot back that the Jerusalem council could hardly be called ecumenical. Only two churches were involved, not the whole *oikoumene* as it then existed. The Jerusalem gathering would be better regarded as a diocesan convocation or a metropolitan sobor at the very most, if it could even be termed a council.

Suvorov of Moscow cautioned against trying to manufacture a whole case from a single passage or two from the scriptures. It was not clear who the presbyters and brethren at Jerusalem actually were. To speak of the apostles as bishops is to force a definition. They weren't bishops in the sense of the word as it was later understood. Bishops were their successors. Furthermore, it was risky to try to imagine what went on in the first two centuries and to assert that whatever it was must have been substantially different from the era of the councils. The genuine expert had to take the whole spectrum of the tradition of the early church into account. As far as the argument from Paul's metaphors on the body are concerned, even the human body is a highly structured organism, not just a haphazard collection of limbs and organs.

Suvorov denounced the concept that a sobor was not legitimate until its decisions had generally been accepted by the clergy and laity at large. What about the competence and authority of the sobor itself? How long did it take until the decisions were considered accepted? Suppose significant parts of the church never accepted council decisions? It was important to note, he felt, that the Eastern Patriarchs had told Pope Pius IX that the believing faithful were the conservers of true belief, not the definers.[13] Details of local and diocesan councils in the history of the Eastern church are hard to come by, he went on. The only continuing indication of what they might have been like was the practice in the Latin church in the Middle Ages. There it was clear that whenever diocesan councils (convocations) met, they were always under the chairmanship of their bishops. Furthermore, clerical and lay members of those diocesan councils never had deciding votes. The same was true with metropolitan sobors. Bishops were always the decision-makers.

Professor Nikolai Glubokovskii of the Petersburg Academy joined Suvorov, warning that to make a distinction between the functions of the church in apostolic times and the era of the ecumenical councils was to create an artificial dichotomy. A critical study of the way the church functioned could be made from the scriptures and the early church historians. A comparison of those sources showed that the church functioned during the council era exactly as it had earlier and that the patterns and norms of the former period carried directly over into the latter. Together they formed a whole picture of the development of ecclesiastical government and procedure. One risked descending into Protestant polemics in marking a dichotomy between the two eras. It was too convenient to isolate scriptural passages and make cases out of them without trying to understand the total context. Hypocrisy was something in which Russian canonists, theologians and historians could not indulge. Sectarians made far too much of half truths. Orthodox were obliged to adhere to the whole of the Christian tradition.

In referring to the council at Jerusalem, Glubokovskii stated that whatever else happened, it was clear that the church at Antioch had had recourse to the judgment of the church at Jerusalem, recognizing it as the mother church and seeking its definition of the issue. It would not have mattered a particle whether or not the majority of the Antioch community liked what Jerusalem decided. The authority of the Jerusalem decision was what had mattered. Furthermore, the theory that presbyters and brothers—interpreted by some to mean clergy and laity—had had a decisive voice in the proceedings was wrong. The decision had been made by the apostles, more specifically Peter and James, and when the word went out at the end of the deliberations, it went out in Peter's name, not James' or anyone else's. James makes it clear (Acts 15:14) that it was Peter's word that was decisive. Bishops were the successors of the apostles, as was clear in the scriptures and attested to by the fathers of the church. They had to define dogma and judge disciplinary matters. Presbyters—clergy, if you like—were the implementers.

Glubokovskii, like Suvorov, realized that the clergy and laity would have to be accorded full participation in the sobor to give the benefit of their experience and research, but it was no good to argue that they had the right to make final and binding decisions. No precedent in apostolic or ecumenical times supported that contention. Advice from clergy and laity would help the bishops, but one could not argue *a posteriori* that they had ever had equal authority in any church council in the past.

Russian bishops, it was true, were strangers to their flocks in many ways. That was the fault of an uncanonical system of administration. The estrangement had to be overcome. But it would be the worst type of blunder to change the present system for another that was not canonical either and to try to justify the new system with arguments that would not stand in the light of the scriptures and church tradition. Times change, but tradition, overall, does not. Another blunder like those made in 1666 and 1721 would not solve the present crisis in the church. Sobor decisions were valid because they were made by the sobor, not because they were subsequently accepted or rejected by one or another group.[14]

Aksakov, seeing one of the cherished principles of *sobornost'* under attack, rose to dispute Glubokovskii. He stridently pointed out that the apostolic meeting in Jerusalem had had the most vigorous participation of the laity and

clergy. Silence on the part of the scriptures did not mean
that they had no voice in the decision. Glubokovskii and his
confederates based themselves upon biblical texts that were
not necessarily accurate in their rendition. If one considered
the oldest extant texts of the Acts of the Apostles—Sinai,
Vatican and Alexandrian—one found wording that clearly
indicated a deliberation and consideration of the problem
of the Antioch Christians that was full and included all
present, not just the apostles and presbyters. Surely, Aksakov
argued, no one could imagine that if there was a large assembly of clergy and faithful present that they simply stood
around in silence. The very fact that those aguing against
lay and clerical participation had found several records indicating that lay and clerical representatives were present
would indicate that they were there for a purpose and not
just to sit in silence. Furthermore, it was necessary to recognize that not all canonical regulations concerning clergy and
laity at councils were in accord. That very fact indicated that
there must have been participation by those parties. If distinctions were to be made between types of councils, it seemed
that ecumenical councils restricted participation by clergy and
laymen while metropolitan councils did not. Aksakov argued
that the coming Russian council was going to fit the description of a metropolitan council, and that would justify the
broader interpretation. The fact that only bishops were recorded at the ecumenical councils merely meant that only
bishops and high-ranking officials were deemed worthy of
having their names recorded. That was the way Byzantine
documents were kept. Metropolitans were so carefully recorded because there were official penalties laid upon them
if they were absent. Aksakov indicated that at the Council
of Alexandria (341), when the problem of local Arianism
was dealt with, St. Athanasius, by then a bishop, summoned
bishops, clerics and laity in his metropolia to root out the
Arian poison "in accordance with the provisions of the
Fathers." Therefore, it was obvious that the Council of
Nicaea, in 325, the First Ecumenical Council, had not done
away with the earlier tradition of summoning all interested
parties for such an important undertaking of the local church.

It could, therefore, be inferred that participation by clerics and laymen was canonical at least at that time. It is true that when such important figures as bishops were excommunicated for heresy, the excommunications were left exclusively to bishops, but that in no way meant that clerics and laymen had been excluded from full participation in other issues. Aksakov noted that when St. Augustine summoned a council to Hippo in 304, he addressed his summons to: "Dillectissimis fratribus, clero, senioribus, et universae plebi ecclesiae Hipponensis cui servio. . . ." *Plebs universa* was not just a quaint phrase. Augustine meant what he said.

After numerous other references to regional metropolitan councils in both the eastern and western parts of the Mediterranean,[15] Aksakov concluded that, at least as far as metropolitan councils were concerned, there was no distinction made between "decision-making" and "consultative" voices at those conclaves. Then he went on to take exception with those who said that the faithful had no voice in defining doctrine and ecclesiastical practice. For one thing, the statement of the Eastern Patriarchs in 1848 could not simply be dismissed out of hand. For another, the celebrated case of the election of St. Ambrose as bishop of Milan gives the lie to that position. In Milan, a semi-Arian conclave of bishops had become deadlocked on who should be bishop. It was the voice of the people, echoing through the cathedral, that forced Ambrose upon the conclave, to the everlasting benefit of the church.

Another point Aksakov disputed was that the government should have the dominant influence in deciding when to summon the sobor, whom to invite to attend and if its decisions would be ultimately sanctioned. Governments came and went, Aksakov said. No one in his right mind would assert that the strength of the government determines the value of the decisions of the church.

It would take careful preliminary preparations for the sobor at the parish and diocesan level and careful deliberations and resolutions at the sobor itself to ensure that the Russian sobor would have a valuable, regenerating and permanently binding influence upon the Russian believing community. If either the government or the church itself tried to ram anything down the throat of the Russian *narod*, there would be another *Raskol* and the church would be worse off than it was now.

Fr. Svetlov and Alexander Rozhdestvenskii took both Aksakov and Glubokovskii to task for overlooking the essence of the church as the body of Christ, the community of love, the whole *ekklesia*. Canonical regulations were derived from that singular fact. They were expendable whenever and wherever they cramped the expression of that community. Distinctions between bishops and presbyters, clerics and laity, decisive and consultative votes, all missed the point. The point was: what type of organization would permit the church to reemerge now as the energizer of the faithful, the light in the darkness of present times?[16] Therefore, one should not go to the Acts or to the canons to prove a point or find a hard and fast regulation. One should try to discover the spirit in which the church arrived at consensus in times past and imparted it to its followers and to posterity.

Kazan's Professor Berdnikov rather tartly replied to the priests that that was all well and good, but it brought them right back to the question: how to constitute a sobor now? He noted several examples, specifically the Spanish councils of Elvira (306) and Toledo (633), and pointed out that there was no way around recognizing that, whoever had participated, the decisions were always made by bishops.

When Archbishop Dmitri asked the sub-commission to divide for their final statement on whether laity and clergy should have consultative or deciding voices in the sobor, twelve members voted that they should have only consultative voices, while seven believed that they should have decision-making voices. They all referred to the canons of the church as the foundation of their arguments.[17] At the general convocation of the Pre-Sobor Commission on May 5, the sub-commission decision was ratified, after a particularly involved argument by Antonii Khrapovitskii that the sobor of Old Believers just concluded in Moscow had permitted only bishops to make final decisions and, therefore, kept the canons.

Though the majority of the members of the sub-commission did not favor the inclusion of representatives of the clergy and laity in the formal decision-making of the sobor, they very definitely did not wish them to be excluded. Their exclusion from the formal promulgations of the sobor was merely intended to preserve canonical norms of the Byzantine church. Given the past violations of those norms and the internal schism the church experienced because of them, the sub-commission majority fervently wished to avoid canonical violations that would give rise to further schism and discord.

They fully agreed with the sentiments of the sub-commission minority that the clergy and laity should be given full opportunity to be heard and that they have a major influence in the sobor's final pronouncements. Zaozerskii made that clear in the session of March 18. He and the archbishops agreed that bishops who actually governed dioceses were the only prelates who should have decision-making authority. That meant sixty-six bishops in all. However, they also envisioned that each bishop would come with a small army of experts and advisers from their diocesan clergy and laity who would have the right of free expression in the formal sessions of the sobor and who would be consulted by the bishops every step of the way. The sub-commission estimated that the sobor would range between 330 and 500 persons. Even Aksakov was heartened at that development, believing that full inclusion of clerical and lay expertise in preparing sobor pronouncements would allay fears that the conclusions of the sobor would be rejected. Professor Viktor Nesmelov of Kazan joined Aksakov in cautioning that the expertise would have to include the humblest country pastor and the missionaries who labored among non-Orthodox Christians and pagans. They warned against letting a small, well-educated ecclesiastical intelligentsia dominate the council. The sobor had to work towards consensus, and it would be a disaster to alienate country pastors and their rural flocks in the process of reforming the church. The Old Believers would be only too happy to welcome them into their fold. The intelligentsia, ecclesiastical and lay, never did understand or sympathize with the simple, ritual-loving Russian believer.

Professor Vladimir Zavitnevich of Kiev Theological Academy, an author of many articles on *sobornost'*,[18] warned that with the political and ecclesiastical atmosphere as heated and controversial as it was in 1906, it would be very difficult to avoid head-on clashes between parties in the sobor. All the potential of a bitter division existed. It would take maximum diplomatic finesse to prevent the sobor from being a disaster. Fiats from on high, forcing the policies of any faction upon the church without consulting and persuading the simple faithful, could wreck the church instead of healing wounds of two and four hundred years' duration. The church would be walking a very treacherous path, steering itself between the pitfalls of its own inner divisions while keeping exterior political interests from perverting or preventing *bona fide* regeneration and reconciliation.

Archbishop Dmitri wondered whether selection of delegates to the sobor should take place in a two- or three-step fashion, much as was being done in electing representatives to the State Duma. Such a scheme had been recommended by Archbishop Sergei Stragorodskii of Finland, but Dmitri put it before the sub-commission tongue-in-cheek because he personally was against it. He felt that the elections to the Duma were causing such turmoil and disruption that to even attempt to repeat the experience was asking for trouble. Professor Suvorov heartily agreed. Such a scheme had never been used in the two thousand years of the church's history, had no canonical precedent and was not advisable in the twentieth century.

Dmitri believed that the selection of non-episcopal delegates to the sobor should be done by the diocesan bishops from among already existing parish elders who had been chosen to review and project parish budgets. Their duties could easily be expanded to serve in the sobor.

No one agreed with Dmitri. Archpriest Svetlov could see no reason why the electoral principle was not as good for the church as it was for the Duma. Just because it had not been tried in two thousand years did not mean it could not be tried in the twentieth century. Besides, it was a very practical measure, one which was even in 1906 being tried in some areas to elect parish councils, *blagochinie* councils, and delegates to diocesan convocations. While electoral procedures might stir up animosities and local passions, it seemed to be the most effective way to see that all contending parties were heard before delegates were chosen. Professor Zaozerskii agreed, saying that once the principle of representation at the sobor was extended beyond the episcopate, there was no reason why every baptized member of the church did not have an inalienable right to be heard at the sobor. The electoral method seemed to be the best way to ensure that that right was exercised. Professors Berdnikov and Pevnitskii, the latter of Kazan Academy also, both of them strict canonists, agreed that the elective procedure was the most feasible, provided that the diocesan bishop had the final right to confirm or disqualify any elected delegate from his diocese. That way the canonical requirement that bishops had the right to determine their advisers and companions at councils would be observed.[19]

On March 22, Archbishop Dmitri expressed reservations about the electoral scheme sketched out previously. He did not think that parish elections should be held to select delegates at the sobor. He argued against parish-level elections primarily because the Duma elections, also conducted in the parishes, were causing such turmoil and bafflement among the peasants that to impose another series of elections at the same time or shortly after would just confuse them altogether. They would have no idea why they were ballotting. They did not even know the difference between the Synod and the Senate now.

Secondly, electoral procedures were completely alien to the spirit and letter of the canons. It would be better to have *blagochinie* councils select a roster of qualified individuals, give it to the bishop and let him make the final selection of delegates. That would be more in keeping with the canons and insure that only individuals acceptable to the *blagochinie* authorities were presented to the bishop and that no one unacceptable to the bishop was selected. Dmitri urged that each *blagochinie* select two laymen and two priests who had the full trust of their parish constituencies.

Nikolai Zaozerskii did not like the archbishop's scheme. The primary purpose of the coming sobor was to reestablish direct relations between the central church administration and the parishes throughout the empire. As the central administration operated now in 1906 it was totally cut off from the parishes. Paperwork and self-serving bureaucrats stifled any living exchange. If the bishops were allowed to have a veto over the selection of representatives of the white clergy and laity to the all-Russian sobor, they would very likely select their own type of delegate and once again frustrate the attempt of the church to hear the voice of its people at the grassroots. The Russian church could not afford to play that kind of charade again. The whole idea of the State Duma was to let the civil authorities hear from the grassroots. The church had to do the same, whatever temporary confusion the process might bring.

The archbishop and Professor Suvorov were dismayed at Zaozerskii's plan. Dmitri said he could in no way go to the sobor himself if he was afraid that any of the lay and clerical members from his diocese would be hostile or antagonistic towards him. His position as pastor would be jeopardized, and it would be impossible to achieve the close working cooperation with them that would be required for the good of the sobor in general and for the Kherson diocese in particular. Suvorov asserted that there was no precedent in the annals of the early church to justify election of delegates to the sobor who did not have the fullest confidence of their bishop. He cited specifically the councils held at Constantinople in 843, 1155 and 1191. In all three, eminent personages spoke and deliberated and had a considerable impact upon the proceedings, but only at the invitation of bishops or the Patriarch.

Suvorov went on to say that while it was true that in the Byzantine church the elective principle, irrespective of the will or office of bishops, had been introduced in 1858-1860 in a series of restructurings of the Orthodox millet, those innovations had been forced upon the church by the Turkish gov-

ernment and western diplomats.[20] They did not correspond
to the true will or interests of the church itself and were in
clear violation of the canonical traditions of the church.

Fedor D. Samarin, one of the members of the State Council who had participated in the deliberations of the Committee of Ministers about church reform in 1904 and 1905,
warmly supported both the archbishop and Suvorov. Delegates elected independently from the clergy and the laity
risked forming antagonistic blocks against their bishops and
directly opened the church to the threat of a new schism.
A community of interest among the delegations to the sobor
had to be assured before the sobor ever sat. The Duma bid
fare to be a discordant assembly divided against itself. The
church could not endure that. It was entirely unreasonable
to expect that if antagonistic parties fought it out in the sobor
they would suddenly find peace and harmony among themselves. Rather, they would return to their parishes and
blagochiniia and spread discord and antagonism there. Turning the bishops into just a party that had to contend with
other parties at the sobor was to negate the whole Orthodox
concept of bishops as shepherds and successors to the apostles.
That had been tried in certain parts of the West in former
times, notably at the Protestant Reformation. The result had
been to reduce bishops to being merely ornaments or to
abolish them altogether. Russian Orthodoxy could not repeat
that absurdity in the twentieth century and still pretend to
bear witness to the unbroken tradition of the church of the
apostles.

Samarin went on to say that the "elective" principle had
become a type of fetish in the twentieth century in the belief that once it was applied, happiness would be the inevitable result. It wasn't turning out that way. In local
villages and *uezdy* its application was deepening the strife.
Such a principle could only work if there was a predisposi-
tion to cooperate. To apply the elective principle in ecclesiastical affairs mechanically at a time when it was failing in
the political arena flew in the face of all logic. The church
had a long tradition and history to which it had to be faithful. Former formulas had been worked out in practical cir-

cumstances and had become the canons of the church. The
slate could not simply be wiped clean and rewritten as if
nothing had happened in the past two thousand years. If
the church wished to take over norms from the political
realm, then she could at least wait to see which of those
norms were successful and which suited the needs of the
church. The new political nostrums everywhere advocated
offered public order little promise at the moment. The
church would adopt them at her own peril. It was true that
many bishops were placeholders, bureaucratic cyphers, who
were completely out of touch with their flocks. A sobor
would have to work to see that their type would not be per-
petuated in the future, but to simply bypass them would be
a mistake. One had to work with the material at hand.
Furthermore, Samarin had grave reservations about whether
a sobor should be contemplated at all now when the political
order in Russia was so unstable.

Archpriest Pavel Svetlov, well known for his disputes in
the press with the archbishop of Volhynia, sailed into
Samarin vehemently. It was precisely because the bishops
were so badly out of touch that they had to be bypassed, he
said. Furthermore, if one were conscious of the church as
the living body of Christ, then the argument that ancient
canons had to be adhered to fell of its own accord. The body
of Christ could very well wipe the slate clean whenever it
deemed that was necessary. The church as body of Christ
transcended existing organizations, canons, rituals and whatever else prevented it from shining forth as God's presence
among men. If the church as body of Christ was conscious
of itself as that body, animated by Christ's benevolence and
love, then it would not matter a bit what forms of elections
were used or what weight placed on the various parties within
a sobor, and the end result would be the harmonious consensus of what was good for that body. It was depressing to
Fr. Svetlov to think that the animosities of the political realm
would be carried over lock, stock and barrel into the church
without any of the uplifting influence of Christ's love. If
that were the case, then the church already had descended to

the level of political and sectarian squabbling, and its future was bleak.

Svetlov made the same plea again at the general session of the Commission, May 5, warning that pedantic arguments about precise adherence to canons missed the fundamental reality that the Russian church was virtually dead. The disorder and violence in the schools and parishes showed them daily that unless the administration of the church were reconstituted in such a way as to give the whole body of believers real involvement, it would soon be too late to argue over the nice points of the ancient canons.

The archbishop cautioned that however high sounding those sentiments were, Svetlov should not lose sight of the fact that the electors were at the same time members of their villages and of their parishes and that their leaders were simultaneously heads of those villages and elders in their parishes. If the average person found it difficult to distinguish between Synod and Senate nowadays, it would be asking a lot to have him distinguish between elections for the sobor and elections for the Duma.

Fr. Alexander Rozhdestvenskii of the St. Petersburg Theological Academy, a leading member of the Religious-Philosophical Society and one of the main advisers of the Petersburg metropolitan during the preparations for the Special Sessions of the Committee of Ministers, countered with the argument that if the church was concerned with maintaining its claim to apostolicity, churchmen would have to be aware that it would have to adhere to the spirit of apostolic times. The scriptures and the canons could not be in opposition to each other. The spirit of apostolic times could be summed up in one phrase: *fiat justitia, pereat mundus*! That meant that earthbound formulas could not hobble the church in its search for authenticity. Canons, it had to be recognized, usually resulted from a compromise between the interests of the church and the interests of secular authorities. When the circumstances that necessitated the compromise had disappeared, the validity of the compromise itself was of necessity also lost. Churchmen in 1906 had to be wary of citing canonical norms simply as a guise for preserving the status quo and for forcing the church to knuckle under to political demands. There should be no mistake that the interests of the government and its organs were very much at variance with the interests and needs of the church, particularly in these times. There was no doubt that the majority of Russian bishops were political appointees, nominated precisely for their subservience to the state and its interests. If they dominated the sobor, the state would dominate the sobor. The liberating life of the church would be stifled again.

It would be very desirable to restore the closeness of bonds between the people and their bishops. But one had to be realistic. These bonds had not existed in the Russian church for a very long time. The sobor would take measures to restore them by arranging to have clergy and laity involved in the election of local bishops, as was the case in the ancient church. The sobor would also have to reduce the territorial size of the average diocese so that the bishop could actually get to know his flock. The sobor would have to put an end to the musical chairs of moving bishops rapidly from one diocese to another. But all this had to come from a sobor that was truly independent of political pressures and bent on church renewal. The current crew of bishops were just as capable now of selling out their flocks to political interests as the bishops of southwest Russia had been in the sixteenth century when they accepted union with Rome and the papacy in return for political favors.

As far as preventing strife and politicking for representation before the sobor was concerned, what difference did it make? History was full of examples of strife and politicking for position and influence in the councils of the church. That could not be helped. The end results of these councils and their impact on the subsequent development of the church were what mattered. What had to be avoided was strife and discord after the sobor ended, and that could be avoided only if all sectors of the church were heard from and the sobor truly achieved a consensus. Rozhdestvenskii noted that in their *Otzyvy* (responses) many bishops called for clerical and lay representatives at the sobor. No more than the Tsar could ignore the voice of the masses in the present situation could the church ignore them. The Duma would restructure the apparatus of government so that it would truly reflect the needs of the time and the interests of the people, and the sobor would do the same for the church. To try to circumvent the consensus of the masses in either case would assure disaster in the future, in both government and church. Rozhdestvenskii vigorously urged the sub-commission to adopt the plan recommended by the St. Petersburg Diocesan Commission: that a three-level election procedure be adopted to choose delegates from the laity and white clergy—at the parish, *blagochinie* and diocesan levels. He noted that the circular from Prince Obolenskii of November 26, 1905, to the bishops to begin creating *bona fide* parish units, with locally chosen elders and councils, would permit parish units to select their nominees for *blagochinie* consideration almost immediately. To Archbishop Dmitri's objection that the local bishop could at least have the opportunity to express his opinion on the fitness of selected delegates, Rozhdestvenskii replied that the local bishops could express their reservations at the sobor just like any other Orthodox.[21]

General Alexander Kireev, an expert on the Old Catholic schism of the 1870s, warmly supported Fr. Rozhdestvenskii. Kireev noted that in the era of the great ecumenical councils the men and movements who were subsequently condemned and anathematized had first been given a full hearing in the councils. Arius was just one.

Kireev warned against trying to exclude undesirable persons from the sobor in advance. No one could tell whose views, however controversial at the moment, might be the proper anticipation of the future. As an example, he said that Alexei Stepanovich Khomiakov (1804-1860), one of the lights of the Slavophile movement, would have been excluded from a sobor if one had been held in the 1850s. Khomiakov's political inclinations were definitely out of favor at the time, and the bishop of Tula was so outraged at Khomiakov's ideas that he publicly denounced him. Had that bishop possessed the right to veto persons unacceptable to him, Khomiakov, one of the church's greatest champions, would have been excluded. So, no veto or review of delegate suitability until the sobor had convened. If there were manifestly unsuitable persons present, let the sobor itself determine who they were and what to do about them. Kireev went on to chide the faint-hearted about wishing to avoid political entanglements with civilian authorities. That was impossible. With the temper of the political arena what it was, with many candidates for the Duma openly out to get the church, entanglements were almost certain. Under the circumstances, then, the only thing to be concerned about was the welfare of the church and to be ready to defend its interests when difficulties arose.

In these opinions, Kireev was stoutly supported by Nikolai Aksakov, who insisted that the business of election or selection or veto of delegates should not be viewed as essentially divisive when the ultimate regeneration of the church and consensus among its members was what was desired. It appeared true that no such thing as formal elections of members of the various councils, regional and ecumenical, had ever taken place. For example, when Emperor Constantine summoned the Council of Arles, he simply told the bishops to bring along one or two priests and laymen who were qualified to participate in the deliberations. The actual method of choosing them was left unspecified. Elections could simply be a method of choosing delegates to the sobor. The thing to avoid was to give the appearance of predetermining the composition of the sobor and risking the loss of public confidence in its deliberations and proclamations. Political interests would have to be dealt with and not allowed to subvert the expression of the spirit and to bend the church to purely temporary political ends. The thing to remember was that all the persons in the sub-commission, together with all the persons participating in the Pre-Sobor Commission and all the eventual persons in the sobor, would be working towards the same goal: the good of the Russian church. That end was never to be lost sight of. The final sobor decisions would have to be accepted by the mass of the believing faithful or a tragedy like the schism of the seventeenth century, which had sapped the vitality of the church for so long, might be repeated. It had resulted from the failure of the 1666-1667 Sobor to address itself properly to the sentiments and beliefs of the Russian masses. That sobor had been perverted to achieve political aims; likewise, the Petrine reform had been accomplished for political ends. No one could doubt that the subsequent history of the church and all its tragedy had stemmed from its political subversion.[22]

Professor Alexander Brilliantov of the St. Petersburg Academy suggested that the Anglican church could be taken as a model in the matter of electing lay and clerical delegates for the all-church conferences. The Petersburg Diocesan Commission had the Anglican model in mind when they suggested a three-step electoral procedure. It was true that the Anglican church was Protestant and, therefore, outside the apostolic succession in the eyes of the Russian church, but it was an episcopal church that had worked out the matter of electoral procedure rather satisfactorily.

When the archbishop asked the sub-commission to divide, three positions emerged: that bishops have the right to veto delegates chosen by lower bodies before the sobor met; that bishops not have that right; and that bishops simply select individuals whom they felt qualified and compatible without elections.[23] There were no hard and fast parties in the sub-commission. Professor Brilliantov had voted to permit lay and clerical representatives at the sobor to have binding votes on the one hand, but voted to give the bishops the right to veto candidates for the sobor on the other. General Kireev had voted to give clerical and lay delegates only consultative votes at the sobor, but now was against giving the bishops any veto over delegate selection.

One of the most vigorous opponents of giving lay and clerical delegates a vote in the sobor was the archbishop of Volhynia, Antonii Khrapovitskii. Khrapovitskii held the most conservative position of the members of the Pre-Sobor Commission in interpreting the canons. Repeatedly, he pointed out to the members of the sixth sub-commission, which he chaired, that no canon permitted laymen and white clergy to participate in a sobor in anything more than an advisory capacity. In making decisions, only the bishops should be allowed even to participate. A sobor was an assembly of bishops of the church, pastors *par excellence*, where they would communicate with each other to arrive at decisions affecting their pastorates. The only capacity in which clerical and lay delegates could take part was as members of the entourage of their bishop. When not asked by their bishops to speak, they had no canonical right to express themselves. Archbishop Antonii was particularly incensed at white priests who insisted that they have an independent voice in the sobor in order to safeguard their interests. Antonii believed that any bishop of a diocese was well enough acquainted with the real problems to be able to present them at the sobor fairly and in the interests of all. Bishops alone were successors to the apostles, not white clergy and certainly not laity. Bishops bore the responsibility before God to teach and reprove. Anyone who even suggested establishing a rival, alternative party in a council was seeking to split the church.

When the sobor made a pronouncement, its authority was guaranteed by the fact that bishops made the pronouncement. The renovated Synod could not contain any lay members or white clergy either. Neither of these two groups shared apostolic succession. They might present arguments to the Synod, they might be in the committees attached to the Synod and in the Synod chancellory, but they had no decision-making authority. Antonii was considerably aggrieved when the Dmitri sub-commission decided that laymen and white priests had a right to be at the council and to have binding votes on some issues.

In the May 5 general convocation, Khrapovitskii re-iterated his position and was supported by Antonii of St. Petersburg. However, the latter softened the harshness of the archbishop of Volhynia's stance by reminding the advocates of full participation and the right to binding votes for white priests and laymen that the tradition of the church, from Gregory the Theologian and John Chrysostom, Augustine of Hippo and Ambrose of Milan, through the ecumenical councils and down to the present day, was that there were two factors in the community of believers: shepherds and flock. The church had been a vigorous community, with all participating, all through those centuries. He reminded the general convocation that whenever the church gathered for the eucharist, all were vital members of the body of Christ. In the mystical sense, the divisions of labor in the vineyard of Christ became irrelevant when the whole was taken together. He told them that he knew their concern. He had been raised in a priest's family and had known the *angst* his father experienced trying to deal with imperious bishops and clerks. In his years of teaching pastoral theology he had kept in close touch with many of his students once they were in the field as pastors. They, too, had experienced the same frustration. Their worries now were not artificial, and he did not believe that they were merely self-serving when they demanded a real voice in the church. However, ways had to be devised to assure their voice was heard without violating the ancient traditions of the church.[24]

After the Easter recess the Dmitri sub-commission reconvened on April 12. Archbishop Dmitri noted that the Duma elections were completed and the Duma would be sitting in fifteen days, and that there was disturbing evidence that a major conflict had developed between the white clergy and their bishops on the one hand and between the white and black clergy on the other. This was most disquieting and convinced him that the question of the right of the bishop to veto candidates in his diocese for the sobor should be reviewed. Otherwise, the conflict would appear in the Duma and be magnified out of all proportions.

His suggestion immediately raised an angry discussion among the members of the sub-commission. Aksakov noted that in the Synod circular sent out by Prince Obolenskii in November, there had been no provision for the veto by the bishop of any lay council members in a parish, parish elders, delegates to the *blagochinie* councils or even to the diocesan convocations. The only potential veto any bishop had was the moral persuasion that a bishop as presider over diocesan convocations could muster. That was where the matter stood at the moment, and that was where it should remain. The Petersburg suggestion of a three-level electoral system— parish, *blagochinie*, diocesan—had been favored by the majority of commission members at their last meeting, and the matter should rest there.

Professor Brilliantov noted that the Procurator's circular, coming as it did from the Synod, might not be considered canonical, though it was legal according to imperial law. To that the archbishop rejoined that if the canonicity of the Synod were to become a stumbling block, then the very Pre-Sobor Commission itself might be called into question because it had been convened at the order of the Synod. Dmitri brought into the sub-commission Professor Alexander Almazov of the Novorossiisk University in Odessa and Alexei Neidgardt, one of the main functionaries of the Synod, to bolster his position *vis-à-vis* the others in the sub-commission. A prolonged and acrimonious debate ensued in which the pro-veto members stressed that the church had to avoid the hassle that was developing in the Duma while the anti-veto members stressed that a hassle could not be avoided. The issue remained unresolved. A collision between the Petersburg metropolitan and his Diocesan Commission, on the one hand, and the archbishop of Kherson, on the other, and their respective viewpoints ensued. Dmitri was particularly irked by an article that had appeared in the *Bogoslovskii Vestnik*[25] urging three-level elections and leaving no veto power to local bishops. The issue became more embittered when Dmitri again asked for a show of hands on the veto/non-veto issue and the veto party mustered eleven votes versus ten for the non-vetoers. By adding Almazov and Neidgardt to the group, Dmitri had won a numerical advantage. However, he had confirmed the worst suspicions of those who felt that episcopal powers and arrogance had to be limited. The acrimony in the ensuing debates reflected suspicion, and the disorder of Russian political life intruded into the church willy-nilly.

On May 15, a general convocation took up the issue of whether or not diocesan bishops should have the right to confirm selection of candidates to the sobor at a final diocesan convocation or whether they should automatically attend if they had been elected, regardless of the bishop's pleasure. The debate was heated and bitter, but when the

division was finally taken, thirty Commission members voted
to permit bishops to have a veto over the delegates from
the white clergy and the laity and fifteen voted against giving them a veto. Both Antonii Vadkovskii and Dmitri
Kovalnitskii voted to give the bishops veto power, as did
fourteen professors, while Professors Brilliantov and Aksakov
voted against it, together with Frs. Svetlov, Koialovich,
Titov, Alexei Maltsev of the embassy church in Berlin and
Metropolitan Flavian. By then, the general convocation was
very conscious of the turmoil in the Duma. Most of the de-
baters feared a similar uproar in the sobor. Despite the lopsided decision, the issue continued to reverberate in the
Dmitri sub-commission and at the general sessions.

Fedor Samarin added a lengthy statement to the record
which he hoped would provide a way out of the impasse. He
recommended that there be no separate elections of lay and
white clergy delegates to the national sobor. Instead, he believed that each diocese should set up its own system and
make its delegate selection in its own way. He suggested
that the final clearance of delegates be done at the diocesan
convocation. Over the past year, the diocesan convocation
had moved in many places beyond being a formality, and
the 1906 convocations promised to be even more productive. Convocations composed of delegates selected at the
blagochinie level came from some form of selection procedure
at the parish level. With the November circular in operation,
parish councils would become even more active and reflect
more than ever the awakened consciousness of local parishioners. It was at the parish and blagochinie levels that local
wranglings and hostilities could be worked out so that by
the time the diocesan convocation had had time to review
candidates, some kind of consensus should have appeared.

Samarin suggested that candidates be recognized by diocesan convocations after being chosen by parish elections or
selected by the diocesan bishop. Then, at the convocation, the
bishop would have the right to oppose any candidate he personally disapproved, but would have to openly explain why,
running the risk of having to change his position in the face
of his convocation. Various other individuals or organiza-

tions would have the right to oppose any candidate they disapproved and, likewise, to explain themselves. Finally, when
manifestly objectionable candidates had been removed from
the roster of eligible candidates, the diocesan lists of delegates would be chosen by lot.

Samarin realized that such a plan would leave many un-
happy, but it was numerically impossible to represent all segments anyway. During elections to the Duma, it was all too
clear that the electoral system had not brought harmony into the political sphere. Therefore, it was incumbent upon the
Pre-Sobor Commission to work out ways to avoid repeating
that kind of discord in the church. With delegate selection
taking place at the diocesan level, irreconcilable clashes in
the sobor could be avoided, and the bishop would be safeguarded as shepherd of and spokesman for his flock, as
required by canon law.

Samarin stressed that he was not scheming to undercut
the voice of the white clergy and laity. At all costs, these
groups had to be given an open and complete hearing at the
sobor. The sobor's conclusions had to be acceptable to the
whole church. It was not the Orthodox way to elevate the
authority of the hierarchy to such a degree that the laity and
clergy were effectively silenced. The Russian church had to
work diligently to prevent the lopsided enhancement of
episcopal and patriarchal authority that resulted in the Roman
church from the decisions of the Vatican Council of 1870-
1871. Samarin and Fr. Fedor Titov of the Kiev Academy
recommended that the Synod chancellory be taken over by
the sobor to provide continuity and to grant the sobor and
subsequent higher administration of the church a working
instrument of record-keeping and communications. The sobor
would alter the structure of the chancellory considerably to
force it to conform to the needs of the restructured church.
Most notably, the office of Procurator would be abolished
and his position taken by the Patriarch or some other first
prelate. The Synod would be restructured to function in the
place of all-Russian sobors when they were not in session.
However, the Synod should always adhere to sobor resolutions and not make policy itself. Samarin and Titov realized

that the transition in ecclesiastical administration would be slowed by taking the Synod chancellory over *in corpore*, but they believed that continuity had to be provided. The slate could not simply be wiped clean, especially in times as troubled as 1906.[26]

The majority of the Dmitri sub-commission favored making the first bishop of the Synod the president of the sobor, rather than leaving the choice of sobor presider to the Procurator. Antonii Vadkovskii, metropolitan of St. Petersburg, would thus become chairman of the sobor. Archbishop Dmitri and six members of the sub-commission opposed that idea, but they were out-voted by nine others, including Alexei Neidgardt, Vasilii Pevnitskii and Brilliantov, who normally sided with the archbishop.

The sub-commission easily agreed that the sobor would have to be divided into various commissions to deal with major issues, much as the Pre-Sobor Commission itself had been divided to expedite matters. All personages would have the right to speak and vote equally in these commissions, since the final decisions would be made in plenary sessions and the problem of decisive versus consultative votes would never come up.

Transcripts of the proceedings should be made available to the press in special briefing sessions after each plenary meeting of the sobor. Protocols of the plenary sessions and of the various commissions would be kept, and the communications commission of the sobor would decide whether or not to release them *in toto* to the press after each meeting. The sobor should meet in Moscow, the seat of the all-Russian patriarchate before the Petrine *reglament*, to give a sense of historical continuity with the pre-Petrine church, to remove it far enough from the seat of government to avoid undue government pressure and meddling and to escape the turmoil that the Duma had brought to St. Petersburg. Moscow offered accommodations in monasteries and hotels that would permit the maximum number of delegates and allow as many of the Orthodox faithful as possible to be present at the sessions of the sobor. The new Spasskii cathedral would be the site of the main sessions, with major religious ceremonies carried out in the hallowed Kremlin cathedrals. Finally, non-Orthodox would be barred from the plenary sessions of the sobor, in order to give as much space to Orthodox as possible.[27]

On April 17, 1906, the Dmitri sub-commission turned to the weighty problems of restructuring the central administration of the Russian church. Mikhail E. Krasnozhen, professor of law at Iuriev-Dorpat University in Estonia, and Nikolai D. Kuznetsov, legal advocate in the Moscow District Court, joined the sub-commission for those deliberations. Archbishop Dmitri noted that the second sub-commission, under the chairmanship of Archbishop Nikandr Molchanov of Lithuania, had dealt with the problem of dividing the Russian church into metropolias and had decided rather quickly against them. Should the first sub-commission follow their lead or not? Archpriest Titov opposed summarily dropping the idea of metropolias. If the voice of the lower levels of the Russian church were to be heard, he felt metropolias were essential. The coming sobor should decentralize administration to allow for local expression and direction.

Titov was supported by Nikolai Aksakov, who noted that the First and Fourth Ecumenical Councils had called for the annual convocation of metropolitan sobors and that those who opposed such frequent convocations often cited the absence of genuine metropolias in Russia as justification. Furthermore, all indications in the descriptions of early metropolitan sobors pointed to regular and influential participation by ordinary clergy and laymen. Here was an excellent opportunity for the Russian church to hear from a broad spectrum of its members. Metropolitan sobors had the advantage of being able to respond to problems peculiar to various regions and to shape the agenda for later all-Russian sobors. Furthermore, metropolitan sobors were supposed to appraise the fitness of bishops-elect before they were formally installed in their dioceses. This function had now been usurped by the Procurator of the Synod, contrary to canonical norms. Furthermore, noted Aksakov, ancient dioceses were much smaller in size than Russian dioceses. The average ancient diocese was no larger than the Russian *uezd*, and the size of the Russian diocese approximated the size of the ancient metropolia. He urged that the number of future metropolias be many more than the seven or eight advocated by the bishops in their *Otzyvy*.

Professor Ioann Sokolov of the St. Petersburg Academy, one of the advisers to the metropolitan in preparing for the Committee of Ministers, replied that Aksakov's idea might bring the Russian church into greater resemblance to the ancient church in administration, but that to transform every province into a metropolia and every *uezd* government center into a diocesan center would stretch the financial resources of the Russian church far beyond their ability to bear. Furthermore, the expansion of the hierarchy to fill all those new dioceses would leave the church administration short of qualified candidates for bishops. In many parts of the empire the population was so thin that it would not justify smaller dioceses. Therefore, Sokolov felt that the creation of a larger number of metropolias than the *Otzyvy* had called for and the reduction of the size of dioceses to *uezd* levels would be something the church could work for over a number of years, but should not be attempted in the upcoming sobor. One of the things most needed right now was to streamline ecclesiastical bureaucracy and to weed out useless cyphers. The rapid extension of the number of dioceses would have precisely the opposite effect.

Sokolov went on to say that the patriarchate of Constantinople did not have the metropolitan subdivision anymore, but instead was closely centralized in the patriarchal Synod. Nevertheless, the principle of *sobornost'* had been maintained, with considerable feedback to the patriarchate from the eighty local dioceses. Russia could use the Constantinople arrangement as a model for her own reform.

Archbishop Dmitri noted that the Russian church had some form of the metropolia already insofar as it was divided into regions. Naturally, the overwhelming power of the Synod made these subdivisions far from true metropolias, but the framework was there. In some of the regions there had been meetings during the Easter holidays among the bishops to prepare agendas and work over common problems in advance of the all-Russian sobor. Dmitri felt that if the sobor overhauled the higher administration of the church, regional organizations would become more important and provide the framework to allow lower levels and the higher administration of the church to come together.

Dmitri went on to lament that the West condemned the Orthodox East for being ossified and benumbed because of Orthodoxy's adherence to the forms and structures of bygone eras. Here was an opportunity to revive an ancient form and make it the very instrument of revitalizing the Russian church. Dmitri warned, however, that the Russian church could not simply restore ancient canons in the twentieth century and expect that new life would come automatically. What had to be restored was the substance and spirit of canonical regulations. Those who urged reviving forms for their own sake would leave the Russian church just as lifeless and just as open to western criticism as before. The church was the maker of the canons and should not view itself as merely a preserver of hallowed customs, a museum of the past.[28]

Aksakov and Neidgardt agreed, while Samarin noted that the arguments that local metropolias with annual sobors would restore the practice of *sobornost'* missed the point. The term *sobornost'* had been lifted from the Slavonic translation of the Nicene Creed and was not really accurate. The term was the translation of the Greek word *katholike*, which means universal, catholic, not conciliar as *sobornost'* does. The extensions of the term catholic included the idea of a universal body of doctrines and practices everywhere accepted. St. Augustine expressed it "ecclesia catholica per totum mundum diffusa."[29]

However, Samarin went on, considering the practical needs of the Russian church, the establishment of metropolias was a good idea. He envisioned the Russian church operating through a number of Synod-like administrations, centralized on the metropolitan level rather than in one closely centralized administration. These administrations would take their direction from annual metropolitan sobors.

Overall direction of the Russian church would come from regularly convened all-Russian sobors. Samarin noted that the revered Moscow metropolitan, Filaret Drozdov, had suggested decentralizing the church into regional metropolias with real local authority more than forty years ago.

Fr. Alexander Rozhdestvenskii of the St. Petersburg Academy noted that there were many qualified candidates for the episcopacy among the white clergy. Since the church was now looking for the administrative means to update itself and truly cement bonds among all its elements, one of the surest ways to do that was to remove the impediments against non-monastic clergy for the rank of bishop. The sobor had the right to change the canons which prohibited non-monastic clergy. The practice of tonsuring widowed white priests before elevating them was a mere formality, a travesty of monastic vows since the candidate never had actually been a monk and an insult to the white clergy, the men who carried the burden of religion among the Russian masses. The western church removed this anomalous relic long ago and for good reasons. Now it was time for the Russian church to do so. Fr. Brilliantov noted that such a solution would immediately make it possible to create new bishoprics in *uezd* administrative towns. The reduction would permit bishops to more effectively know the needs of their flocks. Elevation of pastors whom the people already knew and loved would facilitate renewal and regeneration of ecclesiastical administration in smaller areas. Professor Nikolai Suvorov of Moscow University believed that a reduction in the size of bishoprics and the creation of genuine metropolias with annual sobors, together with the consecration of qualified white priests as bishops, would be especially helpful in the western and southwestern *uezdy* of the empire. In those areas there was a strong legacy of Uniate practices. Uniates had followed the Latin practice of making any qualified candidate bishop, regardless of whether or not he was formally under monastic vows. A monastic hierarchy in these regions was still regarded as alien. Where there was such stiff competition from the legacy of Unia as well as a very active Latin clergy, an ancient prohibition against elevating white priests could easily be abolished.

Professor Vladimir Zavitnevich of Kiev Academy pointed out that Metropolitan Filaret had coupled his pressure for establishing metropolias with a demand that the police and tax record-keeping be suspended also. That abnormality had been imposed at the same time sobornal administration had been suspended. The two went together: restore sobornal administration through the metropolia and at the same time end policing activities. Zavitnevich found renewed pressure from the Ministry of the Interior upon clergy to turn in political agitators extremely offensive to the nature and purpose of the church and the surest way to rob the church of the last vestiges of public trust.

Though there was overwhelming sentiment for restoring metropolias, when practical considerations were scrutinized the majority of the sub-commission decided, fifteen to five, against the idea. Many problems—financing the new metropolias and the greatly increased number of dioceses that would be created, finding qualified men to consecrate as bishops, removing canonical prohibitions against consecrating white priests, plus the lack of time to work out a scheme of metropolias to present to the sobor—forced the sub-commission to table the idea.[30]

The issue of metropolias was also discussed in several sessions in the sub-commission under Archbishop Nikandr Molchanov of Lithuania in March. Professor Evgenii Golubinskii, a member of the Imperial Academy of Sciences and a prominent church historian, informed the sub-commission that a plan had been worked out under the reign of Alexander I for dividing the Russian church into metropolias, but it had to be shelved because it would have been too costly for the Treasury to bear in the aftermath of the Napoleonic wars and because there simply were not enough qualified candidates to fill the new bishoprics.

The Nikandr sub-commission then explored ways to partially implement the metropolias, especially in those areas where local problems existed not common to the rest of the church. One such area was the Volga region, where the church was faced with resurgent Moslem revival on the one hand and a new growth of Old Believer proselytizing on the other. The Volga area church needed a metropolitan at Kazan able to coordinate local dioceses and missionary brotherhoods. The church was losing ground in the region as political reforms became more concrete. The church would not be able to rely upon government services to stem the tide.

An area where the need was felt to be even more pressing in view of the international political implications with Austria-Hungary was the western and southwestern provinces. Archbishop Nikandr believed that there should be an Orthodox metropolitanate at Vilna. He noted that since 1905 there was a groundswell of Uniate sympathies on the one hand and of Latin Catholic activities on the other. Msgr. Edward von Ropp, Latin metropolitan-archbishop of Mogilev, was a vigorous prelate who threatened Orthodoxy once the restrictions on proselytizing among the Orthodox, particularly one-time Uniates, had been removed. Nikandr traced an alarming picture of the rate of defection, numbering 250,000 people since April 1905. He pictured an army of Catholic priests drawn up in a quasi-military command assaulting the Orthodox and gaining sweeping successes. Their aim, he asserted, was nothing less than seeing every Orthodox church in the western parts of the empire transformed into a Catholic church and the simple people responding to the commands of Rome. Especially troublesome were their open designs to reclaim churches that had at one time been Uniate or Latin.

Archpriest Iosif Koialovich, pastor of the cathedral of Lida, a market town forty-five miles directly south of Vilna, warmly supported Archbishop Nikandr. At Lida there was a particularly alarming resurgence of Unia and Latinism. Koialovich supported the idea of a metropolitanate for Vilna. It would enhance the dignity of the Orthodox administration in that region, besides drawing the clergy together to combat the propaganda directed against the "schismatics." That term in itself was one that the simple people found sinister because they did not understand it and the historical bias that it carried. The archbishop and Koialovich both felt that the dioceses in the western areas should be reduced in size immediately, even though the expense involved would be much greater because the Orthodox people were poor and could not even support the bishops they now had. The flock needed more shepherds in these trying times. The Brotherhood of the Holy Spirit in Vilna had been doing yeoman service, but there was no way they could stem the propaganda from the Catholic side, much less launch a counter-offensive among the Catholics themselves. Koialovich noted darkly that desertion to Catholicism meant coming under the influence of Latinism and Polish nationalism, since the law did not permit the Uniate church to operate.

In the southwestern provinces the same kind of need existed, but there was the danger that if the church administration was decentralized and new bishops appeared in smaller dioceses, they would have to be drawn from the local population and would probably be politically soft on Ukrainian nationalists. However, if they were not from the local area, they would be looked upon as Muscovites, and the local population would not trust them. Both Frs. Koialovich and Timofei Butkevich, professor at Kharkov University, together with Professor Nikolai Suvorov, worried that decentralization would give encouragement to these local cultural and political interests and that local bishops would become divisive in the church administration because they would sympathize with them. The very appearance of metropolias at this time would be interpreted as a sign that political autonomy was forthcoming, and that political danger made it expedient not to consider metropolias for the time being.

This argument made Fr. Fedor Titov very angry. Political considerations were not the concern of the church, he thundered. What did it matter if local cultural differences manifested themselves among the bishops and clergy of the western and southwestern regions? Such a development would put the lie to the charge that the Orthodox church was an alien thing, used purely for political ends. The church was supposed to transcend political purposes. Titov referred to the Georgian church, which had a large measure of internal self-administration and used a different language and ritual, but posed no threat of political division in the empire.[31]

Butkevich roared back that in the southwest the church was still riven with non-Orthodox corruptions and attitudes that the creation of metropolias now would help to perpetuate and threaten the very unity of the state church. The Orthodox church was the instrument through which the loyalties of the local population were focused on the Russian Empire and its Tsar, and those ties could not be weakened now. That was the historical fact of the situation, and pious utterings to the contrary would not change it.

But Fr. Koialovich thought that was going too far. The Orthodox clergy were losing the respect and loyalty of their people just now, he said, precisely because they were utilized for political purposes. Political agents forced the priests to spy upon and report their people, and the people hated the priests for it.

The problems outlined and the bitterness they evoked caused the second sub-commission to shelve the question of metropolias, just as would the first.[32]

On April 19, the Dmitri sub-commission examined the question of the reorganized central administration of the church. Three points of view quickly emerged as to how the new administration should function: through a Synod, headed by a Patriarch; through sobors that would sit regularly, with the Synod and Patriarch merely their instruments; or through a Patriarch possessed of powers rather like a Pope, with the Synod absorbed into his chancellory.

The majority of the sub-commission favored making the sobors the supreme authority in the church. They would define policies, establish programs, iron out doctrinal disputes and update the traditional teachings of the church. Periodic sobors would act as courts of highest instance in the ecclesiastical legal structure, hearing complaints against the Patriarch or metropolitans and moving to defrock and excommunicate them when necessary.

Suggestions about how frequently to summon the sobors ranged from every two to every fifteen years, with the majority eventually believing that ten-year intervals were the most realistic. If major crises arose, sobors would be summoned more frequently. If the proper authorities failed to summon the sobor, then it would automatically summon itself every ten years. Otherwise, it was feared, political pressures from outside the church or self-seeking interests inside the church would delay its being summoned.

A related problem was how to finance the sobor. Alexei Neidgardt observed that sobors were the surest way to prevent the state from gradually encroaching upon the prerogatives of the church. Therefore, they had to come with regularity, but it would cost about 500,000 rubles every time. Who would foot the bill? Several members of the sub-commission felt that the State Treasury was the only source they could tap. Sobor expenses would be extraordinary expenses, and the church did not have that kind of money at its disposal. But Samarin pointed out that if the church had to go hat-in-hand to the State Treasury every time it wanted to summon a sobor, the state would use that dependence to exact concessions from the church. The Russian state had proven itself notoriously suspicious of the church in the past, and it would not fail to utilize its hold of the purse strings to thwart the freedom of the church again. New sources of income would have to be devised that in no way depended upon the favor of the Treasury. The already loud clamor among leftists in the Duma about church budgets was just the beginning of a long siege. Bishop Dmitri thought that perhaps the Treasury would bear the expenses of the first extraordinary sobor, but after that the church would have to find its own resources. Dmitri thought that once every five years was about all the church could afford.

Mikhail Krasnozhen of Iuriev-Dorpat believed that five-year intervals were too frequent—both for the amount of money that would be required and for the amount of business that sobors would actually have to transact. In Germany, he noted, the Evangelical Lutheran church convened its general assemblies once every ten or fifteen years and had regional consistorial meetings every two or three years. This pattern could serve useful in the Russian church, too. Finally, ten-year intervals were agreed upon.

Safeguarding the independence of the church was a major concern during most of the deliberations of the Dmitri sub-commission. Alexander Almazov of Odessa and Stefan Golubev of the Kiev Academy cautioned, however, that the Russian church should retain intimate relations with the state, whatever forms those relations ultimately took. The church shared with the state a co-responsibility over the same mass of people, and not simply in affairs of the spiritual realm. The church's roots were deep in the Russian soil, and the government regarded the church as one of its mainstays. For that reason, the government would insist upon having a major influence in the proceedings of the coming sobor and any subsequent sobors that would meet. Furthermore, Russian church-state relations had their roots in the Byzantine tradition, which envisioned a close harmony of interests between religious and civil authorities. On a number of occasions, the Byzantine government had removed Patriarchs who had not harmonized with the purposes of the state, but at the same time the Byzantine state had supported the church and greatly expanded its authority at the expense of the other Patriarchs in the East. Constantinople had given its Patriarchs the right to intervene and settle disputes among the clergy and hierarchy of the jealously independent patriarchates of Alexandria and Antioch.

Likewise, in Russia, the initial conversion to Christianity had come at the behest of the state. Right from the outset there had been a struggle to prevent the ecclesiastical connection from subverting the state to Byzantine political control and autocephaly resulted, which was made permanent in the 1440s when the princes of Moscow refused to accept the Council of Ferrara-Florence and after 1453 when the Turkish conquest rendered the very tenuous subjection to the Byzantine patriarchate obsolete.

The Russian patriarchate itself had been established in 1589 on the initiative of the state. The state was fully aware of the services rendered by the church in retaining Russian unity during the Time of Troubles. The state summoned the

Sobor of 1666-1667 to curb papalism and defrock Nikon, and the state had imposed Peter's *reglament*. Thus, it would be utter foolishness to overlook or try to negate the right of the state to have a voice in ecclesiastical matters. The state would regard it as another sign of Nikonism and would interfere again with a heavy hand. Golubev had taken part in the preparations for the Law of Toleration under Witte and knew whereof he spoke.

Restructuring the Synod became the next problem on the sub-commission's agenda. The present structure was not canonical because it did not have a presider or chief bishop, because it did not have control of its own affairs and because there were non-canonical members seated on it. Its members, their titles, their term of membership, their agenda and their ultimate decisions were controlled by the civilian Procurator. Canonically, such an official had no business interfering in the internal affairs of the church and governing it without sanction from the bishops.

To rehabilitate the Synod was to make it conform to the ancient canons and to make it truly the instrument of the bishops. Since all-Russian sobors would be the authority-granting bodies in the Russian church, the Synod would govern only between the sobors. It would have no authority independent of them and could not contravene their decisions or refuse to implement policies they had authorized. It followed that the chairman of the Synod, whatever he was titled, would be the head of the Russian church, its first prelate. Most of the members agreed that he would be the metropolitan of St. Petersburg in any case. He would deal with the civil authorities on an equal footing on behalf of the church and would stand with heads of other autocephalous churches as their equal. The most important need for a recognized head of the church, chosen by the church, was that his office would stand between the church and meddling politicians and bureaucrats.

In this context, attorney Nikolai Kuznetsov made a lengthy and impassioned plea to the sub-commission to work out means to intimately involve white clergy and laity in the administration of the church, from the sobor and the restructured Synod down to the parish level. It would be a terrible mistake, he warned, to let even the appearance of restructuring the Synod and the synodal chancellory be a means to jettison hundreds of lay bureaucrats and tighten control by the bishops at the expense of laymen and white clergy. The reasons for avoiding that were all too apparent. In those critical months, a deep fissure had developed between the hierarchy and the lower levels. Bishops were regarded as nothing more than *chinovniki* in cassocks, agents of the government like any other bureaucrats. The restructured Synod had to have laymen and white clergy among its membership. Clergy and laity had to have visible representatives, actively participating in the day-to-day administration of the church. They had to have decision-making votes and voices in the Synod, not just advisory ones.

With the Tsar's authority at that moment undergoing considerable diminution in the civil administration, there had to be corresponding diminution of his authority—or rather that of his agent, the Procurator—in the church. If the church was left propping up the crippled bureaucracy of the state, the church would be blamed by the people for whatever losses they might experience. The church had to make clear its distinctness from the state and work to bind its various elements together in a new structural stability.

The first thing the church had to achieve was total administrative autonomy. This had to be achieved within a few months. An internal autonomy like that enjoyed by non-Orthodox denominations had to be acquired, an autonomy that could not be infringed upon except by the consent of the ecclesiastical administration. The rapid development of Old Believer strength since the declaration of toleration was something that had to be taken seriously. A precious year had already elapsed. Another precious twelve months could not be lost. It was all very well and good to speak of the church as viewing itself in the light of the times and canonical norms of the ecumenical era, but this was now 1906, and if the church did not act decisively and immediately, events were going to sweep it along again.[33]

Kuznetsov's plea made an enormous impression upon the

members of the sub-commission. Kireev, I. I. Sokolov, Fr. Rozhdestvenskii, Almazov and Zavitnevich all enthusiastically endorsed his statement. The archbishop quietly noted, however, that that meant making the voice of laymen and white clergy equal to that of the bishops in the Synod. Professor Stefan Golubev of Kiev took up that theme and made a vigorous statement, warning that the times could not be allowed to stampede the church into structural changes that were not consistent with the Orthodox tradition. Kuznetsov's plea had merits, he said, but the involvement of laity and white clergy in the day-to-day administration of the church should come at the diocesan and *blagochinie* levels. Those were the levels where involvement from those elements were most needed and where they would have the greatest effect. There was no canonical precedent for involving them at the highest levels in the way Kuznetsov had suggested. In fact, Kuznetsov's plan was Protestant, showing Stundist tendencies, in that it levelled all elements in the church and made no distinction between lay and hierarchical personages. At this late date the Orthodox church did not need any more Protestant innovations. It needed to free itself from them. On the other hand, Orthodoxy did not regard the laity as an inert mass the way Catholicism did. The Orthodox way lay in the middle. Peter Moghila was a model of how to involve the laity and the white clergy effectively in the church's government and defense. Moghila mobilized the church in times that were as hectic as these, but had each element within the church functioning distinctly. Fraternities of laymen, associations of priests, monks and nuns all played their unique roles and helped launch the counter-offensive that both religiously revived the church and permitted it to fend off the encroachments of the political authorities. Something of that nature had to be achieved in 1906, too. One could not just overthrow the canons and historical experience of the Orthodox tradition.

Professor Nikolai Suvorov of Moscow University agreed, but suggested that the Russian church adopt the practice of the Byzantine church of having a mixed council as an adjunct to the patriarchal Synod. White clergy and laity predominated in the mixed council in Constantinople and provided valuable insight and information into the administration of the church and the Orthodox millet, particularly in financial and educational matters. However, canonical norms and episcopal dignity were preserved by having all strictly doctrinal and disciplinary measures concerning clergy and hierarchy left in the hands of the Synod. A similar arrangement allowed extensive involvement of clergy and laity in the administration of the Orthodox church in Austria-Hungary. Besides instituting something on the order of a mixed council, Suvorov envisioned extensive involvement of lay advisers in such problems as mixed marriages, divorces and annulments when they came before the Synod. That way the principle of *sobornost'* would be preserved and activated. But, he cautioned, the bishops were the successors to the apostles. There could be little doubt that the apostles governed the early church. It would be untrue to the apostolic succession to make them figureheads only.[34]

Eventually, the sub-commission resolved the thorny problem of hierarchical versus lay and clerical representation by including representatives of all three elements. All three segments of the church would have the right to participate in general sessions of the sobor and to cast binding votes in all cases that did not involve questions of dogma, definition of moral law and liturgy. In those questions, binding decisions would be made by the bishops alone, but with the full participation, however, of the other elements in the discussion of those questions. It would be left to the sobor itself to decide at each step whether or not a question was of so grave a nature that only the bishops would make the decision. The sub-commission defined the authority of the upcoming sobor as having all legislative, governing, investigating and judicial authority in the Russian church, plus the right to elect the head of the Russian church.

The Synod, the sub-commission concluded, should be made up exclusively of bishops in order to preserve the principle of succession from the apostles. That recommendation was upheld by the full Pre-Sobor Commission on June 1. There would be several committees attached to the Synod,

much as there were now, in which non-bishops would pre-
dominate. The Synod would be the implementer of the decisions of the general sobors of the church and at the same
time the cabinet of the head of the church. The members of
the sub-commission were keenly aware and vigorously reminded
by Professor Brilliantov that there was always the danger
that the patriarchal Synod would in time evolve itself into a
type of papal curia. The patriarchal chancellory of the Greek
patriarchate was evolving in that direction right at the time,
with the full support of the Turkish government, which could
utilize it better to control the Orthodox population. The
church could avoid a type of papal curia in Russia by regularly
convening sobors. Professor Suvorov heatedly reminded his
colleagues that in the seventeenth century the government
had to intervene to prevent a papalist development and that
Peter's Regulation was imposed for the same reason. The
church had to avoid both papalism and Protestant splintering.
Complete hierarchical control was clericalism. Subordination
to lay control was Protestantism. The Orthodox way lay between, devolving authority to the dioceses while maintaining the authority of the bishops.

Opinions on how many people should be on the Synod
ranged from six to sixteen, with most of the members of the
sub-commission favoring twelve. At least three of the members of the Synod should be permanent—the metropolitans of
St. Petersburg, Moscow and Kiev. They would have co-
adjutator bishops to look after the administration of their
dioceses while they were active in the Synod. Some sub-
commissioners felt that the other episcopal members of the
Synod, three or six more, should rotate in such a way that
over a period of time all of the bishops would serve on the
Synod. Rotation of bishops in the Synod would be much
slower than at present, with their terms ranging from two
to six years. Another alternative was that the sobor would
elect the full Synod every time it met and that that Synod
would remain until the next sobor replaced it. Then there
would be no rotation at all. The sobor would know best
where to lay emphasis in meeting current needs and would
know whom to choose to meet those needs.

When final positions were clarified, twelve of the sub-commissioners favored a Synod of bishops alone and nine favored a Synod that included laymen and white priests. In the end, all favored a Synod of twelve members. Those who would restrict Synod membership to bishops envisioned some other way, possibly a Synod Council (*soviet*) of twelve members that would function as a type of lower house in the higher church administration but would leave all doctrinal and final decisions of discipline in the hands of the Synod proper. There was no agreement on how many of the Synod members would be permanent and how many would be regularly replaced. The full Pre-Sobor Commission resolved that question on June 1 by deciding that five members of the Synod would be permanent—the bishops of Petersburg, Moscow and Kiev, because of their importance; Kazan, because it was in an Old Believer and Moslem area; and Vilna, because of its proximity to Uniates, Latins and Lutherans.[35]

On May 1, while processions of laborers coursed through the city, the Dmitri sub-commission decided that temporary members of the Synod should be automatically rotated according to their seniority in the hierarchy, depending upon the date of their consecration to the episcopate. A strong secondary position, supported by the archbishop, suggested that the church administration be divided into four or five basic regions, with bishops from each region always on the Synod and the rotation taking place at the regional level rather than at an all-empire level.[36]

When the sub-commission turned to the problem of what to title the head of the Russian church, the archbishop, Professor Suvorov and Alexei Neidgardt all pointed out that the office of Patriarch in ancient times had evolved by itself and was never at any time considered dependent upon any kind of Synod. Synods in the sense of the current Constantinopolitan Synod and the Petrine hybrid in Russia were new things and, if canonical authenticity were to be the norm in restoring the Russian church, it would be difficult to make the Patriarch a tool of the Synod. Professor Zaozerskii rejoined that if the Patriarch were regarded as mainly the presider, the title of Patriarch would itself become a stumbling block. In that case, it would be better to forget the restoration of a patriarchate. Fr. Titov noted that when the Russian patriarchate had been established in the first place, there had been no idea of giving it much authority. It was an honorary title which signified that the Russian church was autocephalous and had come of age. Its political usefulness lay in the fact that having a patriarchate helped strengthen Moscow's claim as Third Rome. Nikolai Aksakov emphasized that if the Synod were the supreme governing authority, subject to the decisions of the sobors, a patriarchate would upset that order. Ioann Sokolov declared that all talk about the Synod as an attachment to the patriarchate or the patriarchate as an attachment to the Synod was mere casuistry. They were supposed to work as a unit and not be trying to out-maneuver each other. The synodal chancellory would be the patriarchal chancellory. Sokolov noted that in the heyday of the Byzantine patriarchate there was no such dichotomy between Patriarch and Synod; they had worked together, in unison. Both the *Epanagoge* of Basil the Macedonian and the *Syntagma* of Matthew Blastares, the most concise definers of the office of Patriarch in Byzantium, stressed the importance of the patriarchate as the embodiment of the authority of the church administration, but not as the dictator of the church. Not only was there a *symphonia* between the Patriarch and the imperial government, but between the Patriarch and the church as well. To lose sight of that and to fret about who was attached to whom was to obfuscate the whole concept of what the Patriarch should be.

Furthermore, Ioann Sokolov added, at the present time the Russian church needed the dignity of having a Patriarch at its head. The Russian church was the most powerful of all the autocephalous churches, it was faced with an active Old Believer hierarchy in its midst, and it could not afford to overlook the prestige that had come to the papacy since the last general council of the Catholic church. Hence, to allow secondary arguments to sidetrack the longed-for restoration of the patriarchate now would be foolish. There was nothing standing in the way of making the head of the Synod a Patriarch. The primary weakness of Peter's Synod was that

it had been left headless. Its subsequent distortion and perversion by the Procurators stemmed from that.

Professor Alexander Brilliantov declared, however, that
he could see no canonical justification for restoring a patriarchate to the Russian church. As long as the Synod was to
be the executive and supreme legal authority of the church,
subject to the general directives and decisions of the sobors,
it would be better to avoid all the difficulties that could arise
in connection with the title and regalia of a patriarchate by
simply styling the head of the Synod by the name chairman,
and nothing more. He took Professor Suvorov to task for
constantly dwelling on the theme that Protestantism was
creeping into the Russian church through various innovations—the Petrine *reglament* and other heavy emphasis upon
the concept of *sobornost'*, to name but two. Brilliantov noted
that the Protestant rebellion against the papacy in the sixteenth century had many of the same features that had
marked the earlier controversy between the Orthodox East
and the papacy. Thus, the Protestant experience was not entirely irrelevant in the historical context. On the other hand,
Brilliantov argued, the Russian church is derived from
the Byzantine East and had early on developed its own
unique style. In that context, whatever happened in the West
was irrelevant to the Russian situation. Brilliantov noted that
Metropolitan Filaret Drozdov had been concerned in the
nineteenth century about the growth of Catholic tendencies in
the Russian church in reaction to the heavy Protestant influence of the previous century. Catholic tendencies to over-
dogmatize and over-centralize were evils that should carefully be avoided now. Thus, while Suvorov warned about
Protestant tendencies, it would be well to guard against the
opposite extreme as well. Merely to cite Greek and Byzantine norms should not be regarded as conclusive arguing.
It should be remembered that the Greek church historically
had a weakness for papalistic tendencies in its internal government. Those inclinations had led it to its fatal submission
to the papacy, which had led directly to Russia's breaking
of ties with Constantinople. Brilliantov noted that the Petersburg metropolitan, the person most likely to be chosen Patri-

arch if the patriarchate were restored, was not convinced of the need for a Patriarch and would most definitely be against it if it caused division in the church.

Ilia Berdnikov rejoined that all the talk about papalism in the Russian church was nonsense. There was not the slightest possibility that the first member of the Synod would usurp power from the rest of the members and the whole hierarchy. The restructured organs of administration would preclude that possibility. The Russian church needed to have a Patriarch at its head mainly to insure that it would be autonomous in its own internal government. The Procurator was going to be done away with. The Patriarch would stand at the head of the church. In dignity, he would stand on a par with the sovereign and would deal with the sovereign in behalf of the church. That in itself was enough of a reason why the restoration of the patriarchate was justified.[37]

By mid-May, most of the members of the sub-commission were annoyed that the question of restoring the patriarchate was being bandied about in the religious and secular presses, some of the sub-commission members themselves contributing articles or off-the-record interviews. Archbishop Dmitri and Professors Suvorov and Glubokovskii noted that the hysteria that a restoration of the patriarchate would cause the revival of Nikonism and the creation of a Russian Pope was disturbing a lot of people among the clergy, the lay public and members of other sub-commissions of the Pre-Sobor Commission. Dmitri made a lengthy statement, noting that Roman papalism was the product of peculiar historical circumstances in the West. The Roman Pope had been a unique synthesis of political and spiritual authority because there was no power in the West for centuries that could rival his authority and prestige. The very breakdown of civil authority in the West and the gradual emergence of new forms of secular power had left the Popes free to move with great authority in the void. Dmitri noted that the Roman Popes had not been able to make their claims stick in the East precisely because there was a strong political authority that would not permit that to happen. The reasons the Popes had been able to exercise such great power in the face of

counter-claims by the medieval emperors in the West was
because the Popes and the emperors did not live in the same
city and because the Popes were able to appeal to anti-
imperial interests to check the normal growth of centralized
authority. Had the emperors been able to approximate the
Byzantine model of imperial authority the Popes would have
been much less authoritarian.

Therefore, it was useless to advance arguments against
restoring the patriarchate on the basis of papalism. The conditions for the rise of papalism in Russia never had existed
and were not likely to exist. The church now needed a strong
figure to lead it, and a Patriarch was required. Anything less
would leave the church in the limbo that had given rise to
the overweening power of the Procurators. With conditions
as they were in 1906, the church had to have a strong, respected spokesman, because the times ahead were going to
be difficult.

Dmitri ended with an impassioned plea for the restoration of a new patriarchate in Russia. Using a Hegelian
analogy, he stated that the old patriarchal system had proven
unsatisfactory because it both allowed the inordinate development of patriarchal tyranny over the other bishops and over
the lower clergy of the church during the Nikon era and
therefore had had to be curtailed, and it had actually become a potential threat to the throne during the reign of
Alexei Mikhailovich. On the other hand, the synodal era had
been unsatisfactory because it had permitted the civil government to literally absorb the church and impose heavy
Protestantizing influences. The patriarchal period could be
regarded as the thesis of the pre-Petrine period, the synodal
era could be regarded as the antithesis, while the new era
about to begin would be a synthesis of the positive elements
of both systems. The church could expect better government
internally and more mutually satisfactory relations with the
state as well. Archbishop Dmitri echoed Kireev's sense of
crisis, emphasizing that the right moment was now. The
church could no longer endure the outdated and crippling
synodal system under Procurators. The times were changing

rapidly, and to be frozen in a decadent mold would be a great misfortune for the church.[38]

When the sub-commission defined the duties of the first bishop of the reformed church, they divided them into two categories: as presider over the Synod and as presider over the church. The seven duties as presider over the Synod were defined as follows:

1. To preside over the Synod and conduct its sessions, according to rules suited to collegial institutions.

2. To supervise the implementation of Synod enactments and to supervise the proper functioning of all organs of the central administration connected to the Synod.

3. To convoke all-Russian sobors, in consultation with the Sovereign and by proclamation of the Synod at stated intervals of time, or at any time that no less than one-third of the Russian hierarchy so demanded, and to preside over the same.

4. To carry on direct relations with other churches concerning modern life, either on his own initiative or in consultation with the rest of the Synod in situations of major importance.

5. To function as the medium of communication between the higher levels of ecclesiastical administration and the higher levels of civil administration in day-to-day (*tekushchim*) affairs.

6. To exercise the right of direct intercession with the Imperial Sovereign in matters concerning the inalienable rights and major needs of the church.

7. To present to the Imperial Sovereign an annual report on the internal condition of the Russian

church, indicating its needs in its quest to exercise an elevating influence on the national life.

Twelve duties were ascribed to the first bishop as presider over the Russian church:

1. To celebrate the sacraments at the anointing (of the Sovereign at his coronation).

2. To closely supervise the vacating of cathedral thrones, as demanded by the First and Fourth Ecumenical Councils and the Council of Antioch.

3. To confirm the elevation of bishops to their cathedrals, as provided by the Seventh Ecumenical Council.

4. To authorize leaves of absence for any bishop within the territory of the Russian church or outside it extending longer than a single month, as provided by the councils of Carthage and Laodicea.

5. To receive complaints against any bishop within the territory of the Russian church and to grant him due process, as provided by the councils of Antioch, Sardica and Carthage.

6. To act as an appellate in disputes between bishops and to bring them to settlements of discords without formal proceedings.

7. To clarify proper ecclesiastical procedure for bishops who have personal misunderstandings of it and, if the bishops in question so demand, to bring such misunderstandings before the full Synod.

8. To convene regional councils under the direction of the Synod in order to attack local problems in the church.

9. To exercise general supervision of the order and well-being of the Russian church and to summon the Synod to restore that good order in circumstances where necessary, as commanded by the Seventh Ecumenical Council.

10. To exercise primacy of honor among the bishops of the Russian church and to have his name commemorated, together with the Synod, in all liturgies celebrated by the bishops and clergy of the church.

11. To issue instructional encyclicals and pastoral proclamations to the entire Russian church.

12. To submit to a court of bishops, nominated by the Synod and confirmed by the Sovereign, in the event of his violating the rights and duties of his office (*sluzhenie*), as provided by the Third Ecumenical Council.[39]

With the foregoing out of the way, the sub-commission decided rather easily, on May 17, 1906, that the first prelate of the church would be titled Patriarch, bearing simultaneously the titles of Patriarch and metropolitan of St. Petersburg. The first Patriarch would be elected at the all-Russian sobor. Subsequently, the Synod would appoint *locum tenentes* when Patriarchs died, to be followed by a three-fold electoral procedure. The clergy and laity of each diocese would assemble, choose a single candidate and forward his name to the *locum tenens*. Each bishop would also forward the name of his personal nominee to the *locum tenens*. Then the Synod itself would nominate three potential candidates and forward their names to the *locum tenens*. When the names suggested by the clergy and laity and the bishops had been processed and the names most frequently mentioned by each group certified, then the names from those two sources would be added to the three nominees from the Synod, making a total of five nominees.

Within a month of the death of the Patriarch, the di-

ocesan bishops would assemble in the capital to hear the
names of the five nominees for the patriarchal throne. Three
days later they would reassemble in sacred conclave and ballot
secretly. The candidate with the most votes would be declared
elected. A second ballot would be taken if there was a tie.
A second tie would be broken by the *locum tenens.* Then the
new Patriarch would present himself to the Tsar, with formal
consecration and installation liturgies to follow.

Fedor Samarin, Archpriest Fedor Titov and Professors
Mikhail Mashanov, Nikolai Suvorov, I. V. Popov, Vladimir
Zavitnevich and Alexander Brilliantov, together with attorney Kuznetsov, were against having a Patriarch at all. Their
main objection, articulated by Suvorov, was that in 1906
there should be no pressure to restore the patriarchate. Political conditions were so severely trying the patience and
stability of the Tsar that he would very likely feel threatened
by the restoration of the patriarchate, and if he felt threatened
he would block the restoration. Furthermore, the very wording of the powers to be given to the first prelate of the
church would raise vigorous antagonism in the ranks of the
civil bureaucracy. Fr. Titov went on to say that the restoration of the patriarchate at this time would be looked upon
by large segments of the white clergy as a threat. Everyone
was aware, thanks to the broad coverage the question of the
patriarchate had been given in the religious and secular
presses during the past half decade, that the patriarchate in
the seventeenth century had heavily oppressed the white
clergy and had given rise to the Old Believer schism. That
danger existed again today, particularly since the first and
second sub-commission had both decided to shelve the establishing of metropolias, which could act as checks upon the
power of the Patriarch.

However, the sub-commission voted, fourteen to eight,
to name the first prelate a Patriarch and grant him all the
honors of that title.

Antonii Khrapovitskii was the happiest man in the entire
Pre-Sobor Commission when the first sub-commission went
on record in favor of the patriarchate. Though not a member
of the sub-commission, he had watched its deliberations at-

tentively and had lobbied for the patriarchate both as chairman of his own sub-commission, where he gave fervent
speeches on the necessity of the patriarchate, and privately,
at gatherings of bishops, priests and lay delegates, wherever
he could gain a hearing. A plan he had outlined before the
Easter recess about how to elect a Patriarch was remarkably
similar to the one adopted on May 17. Antonii had pressed
vigorously to give the Patriarch real powers and not just
ceremonial functions and to have the Patriarch be the sole
agent of official communications between the church and
the sovereign, so that the Photian idea of "symphony" would
become a living reality in Russia. On June 1, the general
convocation voted to title the head of the church Patriarch,
by a vote of thirty-three to nine. It marked the end of 206
years of a headless church—or so thought the commissioners
at the time.[40]

CHAPTER VII

The Pre-Sobor Commission (1906): Revitalizing the Church

Having settled the question of the patriarchate, the most important problem became the proper relationship between the church and the state. On May 30 and 31, General Kireev explained in the Dmitri sub-commission that since the political situation in 1906 was in such flux, the church should formalize as tenuously as possible its ties to the state. The state was undergoing a fundamental transformation. The Duma was locked in conflict with the Tsar; the Tsar was the legal protector of the church. It was inevitable that the Duma and the church would collide, too. The church's relations to the Tsar of necessity were in question. The Tsar was Orthodox. The Duma definitely was not.

Professor Ilia Berdnikov noted that the traditional relationship between the church and the state, established by Constantine the Great and preserved in the Russian state since the days of Vladimir the Great, were now coming to an end. The church was reverting to a situation where it had to fend for itself in the face of a civil administration that was at best indifferent and might soon be openly hostile. The phenomenon of government neutrality towards religious matters that had appeared in western governments in the wake of the conflict of the Reformation, and which found its most extreme expression in the government of the United States of America, had now made its appearance in Russia

267

as well. The process had steadily infiltrated, first in the publication of the Manifesto of February 26, 1903, then in the *Ukaz* of December 12, 1904, and finally in the Law of Religious Toleration of April 17, 1905. The protection afforded the church had been weakened. Now the Russian church was entering a relationship to the state either similar to that which obtained in the German Empire with regard to the Catholic church, or possibly even a hostile one as in the case in contemporary France, where total separation had been decreed and church properties and schools had been seized.[1]

Professor Mikhail Ostroumov of Kharkov University stated that there was a group of deputies in the State Duma right at the moment working on a constitutional project aimed at separating the Orthodox church from the state and making the Orthodox faith just another confession among the many coexisting within the confines of the Russian Empire. Under this project, the Orthodox would have no more prestige or privileges than any other denomination—Catholics, Lutherans, Moslems or even the pestiferous Stundists. Any recognition extended to one of them, like in the German model, would be extended to all. The secular press, beginning with *Novoe Vremia*, which had become more and more hostile to the church, was full of the scheme, and it bode ill for the future of the church. The whole thinking behind these moves was to try to put all religions on the same level without distinction. In the long run such a scheme could only bring harm to the Russian people and the Russian state. Without the persistent uplifting influence of the Orthodox church, the cementing element in Russian culture would cease to exist. The whole history of Russia was testimony to the indispensable presence of the church. Without the church, Russia would either have been swallowed up by some other power and culture or would have disintegrated by herself. If one only looked at the canonical norms established by the ecumenical councils and incorporated into the *Novellae* of Justinian, it would be quite clear that the sovereign had an obligation to defend the special interests of the church.

Ostroumov cited several instances in Byzantine and Russian history where the princes or the emperors had failed or refused to defend the church and its interests and had justly come to grief. In the end, it would be the church which would stand in judgment on the civil rulers, and it was in the interest of the latter not to seek temporary gain at the expense of the Orthodox faith. Nikolai Kuznetsov added that just because the Committee of Ministers and the Toleration Law of 1905 regarded other religious bodies in the empire as equals of the Orthodox church, that did not oblige the church itself to do so. There were many ways that the church could defend itself from this levelling process. Refusing to bless mixed marriages to those of other faiths, but granting Orthodox marriages to those of other faiths who were divorced and who now promised to live exemplary Orthodox lives, was only one he mentioned. If the church were truly autonomous, then the state could not impose toleration upon it.[2]

Nikolai Kuznetsov cautioned the members of the subcommission not to be panicked into statements that might be taken wrongly by the embattled Tsar. It was true that the Duma was not an Orthodox body, but the Tsar was still Orthodox. There were powerful lobbies in the Duma from Catholics, whose interests were directed towards weakening the preponderance of the Orthodox church, particularly in the western and southwestern provinces of the empire. Together with Catholic deputies, Lutheran deputies to the Duma had been heard to remark that their denomination was as much Russian, in the sense that its communicants were subjects of the Tsar, as was Orthodoxy. Nothing could be further from the truth. The nationals of those confessions had always worked to undermine the position of the Orthodox church and to turn away Orthodox faithful from their true mother. Thus, it was clear that a major conflict existed between the Duma and the state church as to what the position of the church in the new Russia actually was.

Until April 23, 1906, it had been possible to equate the Duma and the State Council with the church, since both recognized the Tsar as their protector and expected him to play a mollifying role in clashes between them. But the April 23 Fundamental Law declared that the Tsar would make laws in conjunction with the Duma and the State Council, putting limits upon his sovereignty and calling into question his neutrality.

At the same time, the church had before it the hallowed tradition of the Orthodox Emperors, beginning with Constantine the Great. They had all protected the Orthodox church, presided over the ecumenical councils and given the church's canons the force of law in the empire. The same was true of the Russian Tsars, including Peter and his successors. Even though there was grave concern about the canonicity of much of Peter's church legislation, there was no doubt that Peter and his successors remained true as protectors of the church and its interests and defended the church before the claims of other religions. Mutual support between church and state had never been in doubt—until the series of laws of the past year and a half, beginning with December 12, 1904, and ending with the law of April 23, 1906. Nor had there been any doubt in all the laws passed between May 7, 1727, by Peter II, and the reissuing of the Complete Laws of the Russian Empire in 1892 that the ruling family of the Russian Empire would always be Orthodox. Now, with the conditioning of the sovereignty of the Tsar, the door had been opened to the possibility that a non-Orthodox might someday sit on the throne.

All of this made the collation and publication of an Orthodox canon law an urgent necessity. The church had to be in a position to know what its rights and privileges were in the face of the Duma. The church would have to defend itself down the line. It would, of course, have to concede some authority to the Duma in the ecclesiastical budget, as the Duma had the right to review requests from the State Treasury. But when it came to internal administration, the naming of prelates, the undertaking of new missions, the opening of schools, the regulations of marriages, annulments and divorces, and particularly the defining of doctrine and moral law, the church would remain totally independent of the Duma or any of its agencies.

The Tsar would naturally expect to be present at the sobor. It would be his decree that would summon the sobor, and as traditional protector of the church his word would weigh heavily. The church should avoid anything that smacked of a challenge to the Tsar.[3]

Alexander Almazov elaborated that the church was an eternal community which transcended the confines of any single empire or any single form of government. Governments rose and fell, but the church remained. If it did not safeguard its own existence it would be of no use in the future to the state. It would be foolish, however, to adopt a hostile stance *vis-à-vis* the Duma, because the church would be dealing with the Duma for the indefinite future.

Fr. Fedor Titov countered that the church and the Duma were dealing with the same constituency. The electorate of the Russian people would not permit the Duma to humiliate the church. Pressures could be applied to the deputies in the Duma, and they would cease to attack the institutions and values held dearest by the Russian people. The government could not overlook the moral and educational role the church played in public life. Titov urged that the sobor be careful to insure that institutional ties with the state be maintained. He reviewed the historical relations of the church to the state at length and did not find cause for alarm that those relations were changing. The church had proven that it could survive and flourish without Byzantium. Now it could survive and flourish without the ties exercised by the Russian state.[4]

Fedor Samarin, however, argued that the church was not institutionally self-sustaining at the moment. Until that condition existed there was little reason to be optimistic about the future. It was not enough that the Tsar was the protector of the church and that he was Orthodox. He also ruled over a constituency that was 40 percent non-Orthodox. The King of Spain had been known from time immemorial as the Catholic King, but the strength of the Spanish church did not depend on that title or the fact that the King was benevolent towards the church. The Spanish church's strength lay in its institutional autonomy, upon which the King had no right to infringe. Samarin sensed that the fact that the Duma was now sitting and participating in the legislative process of the empire meant that the likelihood of the church's achieving full governing autonomy was less than it had been in the crucial months between the issuing of the Toleration *Ukaz* and the April 1906 decree. Professor Nikolai Glubokovskii of St. Petersburg Academy energetically seconded Samarin's warning, citing articles the former had just published. Until it was granted the same institutional guarantees that were now guaranteed non-Orthodox religions, the church was in mortal danger. The longer this anomalous situation continued to exist, the greater the threat for the church. No one could tell what events might take place in the next few months and years to change the existing trouble. Unless the church were self-governing, it would be liable to any kind of interference, good or evil, that the government or its agents wished to impose upon it. A bland optimism that all would work out in the end was entirely out of place.[5]

In the hectic days of June 1906, the experts in the first sub-commission heatedly and agonizingly worked out a consensus as to the proper relationship of the church and the state for the future. The means of summoning and confirming the decisions of the extraordinary all-Russian sobor provided the model for the rest of the relations between church and state. It was clear that most of the members of the sub-commission were worried about the relations between the church and the Duma and between the sobor and the Duma, even though they would not be meeting in the same city. Very gradually, the experts came to the conclusion that the Tsar, as legal and canonical protector of the church, would formally summon the sobor and open it. He would not, however, preside over its sessions. The newly elected Patriarch would do that. The Tsar would be kept *au courant* of the day-by-day meetings of the general sessions of the sobor and of the decisions the sobor reached. At the end the Tsar would confirm the decisions of the sobor that he found acceptable and issue a formal proclamation of them. They would then become operative in the church. Nothing was concluded as to validating them through the Duma and the State Council, however.

Once the sobor was finished, the new Synod chosen and the means established to rotate bishops in and out of the non-permanent seats, the church would have a virtually autonomous internal administration. A Procurator would remain, but would no longer have the powers he had acquired in the nearly two hundred years since Peter's Regulation. He would not participate in Synod discussions, but would be allowed to audit them. When the Synod made decisions, the Procurator would review them to see if they conflicted with civil law and inform the Synod in writing if they did. His written reports, however, would have no binding effect on the Synod. Points of conflict would be worked out with the appropriate ministries of the civil government, with the Duma or with the State Council. All Synod transactions would be reported to the Tsar by the Procurator, but any direct sovereign-to-church communications or consultations would be carried out in meetings between the Tsar and the Patriarch. The Procurator would be someone mutually acceptable to the Synod and the Tsar. He would sit in the State Council, the Committee of Ministers and the Council of Ministers. He would have the right to speak on behalf of the church in those councils and would transmit in writing decisions taken in those bodies to the Synod. As an appointee of the church, he would not be replaced every time a political crisis necessitated the changing of civil ministers. Either the Procurator or some other person designated by the Synod would go before the Duma or any of its committees or agencies to represent the church. Negotiations between agencies of the Synod and suitable government agencies would be conducted to resolve points of conflict between them.

In keeping with their concern not to have hostile civil agencies intervening in the church, the sub-commission decided that if the state had to interfere because of disorder in the church, the Tsar would do so personally. He would collaborate with the bishops or the Synod, for example, to bring a wayward Patriarch to heel. Normally, however, matters of church discipline would not involve political authorities at all. In a serious issue, the Synod and the Patriarch would ask the Tsar to grant approval or issue condemnation in his role as defender of the church.

The recurring concern was that the church have full in-

ternal autonomy when reform was completed. Alexander
Brilliantov, however, objected strongly to autonomy, arguing that it was alien to the eastern tradition of symphony
between the civil and ecclesiastical administrations. Other
members agreed that autonomy might jeopardize the principle of symphony, but maintained that, given the existing
circumstances, the welfare of the church had to be safeguarded. Brilliantov's objection that insistence upon autonomy
was a Catholic, not Orthodox, principle fell mainly upon deaf
ears.[6]

The sub-commission adopted a twelve-point recommendation governing relations between church and state on June
7, 1906. Some of the recommendations were intended to go
into effect even before the sobor met.[7]

> 1.   The Russian Orthodox church possesses the right
> to establish for itself new enactments, with the con-
> currence of the Sovereign Emperor. In keeping with
> this, the Sovereign Emperor will have the right to
> review enactments of the anticipated extraordinary
> all-Russian sobor and will have the same right with
> regard to decisions of periodic sobors, together with
> any dispositions of a governing nature from the Holy
> Synod.

> 2.   Enactments of the extraordinary all-Russian sobor,
> of periodic sobors and of the permanent Synod which
> deal with disbursements from the State Treasury,
> either as grants to ecclesiastical personnel or to civil
> personnel, will acquire the force of law through or-
> dinary legal procedures.

> 3.   The Orthodox church of Russia is administered
> freely in its internal affairs through its own institu-
> tions, under the protection of the Sovereign Emperor.

> 4.   An official report will be presented to the Sover-
> eign Emperor annually, detailing the affairs of the
> church.

5. Ordinary periodic sobors will be summoned with the concurrence of the Sovereign Emperor.

6. Periodic sobors will be summoned by the Sovereign Emperor at the time of the election of a Patriarch. In the event of a sobor to examine misconduct of a Patriarch, the same shall be summoned and supervised by the Sovereign Emperor.

7. The extraordinary all-Russian sobor and the periodic sobors will present their enactments for the consideration of the Sovereign Emperor through the Patriarch. Likewise, the Holy Synod will present its decisions, in cases so requiring, through the medium of its chairman, the Patriarch.

8. If the Sovereign Emperor cannot be personally present at any sessions of the extraordinary all-Russian sobor or the periodic sobors, he will nominate a representative.

9. The Sovereign Emperor will have his personal representative in the Holy Synod in the person of the Procurator, who will not participate in deliberations. He will audit decisions and enactments of the Synod to see that they are in agreement with the laws. In the event of a conflict between Synod enactments and civil law, he will notify the Synod and the Sovereign to that effect, observing usual forms devised for that purpose.

10. As the representative of the Sovereign Protector of the church, the Procurator will participate in higher government bodies whose deliberations and decisions affect ecclesiastical affairs. He will present issues of a legislative or administrative nature for consideration to those bodies.

11. The Procurator will not formally be a member

of the Council of Ministers. A change in the membership of that Council because of political turmoil will
not necessitate a change in the person of the Procurator.

12.   Paragraphs 42 and 43 of tome I, part I of the
Fundamental Laws of the Russian Empire will be
amended as follows. Paragraph 42 will be changed
from:

> The Emperor, as a Christian Sovereign, is the
> supreme protector and safeguarder of the dogmas
> of the state church and the supervisor of true
> belief and all sacred decorum in that church.

to:

> The Emperor, as an Orthodox Sovereign, is the
> supreme protector of the state Orthodox church
> and the safeguarder of its good order.

And paragraph 43 will be changed from:

> In the administration of the church, the auto-
> cratic power acts through the medium of the Most
> Holy Governing Synod established by it.

to:

> In its relations with the Orthodox church, the
> autocratic authority acts in concordance with the
> all-Russian ecclesiastical sobor, which it acknowl-
> edges, the permanent Holy Synod and the pre-
> sider over the Russian Orthodox church, the Patri-
> arch.

Thus, the sub-commission guaranteed full internal autonomy for the church while preserving vestiges of the traditional Byzantine order of church-state relations. The Duma

was pointedly ignored. Members of the Pre-Sobor Commission were offended by the position paper of the dominant Constitutional Democratic Party in the Duma, which advocated a posture of benign neglect towards the church. When pressed on this point by the attorney Nikolai Kuznetsov, Pavel Miliukov told him, "Oh, we have forgotten about the church." The paper and the slight made a very bad impression upon the members of the Pre-Sobor Commission.[8]

* * *

Once Archbishop Dmitri's sub-commission had worked out a scheme for restructuring the central church administration to present to the sobor, schemes for restructuring the diocesan administration became relevant. Under the chairmanship of Archbishop Nikandr Molchanov of Vilna, the second sub-commission formalized plans for reviving diocesan administration. The second sub-commission overlapped the first on many issues, and many of the same personnel took part in discussions on both sub-commissions. Archbishop Nikandr's sub-commission noted that already in the early part of the nineteenth century, Metropolitan Filaret Drozdov had complained that the diocesan consistory had become so overgrown that it had replaced the bishop as the actual wielder of authority.

Archpriest Timofei Butkevich, formerly a *blagochinie* dean but in 1906 a professor at Kharkov University, said that from his experience as well as from his reading of the *Otzyvy* it was clear that the consistory was the reason for the impersonal and frequently antagonistic relations between the diocesan administration and the parish clergy. The laity were sick and tired of the rigid formalities to which they were subjected for even the slightest problem. As a result they often had recourse to state authorities to resolve problems that normally should be handled by the church. Problems like evicting pastors, recovering church funds and securing annulments or divorces were so complicated and so cruelly handled by consistorial clerks that state courts or *zemstvo* organizations appeared humane and benevolent by comparison. Churlishness on the part of consistorial clerks had been responsible for frustrating the expansion of the church school system in many places.

Archbishop Nikandr did not agree. He felt that Butkevich, the *Otzyvy* and the press in general had overstated the faults of the consistories. Often, he said, the fault lay with bishops who did not care to spend the time reviewing reports sent to them by their consistories and merely affixed their signatures like any other clerk. Those bishops who were determined could and already had in some places effected a change in the attitudes of their consistories and in the character of their diocesan administrations.

Professor Nikolai Zaozerskii of Moscow countered that presently the law excluded the bishop from direct participation in sessions of diocesan consistories, especially when the consistories sat as courts of instance or courts of appeal. That directly violated the pastoral function of a bishop. The law made the bishop into a legal counterpart of a provincial governor in its attempt to separate legal and administrative functions, a concept that was contrary to pastoral principles and canon law. Nikandr objected that he himself was present during many such cases that came before his consistory. Zaozerskii pointed out to the bishop that every time he had participated in his consistory when it acted as a court he had been in violation of imperial law.[9]

On April 20, the Nikandr sub-commission had turned to the problem of how to bring the bishops into closer contact with their flocks. Professor Ilia Berdnikov presented a paper to them, already published in the January issue of *Pravoslavnyi Sobesednik*,[10] in which he made two major suggestions. The first was that the diocesan bishop have a lifetime tenure of the diocese and cathedral to which he was originally appointed. With the prospect of moving from place to place removed, the bishop would then not find it incumbent upon himself to jockey for position and favors with higher church administrators or government officials. At the same time, he would not feel that his future depended upon the good will of local provincial governors or their aides, who would come and go while he remained. Furthermore, a bishop who knew that he was going to live out his life and die in the place of his initial appointment would be more likely to concern himself intimately with the details of governing his diocese, with the clergy who served him and with as many of his flock as he could become acquainted. Nothing but good could come from that, in sharp contrast to the present situation, where some bishops were transferred to a diocese which they publicly indicated they did not want. Berdnikov noted that eastern canon law permitted one transfer of a bishop, but no more. Professor Brilliantov noted that in the West the transfer of a bishop from place to place was a rarity to this day. Canon law permits a transfer in the event of a diocese's being without a bishop. The West frequently rebuked the Eastern church for its musical chairs of transferring bishops. Professor Zaozerskii added that Pope Leo the Great compared a bishop who left a diocese for a more lucrative place to a man who would abandon his bride to a rapist.

A second recommendation was that, in view of the unfeasibility of creating metropolias and a much larger number of dioceses, *uezd* bishops be created. *Uezd* bishops would be virtually autonomous, but loosely subordinate and ultimately answerable to the diocesan bishop. The genius of the *uezd* bishop plan was that the *uezd* bishop would not have to have the complicated and expensive entourage of a complete diocesan consistory, bishop's residence and all the other acoutrements of an episcopal establishment. All the *uezd* bishop would need would be an archpriest to assist him administratively and liturgically in his cathedral, a sacristan and an accountant. He could live in a local monastery or humbler residence than a diocesan bishop required. The complicated details of administration, legal processes and major finances would be taken care of by the regular diocesan consistory. The *uezd* bishop would be autonomous in all local matters and would be much more truly the pastor his flock needed. He would present a written report of his pastorate to his diocesan bishop once a year. His very proximity would permit an understanding of the pastoral concerns of his white clergy and the social-religious needs of his people and would go far to narrow the gap that currently existed between bishops and their charges. The maintenance of an *uezd* bishop would be little more than the maintenance of the pastor of a large parish. Berdnikov noted that in many towns in the Kazan-Viatka region, local citizens had offered to provide the maintenance of a bishop themselves, if only they could have one.

Most of the members of the sub-commission were pleased with Berdnikov's scheme, though the archbishop did not believe that the gap between bishops and their clergy and laity was as serious as commonly believed. Fr. Butkevich was pleased in part because the *uezd* bishop would replace the vicar bishops, whom he felt too closely resembled Catholic auxiliary bishops, which were uncanonical. In all polemics with Latinism on the question of bishops, Orthodox had argued for the essential equality of all bishops. Furthermore, Nikandr argued, the whole concept of vicar bishops was taken from the heretical West[11] and was based on the pattern of suffragan bishops. It was not eastern. It was initiated only in 1708 by Peter the Great and was extended to all dioceses in 1865 by Alexander II. It had Catholic precedent as its justification at that time, and for that reason it should be abolished. Berdnikov objected, however, that the vicar bishops, or whatever one called them, were useful. They were much more directly under the control of the diocesan bishop and were an extension of his person and authority in places where he could not be. Berdnikov felt that a combination of the *uezd* and vicar bishops would work very well. Professor Glubokovskii warned against taking the archbishop of Vilna's statements too literally because he usually exaggerated when he discussed heretics and Catholics.

Berdnikov agreed with Alexander Almazov, who objected that not every *uezd* had the population or the financial resources to support an *uezd* bishop, even with the minimal expense such an establishment would entail. But, Berdnikov said, several *uezdy* currently lost in the vastness of some diocesan boundaries would be able to band together and support their own *uezd* bishop. Furthermore, all *uezd* bishops would have the same status and duties, defined by the central church administration. Nowadays, all vicar bishops did not operate under the same regulations but under instructions drawn up on an *ad hoc* basis by their diocesan consistories.

Uezd bishops would be transferred only for the most serious reasons, such as the sudden death of the diocesan bishop and the unavailability of another suitable candidate or if the special talents of a certain *uezd* bishop might necessitate his transfer to another place. But in all cases, these transfers would be rare and contrary to usual procedure. In due time, when conditions were favorable, *uezd* bishoprics could be elevated to full dioceses, complete with their own administration.

The sub-commission adopted Berdnikov's plan seven to three.[12]

Berdnikov also introduced a memorandum on powers that should be removed from the control of the Synod and restored to the diocesan bishop, as they had been in pre-Petrine and Byzantine times. Among the authorities he recommended to be restored to the bishops was, first of all, the right to establish or to change the status of parishes. Currently, all parishes had to have Synod approval before they could be opened. Sometimes parishes were decreed by the Synod for which there were no funds to build churches or to maintain priests and their families. After much discussion, it was agreed that new parishes would normally need only episcopal authorization, unless they required assistance from the State Treasury. Then the Synod would have to grant authorization and seek the necessary funds from the Treasury. The sub-commission was informed by Frs. Iosif Koialovich and Fedor Titov that all the parishes in the western and southwestern provinces received substantial state subsidies and would, therefore, need extraordinary authorization and funding under the new order. Fr. Koialovich and Professor Almazov noted that the dependency upon the state, whether it was through the Synod or the State Treasury, sometimes worked against the interests of the church. For example, in the years 1869-1872, many small parishes which could not pay their own way were closed in the southern and western provinces, and their closing had permitted an increase in successful proselytizing by Stundists and Catholics. Fr. Koialovich noted that there were several parishes in the vicinity of Lida that were still closed and that the empty churches only served to embarrass the Orthodox. Latins and hard-core Uniates pointed to them as an example of the moral bankruptcy of the Orthodox church.

Secondly, it was decided that the normal authorization for the opening or closing of monasteries should remain in the hands of the diocesan bishop rather than in the hands of the Synod, as had been the case since the Regulation. The reason for that was that the local bishop would have a better idea of the need for and feasibility of a monastery than the authorities in St. Petersburg did. Again, only if a monastery needs state subsidies should the central church authorities be involved in its establishment. Nowadays, not only the Synod but also the Treasury and the Ministry of the Interior had to be informed and their sanctions received. As far as the Ministry of the Interior was concerned, it regarded all monks as social parasites and all lands dedicated to the support of a monastery as wasted. Hence, the freer of that Ministry the church could be, the better. The local bishop would also confirm or reject the nomination of an *igumen* or superior to a monastery or a convent, unless they were stauropigial monasteries like the Nevskii, Troitskii, Pecherskaia and Pochaev. The bishop would also have the right to approve or disapprove prolonged absences of members of his diocesan consistory, and to grant honors and distinctions to members of his local clergy. The bishop would have the right to defrock members of his local white and monastic clergy after a proper hearing.

The local diocesan consistory, with the bishop as its head, would have the right to annul marriages and grant divorces, rather than passing merely preliminary judgments at the diocesan level and then sending cases to the Synod. Only when such cases needed higher judgment would the local bishop and his consistory send them to the Synod, at their own discretion.

The outbreak of superstitious practices in a diocese or the sudden appearance or growth of sectarian or Old Believer activities would be reported to the central church authorities only if local diocesan officials believed the situation warranted it. Notable conversions of personages or groups from sectarianism, the Raskol or non-Orthodox denominations would likewise be reported only if the local diocese felt them significant.

The desecration or burning down of churches and other church properties would be reported to the central authorities only at the discretion of the local diocese. Excommunications and lifting of excommunications would be handled at the diocesan level, unless it was a case of special importance, like the excommunication of Tolstoi in 1901. Even then, dioceses should have the right to remonstrate with the central authorities in such matters, and central authorities should retain the right to review diocesan decisions when appealed.[13]

Normally, the only notification of activities in a diocese or policies undertaken by a diocese would be in the annual report submitted by the diocese. In most cases, dioceses would deal with the government on a local level to resolve issues that needed their mutual attention. Civil authorities could appeal to the Synod if they felt diocesan officials were uncooperative or unreasonable.

Local parishes, clergy and laity would have the right to lodge complaints against their bishops whenever their remonstrances went unheeded or were unsatisfactorily resolved.

Religious societies, brotherhoods and sisterhoods would have the right to establish themselves without diocesan or central church authorization, providing they were financially self-sustaining and not incorporated formally under monastic rules. They would require diocesan authorization if they planned to participate in diocesan programs, such as the setting up of *Edinoverie* chapels.

Archpriest Butkevich warned that setting up *Edinoverie* chapels sometimes bewildered the local Orthodox, who regarded them as Old Believer chapels and could not see why Orthodox were asked to contribute to their maintenance. Butkevich felt that the plethora of new chapels should be restricted. Pavel Mansurov, an expert on Anglican-Orthodox relations, retorted that the reason *Edinoverie* chapels were springing up was to prevent Orthodox who were dissatisfied with the state cult from defecting to Stundism. *Edinoverie* chapels in the southern and western provinces employed local chaplains, sometimes used vernacular liturgies and prevented defections to sectarianism or the Raskol. One of the Stundists' chief means of attracting the unwary was to advertise that they worshipped in local dialects. A bishop was far more able to determine need in such cases and take preventive action before whole villages were lost to Orthodoxy.

One of the major purposes for devolving administrative work from the Synod to the diocese was to cut the amount of paperwork and the number of redundant bureaucrats needed to compile it. One annual report should be the only regular means of communication with the Synod. Paper traffic between diocese and Synod could be cut by two-thirds to three-fourths. If the Synod had reason to disapprove the operation of a diocesan administration or did not understand fully from the annual report what diocesan programs and policies were, then it could demand fuller information from the bishop. In cases where there were ongoing problems or disorders in the administration of a diocese, the Synod would have the right to send an inspector or a team of inspectors to investigate the situation. If the problem could then be worked out with the participation of the inspectors, it would be concluded on the spot and a report would be sent back to the Synod. If it were not, then the Synod could take whatever steps were needed, including the removal of the local bishop. Regular visitations from Synod officials to the dioceses were not provided for, because that would evidence distrust of local personnel and would diminish diocesan autonomy.[14]

A pressing need was to restore the consistory to the direct control of the diocesan bishop and to abolish the independence of the consistory secretary and his direct ties to the Procurator. Instead, the consistory secretary would be subordinate to the bishop. The consistory would be renamed a diocesan council and would conduct day-to-day administrative activities. The bishop would be its chairman, except when he was absent because of pressing duties or illness. In those cases he would name his representative to chair the consistory till his return. The present Fundamental Law, which barred the bishop from participating in his consistory's activities, would be abolished, and he would be given the right to summon and dismiss his consistory at his pleasure. The consistory in the future would be made up of clergy only, elected at the diocesan convocation by clergy and laymen. The term of office would be six years, with half the membership rotating every three years.

The consistory, when sitting as a local court of ecclesiastical appeal on divorces, annulments or consanguineous or mixed marriages with non-Orthodox, would never make transcripts of its proceedings available to civil authorities, as was now required by law. Unfrocking priests, monks or nuns would be exclusively the affair of the church, as would be cases of excommunication. Outside commands or pressures would not be acceptable. Official communication of consistory transactions to civil agencies, provincial and central, would be discontinued. It was none of the civil authorities' business to know what was conducted in the consistory. The consistory was a pastoral institution, not a civil agency.

Professor Berdnikov warned that restructuring the diocesan administration was desperately needed before the convocations of the summer of 1906. The 1905 convocations had been very clamorous and unruly, and with the sobor coming and the political atmosphere as charged as it was, Prince Obolenskii should temporarily restructure the relation of bishops to their consistories and convocations to permit maximum input from the lower clergy and to minimize the risk of ill will. The sobor could then give final form to this reorganization.[15]

In a number of dioceses the upheavals of 1905 had turned the diocesan convocations into forums for a real exchange of ideas and programs for tackling the moribund life of the Russian church. The hierarchy was confronted with an often militant parish clergy, which demanded that the church involve itself in political and social turmoil and reform itself in such a way as to give the white clergy and laity a grass-roots voice in ecclesiastical government. It had been a very unsettling experience for a number of bishops accustomed to dreary diocesan convocations held only because the law required them.

Some dioceses, following the lead of the St. Petersburg metropolitanate, instituted pastoral conferences which gave the clergy an unofficial forum for exchange of ideas and allowed them to communicate to their bishops ideas about the social and religious needs of their parishioners. The need that diocesan convocations be not merely rubber-stamp sessions but be combined with pastoral conferences in every diocese was acute. They should be a kind of ecclesiastical parliament, as Fr. Butkevich hoped. Convocations should function as local sobors, meeting annually, establishing diocesan programs, overseeing diocesan income and expenditures, electing members to the consistories and resolving matters that the consistories laid over for their attention. The care of orphanages, clergy retirement funds, scholarships, school administration, management of candle factories and the like would be handled by special committees of clergy and laymen. Those committees would annually report at the convocations.

Pastoral conferences would be distinct from diocesan convocations. At the former, only clergy would be present, unless lay experts were specially invited or local custom habitually included laymen—as in the south. Pastoral conferences would either meet at the same time as the annual diocesan convocation or at other times and places in the diocese, depending upon the time available and the nature and urgency of the issues. Fr. Butkevich noted that an issue currently agitating diocesan pastoral conferences was the manner of performing baptism—through total immersion or by pouring water on the head of the person being baptized. The former was the traditional Orthodox method, but pouring had become widely used in the southern provinces under the influence of Catholicism. Some Orthodox clergy, under the influence of Unia, insisted that pouring was sufficient, indeed, the only correct way. It took some rather emotion-charged conferences to persuade them to baptize by immersion.

Parishes would send lay delegates chosen by parish assemblies or appointed by parish councils to diocesan convocations. Parish pastors would attend both diocesan and parish convocations *ex officio*. Each diocese would tailor the structure and frequency of meetings of either type of convocation to its own needs. In Moscow and St. Petersburg convocations might be monthly or bi-monthly, while in Turkestan or Irkutsk they would probably be annual at the very most. All civil regulations governing the activities and organization of diocesan convocations would lapse. Transcripts of proceedings would no longer be forwarded to provincial and central government agencies.

All-diocesan convocations would be attended by *uezd* bishops together with representatives from their clergy and laity. Involving the believing masses in the consideration and making of ecclesiastical policies would erase the deep suspicion that the church remained indifferent to and aloof from them and their problems. Such involvement was nowhere forbidden by the canons and would go a long way towards implementing the principle of *sobornost'* in the church.

Once the consistory became part of the bishop's administration and diocesan administration became much more autonomous, the nature of *blagochiniia* would be transformed. The lay members of the Nikandr sub-commission believed that laymen should be included in both the *blagochinie* administration and in the *blagochinie* council, elected by parish councils. Parish clergy would belong *ex officio*. The dean of a *blagochinie* should be nominated by the members of the administration and his name submitted to the bishop for approval. Members of the *blagochinie* administration would be elected by the *blagochinie* council. A vehement debate arose over whether the bishop should have the right to confirm the election of members of the *blagochinie* administration. The issue was left unresolved.

With the *blagochiniia* liberated from the direct control of the Synod procuracy, they would no longer have the burden of policing the local clergy and would become a catalyst for pastoral action and social reform. The sub-commission was concerned that the *blagochiniia* be changed immediately to end curbing and punishing priests who refused to act as police agents. Ties to the Ministry of the Interior and the agents of the Okhrana should be immediately suspended.

Certain dioceses in the patriarchate of Constantinople had recently instituted organizations like the diocesan convocation, as had some places in Syria in the patriarchate of Antioch and in the church of Greece. There was comfort in the knowledge that the convocation was becoming a practice in the Orthodox East, whether or not a canonical norm could be found for it.

Would the diocesan bishop automatically chair diocesan convocations and pastoral conferences, and would the decisions of such convocations and conferences be binding upon the bishop and the consistory? Archbishop Nikandr hotly insisted that the bishop, as pastor of the diocese, preside. Zaozerskii, Almazov and Butkevich vigorously argued otherwise, but when the sizzling debate ended the archbishop was in the majority. The sub-commission finally decided that the decisions of convocations would only be advisory and not binding upon the bishop and his consistory.[16]

*   *   *

The fourth sub-commission, under the chairmanship of Archbishop Stefan Arkhangelskii, worked out schemes for reforming the Russian parish. Since the Law of Toleration of April 1905, competition from non-Orthodox religious groups had become intense. On November 18, 1905, the Synod had set forth guidelines for reorganizing the parish. They were a partial step towards meeting the competition, but did not give the Orthodox parish a legal identity. There was no deadline by which the reorganization of the parish was to be completed. Hence, by March of 1906, very little had been done. In the absence of definite guidelines, the Stefan sub-commission felt that Russian parishes should organize as legal entities, elect officers for parish councils and hold parish assemblies at once. Professor Nikolai Zaozerskii attended the sessions of the Stefan sub-commission and supported Lev Tikhomirov in evolving a consensus that substantially reproduced a scheme outlined by Alexander Papkov in 1902.[17]

If Russian parishes proceeded to organize immediately,

the Synod would have to recognize a *fait accompli*. Most members of the sub-commission felt that a strong parish organization should exist before the sobor so there could be input into sobor sessions from the parishes. In the next few months, constantly changing political and social conditions would be reflected at the parish level first. Strong parish units would prevent political pressure groups, within and without the Duma, from utilizing parishes as their forums without any really religious function being served. They would also prevent left-wing and right-wing factions from harassing the clergy.

During 1906, parish life in large areas of the empire simply disintegrated. Priests who had been home during the Easter recess or who periodically travelled back to their parishes during the spring sessions of the Pre-Sobor Commission reported that hooliganism in the parishes had become extremely serious. Liturgies were disrupted, and gatherings in or near churches had become free-for-alls in which rioting and bodily harm was done to worshippers. The degeneration of parish life became much worse during the summer, and by fall many of the commission delegates reported it functionally dead.

Throughout May 1906, the fourth sub-commission outlined a two-fold function for the parish—as a center of worship and religious education, and as an *obshchina* of the pre-Petrine type, a community that would embrace part of a major city or provincial town, a large village or several small villages. As an *obshchina*, the parish would be responsible for establishing self-help financial funds that would be available for such projects as instituting small handicraft factories, improving community agriculture, hiring horticulturalists to teach better crop usages and hiring veterinarians to teach better animal care and breeding. *Obshchina* funds would made available to youths and girls from the parish to attend specialized schools to bring skills back to the community. Students not returning to their home villages would pay back their tuition and expenses at an established rate.

The parish would maintain cemeteries, build schools, orphanages and homes for the poor and disabled, run dispen-

saries and soup kitchens, establish study circles to teach literacy to adults and instruct them in Christian literature to
prevent activities by atheistic groups and sectarian proselytizers. The *obshchina* would bind the people of the town,
village or countryside together into a strong community, self-
sufficient economically and culturally. In cities, parish societies would operate in manners befitting their localities. Flexibility of approach would allow the involvement of a maximum number of people and reinforce the influence of the
Orthodox church.

The sub-commission recognized that granting full financial autonomy to the parish was necessary to give cohesion.
Funds for church buildings and cult activities should be kept
separate from *obshchina* funds. Church revenues would come
from the treasury of the *obshchina*, established annually by
the parish assembly. Repair and supply needs, together with
clergy salaries, would be budgeted so there would be no
squabbling with the *obshchina* over finances. Archbishop
Stefan emphasized the need for clear lines between community and church finances.[18]

As Archpriest Konstantin Brechkevich, a *blagochinie*
dean from Odessa, repeatedly stressed, the parish should
strive to become self-sustaining as soon as possible in order
to cut ties with government agencies. Each parish should
generate income surpluses to lighten the burden upon individual families. Ultimately, the parish should not have to
ask individual families for tithes or annual pledges, a cause
of much anticlericalism. The surplus returning to the
obshchina treasury would provide overhead for church buildings and clergy salaries. The end of fees for administration
of sacraments and liturgies would end the haggling between
parishioner and pastor over the latter's income.

The parish pastor would have the right to either name
directly or confirm members of the parish council. In larger
parishes, particularly in the cities, the church and *obshchina*
councils would be separate, with the pastor presiding over
the former and acting as merely adviser to the latter. In
smaller parishes there would be but one council.

Parish assemblies would meet at least twice a year, more

often where size and need demanded, even once a month. Parish assemblies would establish both church and *obshchina* budgets, approve plans for investing funds and granting aid and review budgets. Parish assemblies would either elect the council directly or provide a list of candidates from which the pastor could choose his council. If *obshchina* and church councils were separate, the pastor would have no veto or selection authority over the members of the *obshchina* council other than the power of his own persuasion.

Parish councils would interview prospective pastors, deacons and psalmists and their families whenever the positions fell vacant and would provide a list of candidates for those positions to the bishop. In cases of stalemate, the bishop would appoint. Parish councils could, on the initiative of the parish assembly, request the diocesan bishop to remove a pastor who was unsatisfactory. If a parish were laid under interdict by its bishop, its council would have the right to have the diocesan consistorial court review the matter and ultimately to appeal to the Synod.

Parish councils would select young men to study for the priesthood with the intention that they would return to minister in their own parishes. Councils could ask parish assemblies to vote funds for their secondary and seminary education.[19]

Parish *obshchiny* would be legal persons, with full rights to acquire and administer properties. In matters of mutual aid, investments, insurance programs and projects of that type, the *obshchina* would be fully autonomous. However, in matters relating to support of the church, clergy and cult and the support and maintenance of schools, orphanages, infirmaries and other functions which involved the charitable and teaching prerogatives of the church, *blagochinie* and diocesan authorities would have the right to supervise and veto any project they felt too large or inconsistent with larger ecclesiastical goals and policies. Each parish would make its annual budget plans available to both *blagochinie* and diocesan authorities. Diocesan authorities would have the final legal disposition of all church buildings, priests' homes, parish schools and other properties needed for Orthodox worship, maintenance of Orthodox clergy and the propagation of Orthodox belief. Archpriest Mikhail Kazanskii repeatedly stressed that in 1906 there was a real danger that whole parishes or the larger part of the parish memberships might defect to sectarianism, Catholicism or Lutheranism. If the parish held exclusive title to properties, they could legally be expropriated for non-Orthodox worship and preaching.

The parish *obshchina* would be fully autonomous in representing itself before civil authorities, in civil court proceedings and in financial undertakings not under higher diocesan supervision. Parish finances and parish administration would not to be subject to the review or interference of land captains, police officers or other civil authorities unless the parish *obshchina* so authorized or the diocesan administration had given its sanction. Whenever such authorization was given, either by the parish or the diocese, it would last for the duration specified and have to be renewed each time civil authorities wished to intervene. The parish *obshchina* could exclude any and all political, social, patriotic or other such organizations from its properties or participation in its assemblies or meetings. Where parish prohibitions were violated, the parish had the right to take offending organizations or persons into civil court and expect diocesan authorities to stand behind them. The need for autonomy was repeatedly stressed by Archpriests Mikhail Gorchakov, a friend of Fr. Gapon, and Mikhail Kazanskii, pastor of the Vyborg cathedral. Both men had experienced and observed numerous occasions when intervention or intimidation by civil authorities or patriotic organizations, with the tacit encouragement of the authorities, entirely perverted the religious-moral focus of the parish and subjected earnest priests to harassment.[20] Their concern was strongly echoed by Metropolitan Antonii of St. Petersburg, who stressed that it was in the parish that the long-festering antagonism between clergy and laity would have to be resolved if a vibrant church life were to survive the current social and spiritual crises buffeting Russia.

Some members of the fourth sub-commission took Prince Obolenskii to task because the Synod had presumed to issue

the special regulations before the Pre-Sobor Commission convened. They believed that the final disposition of the parish
lay with the sobor, which they expected would sit in the
latter part of 1906. Synod interference meant government
interference, and that was out of order. The Procurator
responded that parish reorganization had to be hastened because of anti-religious revolutionary pressures, on the one
hand, and anti-Orthodox sectarian pressures on the other.
There was no certainty that the sobor would be sitting by
the end of the year, because there was pressure being brought
in the Council of Ministers to postpone the sobor until the
current crisis with the Duma had been settled. The metropolitan of St. Petersburg supported the November 18 regulations as a means of safeguarding the Orthodox parish until
a sobor could sit. The November regulations had been based
upon the council and assembly type of organization introduced into the diocese of Finland by the Petersburg metropolitan when he was archbishop there and since extended to
all parishes in the Finland diocese. Parishes in Finland had
become encouragingly viable under this type of organization
and no longer took an inferior attitude *vis-à-vis* the much
more numerous Lutheran congregations. Fr. Kazanskii urged
that the Finnish parish become the model for the church in
general.

Parish councils, under the direction of their pastors, could,
if all parties concerned were agreeable, function as a type
of fraternal court. Fraternal courts could settle various disputes—marriage difficulties, personal injuries by one parishioner to another, injuries to property, defaulting upon loans
or imposing usurious interests, divorce settlements after a
diocesan marriage tribunal had granted them—so that the
parties involved would not have to bear the expense or humiliation of civil cases. Any local dispute could be settled
amicably without recourse to the formalities and expense of
a civil proceeding. Professor Almazov stressed that parish
courts could be useful, off-setting the spirit of private property and other western social concepts penetrating Russia.
Private property was the source of much competitiveness, oppression and misery and was foreign to the spirit and tradi-

tion of the Orthodox church. Hence, it was desirable that parish *obshchiny* be organized to foster social responsibility. Usury, for example, was contrary to the spirit and canons of the church. On the other hand, the parish *obshchina* should make use of laws governing private property to insure that as a legal person the *obshchina* had full and unfettered title to and disposal of its properties.

Parishioners who worked against the interests of their parishes, particularly their religious and moral interests, could be brought before the parish council, sitting as a court, and be formally condemned. The council could then issue a public declaration of their transgressions and the sanctions to be brought against them, including exclusion from liturgies and the eucharist. If such actions did not bring wayward parishioners to heel, they could be reported to diocesan officials with a recommendation for formal excommunication. Wayward parishioners who still did not mend their ways would face formal legal steps instituted in civil courts to expel them from parish financial, educational and insurance agencies. Parishioners falling away from the Orthodox faith, and therefore terminating membership in their parishes, would lose all financial, fraternal and insurance benefits, plus shares in parish properties.

The Orthodox pastor needed concrete authority, stressed Alexander Almazov. The power of sectarian and Old Believer clergy had been greatly enhanced in their communities by the law of April 17, 1905, and the Orthodox priests needed comparable authority. More importantly, the authority of the Orthodox pastor had been eroded seriously over the past nearly two centuries, and now it was necessary to reverse that process.[21]

*   *   *

Securing independence for ecclesiastical administration carried with it the immediate and necessary corrollary of independence in managing church properties. Since the Regulation, the church had slowly lost title to its properties, and it was a moot point whether there was much hope that it could ever regain title to them or even to a minor portion of them now. The reign of Catherine II had been particularly devastating to church properties. With the loss of control of properties the church had lost a significant part of its ability to operate autonomously, even within the safeguards that the Regulation had tried to assure. With the Duma in the mood that it was in in 1906, it was very unlikely that there would be a willingness on the part of the government to retrocede former ecclesiastical properties to the church or even to authorize funds that would permit the church to acquire new properties. The state was likely to utilize its guardianship over monastic holdings to further its encroachments upon church properties. Many deputies in the Duma were all too eager to emulate their counterparts in France and strip the church of most of its holdings. Among others, the two Antonii's stressed the vital necessity of securing from the government absolute control of ecclesiastical properties at the earliest opportunity.

At the same time, it was necessary to avoid a prolonged wrangle with the government and its agencies about properties because that would reinforce the Duma and the bureaucrats in the Ministry of Finance in their determination to trim subsidies for the church. If cuts were made in the annual subsidies, which totalled one-third to one-half of the ecclesiastical budget, the church would be strapped, especially in the western and southwestern areas where all of the clergy were on state salaries. The school budget depended upon subsidies from the Treasury and from *zemstvo* organizations, as did many of the charitable functions of the church. Hence, the church would have to walk cautiously to avoid losing the subsidies it currently received. Frs. Butkevich, Koialovich and Archbishop Antonii Khrapovitskii warned that it was possible that Old Believers, Catholics and Lutherans would demand state subsidies for their religious activities as a consequence of religious toleration and the assumed equality of religions in the empire. There was comfort in the realization that the state found it necessary to maintain ecclesiastical institutions of the Orthodox faith in some areas and to deny assistance to similar institutions operated by other religious bodies simply as a means of its own survival.[22]

Diocesan seminaries were the key to the future of the Russian clergy and their effectiveness as pastors and leaders among the masses of people. Seminaries had a threefold function: to provide higher education to the children of clerical families, to provide future pastors for the Russian church and as the source of inspiration for Orthodox life in the empire. In the future, the seminary would have to uplift the spiritual tone of parish life and be a vital center of Orthodox learning among the non-Russian and non-Orthodox peoples.

Most experts at the Pre-Sobor Commission, especially in the sub-commission under Bishop Arsenii Stadnitskii of Pskov, agreed that seminaries in 1905 and 1906 had broken down completely in practically every diocese of the empire. Seminarians were in open rebellion, often providing the leaders for public disorders.[23] In several dioceses, classes in the seminaries had been suspended indefinitely. The dispiriting realization that student violence was not merely the exuberance of the times but revolt against the archaic administration of seminaries and against their perception of the church as an antiquated institution unable to respond to the conditions of the era lay heavy upon the whole Pre-Sobor Commission. Seminary students deeply detested the harsh regimen they were subjected to and resented harsh police measures brought against simple parishioners by higher ecclesiastical authorities, in open collusion with oppressive political agencies. The staggering challenge to the experts in the Arsenii sub-commission was to come up with plans for seminary administration and curriculum that would make seminaries the training ground for an effective Orthodox clergy in the future.

With the level of education among the laity rising every year, the number of years a seminarian would have to be in school before ordination would necessarily increase. The problem consisted of giving students a proper background in the traditional curriculum of any seminary—sensitivity and perceptivity in scriptural studies, the writings of the church fathers, the liturgy and music of the Eastern church—and an acquaintance with the intellectual and political currents of the times, so that they could bring traditional learning to bear upon the problems of the twentieth century. Orthodox clergy labored under the handicap of not being very well educated, in addition to their characterization by secular intellectuals of being obscurantist, obtuse and obsolete.

Seminaries in 1906 were still operating under regulations issued by Konstantin Pobedonostsev in 1884. Those regulations had been issued with the precise intention of making seminaries bulwarks of anti-revolutionary propaganda and bastions of traditional patriotism and monarchism. At the same time, they trained a very intellectually limited priesthood. The Pobedonostsev regulations had succeeded in crushing adventurous activities and thinking among seminarians, at the price of creating an atmosphere of sullenness and apathy which periodically boiled over into rioting that had no other motive than to express antagonism towards the type of administration that benighted the seminaries. As professors and clergy, including the metropolitan of St. Petersburg, pointed out, rioting and disorders in the seminaries were nothing new. Seminaries were natural settings for disorders when a tide of anarchism swept the empire. It was no surprise that these past two years had been a time of unusual violence in the seminaries. It was galling to hear civil police agencies blame the church for helping to create violence on the one hand and to hear revolutionary groups charge that the violence in the seminaries was due to the decadent condition of the church on the other.[24]

Many of the members of the fifth sub-commission noted that in the period between 1867 and 1884, when the seminaries were under a relatively liberal administration, student disorders had been much less pronounced than in the quarter century since. However, as Lev Tikhomirov noted, the seminaries had not been designed to train young men for pastoral duties before 1884. Even anti-religious teachers had been employed in them, and many graduates never intended to take holy orders or took them only to acquire a living. The 1884 crackdown had improved that aspect of the problem.

In the future, seminaries would have to combine a curriculum and discipline that both permitted the personal liberty necessary for a student to mature according to his own abilities and inspired him with a love and compassion that would make him an effective pastor in the changing parish. A diversity of seminary types would have to be developed that would correspond to the needs of the widely variegated areas of the empire.

Eventually, the fifth sub-commission decided to recommend two basic types of seminaries: one whose curriculum was designed to train pastors and would follow a curriculum weighted towards that end, and another that would train young men from clerical families for other vocations in life but would be distinguished from schools of the Ministry of Public Education by a deliberate emphasis upon the Orthodox way of life. Graduates of this second type of seminary would take their places in secular life alongside graduates from other types of schools and would provide a counter cultural influence. They would also be employed in parish *obshchina* organizations, diocesan administrations and central church organs and would bring a culturally sympathetic and technically appropriate background to their duties. Their type of education would make them natural partners of pastors in their communities.

The curriculum of the second type of seminary would compare with that taught in higher schools of the Ministry of Public Education, the Ministry of the Interior and military schools, so that students from the seminaries could readily transfer to these other schools for specialized instruction and students from the other types of schools could transfer to the seminaries to gain a deeper appreciation of the teachings and culture of the church.

A repeated concern of the fifth sub-commission, and one in which Antonii Vadkovskii and Antonii Khrapovitskii were of one mind, was that administrators and teaching staff in diocesan seminaries be appointed entirely by church authorities and that a wholesale house cleaning of retired military officers and other incompetent civil servants in the seminaries be undertaken. Metropolitan Antonii warned the members of the Arsenii sub-commission that this house cleaning could not wait, but had to be undertaken in the hope of re-opening closed seminaries in September. Antonii Khrapovitskii himself had experienced discouraging disorders in his sem-inaries, where he thought he had a good rapport with the stu-dents. He found even worse disorders in the summer and autumn of 1906 and all during 1907. The sub-commission was aware that civil authorities looked with a jaundiced eye upon any scheme to separate seminaries from direct police inspection and intervention.

Most of the Arsenii sub-commission felt that once the administration and staff of the seminaries were in the hands of the church, students who either were lackadaisical about the curriculum or who utterly refused to enter into the re-ligious spirit and discipline of seminary life would simply be expelled. It was time that the education of sons of clergy just because they were sons of clergy be discontinued by the church. The state and its agencies had long had an obliga-tion to aid in their education, but seminaries all too often became places where students who had not succeeded in other schools or who had been expelled for disciplinary problems thought they had an assured route to a leaving certificate. No student should be admitted to the seminaries who did not show clear signs of having a vocation to the priesthood or lay service and a love of the teachings and discipline of the Orthodox church. Major efforts should be made to attract students from working classes and other social classes out-side the clergy.

Antonii Vadkovskii cautioned, however, that the church had an obligation to continue to educate children of clerical families. Families were large, usually destitute, and unable to afford education in technical schools and gymnasia. Unless diocesan schools and seminaries prepared them for life, they would be disgruntled and readily attracted to revolutionary activities and violence. Properly educated, however, they could become satisfied, productive members of Orthodox com-munities and an influence for the church and the social and intellectual atmosphere it wished to create. The fifth sub-commission noted that Catholic and Lutheran seminaries in

the empire were not afflicted by the same disorders as Orthodox seminaries and that Catholic and Lutheran clergy made
the maximum propaganda out of that fact. Furthermore,
those seminaries had a strong intermingling of students from
various social classes, and the religious tone of their instruction and cultural atmosphere left little to criticize. Vadkovskii
warned again and again that all the reforms in the world
would fail unless a competent, dedicated pastorate were created. Professor Viktor Nesmelov of the Kazan Academy
urged that an extensive system of scholarships be set up to
encourage students who were truly imbued with a pastoral
vocation to enroll in the seminaries. They would be closely
scrutinized before scholarships were granted to insure that
they were not simply entering seminaries for a free education.
Seminaries would recruit talented and serious students from
technical schools, gymnasiums and *zemstvo* schools as well
as church schools.

However, Archpriest Tikhon Kozlovskii, a *blagochinie*
dean from the Mogilev diocese, insisted that the clerical
family was the surest source of truly Orthodox candidates for
seminaries. He warned that in certain areas, notably the
western and southwestern dioceses, non-clerical students were
infected with crypto-Catholic or sectarian attitudes that were
hard to detect and hard to root out. The shades of difference,
especially with Catholic influences, were difficult to delin-
eate, but when they were all taken together they fostered an
attitude and a point of view that was alien to the spirit of
Orthodoxy.[25]

One of the fondest dreams expressed in the Pre-Sobor
Commission was to bring the Old Believers back into the fold
of the state church. Archbishop Antonii Khrapovitskii of
Volhynia had studied the teachings and rituals of the Old
Believers since his days in the seminary and had concluded
that, with minor alterations in their beliefs, there was no
major difference between them and the state church. The
archbishop had strong doubts about the manner and reasons
for the excommunication of the Old Believers in the seventeenth century, and he hoped that the imminent all-Russian
sobor would welcome them back as *Edinovertsy*. To that

end, he pushed the Pre-Sobor Commission to recommend to the sobor that a special *Edinoverie* bishop be permanently seated in the Synod and that *Edinovertsy* have a large measure of internal autonomy.

The archbishop of Volhynia was very much aware that there were minimal differences of rite between Old Believers of Austrian succession and underground Uniates in the southern and southwestern areas of the empire and feared, as a result of the Law of Toleration, that they might make common cause if the state church did not seize the initiative and make strong overtures to the Old Believers. The Petrine reform was the Old Believers' primary argument against the state church's validity. Therefore, restoration of an all-Russian patriarchate and the summoning of the sobor had to be accomplished within the next few months, lest the opportunity for approaching the Old Believers passed. They were already inclined to elect their own Patriarch. If these events occurred before the state church acted, the division would be prolonged, and the state church would have lost a major round in the struggle for the loyalties of the masses.

Antonii warned again and again that one of the most effective forms of Catholic propaganda in the western and southern provinces was that the Uniate church would be restored soon. Among the unlettered masses, that made a powerful impression. Catholic clergy even had the audacity to specify before their audiences and in their publications which churches and ecclesiastical monuments would be restored to the Uniate church. Antonii reiterated that if the Austrian hierarchy of Old Believers and the Uniate church now headquartered in Austrian Galicia were allowed to join forces, the political implications for the Russian Empire would be ominous. However, if a reconciliation with the Old Belief were affected, the powerful psychological impact of their condemnation of the state church as illegitimate would be gone. This would in time take away some of the opprobrium of the state church as "schismatic." Moreover, the solid conservatism of Old Believer political attitudes would be of inestimable value to the Russian autocracy. Remove the caesaropapism of the Petrine *reglament* and the political opposition of the Old Believers would be weakened. The Old Believer administration that had taken shape since the Law of Toleration had structured itself along the very lines of *sobornost'* that Russian theologians and canonists had been advocating—a fact that was being noted by the laity and clergy of the state church.

Antonii believed that if a reconciliation could be truly effected, then over a period of time the differences in ritual could be worked out to the satisfaction of everyone. Once the psychological barrier against the state church had been removed, many Old Believers might find differences in ritual less significant than before and be won over gradually to the rites of the state church. For this reason, he heartily approved permitting mixed marriages between the members of the state church and Old Believers, on the condition that the latter allow themselves to be instructed in the doctrines of the state church—without the obligation to formally convert— while he most stridently refused to permit mixed marriages between Orthodox and Catholics. It was not that Catholic sacraments were not as valid as Orthodox, but Catholic pressure upon the non-Catholic partners in mixed marriages was so great that the Orthodox partners were usually lost to Catholicism. Archbishop Nikandr Molchanov of Lithuania heartily supported Khrapovitskii. Antonii made extensive use of the writings and public addresses of Mikhail Semenov of the St. Petersburg Academy, who believed that there were no canonical problems preventing full reconciliation of Old Believers to the state church.[26]

The Pre-Sobor Commission held its last meeting on June 14, 1906, and dispersed for the summer holidays under the gathering cloud of crisis that accompanied the dissolution of the State Duma three weeks later. Bishops had to convene diocesan convocations to gain fuller insight into the fluid conditions of their dioceses. Violence became more and more terrifying during the summer and fall of 1906. Many of the delegates to the Pre-Sobor Commission felt that they would not be allowed to reconvene in the autumn because conditions in the empire would be too troublesome. Some of them advocated that the Synod chancellory finish their labors for them, that the Tsar be asked to set a specific date for the sobor before the summer ended, or that they themselves set a date before adjourning.

The delegates were concerned about the Duma. Confrontation between it and the government had reached a climax, and it appeared that the Tsar might give way to its demands to control government policies entirely. Laws had been drafted that would forcibly alienate lands to redistribute to the peasantry. The church had legal title to millions of acres but had not had independent disposal of them since the reign of Catherine II. Loss of title to these lands, together with cuts in the ecclesiastical budget, would demolish the church's bargaining position in the Duma for subsidies from the Treasury. Without guaranteed subsidies for the indefinite future, the restructuring of church administration, overhaul of church schools, establishment of an independent ecclesiastical court system and even the sobor itself were all in question. In such circumstances, the position of the church in the Russian Empire would be in serious jeopardy. Many of the delegates in the Commission urged bishops, priests and laymen to put pressure upon their Duma representatives not to harm the interests of the church. Some who believed that the present Duma would not last very much longer felt that the diocesan convocations would provide an excellent opportunity to organize campaigns to elect priests and laymen for the next Duma who were sympathetic to the needs of the church.

Thus, on June 12 and again on June 14, intricate discussions were held on what precisely was the relationship of the government and the church in the spring of 1906. Professor Mikhail Ostroumov of Kharkov University argued that the December 17, 1905, rescript of Nicholas II to the three metropolitans authorizing them to determine when to summon the sobor for a total reconsideration of the relationship of church and state and complete revival of the canonical bases for the administration of the church meant *de facto* that the Tsar had already restored self-government to the church and that therefore the church, headed temporarily by the three metropolitans, could now determine its own course. Ostroumov was especially concerned that the Duma not be regarded as having put limitations upon the Tsar before that date and therefore upon his relationship to the church. He was warmly seconded by Fr. Mikhail Gorchakov of Petersburg, who warned that if the Duma had already reduced the Tsar to being a constitutional monarch and the church still legally remained subject to the Tsar's will, then the church was also subject to the Duma. On the other hand, Gorchakov argued, if the Toleration Law of April 17 and the rescript of December 17 were taken together, it was clear that the church had gained its administrative autonomy already and was free to proceed entirely independently of government agencies.

The Procurator objected that such an argument reduced his position to being nothing more than an observer and that until the laws regarding the relationship of the Synod to the Tsar and the Procurator to the Synod were explicitly changed, they remained in effect. He was joined by Antonii Khrapovitskii, who argued that to proceed as if the church were autonomous and no longer dependent upon the will of the Tsar meant that the special position of the Orthodox church in the empire had already been abrogated. He concluded that if that were so, then the relationship of the Orthodox church to the Tsar was no different than the relationship of the Catholic or any other church to the Tsar, something that ran counter to the whole national history of Russia and the canonical responsibility of the Tsar as protector of the Orthodox church. As far as a hostile Duma invading the precincts of the church was concerned, he went on, the canons explicitly forbade that, and no government body or agent could alter that, now or ever. No one could overlook the vital link between the tsardom and the church, whatever powers the Duma arrogated to itself or the Tsar agreed to give up.

The Pre-Sobor Commission adjourned with the church in a legal limbo.[27]

*   *   *

On April 17, 1906, exactly a year to the day after the Toleration proclamation, Witte had been relieved of his post as Prime Minister. Together with him went the liberal and sympathetic Prince Obolenskii, though Obolenskii had wished to remain as Procurator and the new Prime Minister, Peter Stolypin, had wanted him to continue. (Obolenskii was a cousin of Stolypin.) Obolenskii's replacement was Prince Alexei Shirinskii-Shikhmatov, Sabler's replacement as Assistant Procurator under Pobedonostsev, whom Pobedonostsev himself had described as a reactionary. Witte derisively referred to him as Shakhmatov ("Checkmate").[28] Shirinskii-Shikhmatov did not believe there was anything fundamentally wrong with the way the Russian church was administered and looked with suspicion upon the clergy for producing such men as Georgii Gapon and Fedor Tikhvinskii, who in the Duma stridently denounced every government attempt to block land reform and government support of such scurrilous organizations as the Union of Russian People and the Black Hundreds. He made little effort to conceal his dislike for white priests and liberal professors at the general sessions of the Pre-Sobor Commission. The new Procurator believed that the Synod should, with the assistance of the Okhrana, crack down upon rebellious clergymen and not encourage them with talk of a sobor or any major reforms of the church. Shirinskii-Shikhmatov did not like the metropolitan of St. Petersburg and lent his influence to trying to have Antonii removed. Needless to say, his appointment sent a shiver through the ranks of the Pre-Sobor Commission. Shirinskii-Shikhmatov was against prolonging the sessions into the summer of 1906 to bring preparations for the sobor to completion, possibly before mid-August.[29]

The Duma was dissolved on July 9, 1906, and in the simultaneous reshuffling of the government Prime Minister Stolypin got rid of the garrulous Shirinskii-Shikhmatov. Antonii Vadkovskii breathed a sigh of relief and went to work to persuade the Prime Minister and the Tsar to reconvene the Pre-Sobor Commission—a difficult project in view of their preoccupation with widespread insurrection and preparing elections for another Duma. Gradually, the next Procurator, Peter Petrovich Izvolskii (1850-1922), became convinced that no harm could come from allowing the Commission to finish its work. Izvolskii remained Procurator till

February 1909. His role was to keep the church in check and to ferret out radical clergy and political troublemakers. He was a heavy cross for the metropolitan to bear. Izvolskii and Stolypin regarded the church as their mainstay in restoring government authority throughout the empire and tolerated no opposition from within its ranks.[30]

On October 25, the metropolitan finally gained clearance for the Pre-Sobor Commission to reconvene by persuading the Synod that the unresolved issues would take the Synod years to work through, while the more than one hundred members of the Pre-Sobor Commission could handle them more rapidly. They reassembled for their first autumn meeting on November 2. Antonii heartily welcomed them and told them that he had nearly despaired of seeing them again. Izvolskii stressed the "direct links" that the government cherished with the church and that the renovation of the church had begun because of the "will of the Tsar." He then limited them till December 15 to complete their work. Antonii ended the opening session by telling the Commission that their first task lay in reconsidering the question of metropolias, which both the first and second sub-commissions had shelved without clear conclusions.[31]

During the summer months, metropolias had become much more necessary in the eyes of most of the members of the Commission. Internal disorder had affected the church as much as the civil administration, which revealed that the church was rapidly losing touch with the once silent masses. Simultaneous remedial activities had to be launched in many areas of the church. Dioceses could attack problems by grouping together to work out programs tailored to the different problems that plagued various regions. In the Volga area the predominant problem was the activity of Old Believers, both of Austrian and priestless derivation. The western and southwestern areas were experiencing a serious confrontation with Catholicism and new attacks from sectarians, particularly Stundists. In the Baltic area and Finland-Karelia, pan-Finnish Lutheranism had gone on the offensive and was destroying the gains made by Orthodoxy over the past decade. Through diocesan convocations the bishops had learned the depth of the challenges, which no diocese could battle alone. The Procurator's chancellory was alarmed by the rate of defection from Orthodoxy, together with the weakness of the church in stifling civil disorders, and was therefore concerned that regional counterattacks be launched.

At a general session chaired by Metropolitan Antonii on November 7, Nikolai Aksakov and Alexander Papkov, together with Professors Almazov and Zaozerskii, defended the timeliness of metropolias for Russia. Fr. Timofei Butkevich just as strenuously warned that decentralization would fuel the flames of Ukrainian nationalism and of other dissident political groups seeking autonomy within or separation from the empire. Professor Mikhail Ostroumov countered that in the early years of the Christian church it was precisely the existence of metropolias that had permitted the church to go on functioning in some areas after the political structure of others had collapsed. It was a grim thing to contemplate, he implied, but the possibility of the Russian Empire's collapse had to be considered. Antonii Khrapovitskii, who had found his diocese a seething caldron during the summer of 1906, heartily supported the establishment of metropolias as a means to give regional bishops solidarity to overcome crises. Archpriest Mikhail Gorchakov lamented that the question of metropolias was turning too much upon political considerations. The delegates should remember that the church had its own *raison d'être* and should view the question of reviving metropolias in that light. Archbishop Nikandr noted that in times like these, political and religious issues become one and the same. Furthermore, metropolias were an excellent way to insure that the principle of *sobornost'* would operate in the government of the Russian church. The Synod could never handle the volume and complexities of governing the church in present circumstances, a fact that had been all too clear even before the current crisis. Dioceses were too small and possessed inadequate resources for dealing with the nature of problems that had become so critical so rapidly. Therefore, metropolias were the best means to alleviate the burden on the Synod and to enlarge the scope of individual dioceses.

Metropolias would permit regional sobors to sit with much greater frequency than all-Russian sobors.

After much heated debate, the general session of the Commission decided, thirty-one to fifteen, to reverse the decisions of the spring sub-commissions and to recommend restoration of metropolias in the Russian church.[32] But on November 9, the Commission also decided by a vote of twenty-eight to fifteen that metropolitans would not have administrative or legal authority in their metropolias, only pastoral functions. They would be authorized to summon regional sobors once every two or three years, with the right to preside over them, but would not have the right, as provided in the canons of the Byzantine church, to interfere in the administration of dioceses. Neither would clergy and laymen with complaints against their bishops have recourse to metropolitans, but would bypass them and go directly to the patriarchal Synod. If metropolitans remained out of the administrative/legal realm, it was felt, their effectiveness as conciliators and pastors would be greater. Otherwise, there would be endless wrangling among bishops and between them their metropolitans. The metropolitans would have the power of moral suasion, nothing more. Antonii Khrapovitskii was vehemently against limiting metropolitans in this manner, but when the vote was taken the three metropolitans, the Procurator, Archbishops Dmitri, Nikandr and Arsenii and Professors Pevnitskii, Almazov, Tikhomirov and Brilliantov, among others, were against him.

At the general session of November 10, the Commission decided to establish new metropolias at Tiflis, Kazan, Irkutsk and Vilna besides those already existing at Moscow, Petersburg and Kiev. Diocesan bishops would be chosen at metropolitan sobors, over which the metropolitans would preside, with final confirmation of the bishop coming from the Synod. There was a sharp exchange about whether or not laymen and white clergy could participate in the selection of candidates for bishop. The three metropolitans—Antonii, Flavian and Vladimir—together with Antonii Khrapovitskii, Dmitri Kovalnitskii, Nikandr Molchanov and two of the professors were in the decided minority (thirteen versus thirty-one) against having white clergy and laity participate. Most of the archpriests and all of the professors who had spoken out for *sobornost'* were in the majority, which favored white priest and lay participation.[33]

On November 24, the Commission got into a battle over an attempt by Izvolskii to retain secretaries directly appointed by and dependent upon him in diocesan consistories. The bishops were adamantly opposed to retaining them and were supported by many of the white priests and lay professors. Professor Ilia Berdnikov noted that paragraph 285 of the *Ustav Dukhovnykh Konsistorii* had been inserted at the behest of N. A. Protasov, a colonel who had been made Procurator in the reign of Nicholas I. Paragraph 285 had made the consistorial secretary the appointee of the Procurator so that the Procurator would have a spy in the inner workings of every diocesan administration. The government had not trusted the bishops then and wanted to be sure that they ferreted out potentially troublesome priests and monks before they ever had a chance to oppose the political interests of the state. Secretaries had been the direct cause of the emasculation of the canonical authority of the bishop. Now that the Commission had decided to restore rightful authority to the bishop, an attempt to retain secretaries under the Procurator's command indicated that the present Procurator had no intention whatsoever of respecting episcopal authority, but was determined to continue to hold direct powers to interfere with bishops and their administrations and in so doing retain his own exaggerated authority in the patriarchal Synod.

Antonii Vadkovskii supported Berdnikov and asked pointedly whether the government trusted the church or not. Peter Ostroimov, the chief assistant to the Procurator, tried to argue that the position of the secretary was not what Berdnikov had made it out to be and that the bishops had all the independence they needed. But Vadkovskii pointed out that, as the law stood, none of the decisions of the Synod had any authority unless they were signed by the Procurator, and none of the decisions of a diocesan consistory had authority unless they were signed by its secretary, the Procurator's

agent. Unless those conditions were changed, all talk of restoring the church was useless. The present situation existed
only because the government did not trust the bishops.

Ostroimov complained that it appeared as though the
Commission did not think the Tsar trusted the church. Was
the Tsar the loyal son of the church, its protector, or did he
think the church should be kept under the supervision of
police agents of the Ministry of the Interior? But Ostroimov's
injured air did not make any impression upon the Commission. The structure of the procuracy, they felt, including the
powers of consistory secretaries, was designed precisely because the government did not trust the church. Fr. Mikhail
Kazanskii reiterated their conviction that unless the make-up
of the consistory were changed, nothing would change.

Fr. Tikhon Kozlovskii made an impassioned appeal for
the abolition of consistorial secretaries. They and the clergy
stood at loggerheads and absolutely distrusted each other—
a situation especially injurious to the church at a time when
the closest ties were needed between bishops and their clergy.
Consistorial secretaries undercut close ties. If the church were
to meet the crisis it now faced, self-serving, imperious little
secretaries had to be swept away. Kozlovskii went on to note
that all this had been decided upon in the spring in the
second sub-commission, and there was no reason to bring
the subject up again and prolong debate on it.

Finally, Antonii Vadkovskii asked for two votes: should
the secretary of the consistory be appointed by the bishop,
and should the bishop personally preside over the meetings
of the consistory or not? On the first question, the Commission voted forty-one to zero yes, and on the second, thirty-
three to eight yes. Both Izvolskii and Ostroimov, seeing the
tide of feelings, absented themselves from the vote.[34]

*   *   *

At the beginning of December, Antonii Vadkovskii fell
ill. The strain of sustaining the Pre-Sobor Commission had
taken its toll during the autumn as he came under enormous
pressure from right-wing political groups to sanction their
terrorist activities and vituperous propaganda against the

Duma, against parties of the center and left and against professional societies working towards political change in the empire. The Union of Russian People, founded by Dr. Alexander I. Dubrovin (1855-1918), was the most notorious group, combining an ideology and program akin to those of the John Birchers, the Orange Order, and the Ku Klux Klan. The Union arrogated to itself the right to define true patriotism, true Orthodoxy and true devotion to the Tsar, held trials of prominent figures whom it considered traitorous *in camera* and arranged their murders. Among their unfulfilled executions was the murder of Witte, whom they regarded as the chief architect of the ruin of autocracy. Nicholas II had become an honorary member of the organization in 1905, together with Pobedonostsev and scores of highly placed officials in St. Petersburg, Moscow and other cities. The Union instigated many of the riots and pogroms that swept through the southern and western provinces during 1906. Vadkovskii had not only refused to join the Union but had preached against it and turned Dubrovin away when he came to enroll the metropolitan. With unlimited funds originating in the Ministry of the Interior, the Union terrorized and propagandized on a large scale during elections to the second Duma. Hundreds of Orthodox priests were forced to either sanction the Union and its activities or were driven out of their parishes. Antonii intervened to protect priests in the Petersburg area, only to convince Dubrovin and his band that the metropolitan was a traitor second only to Witte.

Finally, on December 6, 1906, Dubrovin published an open letter in the *Russkoe Znamia*, the Hundreds' smear sheet, accusing Antonii of betraying the Tsar, of aiding and abetting political enemies of the empire and of subverting the church to atheistic and revolutionary ends. Dubrovin called for the metropolitan's resignation or, if it were not forthcoming, his deposition and defrocking.

The Pre-Sobor Commission, now chaired by Metropolitan Vladimir Bogoiavlenskii of Moscow, was shocked and outraged. Attorney Nikolai Kuznetsov introduced a resolution of support and sympathy for Antonii at the December 7 session which denounced Dubrovin for conniving to pervert the church for political ends and to use it and its personnel to spread violence and hatred in the name of Christ the Savior. The resolution denounced Dubrovin for going far beyond the limits of common decency and courtesy and declared that the Union, by attacking Vadkovskii, had launched an attack on the entire episcopacy of the Russian church. Dubrovin was put on notice that his activities only more firmly rallied the flock of the Russian church around its first shepherd and that attacking the metropolitan while he was so seriously ill revealed a cowardly character.[35]

Those two events—the pointed discussion about the Tsar's not trusting the church and the show of solidarity with Antonii Vadkovskii—infuriated Nicholas and sounded the death knell of the Commission and, as it turned out, of the sobor as well.

The last general session of the Pre-Sobor Commission sat on December 15, 1906. The Protocols of all the remaining separate sessions of sub-commissions together with those of the general sessions were collated by the end of December and published in four volumes before the end of January 1907. During the hectic months of February and March 1907, Nicholas read the Protocols. He informed Antonii and Izvolskii on April 25 that he had finished them. Antonii still hoped that the Tsar would announce the convocation of the sobor for Pentecost 1907 or on Assumption Day in August at the very latest. The church was in a desperate condition and needed the sobor immediately.[36]

CHAPTER VIII

Twilight of Freedom

The summons to the all-Russian sobor never came.

Nicholas and Prime Minister Stolypin locked horns with the second Duma, just as they had with the first, and would not consider summoning a sobor until the dispute with the Duma was resolved. The second Duma went the way of the first and was dissolved on June 3, 1907—too late to permit the summoning of the sobor for Pentecost of that year.

Nicholas was offended by the determination to disengage the church from the embrace of the state repeatedly expressed in the Protocols of the Pre-Sobor Commission and the *Otzyvy* of the diocesan bishops. With government political controls as unstable as they were, the independence movement in the church looked like another challenge to the state, one as serious as Nikon's challenge to Tsar Alexei Mikhailovich in the seventeeth century. Antonii's friendship and collaboration with Witte, and the certainty that he would be elected Patriarch when the all-Russian sobor sat, made him suspect in wide circles at the top of the government. Nicholas held Vadkovskii partially responsible for the Gaponovshchina of 1905, viewed him as the inspirer and sustainer of continued agitation in the church and sought to have him removed from office to clear the way for the election of a conservative to the patriarchal throne when the sobor convened. Vadkovskii's harboring of Bishop Antonin of Narva was but one affront to the Tsar, whose preference for St. Petersburg metropolitan was Antonii Khrapovitskii. Khrapovitskii had moved de-

313

cidedly to the right of the political spectrum during the past two years and had collaborated with and assisted the Black Hundreds and the Union of Russian People. Priests in his diocese who did not crack down upon political dissidents and actively support the Okhrana in rooting out revolutionary agents and Ukrainian nationalists were defrocked and dismissed from their parishes. The Pochaev Monastery was a politicized institution serving as the headquarters of the Black Hundreds for southwest Russia, and the monastery's presses were put at its service.[1]

Nicholas was thwarted, however, by Khrapovitskii's insistence that he would succeed to St. Petersburg only if Vadkovskii freely resigned and all canonical regulations for naming a successor were followed. Vadkovskii refused to resign, realizing that if he vacated his office the heavy hands of the Okhrana and the Procurator would descend upon his clergy with a vengeance, while the tenuous rapport with the St. Petersburg intellectuals and labor leaders would vanish forever. Vadkovskii was forced, in fact, to defrock several leading priests in any case. Frs. A. Arkhipov, Alexander Brilliantov, K. Kolokolnikov and Fedor Tikhvinskii were all deprived of their priestly functions because of their refusal to break with the Trudovik (Labor) Party in the third Duma. Had Vadkovskii not done so, the Synod would have gone over his head. The whole of his Pastoral Council was in disfavor with the authorities, and they feared that at any time the Synod would strip them of their offices and incomes. Fr. Alexei Grinevich bowed to the political demands of the Synod and severed his ties with the Trudoviki, only to have his action compared to that of Judas and to have his pastoral effectiveness greatly impaired.[2]

Another of Metropolitan Antonii's leading supporters, Archimandrite Mikhail Semenov, an original member of the Religious-Philosophical Society and closely associated with the St. Petersburg Pastoral Council, became so discouraged with political interference in the state church and the mindless poisoning of the wellsprings of reform that he formally went over to the Old Believers in 1909. It was a major blow to the moderate reformers left in the church.[3] Semenov had been one of the main publicizers of reform in the press and in a series of lectures given in 1905 and 1906.[4] He had supported both Vadkovskii and Khrapovitskii in their efforts to achieve a rapprochement with Old Believers in the springtime of Toleration. At the same time, he had publicly criticized the archbishop of Volhynia for his support of the Hundreds and Unionists and for his anti-Semitism. Politically, Fr. Mikhail sympathized with the Social Democrats and had written a brochure entitled "Christian Freedom" in which he had expressed the opinion that some of Karl Marx's theories were Christian and were comparable to some of the teachings of the early church fathers.

The swath of anti-reform cut wide among the clergy of the Orthodox church in the backlash from the 1905 Revolution. Among the scores of priests defrocked and publicly persecuted was Fr. Vasilii Popov of St. Afanasii parish, Shenkursk village, Arkhangelsk diocese, a prominent member of the Peasant Union. At one point, he had publicly cursed Nicholas II as "bloody Nicholas" and had charged that much of the suffering of the Orthodox Russians could be laid at the feet of his dynasty.

Sentiment to adhere to the canonical norms of Eastern Orthodoxy in the future selection of prelates was so strong, however, that the Procurator could not simply remove the St. Petersburg metropolitan and replace him with someone more pliable, as had been the habit in the past. Even though many of the clergy and bishops of the church would have been only too happy to see Vadkovskii go, they would have insisted that they be involved in the defrocking and replacement proceedings. They would probably have replaced Antonii with Sergei Stragorodskii of Finland anyway, Vadkovskii's former student and personal friend. Sergei would have been as unmalleable as Antonii, and Nicholas harbored a grudge against him for having publicly denounced police brutality in breaking up Fr. Gapon's procession in 1905. Any attempt, therefore, to dump Vadkovskii would have resulted in a stalemate, and the metropolitanate would probably have gone without an incumbent altogether. Since the government was not in a position to assail the church head-on in 1907 and

1908, a slow process of enfeeblement had to be applied.[5]

Publications with government connections attacked the lackadaisical attitude of the clergy towards suppressing political dissidence and excoriated them for failing to whip up popular support for the government and its policies. Ominous references to the wealth of such institutions as the Pecherskaia Lavra of Kiev and the Troitskii Lavra near Moscow kept churchmen mindful of where the government could strike if the church failed to tow the line sufficiently. Attacks like that stunned even Khrapovitskii, who vigorously pointed out to M. O. Menshikov (1859-1919), editor of *Novoe Vremia*, source of many slurs on the church, that the church had spent millions of rubles circulating brochures and magazines defending the state and housing state-supported organizations like the Union and the Hundreds. He reminded the editor of the work done by the Pochaev Monastery in countering the revolutionary and liberal press and of the major role played by Vitalii Maksimenko, head of the Pochaev presses, in getting votes for government candidates in the elections to the second and third Dumas in Volhynia. *Novoe Vremia* countered by circulating stories of lives of wayward monks, illustrating them with examples provided by the popular actor Grigorii Ge, who told of seeing monks of the Kitaev Monastery escorting women friends to picnics. The implication was that that was rather normal behavior for Russian monastics, but Menshikov and Ge overlooked the detail that the Kitaev was a subordinate house of the Pecherskaia to which wayward monks were sent either to reform or to leave monastic life entirely. Besides the muckraking dealing with monastic clergy, Menshikov relished detailing stories of the drunkenness of the white clergy, implying that alcoholism afflicted virtually every white priest and that was the reason they were so ineffective as pastors. The disparagements of *Novoe Vremia* and other influential, widely read organs served very well to remind clergymen of how tenuous their incomes were and how easily their public image could be besmirched.[6]

The clergy champed at the bit, impatiently awaiting the sobor, so that the growing chorus of criticism from the secular press—particularly conservative journals like *Slovo* of St. Petersburg and *Moskovskiia Vedomosti, Golos Moskvy* and *Russkoe Slovo*, which formerly had supported the church and the calling of a sobor but lately had become sharply critical of the church and its leadership for not having the energy to reform and play a positive role in the post-1905 situation—could be countered. It was especially painful to see the right-wing press take up the themes and criticisms that formerly had been the exclusive domain of the left-wing press. A sobor would make it plain for all to see that the church was bursting with vitality and new life and would give the lie to the smears of the press.

Attacks on the metropolitan of St. Petersburg in *Golos Moskvy* by Professor I. M. Gromoglasov, a prominent graduate of Moscow Academy, an authority on the Old Believers and a writer on ecclesiastical affairs, took another angle which left a painful impression upon the clergy. Gromoglasov accused Antonii of being the one who was frustrating the summoning of the sobor. The professor reminded his readers that Nicholas had stated in the rescript of December 1905 that the three metropolitans would determine the date of the sobor once the preliminaries had been worked out. So, now was the time, and Antonii's pious utterings to the effect that the time of the summoning lay in the hands of the Tsar and that the Tsar lay in the hands of God did not impress him.

Press harassment was so dispiriting that on February 19, 1908, a delegation from the Petersburg Pastoral Council—consisting of Archpriests Filosof Ornatskii, Mikhail Gorchakov (1839-1910), a one-time associate of Fr. Ivantsov-Platonov, L. P. Petrov and V. I. Marenin—called upon the metropolitan to urge him to defend himself publicly against *Novoe Vremia* and the Hundreds' fellow-travelling sheet *Russkoe Slovo*. Mikhail Menshikov had just published an article blaming all the disorders in the Russian church on Antonii. An echoing article had simultaneously appeared in *Russkoe Slovo* authored by its editor, Varvarin. Varvarin accused Antonii of harboring revolutionaries and traitors among his clergy. Any priest or bishop in the empire who wanted to defy the authorities

could find refuge under the wing of the metropolitan. That
was why there were so many radical priests, socialist archimandrites and Cadet bishops swarming around St. Petersburg
as members of the Duma. Varvarin had no doubt that if
their comforter and patron were removed from the scene,
they would also disappear.[7]

The very next day, February 20, the Ecclesiastical Committee of the State Duma addressed an impassioned plea to
Metropolitan Antonii to use his influence and prestige to get
the momentum for summoning the sobor moving again. The
Committee's chairman, Vladimir N. Lvov (1872-1930?),
pleaded that until the sobor had sat and the church had defined its organization and position in the social and political
life of the empire, it would be very difficult for its sympathizers in the Duma to work for its welfare. Lvov and his
committee told Antonii that there was no longer any excuse
for not summoning the sobor on the grounds that political
conditions in the empire were too fluid. By 1908 that was no
longer true. The Duma, after two traumatic attempts, had
settled down to fruitful labor, and it was important for the
church to establish a harmonious pattern of relations with
it. If the church were self-governing and independent it could
win and retain the respect of deputies who were indifferent
or hostile. During the elections to the third Duma, Lvov and
his associates had become aware of the grassroots support
for a sobor. It would be a tragedy if this interest were not
reciprocated by ecclesiastical leaders. Lvov impressed upon
Antonii that 1908 was the most opportune time to summon
the sobor. After the trauma of the past three years, the public
mood was chastened and more receptive than at any time in
the past quarter century to a vigorous role on the part of
the church. A self-reliant church, governed by its own canons,
would win the respect of secular intellectuals and politicians
and would counter the insidious propaganda of Old Believers, Catholics and Stundo-Baptists. In the Duma itself,
Fr. I. V. Titov vigorously lobbied for passage of legislation
that would give the church true autonomy, continued protection by the authorities and the same freedoms now enjoyed
by non-Orthodox bodies.

Antonii replied directly to the point, stating that everything was ready for the sobor. He agreed fully that the time was ripe for the sobor, but that the final summons had to come from the Tsar. Nicholas had repeated several times over the past two years that he would summon it at "an opportune time." His failure to do so meant that, for whatever reasons, the time was not yet opportune. Antonii could only hope that the time would come soon.[8]

March and April 1908 saw the first crackdown on theological academies. Antonii Khrapovitskii, who had had heated controversies with several professors from Kiev, pressured the Synod for a crackdown upon Kiev at the earliest opportunity and was appointed inspector-general of the academy to root out the nest of revolutionaries and heretics, whose existence he traced back to 1904.[9]

Khrapovitskii believed that Prince Obolenskii was primarily responsible for the degeneration of life in the academies because he had issued the Temporary Regulations of February 1906. The Regulations had made the academies autonomous in the same manner as the universities and had made the faculty council in each academy the highest governing authority. The right of interference from local bishops and the Synod had been terminated. Khrapovitskii believed that that caused student pressure for more change, for curtailing surveillance of students, for the decline of religious life in the academies and for the infection of the academies with revolutionary and atheistic attitudes.[10] Khrapovitskii was particularly incensed that rectors had allowed students to hold requiems for revolutionaries and to preach publicly that Christ himself had been a revolutionary. Graduates from the academies had gone out to seminaries and diocesan schools and into pastorates with results that were only too plainly evident. The whole church was being infected with revolutionary attitudes. It was hardly a wonder that the government suspected the church of no longer playing its traditional supportive role.

Khrapovitskii was offended that the academies had made attendance at liturgy optional and had immediately experienced a sharp decline in regular chapel attendance. Allowing students to determine the use of their leisure time was another blunder. He condemned the discontinuance of dossiers kept by the faculty and administration on each student. He recommended that if the Kiev Academy in particular, and the rest of them in general, did not return to their former discipline and supervision, they should be closed altogether. Barring that, between three-fourths and two-thirds of all academy students should be dismissed and their places filled with more reliable and less precocious students. Professors with sympathies for revolutionaries should be forthwith removed and replaced with faculty more dedicated to religious pursuits. Antonii warned that simply filling teaching positions with priests would not be sufficient because many priests openly supported parties of the left. A thorough investigation of the backgrounds of new professors would have to be undertaken before appointments could be made.

The immediate upshot of Antonii's inspection was that Fr. Fedor Titov lost his professorship for a time. The rector, Bishop Platon Rozhdestvenskii, had already been dismissed. Platon was a deputy in the second Duma, had joined the Cadet Party, and had become one of the most vigorous critics of the Hundreds and Unionists. Platon had infuriated Vitalii Maksimenko and the Unionists in the Ukraine by trying to stop the October 1905 pogrom in Kiev and for anathematizing the Union afterwards for starting it. The dismissals created an uproar which further discredited the church in the public eye, but the effect was exactly as Khrapovitskii had intended. Liberal professors became less outspoken and academy autonomy was gradually whittled away. Dmitri Kovalnitskii performed a similar, if less thorough, purge of the St. Petersburg and Moscow Academies.[11]

Shortly thereafter, Professor V. I. Ekzempliarskii, an expert in moral theology and a popular lecturer, was indicted by the Kiev metropolitan, Flavian Gorodestskii, for an article entitled "The Moral Teaching of John Chrysostom," in which he noted that many of the positions taken by secular reformers and revolutionaries in Russia were the same as those taken by the great Greek theologian. Ekzempliarskii appealed to the Synod that there was nothing heretical in his article, but nevertheless was dismissed from his chair at the Kiev Academy. The negative impression that episode made materially affected the debate on the Synod's budget estimates for 1908.[12]

Those who raised the outcry for immediately summoning the sobor and blamed church leaders for the delay completely failed to understand that Peter Stolypin, the Prime Minister and Chairman of the Council of Ministers, backed by avid right-wingers, was the man who was actually blocking the sobor. Stolypin was flatly against both summoning the sobor and restoring the patriarchate. A sobor, as far as he could see, would serve to revive political and social passions that had boiled over during the terrifying past three years. It had taken extreme juggling measures to bring the Duma into line after it had been twice dissolved, and there was no point running the risk of a sobor over which the government would have little control. Stolypin had no doubt that the sobor would be antagonistic towards the government and that a restored patriarchate would institutionalize that antagonism. Therefore, he remained the most powerful opponent of the church until his assassination in September 1911.

Stolypin's plan was instead to subject the Orthodox church to an all-encompassing Ministry of Denominations, which would include all the religious bodies operating within the boundaries of the empire. The Synod would be simply the chief governing apparatus of the Orthodox religion, occupying a position on an equal level with the administrations of the Catholic church, the Lutherans, Old Believers, sectarians, Moslems and Buddhists. It took the strongest opposition from the hierarchy, especially those in the State Council, to prevent Stolypin's scheme from ever coming before the Duma.[13]

After the assassination of the Prime Minister, an even more sinister threat plagued the church. Grigorii Rasputin, a former peasant and a Khlyst sectarian, had worked his way into the confidences of the imperial family and had become a menace to churchmen and politicians alike.[14] To the public, Rasputin appeared as an Orthodox in full communion with the church. In fact, however, he had been condemned by the Tobolsk Diocesan Consistory as a heretic, and the bishop had warned the Synod against him, his teachings and his influence. Rasputin had used his influence to have the bishop of Tobolsk replaced by an unknown monk, Varnava Nakronin (1860-1921), who had spent most of his monastic life as a humble gardener and had little understanding of the demands of a bishop's role. The Synod also removed the consistorial secretary and several of the members of the diocesan consistory—something that could not have happened had the church been autonomous.

Rasputin was introduced to students and staff at the St. Petersburg Academy in the early years of the century. Recognized and befriended initially by one Mitka Koliaba, a deaf-mute who had been partially healed by the late Amvrosii Grenkov, Rasputin became a holy wanderer and concealed the seamier side of his nature. He made a favorable impression on such prominent clergy as Archimandrite—later Bishop—Feofan Bystrov, then inspector of the academy; Bishop Sergei Stragorodskii, then rector; and Fr. Roman Medved (1875-1929), a prominent Petersburg priest, all of whom were interested in healing and mysticism. They in turn introduced him to the Grand Princesses Militsa and Anastasia Nikolaevna, daughters of the King of Montenegro and wives of the Tsar's uncles, the Grand Princes Peter and Nikolai Nikolaevich. Having gained access to that company, Rasputin was soon introduced to the Tsar and the Tsarina. His story after that is well known.

By 1909-1910, some of the clergy who had initially befriended him had become aware of his sordid activities through hearing confessions of some of the women he had disgraced. Bishop Feofan Bystrov tried to warn Empress Alexandra that Rasputin was not what he appeared to be, only to be warned by her that he should not slander her "friend." Feofan persisted, however, with the result that the worried Rasputin temporarily absented himself from St. Petersburg and took refuge in the company of Germogen Dolganev, the bishop of Saratov and a member of the Synod, and Illiodor Trufanov (1880-1958), popular archimandrite of a Tsaritsyn (later Stalingrad) monastery. The irony was that Rasputin had been introduced to both of them by Feofan himself several years earlier at the academy. Feofan was transferred in 1910 to the Crimea as bishop of Taurida, a stern punishment meted out for having offended the imperial family, to whom he had been confessor.

Both Germogen and Illiodor, together with a growing number of the hierarchy, realized that the wanderer was not at all a saint and broke publicly with him in 1911. Germogen, Illiodor and others tried forcibly to exorcise Rasputin in a desperate attempt to break his hold on the imperial family and other powerful Petersburg personalities. The terrified Rasputin told the Tsarina about the event, and Nicholas II ordered the Synod to strip both clerics of their offices. Germogen was banished to the Zhirovitskii Monastery in the Grodno diocese in January 1912, there to remain until it was evacuated during the German invasion of 1915. Illiodor was reduced to lay status and subsequently went into exile abroad. Rasputin's position was virtually unassailable after that. He soon was selecting candidates to fill ecclesiastical offices, discrediting the church tragically in the years just prior to the Bolshevik Revolution.[15]

The two bishops in the Duma, Evlogii Georgievskii of Kholm and Mitrofan Krasnopolskii (1869-1918), together with Antonii Khrapovitskii, a member of the State Council since 1906, vigorously protested to Vladimir K. Sabler, now Procurator, that the appointment of Varnava Nakronin to Tobolsk and the Germogen-Illiodor scandal made the church the laughing-stock of the empire. Secular intellectuals, atheists and non-Orthodox sectarians saw Rasputin as proof of the spiritual bankruptcy of the church. Sabler squirmed in great discomfort, but said that there was nothing he could do because pressures had come "from above."

The last line of defense for the church gave way in November 1912, when Antonii Vadkovskii finally died after a long and painful illness. Sergei Stragorodskii should have succeeded him, if the normal line of succession were adhered to, just as Vadkovskii himself had been transferred from Finland. But Sergei was a student of the deceased

Antonii and a life-long friend who shared his teacher's thinking about the proper character of the St. Petersburg metropolitanate and had been one of his chief advisers. Ever since 1903, he and Antonii had worked together to reform the church, and he had sided with the bishops who protested the Varnava appointment and had failed to silence Germogen in the Synod. Nicholas flatly refused to allow his appointment to St. Petersburg. Sabler then suggested Khrapovitskii, the man Nicholas had wanted in St. Petersburg several years earlier. By now the Tsar had cooled towards the archbishop of Volhynia too, but he did suggest that Khrapovitskii might be transferred to Moscow to replace Vladimir Bogoiavlenskii, who was finally selected for the St. Petersburg see. Vladimir, the honorary chaplain of the Hundreds, was old enough not to offer any serious challenge to the established church government, had collaborated gladly in crushing radical clergy in his own diocese and was expected to be quiet and grateful for the appointment. Khrapovitskii's appointment to Moscow was leaked to the press, but in the final analysis it was Archbishop Makarii Nevskii (1836-1918) of Tomsk, then seventy-seven years old and also expected to be quiet and grateful who became the Moscow prelate. Khrapovitskii was mortified and had to return more than one hundred letters and telegrams of congratulations to their senders.

Thus, by once again ignoring the canons of the church and adhering strictly to political interests, three aged men came to sit in the metropolitan cathedrals of the empire. By passing over Sergei, Antonii, Tikhon Belavin, Konstantin Bulichev and Arsenii Stadnitskii, among others, the government blocked, paradoxical as it may appear, energetic men who would have strengthened support for the dynasty as well as strengthened the church.

Vladimir, however, turned out to be not as docile as expected. He became so outraged at Rasputin's interference in the church and the feebleness of the sycophantic Sabler that he made himself *persona non grata* in St. Petersburg and was demoted to Kiev in 1915, when Flavian Gorodestskii finally expired. He was replaced in St. Petersburg by the sycophantic and simpering Pitirim Oknov, a protégé of

Rasputin, who brought final humiliation to the church. Pitirim and Makarii both sought Rasputin's favor and in turn blocked any effort in the Synod during the war years to curb him.[16] The crippling hand of Rasputin thus closed around the church even before it worked its final paralyzing effect on the political machinery of the Russian Empire. Suspected and mistrusted by the state, the church went into the final years of the tsarist regime paralyzed by an uncanonical administration and blamed for much of the worst aspects of government maladministration.

A particularly energetic renewal of Russification in the western provinces occurred, in which the church was fully utilized in the attempt to de-Polonize the former Uniate population, to forcibly return two or three hundred thousand nominal Orthodox who had defected to Latinism and to transform the religious character of Warsaw through the efforts of the arrogant Archbishop Nikolai Ziorov (1850-1915). Eventually, in 1912, the region of the Kholm (Chelm) diocese was completely detached from the government of Poland, to be directly governed from St. Petersburg, largely through the efforts of Bishop Evlogii Georgievskii. In Finland, various laws were passed limiting the autonomy of that grand duchy, most notably the law of June 17, 1910, which allowed a more direct attack upon Lutheranism and pan-Finnish nationalism. The attack upon the Old Believers was renewed, which drove some of them either into sympathizing with the Uniate exarch, Leonid Fedorov—appointed by Metropolitan Sheptyskii for Russia—on the one hand, or into the arms of Stundo-Baptism on the other. With the imminent disintegration of the empire, all these endeavors created a backlash among minority populations that worked great harm upon the church when the empire finally did collapse in World War I.[17]

Ten years after the Pre-Sobor Commission had completed its labors, the old regime fell. The church was about to be engulfed by the holocaust of the Bolshevik Revolution. During the war, the image of the church deteriorated swiftly and sharply under the Rasputin-ridden pastorate of Metropolitan Pitirim who, with Makarii of Moscow, reduced the Synod to immobility. The Romanov dynasty rendered the church unable to play its accustomed role of helping to rescue the tsardom from its enemies.

Relief came tragically late. Rasputin was assassinated in December 1916, too late to permit the government to regain its balance. Nicholas II abdicated in February 1917, and Russia went from disintegration to chaos. Pitirim Oknov, Makarii Nevskii and Varnava Nakronin, among others, were driven from their sees, but the shadow of Bolshevism already was falling over Russia when they finally went. They had remained for too long.

CHAPTER IX

Epilogue

This study was undertaken to examine the validity of the view that the Russian Orthodox church was hopelessly anachronistic in matters ecclesiastical, cultural and political in the opening years of the twentieth century. The evidence suggests that, despite enormous and complicated problems, and despite stifling controls exercised by the tsarist state since the time of Peter the Great, the Russian Orthodox church was not moribund. In fact, the opposite was true. Numerous signs of renewal and reform were visible as the church sought to burst out of the cocoon spun around it since the eighteenth-century reforms. The Russian clergy was not a grey mass of indistinguishable nonentities, as was so commonly imagined by a significant proportion of the pre-Revolutionary Russian intelligentsia and the majority of western students of Russia. In retrospect, it seems peculiar that the observations of such contemporary, astute students of the Russian scene as Bernard Pares (*Russia and Reform*, London, 1907) have been so easily overlooked when they deal with the Russian clergy, or that the efforts of exiled intellectuals such as Nicolas Zernov (*The Russian Religious Renaissance of the Twentieth Century*, New York, 1963), who indicated clearly that a religious revival was discernible, did not stimulate western scholars to pursue further study of the church until very recently.[1] The Russian clergy consisted, on the average, of men of God, deeply concerned with revitalizing their church and bringing it into synchronization with the spiritual, social and political demands of the century. They had deep reservations about the pattern western churches had taken in adapting to the modern era and were conscious that in many cases the western adjustment had not been successful. They were conscious that the Russian church was rooted in its Byzantine heritage and that they would have to find the wellsprings for renewal in that heritage. As demonstrated in their writings and in their often turbulent debates in the Pre-Sobor Commission, Russian religious intellectuals were aware that the canons and regulations of the Byzantine era had been hammered out in times equally as turbulent as they were facing and that distance of time and place was not as insurmountable as might at first appear.

Although the canons contained no ready solutions for the pressing problems of the day, they could neither be ignored nor regarded lightly. For every serious-minded priest, prelate or professor, the canons were the touchstone upon which they based their thinking. The authenticity of the Orthodox church depended upon its adhering to an established tradition that had been handed down from the time of the apostles and the church fathers. The problem was to maintain authenticity and yet bring tradition into focus with the times. Whether the concerned churchman was a Fr. Gapon organizing industrial workers, a Fr. Georgii Petrov counselling parishioners, a Metropolitan Antonii trying to steer measures for reform between the pitfalls of political exigencies, a lawyer Kuznetsov warning against antagonizing the political magnates beyond reconciliation or a Bishop Feofan or Germogen deliberately antagonizing them, all remained conscious of the canons and the need not to emasculate or violate them. Violent arguments ensued as to how canons were to be interpreted or how they had gained their authority, but few suggested simply scrapping them.

The documents of the time speak for themselves. The wide spectrum of experts and pastors knew that serious changes had to be made and that the church had to regain autonomy. The pressure of time and events forced them to consider and resolve a staggering number of issues in a relatively short period of time in 1905 and 1906. Despite very different vantage points and experiences, they came to remarkable harmony in their resolutions. Generally speaking, the theologians were liberal as a group while the canonists and historians were relatively conservative. They usually discovered that their points of view were not irreconcilable, in spite of the fact that the rapidly changing social and political scene was creating divisions at the very time they were deliberating. Nicholas II failed to summon the sobor in 1907. Had he done so, the devastating swath of reaction and political opportunism would not have cut into the church so deeply. But the state feared an open forum in the church, as it did in other spheres of political and social activity, and, above all, it feared that the church itself would become politically antagonistic. So the brief dawn of hope for church emancipation and reform was deliberately darkened.

Many leading church figures, working indefatigably to renew the church, had premonitions about the future if they failed to effect significant reforms. None of them could have imagined the persecution that was to be the fate of the Russian church as a result of the Bolshevik Revolution, with many of the champions of reform becoming victims of the Revolution and martyrs for their beliefs. One should not suggest that a reformed and revived church could have changed the political and social course of Russian history entirely in the decade before the Revolution. At best, it might have affected certain phases of it. But a reformed church would have had the opportunity to prepare itself for its next struggle against the most formidable enemy in the history of religion in general and Russian Orthodoxy in particular: the Soviet regime. That story awaits another volume.

The following abbreviations are used throughout the notes:

Evlogii   Evlogii Georgievskii, *Put' Moei Zhizni. Vospo-minaniia Mitropolita Evlogiia* (Paris, 1947).

Nikon   Nikon Rklitskii, *Zhizneopisanie Blazheneishago Antoniia, Mitropolit Kievskago i Galitskago,* 10 vols. (New York, 1953-1963).

OEA   *Otzyvy Eparkhial'nykh Arkhiereev po Voprosu o tserkovnoi reforme,* 3 vols. (St. Petersburg, 1906).

PG   J. P. Migne, ed., *Patrologiae cursus completus,* Series Graeco-latina, 162 vols. (Paris, 1857-1866).

PL   J. P. Migne, ed., *Patrologiae cursus completus,* Series Latina, 217 vols. (Paris, 1844-1855).

PSZ   *Polnoe Sobranie Zakonov Rossiiskoi Imperii,* 1st series (1649 to December 12, 1825), 45 vols.; 2nd series (December 12, 1825 to March 1, 1881), 55 vols.; 3rd series (March 1, 1881 to 1913), 33 vols. (St. Petersburg, 1830-1916).

SZ   A. F. Volkov and Iu. D. Filipov, eds., *Svod Zakonov Rossiiskoi Imperii,* 4th ed., 2 vols. (St. Petersburg, 1904-1905).

Vadkovskii   Antonii Vadkovskii, *Rechi, Slova i Poucheniia,* 3rd ed. (St. Petersburg, 1912).

VO   *Vsepoddaneishii Otchet Ober-Prokurora Svia-teishago Sinoda (K. Pobedonostseva) po Ve-domstvu Pravoslavnago Ispovedaniia* (St. Petersburg, 1891-1916). The numbers in italics in the notes represent the years which the reports cover.

ZhKM   *Zhurnaly Komiteta Ministrov po Ispolneniiu Ukaza 12 Dekabria 1904g.* (St. Petersburg, 1905).

ZhP   *Zhurnaly i Protokoly Zasedanii Vysochaishe Uchrezhdennago Predsobornago Prisutstviia,* 4 vols. (St. Petersburg, 1906-1907).

Notes

CHAPTER I

[1]*VO 1900*, prilozhenie, 14; *SZ*, I, ch. 1, raz. 1, gl. 7, 40-44; VIII, ch. 2, kn. 10, gly. 1-8, prilozhenie.

[2]Michael T. Florinsky, *Russia, A History and an Interpretation* (New York, 1966), I, 409-416; Ivan Vlasovs'kii, *Naris Istorii Ukrains'koi Pravoslavnoi Tserkvi* (New York, 1959), III, 252-253; Robert F. Byrnes, *Pobedonostsev, His Life and Thought* (Bloomington, Ind., 1969), 167-168; Evlogii, 194-195; *VO 1888-1889*, 9-10; *1890-1891*, 3-4; *1892-1893*, 29-30; *1894-1895*, 44-45; *1896-1897*, 20-46; *1898*, 1-28; *1899*, 4-13; *1900*, 4-8; A. Schmemann, *The Historical Road of Eastern Orthodoxy* (New York, 1963), 310-355; Alexander Muller, *The Spiritual Regulation of Peter the Great* (Seattle, 1972), ix-xxxviii; Steven Runciman, *The Orthodox Churches and the Secular State* (Trentham, New Zealand, 1971), 45-63; George A. Maloney, *A History of Orthodox Theology Since 1453* (Belmont, Mass., 1976); 30-49. Two succinct accounts of the operation of the Synod are in Timofei V. Barsov, *Sviateishii Sinod v ego proshlom* (St. Petersburg, 1895), and Barsov, *Sinodal'naia Uchrezhdeniia nastoiashchago vremeni* (St. Petersburg, 1899). Flavian Gorodestskii was moved to Kiev in February 1903 when he succeeded Metropolitan Feognost and was there for all important pre-World War I events.

[3]Vasilii V. Rozanov, "O neudobstve chastykh peremeshchenii v dukhovnom vedomstve," *Okolo Tserkovnykh Sten* (St. Petersburg, 1906), I, 372-375; Evlogii, 134; *VO 1890-1891*, 29-34; *PSZ*, 1st series, I, par. 4001, 676; F. V. Blagovidov, *Ober-Prokurory Sv. Sinoda v XVIII i v pervoi polovine XIX stoletiia* (Kazan, 1899-1900), gives a succinct account of this process.

[4]*VO 1892-1893*, 194-195, 412; *1894-1895*, 45; *1898*, 127-137; *1900*, 7-17, 256-272.

[5]*VO 1888-1889*, 10-20; *1890-1891*, 3-8; *1892-1893*, 30-76; *1894-1895*, 45-60; *1898*, 5-7; *1899*, 4-8; *1900*, 9-17; Stepan G. Runkevich, *Russkaia Tserkov' v XIX veke* (St. Petersburg, 1901), 140-143.

[6]*VO 1888-1889*, 25-27; A. P. Lopukhin, *Istoriia Khristianskoi Tserkvi v XIX veke* (Petrograd [sic], 1900-1901), 616-623, 721-725; Donald Mackenzie Wallace, *Russia* (New York, 1908), 51-52; Muller, 20, 109 (nn. 36, 37).

[7]*VO 1888-1889*, 21-24; *1892-1893*, 77-91; *1894-1895*, 66-70; Wallace, 50-52, 262; *ZhP*, I, 428-430.

[8]*VO 1888-1889*, 12-15, 34-36, 286-292; *1890-1891*, 4-22, 65-66, 342-351; *1892-1893*, 32-35, 139-142, 427-429; *1894-1895*, 53-55, 111, 294, 299;

331

1896-1897, 21-28, 50-52, 173-177; *1898*, 2-3, 8-9, 24, 141-144; *1899*, 4-7, 26-27, 167-170.

[9]*PSZ*, 1st series, VI, par. 4002, "Pribavlenie k Dukhovnomu Reglamentu," 699-715.

[10]*SZ*, IX, kn. 1, gly. 407-408, 426-431; Wallace, 46-51; Bernard Pares, *Russia and Reform* (London, 1907), 128-129; Georgii Gapon, *Story of My Life* (New York, 1906), 22-27; Anatole Leroy-Beaulieu, *The Empire of the Tsars and the Russians* (New York, 1902), III, 222-223.

[11]Pavel Miliukov, *Ocherki po Istorii Russkoi Kul'tury* (St. Petersburg, 1909), V, 149-152, 158-162, 168-169; *VO 1890-1891*, 29-43; *1896-1897*, 278-279; Pares, 127-136, 142-150.

[12]*ZhP*, I, 446-449; 549; II, 1-2, 21-28, 52-60, 409-410; III, 322-363.

[13]Pares, 130-146; Leroy-Beaulieu, 231-233; *VO 1888-1889*, 313-314; *1890-1891*, 367-368; *1892-1893*, 458-459; *1894-1895*, 324-325, 352-353; *1900*, 288-296.

[14]Evlogii, 96-97; *VO 1892-1893*, 163-185; *1896-1897*, 78-86, 141-158; S. Iu. Kamenev, "S. Iu. Vitte i K. P. Pobedonostsev o sovremennom polozhenii Pravoslavnoi Tserkvi," *Vestnik Evropy*, I, 2 (February 1909), 659-663.

[15]Gregor Prokoptschuk, *Metropolit Andreas Graf Scheptyskyj, Leben und Wirken des grossen Förderers der Kichenunion* (München, 1967), 23-25; Vlasovs'kii, II (1957), 5-10; Nikolai E. Kapterev, *Kharakter Otnosbenii Rossii k Pravoslavnomu Vostoku v XVI i XVII stoletiiakh* (Sergiev Posad, 1914), 14-25; *VO 1900*, 189-191. The best study in English covering the Ecumenical Patriarchate at that time is Stephan Runciman, *The Great Church in Captivity* (London, 1968).

[16]Vlasovs'kii, II, 140-183, 292-308. An independent Orthodox hierarchy had been reconstituted in 1632.

[17]George Vernadsky, *A History of Russia*, V, pt. 2 (New Haven, 1969), 609-634; Vlasovs'kii, II, 259-279; Kapterev, 349-382.

[18]Vlasovs'kii, II, 292-328; Prokoptschuk, 33-34.

[19]Vlasovs'kii, 328-343. The uncanonical manner in which Kiev was subjected to Moscow became grounds for Constantinople's recognition of the autocephaly of the Orthodox Church in Poland in 1925 over the protest of the Moscow patriarchate. See Alexander Svitich, *Pravoslavnaia Tserkov' v Pol'she i ee Avtokefaliia* (Buenos Aires, 1959).

[20]Vlasovs'kii, II, 11-128; III, 175-182; Nikon, II, 262-263; *PSZ*, 1st series, VI, par. 3718, 314-345. The diocese of Kholm, a region of considerable controversy in the twentieth century, did not revert to Orthodox jurisdiction in 1632. It remained Uniate from 1596 to 1875.

[21]Vlasovs'kii, III, 182-213; Polish Research Center, *The Orthodox Church in Poland* (London, 1942), 17-25.

[22]*VO 1888-1889*, 138-148, 186-192; Vlasovs'kii, III, 213-244; Iulian F. Krachkovskii, *Piatidesiatletie Vossoedineniia zapadno-russkikh Uniatov s Pravoslavnoiu Tserkov'iu (1839-1899gg.)* (Vilna, 1889), 2-79; S. P. Mel'gunov, *Iz Istorii Religiozno-obshchestvennykh dvizhenii v Rossii XIX veka* (Moscow, 1919), 71-78, 89-90; Runkevich, 98-107; Grigorii Kiprianovich, *Zhizn' Iosifa Semashki* (Vilna, 1893).

[23]*VO 1890-1891*, 61-69; *1894-1895*, 15-16; Evlogii, 95-96, Mel'gunov, 78-83.

[24]*VO 1900*, 179-198; Vlasovs'kii, III, 244-250, 260-262; Evlogii, 91-97, 135-141, 253-277, 325-334; Pares, 63-64; Mel'gunov, 83-88, 91-110;

Prokoptschuk, 123-157; *ZhP*, I, 427; Edward Chmielewski, *The Polish Question in the Russian State Duma* (Knoxville, 1970), iii-117; Nikon, II, 65-68.

[25]*VO 1896-1897*, 58-69, 72-73; *1898*, 210-211; Nikon, II, 257-291; Evlogii, 91-96.

[26]*VO 1896-1897*, 61-63, 71-77; *ZhP*, I, 388-389. A typical problem was the rapid spread of Catholic devotional cults among the Orthodox of the western dioceses, such as the Fraternity of the Sacred Heart. Russian bishops had to counter its influence with their own organizations, like the Brotherhood of the Holy Spirit.

[27]Vernadsky, V, pt. 1, 346-350, 355, 382-383; Metropolitan Makarii Bulgakov, *Istoriia Russkoi Tserkvi* (St. Petersburg, 1889-1903), XII, 111-114, 200-221; Pierre Pascal, *Avvakum et les Débuts du Raskol* (Paris, 1938), 1-73.

[28]Makarii, XI, 82-89, 217-227; *PSZ*, 1st series, I, par. 1, 3; Vernadsky, V, pt. 1, 411-415; Pascal, 54-61.

[29]Vernadsky, V, pt. 1, 415-417; Pascal, 50-52, 62-64.

[30]Vernadsky, 417-428; Pascal, 134-135, 156-178; Vlasovs'kii, II, 159-183, 189-207, 212-242, 251-258; Makarii, XI, 444-505, 564-610; XII, 50-55, 69-72, 280-283.

[31]Makarii, XII, 118-130; Vernadsky, 421-423, 428-430; Pascal, 57-59, 175-178, 202-205; Vlasovs'kii, 247-258; Kapterev, 353-368.

[32]William K. Medlin, *Moscow and East Rome* (Geneva, 1952), 168-170, 182-205; Makarii, 140, 281-290.

[33]Makarii, 115-120; Pascal, 205-212; Vernadsky, V, pt. 2, 568-570.

[34]Makarii, 120, 125-144; Pascal, 213-214, Vernadsky, 570-571.

[35]Makarii, 227-248, 262-268, 301-522; Vernadsky, 584-592.

[36]Makarii, 525-534; XIII, 686-751; Vernadsky, 592-604.

[37]Sergei A. Zenkovsky, "The Russian Church Schism: Its Background and Repercussions," *Russian Review*, 16 (1957), 37-58; Theofanis G. Stavrou, "Nikon," *Threskeftike kai Ethnike Egkyklopaideia*, IX (Athens, 1966), 559-564; Makarii, XII, 593-628; Vernadsky, 604-607; Pascal, 373-381; Miliukov, V, 43-45.

[38]Makarii, 638-640, 669-682; Miliukov, 49-51; Vernadsky, 609-627.

[39]Miliukov, 46-94; *PSZ*, I, par. 412, 705-706; Vladimir Anderson, *Staroobriadchestvo i Sektanstvo* (St. Petersburg, 1904), 168-187; Robert O. Crummey, *The Old Believers and the World of Antichrist* (Madison, Wisc., 1970), 58-70; A. S. Pavlov, "Otnoshenie Tserkvi k neprinadlezhashchim ei khristianskim obshchestvam," *Bogoslovskii Vestnik* I, 4 (1902), 656-657.

[40]Miliukov, 54-62; Anderson, 222-230; A. S. Prugavin, *Staroobriadchestvo vo Vtoroi Polovine XIX veka* (Moscow, 1904), 7-18; *ZhKM*, 213-214; *VO 1900*, 21-22. The formal submission of *Edinoverie* to the Synod came on October 28, 1800, an event commemorated in 1900 at the Sts. Peter and Paul cathedral in St. Petersburg.

[41]Miliukov, 63-67; Anderson, 204-222; *VO 1898*, 82-88; *1900*, 210-223.

[42]Miliukov, 107-133; Anderson, 289-352, 371-427; René Fülop-Miller, *Rasputin, the Holy Devil* (New York, 1929), 18-26; *VO 1896-1897*, 141-158; *1898*, 104-121, 132-133; *1899*, 129-135; *1900*, 243-245.

For example, authorities in Elisavetgrad *uezd*, Ekaterinoslav diocese, had found a secret Stundist clique in the village of Novoselovka. The village clerk was Stundist and had vouchered state funds to establish a Stundist school.

When this was discovered and the school closed, the clerk simply reopened it in his own home. Church authorities in the Crimea, the main stronghold of Stundism, found that Ukrainian communities in the neighborhood of German-speaking communities were the most susceptible to Stundist propaganda. The same was true in the diocese of Volhynia. Commercial intercourse, combined often with economic dependency, permitted Stundist proselytizers to distribute literature imported from the International Tractarian Society of Hamburg. Baptist missionaries trained in Hamburg rendezvoused at Tulcea, Rumania, before crossing the frontier into the Ukraine. Ukrainian and Russian converts were sent to Tulcea for training as missionaries.

Financial advantage came with conversion. Loans and gifts were arranged for converts in the Kherson diocese, where the Rikkenhaus Society gave seven rubles for every male convert. The Society was underwritten by wealthy merchants of Sevastopol.

Stundist preachers frequented fairs and taverns, engaging supposed Orthodox spokesmen in debates. The Orthodox was really a Stundist who made the traditional faith appear ridiculous.

[43]Anderson, 427-440; A. S. Prugavin, *Raskol Vverkhu* (St. Petersburg, 1909), 242-253; Miliukov, V, 133-146; Vladimir Bonch-Bruevich, *Iz Mira Sektantov, Sbornik Statei* (Moscow, 1922), 171-191; S. Durasoff, *The Russian Protestants* (Rutherford, N.J., 1969), 35-49; *VO 1894-1895*, 220-221.

[44]*VO 1894-1895*, 222-226, 229-230; *1896-1897*, 150-158; *1898*, 89-104, 119-120.

Like Uniates and Old Believers, sectarians believed that the coronation of 1896 would bring an *ukaz* of religious toleration. Stundist proselytizers correspondingly again subjected Orthodox practices and clergy to harsh attack, while spreading the rumor that the heir to the throne and Tsarina Alexandra were secret converts, together with hundreds of priests from the Orthodox church.

Thus, in 1896 and 1897, Stundism erupted into the dioceses of Nizhni-Novgorod, Kaluga, the Don and Orel. Only by 1900 did the Synod feel the rate of Stundist growth had been tamed.

[45]*VO 1898*, 64-78, 121-126; *1899*, 140-144; *1900*, 230-241; *1913*, 74-78; Nikon, III, 202-259.

[46]Evlogii, 192-194; *VO 1908-1909*, 17-18.

Rachinskii had studied in Germany and had taught zoology at Moscow University. He resigned his post over the appointment of a dean of the law faculty whom he regarded as incompetent. Translator of Darwin's *Origins of the Species*, he was a champion of basic Christian education of a practical nature for the masses. He had established several schools, the most successful of which was in Tatev, Smolensk diocese.

[47]*VO 1888-1889*, 91-94; *1890-1891*, 69-72; *1894-1895*, 48-49, 126; *1896-1897*, 24-26; *1899*, 225-243; *1908-1909*, 18-19; Byrnes, 274-278; Nikon, 98-99.

[48]*VO 1888-1889*, 320-384; *1890-1891*, 424-479; *1892-1893*, 504-550; *1894-1895*, 364-401; *1896-1897*, 219-271; *1898*, 179-210; *1899*, 225-242; *1900*, 337-359.

[49]*VO 1888-1889*, 436; *1894-1895*, 366-367; *1896-1897*, 227-229; *1898*, 174-185; *1899*, 240-243; *1900*, 338-342.

[50]*VO 1888-1889*, 57; *1890-1891*, 436-442, 512-513; *1892-1893*, 528-533;

1894-1895, 371-373; *1896-1897,* 250-253; *1898,* 170-174; *1899,* 50-59; *1908-1909,* 21-22.

Financial support from wealthy peasants, the Kulaks whom Lenin despised and Stalin destroyed, was exemplified by the Kornilov brothers who donated 5,000 rubles for the construction, equipping, and staffing of St. Andrew's school in Alexandrovsk *uezd,* Vladimir diocese, in 1891. They contributed large sums regularly in the years that followed for other schools. In 1898 another peasant, Anatolii Aliutin, gave 5,000 rubles for a school in Bobrovo village, plus a per annum commitment for its maintenance. In the Vologda diocese that same year a peasant named Vasilii Nikulichev gave 5,000 rubles for the school in Ustianka village, while another peasant, A. Smirnov, gave 4,500 rubles to a school in Fedotov village in the Kaluga diocese.

In addition to encouraging peasant support the various dioceses received increasing monies from merchants, medical doctors, public officials, university professors and many other elements in the changing kaleidoscope of society.

[51]*VO 1890-1891,* 450-459; *1894-1895,* 361-395; *1896-1897,* 230-231; *1898,* 170-174, 187-188; *1900,* 303-304, 335-337, 342-350.

Priests like Fr. Vasilii Danilov of Potanev village exemplified the efforts the clergy were making for the schools. He scraped up 2,500 rubles and then provided much of the manual labor to build and equip his school in the Tambov diocese, while in the Arkhangelsk diocese Fr. Stefan Afanasiev personally built the school of the Annunciation in Ukhtostrov. In the same diocese Fr. Gregorii Kudriatsev of Chelmokhod village and a peasant parishioner, Nikita Soksar, raised 1,300 rubles for their school and then provided the labor to construct it. Then Fr. Kudriatsev was its faculty. In Kiev diocese a similar effort was made by Fr. Afanasii Nedelskii in Kodryshov village.

[52]*VO 1890-1891,* 450-462; *1892-1893,* 531-540; *1894-1895,* 382-385; *1896-1897,* 224-226.

[53]*VO 1890-1891,* 450-462; *1892-1893,* 531-540; *1894-1895,* 382-385; *1896-1897,* 224-226, 242-244; *1898,* 198-206; *1900,* 351-355.

In some parish schools, special courses were introduced. For example, icon painting in the style of the Stroganov school was introduced in the school in Mstersk village, Vladimir diocese.

[54]*VO 1890-1891,* 450-459; *1892-1893,* 528; *1894-1895,* 376-377, 396-398; *1896-1897,* 78-86; *1900,* 113-120.

In January 1898, there were 10,079 Old Believer students in the parish schools and in January 1899, there were 12,694. In January 1898, there were 13,812 Catholic and Lutheran students in the system, while a year later there were 16,956. Jews and Mohammedans numbered 2,460 in the former year, 3,948 in the latter. There were fewer than 2,000 Stundist and other sectarians both years.

[55]*VO 1888-1889,* 280-285, 299-307; *1890-1891,* 69-72, 189-194; *1892-1893,* 460-465, 480-481; *1894-1895,* 48-54, 128-132, 352-353; *1900,* 24-31.

In 1890 there were fifty-four seminaries, 177 men's schools, and forty-nine women's schools, plus twelve special women's schools established by Empress Marie Fedorovna early in the century for daughters of parish clergy. In 1900 there were fifty-eight seminaries, 187 men's schools, and fifty-three women's schools, plus the Empress Marie schools.

In 1900 there were 19,112 students in the seminaries, 31,175 students in the men's schools, and more than 15,000 in the women's schools, plus 2,468 in the Empress Marie schools.

[56]VO 1888-1889, 289-290, 302-304, 306-307; 1890-1891, 362-366, 402-407; 1892-1893, 458-462.

[57]VO 1888-1889, 336-337; 1890-1891, 407; 1892-1893, 458-461; 1898, 182-184; 1905-1907, 134-140.

[58]VO 1888-1889, 280-289, 290-298; 1890-1891, 342-358; 1892-1893, 327-416; 1894-1895, 318-364; 1896-1897, 189-218; 1898, 154-157; 1899, 182-224; 1900, 288-336.

[59]VO 1888-1889, 290-294; 1890-1891, 347-348, 356-358; 1899, 181-182; 1892-1893, 410-414; 1900, 89-92, 287-288; Evlogii, 179-181; Vadkovskii, 7-11.

The Petersburg Society for Religious and Moral Propagation had its origins in January 1888, under the ispiration of Archimandrite (archabbot) Antonii Vadkovskii and with the approval of Procurator Konstantin Pobedonostsev. One of its better known student organizers a decade later was Fr. Georgii Gapon.

[60]VO 1888-1889, 348-349; 1890-1891, 346-351; 1892-1893, 431-470; 1894-1895, 302-314; 1896-1897, 180-181; 1899, 172-179; 1900, 319-324.

CHAPTER II

[1]Robert F. Byrnes, Pobedonostsev: His Life and Thought (Bloomington, Ind., 1969), 44-92, 383-396; V. V. Ognev, Na Poroge Reforma Russkoi Tserkvi i Dukhovenstva (St. Petersburg, 1907), 6-7. One of the first restrictions imposed upon the church was the decision of April 5, 1881, to have blagochinie deans appointed by St. Petersburg—rather than having their peers elect them—in an effort to tighten control over the parish clergy.

[2]VO 1888-1889, 301-310; 1890-1891, 402-409; 1892-1893, 460-468, 480-481; 1898, 184-188; Byrnes, 341-367; Evlogii, 18-30.

[3]Gerhardt Simon, "Antonij Vadkovskij, Metropolit von St. Petersburg (1846-1912)," Kirche im Osten, 12 (1969), 22-23; Peter Scheibert, "Die Petersburger religiösphilosophischen Zusammenkünfte von 1902 und 1903," Jahrbücher für Geschichte Osteuropas, 11 (February 1965), 528-529; V. V. Rozanov, Okolo Tserkovnykh Sten (St. Petersburg, 1906), I, 209; Ivan Vlasovs'kii, Naris Istorii Ukrains'koi Pravoslavnoi Tserkvi (New York, 1959), III, 261.

[4]The Optina Monastery at Kozelsk, Kaluga diocese, was probably the most influential spiritual center. There lived Fr. Amvrosii Grenkov, the model for Fr. Zossima in Dostoevskii's Brothers Karamazov. Besides Dostoevskii, Amvrosii counselled Leo Tolstoi, Pobedonostsev, Vadkovskii, Khrapovitskii, Vladimir Soloviev, Sergei Witte, many prelates of the church, the Empress Marie (the wife of Alexander III and mother of Nicholas II) and countless lesser personalities. Two useful works on Amvrosii are Sergei Chetverikov, Opisanie Zhizni Optinskago Startsa Ieroskhimonakha Amvrosiia (Kaluga, 1912), and John B. Dunlop, Staretz Amvrosy: Model for Dostoevsky's Staretz Zossima (Belmont, Mass., 1972).

⁵I. Korol'kov, "Pamiati Mitropolita Antoniia," *Trudy Kievskoi Dukhovnoi Akademii*, no. 4 (1916), 481-482; Simon, 11-12; *VO 1911-1912*, 56-57.
⁶Korol'kov, 483-485.
⁷Ibid., 486-494; Simon, 12; Vadkovskii, 349-353.
⁸Richard Pipes, *Social Democracy and the St. Petersburg Labor Movement, 1885-1897* (Cambridge, Mass., 1963), 22-56; *VO 1911-1912*, 57-58; Vadkovskii, 7-11. Among the first supporters of Vadkovskii's *kruzhki* were Bishops Veniamin Bornukov and Innokentii Beliaev, and Frs. Filosof Ornatskii and Afanasii Nikitin.
⁹Korol'kov, 494-496; Simon, 14-17; *VO 1912*, 58-60; Vadkovskii, 55-57.
¹⁰*VO 1888-1889*, 192-195, 336-337; *1890-1891*, 402-409; *1892-1893*, 460-468; *1896-1897*, 52, 74-86; Arthur Ruhl, *New Masters of the Baltic* (New York, 1921), 114-116; L. G. Sakharova, "Krizis samoderzhaviia nakanune revoliutsii 1905 goda," *Voprosy Istorii*, 8 (1972), 138-139; Michael Haltzel, *Der Abbau der deutschen ständischen Selbstverwaltung in den Ostseeprovinzen Russlands* (Marburg/Lahn, 1977).
Besides at the Orthodox seminary in Riga, the government established a number of special full scholarships at the Vitebsk and Polotsk Seminaries for Latvian students to study for the Orthodox priesthood. There were also special stipends for Estonian students at the Riga Seminary. Some of the more promising parishes had been opened at Friedrichstadt, Frauenburg, Pfaltzmark and Joachimstam.
¹¹*VO 1896-1897*, 91-96; *1898*, 2, 9-10; *1899*, 108-109; *1900*, 205-207; Simon, 18; Korol'kov, 497; Vadkovskii, 63-65.
¹²Korol'kov, 497-499; *VO 1900*, 89-92; *1911-1912*, 61-62.
¹³Scheibert, 513-523; V. I. Lenin, "The Attitude of the Workers' Party Towards Religion," *Proletary*, 45 (May 13, 1909), quoted in *V. I. Lenin on Religion* (Moscow, 1966), 17-27; Rozanov, "Lev XIII i Katolichestvo," in *Okolo Tserkovnykh Sten*, II, 208-224.
¹⁴Scheibert, 525-531; Rozanov, "Ob Otluchenii Gr. L. Tolstogo ot Tserkvi," in *Okolo Tserkovnykh Sten*, II, 451-454; Nikon, I, 102-105; *VO 1900*, 276. A recent Soviet work on the group associated with the Philosophical Society is A. Gussarova, *Mir Iskusstva* (Leningrad, 1972), while an American work is John E. Bowlt, *The Silver Age: Russian Art in the Early Twentieth Century and the "World of Art" Group* (Newtonville, Mass., 1979).
Two men particularly embarrassed the church during these years and consequently became topics of heated debate at the Society sessions: Leo Tolstoi and Vladimir Soloviev. Tolstoi had become increasingly critical of the church in the 1890s and by 1900 was espousing a type of secular humanism that preserved the moral context of Christianity but abjured all allegiance to any specific confession. His criticisms of the Orthodox clergy were especially biting, and he made it clear to his expanding student and intellectual constituency that the church was irrelevant. In the Society debates, Merezhkovskii, Gippius, Andrei Belyi, Vasilii Rozanov, Nikolai Minskii and their supporters made particularly telling points in their defense of Tolstoi. Various figures from the church side—Anton Kartashev, Vasilii Terniavtsev, V. V. Uspenskii and Fr. S. A. Sollertinskii—agreed that Tolstoi's moral teachings were Christian and that his excommunication by Pobedonostsev in 1901 from the Russian church was more for personal and political reasons than for anything else.

Vladimir Soloviev was the son of the great historian Sergei M. Soloviev. Like Dostoevskii and Tolstoi, to say nothing of other eminent but lesser known Russian thinkers, Soloviev sought an intellectual and moral synthesis that would explain the social and political problems of the turn of the century. Ultimately, he set forth his views in a work published outside of Russia, entitled *La Russie et l'Église Universelle* (Paris, 1889), in which he advocated reconciliation between the Russian church and the papacy so that the Tsar and Pope could collaborate to give political stability and moral direction to Europe. Among those he had a considerable impact upon were Khrapovitskii, who ultimately rejected him, and Sergei Bulgakov, who remained attached to aspects of his thought all his life (see Bulgakov's *Avtobiograficheskiia Zametki*, Paris, 1946). Soloviev's suggestion was a scandal among the Orthodox and a sensation among the Catholics.

[15]Scheibert, 556-560; *Novyi Put'*, II (1903), 66-67, quoted in F. V. Blagovidov, *K Rabote obshchestvennoi Mysli po Voprosu o Tserkovnoi Reforme* (Kazan, 1905), 7; Simeon Nikol'skii, "Sekta 'Ioannikov' v Stavropol'skoi eparkhii," *Stavropol'skiia Eparkhial'nyia Vedomosti*, no. 8 (April 16, 1907), 454-467; Richard Pipes, *Struve: Liberal on the Left* (Cambridge, Mass., 1970).

[16]In a speech given shortly after the assassination, Ivan Sergeevich Aksakov asserted that the very assassination would produce a moral revival in Russia and raise her in the eyes of other Slavic peoples. For a study of Aksakov, see Stephen Lukashevich, *Ivan Aksakov, 1823-1886: A Study in Russian Thought and Politics* (Cambridge, Mass., 1965); for a thorough examination of Slavophilism, see Andrzej Walicki, *The Slavophile Controversy* (Oxford, 1975).

[17]Nikon, I, 1-59.

[18]Ibid., 60-107.

[19]Nechaev had tried first of all to smear Antonii's character politically by reporting that he stirred up student dissent and preached subversion of the political order. Khrapovitskii had no trouble proving that he had always been an ardent monarchist and Russian nationalist. In a futile attempt, Nechaev even accused him of misusing funds from the student medical service for his own personal use.

[20]Nikon, I, 112-179; Nikolai D. Kuznetsov, *Preobrazovaniia v Russkoi Tserkvi* (Moscow, 1906), 12-13.

[21]Nikon, I, 206-212; II, 1-52, 330-331; *Stavropol'skiia Eparkhial'nyia Vedomosti*, no. 11 (June 1, 1906), 617-618.

[22]A. M. Ivantsov-Platonov, *O Russkom Tserkovnom Upravlenii* (St. Petersburg, 1898), 1-86.

[23]Ibid., 17-22, 66-67.

[24]Ibid., 22-46.

[25]Ibid., 46-86; Lev A. Tikhomirov, *Monarkhicheskaia Gosudarstvennost'* (Buenos Aires, 1968), 320-324; see also Nicolas Zernov, *The Russian Religious Renaissance of the Twentieth Century* (New York, 1963) for a broad overview of the ramifications of the new stirrings in the church.

[26]*Bogoslovskii Vestnik*, I, 2 (1902), 215-224; I, 3, 436-457; A. A. Vasiliev, *History of the Byzantine Empire* (Madison, 1961), I, 234-290; Alexei P. Lebedev, *Vselenskie Sobory VI, VII, i VIII vekov* (St. Petersburg, 1904), 15-17.

[27]*Bogoslovskii Vestnik*, III, 10 (1902), 200, 216.

[28]Samuel Baron, *Plekhanov: The Father of Russian Marxism* (Stanford, 1963), 38-47, 82-93; Georgii Gapon, *Zapiski Georgiia Gapona* (Moscow, 1918), 34-35; Tikhomirov, 1-6.

Lev A. Tikhomirov had been a *narodnik* revolutionary during the peak of violence culminating in the death of Alexander II, and was one of the five key founders of the People's Will organization, which engineered the assassination. After the assassination he had worked to bring about the expected general upheaval that was supposed to follow. However, with the reorganization of the secret police into the efficient and dreaded Okhrana, most revolutionaries were either arrested or forced to flee the country. Tikhomirov fled to Switzerland in 1882, one step ahead of the Okhrana. There he hoped that the People's Will would be able to regroup and give new inspiration to the rapidly dying revolutionary movement at home. Once in Switzerland, however, he found that contacts with home were impossible to maintain. The news of the success of the Okhrana in extirpating every vestige of their organization made the *Narodnovoltsy* a very despondent group.

At first, Tikhomirov studied Marxism with other former Land and Liberty enthusiasts in the hope of finding a new revolutionary doctrine to which he could give his allegiance, but he found it was not possible. He believed that Marxism was too facile and definitely out of touch with the Russian scene. Bitter arguments with Georgii Plekhanov and his followers, one-time *narodniki* who were now going over to Marxism, only split the revolutionaries into smaller and smaller factions. Plekhanov was to develop Marxism in a Russian context during the 1880s so well that he came to be the intellectual father of the generation of young Marxists who seized power in 1917. Tikhomirov returned to Russia in 1888 and became an associate of Sergei Witte, the Minister of Finance and soon to be Prime Minister, and a friend of Peter Stolypin, who would follow Witte into the position of Prime Minister and would make Tikhomirov a member of the State Council during the most crucial years of the monarchy. Tikhomirov died before Lenin had a chance to deport him.

[29]For a recent discussion of Prokopovich see James Cracraft, "Feofan Prokopovich and the Kiev Academy," in Robert L. Nichols and Theofanis G. Stavrou, eds., *Russian Orthodoxy under the Old Regime* (Minneapolis, 1978), 44-64; see also George A. Maloney, *A History of Orthodox Theology since 1453* (Belmont, Mass., 1976), 42-49; Tikhomirov, 292-298; A. S. Pavlov, *Kurs Tserkovnago Prava* (Moscow, 1882), 505-507.

[30]The Old Catholics, led by Johann von Döllinger, archbishop of Munich, refused to accept the definition of papal infallibility made in 1871 by the First Vatican Council. A small group, confined mainly to southern Germany and Switzerland, broke with Rome, but they were not able to effect a reversal of the doctrine or persuade other Catholics in general. Prior to World War I, Russian church figures such as Alexander A. Kireev and Archpriest Pavel Svetlov, a professor at the Kiev Theological Academy, worked to bring the Old Catholics into union with the Russian church—a kind of reverse Unia. The war ended their attempts, however, and Old Catholicism faded into irrelevance. See Josef L. Altholz, *The Churches in the Nineteenth Century* (Indianapolis, 1967), 85-87, 187; Alexander A. Kireev, "Sovremennoe Polozhenie Starokatolicheskago Voprosa," *Bogoslovskii Vestnik*, III, 11 (1908), 423-454; and Pavel Svetlov, "O Novom Mnimom

Prepiastvii k edineniiu Starokatolikov i Pravoslavnykh," *Bogoslovskii Vestnik*, II, 5 (1903), 134-150.

[31]Lev Tikhomirov, "Zaprosy Zhizni i Nashe Tserkovnoe Upravlenie," *Moskovskiia Vedomosti*, nos. 343-345 (December 13-15, 1902); Tikhomirov, *Monarkhicheskaia Gosudarstvennost'*, 287-303.

[32]ZhP, I, vi-vii; ZhKM, 152-153; S. Iu. Kamenev, "S. Iu. Vitte i K. P. Pobedonostsev o sovremennom polozhenii Pravoslavnoi Tserkvi," *Vestnik Evropy*, I, 2 (February 1909), 651-691.

[33]ZhKM, 154-173; Byrnes, 363-366; Igor Smolitsch, "Der Konzilsvorbereitungsausschuss des Jahres 1906," *Kirche im Osten*, 7 (1964), 53-59; Vadkovskii, 77-79, 221-222, 277-278.

[34]ZhKM, 174-239; Sergei Witte, *Vospominaniia: Tsarstvovanie Nikolaia II* (Berlin, 1922), I, 319-331; Kamenev, 651-667; Blagovidov, 1-2, 49-50. Restoration of the Uniate church was not included in the recommendation of the *ukaz*.

CHAPTER III

[1]In a sermon at the liturgy for the dead soldiers of Port Arthur, Antonin Granovskii, vicar-bishop of Narva, warned that the defeat in the Crimea had led to violence and murder in Russia, and he feared that the defeat at Port Arthur would lead to the same. See Vasilii N. Myshtsyn, *Po Tserkovno-obshchestvennym Voprosam* (Sergiev Posad, 1905-1906), I, 41- 42; for a concise review of events leading to the crisis of 1904-1905, see A. A. Kizevetter, *Na Rubezhe Dvukh Stoletii* (Prague, 1929), 351-376.

[2]For a recent survey of Fr. Gapon's life, see Walter Sablinsky, *The Road to Bloody Sunday* (Princeton, 1976); see also Georgii Gapon, *Story of My Life* (New York, 1906) and *Zapiski Georgiia Gapona* (Moscow, 1918), the latter a translation of the former.

[3]Ibid., 7-11; Sergei Witte, *Vospominaniia: Tsarstvovanie Nikolaia II* (Berlin, 1922), I, 260-268.

[4]Archimandrite Feofan, a protégé of Fr. Amvrosii Grenkov of Optina, was the favorite confessor of many students at the academy, many officials outside the academy and the young princesses of the imperial family.

[5]Gapon, *Zapiski*, 12-32; *PSZ*, 1st series, I, par. 11, 619-715; Alexander Muller, *The Spiritual Regulation of Peter the Great* (Seattle, 1972), 60-62; *VO 1901*, 8. Gapon was inspired by the work of Fr. Alexei Kolokolov (1836-1902), who had set up orphanages, medical dispensaries, camps and special training classes for Petersburg youths during the last two decades of the nineteenth century. Like Gapon, Kolokolov had been a rural priest and had come to the capital specifically to aid the peasant proletarians who were abandoning their villages. After Kolokolov's death, his work was continued by the Alexeev Society, which was founded for that purpose. Vadkovskii was its chairman, Sabler its vice-chairman. See *VO 1902*, 16-22.

[6]Richard Charques, *The Twilight of Imperial Russia* (London, 1965);

59-87; Jeremiah Schneiderman, *Sergei Zubatov and Revolutionary Marxism* (Ithaca, N.Y., 1976), 173-181; Sablinsky, 56-68; "Doklad Direktora Departamenta Politsii Lopukhina Ministru Vnutrennykh Del o sobitiiakh 9-go Ianvaria," *Krasnaia Letopis'*, I (1922), 330.

[7]Gapon, *Zapiski*, 32-41; Bernard Pares, *Russia and Reform* (London, 1907), 309-311, 477-481; Solomon Schwartz, *The Russian Revolution of 1905* (Chicago, 1969), 279-282; Sablinsky, 68-73.

[8]*Gapon, Zapiski*, 41-48; N. A. Bukhbinder, "Iz Zhizni G. Gapona," *Krasnaia Letopis'*, I (1922), 101-103; I. Korol'kov, "Pamiati Mitropolita Antoniia," *Trudy Kievskoi Dukhovnoi Akademii*, no. 4 (1916), 483-497; Semen Kladovnikov, "Protokol Otdel'nago Korpusa Zhandarmov, 27 Ianvaria, 1905," *Krasnaia Letopis'*, I (1922), 322-325; Alexei E. Karelin, "Deviatoe Ianvaria i Gapon: Vospominaniia," *Krasnaia Letopis'*, I (1922), 111-115; Kizevetter, 342-350.

[9]Gapon, *Zapiski*, 48-54; "Upravlenie Moskovskago General-Gubernatora Gospodinu Ministru Vnutrennykh Del," *Krasnaia Letopis'*, I (1922), 300-301; "Spravka Ministerstva Vnutrennykh Del," *Krasnaia Letopis'*, I (1922), 297-298; Sidney Harcave, *First Blood: The Russian Revolution of 1905* (New York, 1964), 36-37; Shmuel Galai, *The Liberation Movement in Russia, 1900-1905* (Cambridge, England, 1973), 183-184; Boris Nikolaevskii, *Azev the Spy* (Hattiesburg, Miss., 1969), 67-88; Witte, I, 188-198;Sablinsky, 74-118; Sergei Zubatov, "Zubatovshchina," *Byloe*, no. 4 (1917), 170-172.

[10]Gapon, *Zapiski*, 54-55; Karelin, 108-110; Vladimir Ianov, "Protokol Otdel'nago Korpusa Zhandarmov, Ianvaria 13-go, 1905," *Krasnaia Letopis'*, I (1922), 311-313; Witte, 288-295; V. D. Nabokov, et al., "Zemskii S'ezd 6 i 7 Noiabria, 1904g," *Kratkii Otchet* (Paris, 1905), 11-14; Galai, 157-193.

[11]Kizevetter, 353-358, 370-372; V. Nevskii, "Ianvarskie Dni v Peterburge v 1905 godu," *Krasnaia Letopis'*, I (1922), 13-15; Ianov, 313-317.

[12]Sablinsky, 143-156; Kizevetter, 372-379; Witte, I, 228-232, 260-268, 301-306; Gapon, *Zapiski*, 55.

[13]Ibid., 56-58; "Doklad . . . o sobitiiakh 9-go Ianvaria," 330-332; Ianov, 313-315.

[14]Gapon, *Zapiski*, 59-86; Nikolai Petrov, "Zapiski o Gapone," *Vsemirnyi Vestnik*, III (1907), 58-61; Ianov, 316-322; "Doklad . . . o sobitiiakh 9-go Ianvaria," 332-337; Nevskii, 25-38; Karelin, 110-111; Maxim Gorkii, *Sobranie Sochinenii* (Moscow, 1954), XXVIII, 346-348; Sergei Stechkin-Stroev, "Protokol Otdel'nago Korpusa Zhandarmov, 3-go Fevralia 1905g," *Krasnaia Letopis'*, I (1922), 326-327; Witte, I, 308-313; Harcave, 88-97; Sablinsky, 157-228. Some of Sablinsky's chronology is in error. For a discussion of possible new models of church-state relations, see Nikolai D. Kuznetsov, *Preobrazovaniia v Russkoi Tserkvi* (Moscow, 1906).

[15]Gapon, *Zapiski*, 86-100; Vadkovskii, 89-91; Schwartz, 75-245; Witte, I, 313-318, 337-409, 420-500; Sablinsky, 229-322; Myshtsyn, I, 38-39; I. V. Preobrazhenskii, *Tserkovnaia Reforma* (St. Petersburg, 1905), 283-285; B. V. Titlinov, *Tserkov' vo Vremia Revoliutsii* (Petrograd, 1924), 9-11.

The literature on the 1905 Revolution and its era is considerable. Theofanis G. Stavrou, ed., *Russia under the Last Tsar* (Minneapolis, 1969), puts the time into perspective, as does Erwin Oberländer et al., eds., *Russia Enters the Twentieth Century* (New York, 1971), and Richard Pipes, *Russia Under the Old Regime* (Cambridge, Mass., 1974), although the latter's coverage of the church is seriously deficient due to the author's prejudice.

Two useful accounts are Bernard Pares, *Russia and Reform* (London, 1907), and P. Miliukov, *Russia and Its Crisis* (New York, 1962; first printed in 1905). Other pertinent works are Harcave, cited above; Howard D. Mehlinger and John M. Thompson, *Count Witte and the Tsarist Government in the 1905 Revolution* (Bloomington, Ind., 1972); M. N. Pokrovskii, *Izbrannye Proizvedeniia*, vol. 3 (Moscow, 1967); Henry W. Nevison, *The Dawn in Russia* (London, 1906); Jacob Walkin, *The Rise of Democracy in Pre-Revolutionary Russia* (New York, 1962).

[16]Kuznetsov, 15-16; Sergei Witte, "O Sovremennom Polozhenii Pravoslavnoi Tserkvi," *Slovo*, no. 108 (March 28, 1905); *Russkoe Delo*, no. 14 (1905), 1; *Missionerskoe Obozrenie*, no. 5 (1905), 806-808; *Tserkovnyi Vestnik*, no. 15 (1905), 451-453; *Ruosskoe Slovo*, no. 78 (1905), 1-3.

[17]F. V. Blagovidov, *K Rabote obshchestvennoi Mysli po Voprosu o Tserkovnoi Reforme* (Kazan, 1905), 17-24, 50-69; Kuznetsov, 15-24.

[18]Preobrazhenskii, 48, 136-137; S. Iu. Kamenev, "S. Iu. Vitte i K. P. Pobedonostsev," *Vestnik Evropy*, I, 2 (February, 1909), 654-656, 666-667.

[19]Kuznetsov, 8-10; Preobrazhenskii, 133-136.

[20]*Slovo*, no. 108 (March 28, 1905), as quoted in Preobrazhenskii, 122-133; Kuznetsov, 26-36.

[21]Preobrazhenskii, 42-43, 142-143; Robert F. Byrnes, *Pobedonostsev: His Life and Thought* (Bloomington, 1969), 363-368; Aurelio Palmieri, *La Chiesa Russa* (Florence, 1908), 1-9. Runkevich's rejected dissertation was published by the Synod's press in 1906 on orders from Pobedonostsev—a direct outcome of this controversy.

[22]Kamenev, 668-678.

[23]Kuznetsov, 39-46; Byrnes, 363-368; F. M. Dostoevskii, "Pisatel'-Khristianin," *Tserkovnyia Vedomosti*, V (1906), 226-230.

[24]Kuznetsov, 48-70; Palmieri, 6-11; *VO 1905-1907*, 78-80. Filosof Ornatskii was pastor of the Kazan cathedral on the Nevskii Prospekt. He was later to be arrested by the Bolsheviks (spring 1918) and murdered. See Michel Polsky, *Les Nouveaux Martyrs Russes* (Montsurs, 1976), 20-22.

[25]*Tserkovnyi Vestnik*, XI (March 17, 1905), 321-325; Antoine Malvy, "La Reforme de l'Église Russe," *Études*, CVII (1906), 166-172.

[26]Preobrazhenskii, 42-47; Alexander Bogolepov, *Church Reforms in Russia, 1905-1918* (Bridgeport, 1966), 12-18; *VO 1905-1907*, 67-68. The bishops on the Synod in 1905 besides the three metropolitans were Alexei, exarch of Georgia, Archbishop Nikolai Nalimov of Finland, Archbishop Gurii Okhotin of Novgorod, Archbishop Anastasii Dobradin of Voronezh, Archbishop Arsenii Briantsev of Kharkov, Antonii Khrapovitskii, bishop of Volhynia, Bishop Veniamin Bornukov of Kaluga, Kliment Vernikovskii of Vinnitsa, Lavrentii Nekrasov of Tula, and Nikon Sofiiskii, bishop of Vladimir. Also specially appointed were Archpriests Ioann Ianyshev, chaplain to Nicholas II, and Alexander Zhelobovskii, chaplain to the armed forces.

[27]Convocations of clergy had been authorized in 1867, restricted to finding ways and means to set up and maintain diocesan men's and women's schools and seminaries. Their functions expanded, however, and they took over the management of the budgets of missionary activities, charitable institutions, candle factories, wineries, oil production for liturgical functions and medicinal uses and dozens of other types of enterprises devoted to supplying churches with items for worship. They also raised funds for philanthropies under the care of the church. By the turn of the century, social

and pastoral problems had become regular items on the agendas of diocesan convocations in many parts of the empire, though these topics had not been authorized by the Procurator.

[28]Kuznetsov, 145-151; Witte, II, 323-330; Preobrazhenskii, 42, 115-117, 155-158, 179-181; *VO 1908-1909*, 45-47, 88-93; Malvy, 160-166, 172-180.

[29]Malvy, 306-311. The Living Church was headed by Alexander I. Vvedenskii, a docent in 1906. Vvedenskii subsequently was named a professor at Petersburg Academy and was made archpriest. See his *Tserkov' i Gosudarstvo: Ocherk vzaimootnoshenii Tserkvi i Gosudarstva v Rossii, 1918-1922gg.* (Moscow, 1923).

[30]Kuznetsov, 59-63; Titlinov, 7-18; Preobrazhenskii, 37-47, 67-73; Palmieri, 161-226; Nevison, 60-86. For a recent discussion of liberal Orthodoxy see Paul R. Valliere, "The Problem of Liberal Orthodoxy in Russia, 1905," *St. Vladimir's Theological Quarterly*, 20, 3 (1976), 115-131.

[31]Preobrazhenskii, 229-230; Malvy, 180-182, 311-312.

[32]*Novoe Vremia* (March 18, 1905), as quoted in Preobrazhenskii, 9-12. Schneiderman calls *Novoe Vremia* "reactionary." See *Zubatov and Revolutionary Marxism*, 177ff.

[33]*Novoe Vremia* (March 20, 1905), 481, as quoted in Palmieri, 65; and Preobrazhenskii, 13-16. See Rozanov's *V Mire neiasnogo i nereshennogo* (St. Petersburg, 1901) and his *Okolo Tserkovnykh Sten*, 2 vols. (St. Petersburg, 1906). On Rozanov himself see Spencer E. Roberts, tr., *The Four Faces of Rozanov: Christianity, Sex, Jews, and the Russian Revolution* (New York, 1978).

[34]*Birzheviia Vedomosti*, no. 8735 (March 23, 1905), as quoted in Palmieri, 115-117, 135; and Preobrazhenskii, 25-29.

[35]Preobrazhenskii, 19-32, 43, 322-324. Discussion of church reform appeared in the provincial press on March 23. The *Odessa Listok*, for example, featured a brief survey of the Russian patriarchate of the pre-Petrine era, but offered very little comment and no interpretation, except that the boyars had thought that the creation of a patriarchate had been a good idea in the sixteenth century but it had been abolished in the eighteenth to placate that same group. Characteristically, *Volyn* (*Volhynia*) on March 25 rejoiced that the Synod had decided to summon a sobor. *Volyn* noted that Metropolitan Antonii was one of the key figures persuading the Synod to so move, and it expected that a Patriarch would be elected at the sobor, which *Volyn* expected would be held within a couple of months. The same day, the *Astrakhanskii Listok* referred to the procuracy as an "artful contrivance" defacing the Orthodox church and welcomed its imminent abolition.

[36]*Rus'*, no. 75 (March 24, 1905), as quoted in Palmieri, 81; and Preobrazhenskii, 47-50.

[37]Ibid., 50-52.

[38]Preobrazhenskii, 52-57, 146-147; Evlogii, 202-203; Dmitri Filosofov, *Neugasimaia Lampada* (Moscow, 1912), I, 16-31.

Petrov had been a parish priest for the first year and a half after his ordination and was then transferred to a parish school in Petersburg. After three years in his second assignment, he received a notification from the diocesan consistory that he was to reconcile a marriage of two of his former parishioners. He did not know them, and they did not know him. When he called on them to exhort them, they did not want him in their apartment, and he was not even sure that the wife he was exhorting to be faithful was actually the woman the man was married to. Petrov was so angry with the bureaucratic incompetence that caused this embarrassing situation that he went directly to the consistory offices to complain to the clerk—a former schoolmate—who had sent him the directive in the first place. However, he could not find him and was informed by another clerk that it was not his business to question the orders sent out from the consistory—he was merely to carry them out. The infuriated Petrov read the coxcomb out, only to be dismissed with "mistakes do happen, don't they?"

Archimandrite Mikhail, on the other hand, would become radicallized politically and would publish *Why I Became a People's Socialist* in 1907. By 1909 he was so discouraged with the pace of reform of the state church that he formally went over to the Old Belief, becoming an Old Believer bishop after the 1917 Revolution.

[39]*Moskovskiia Vedomosti*, nos. 83-84 (March 25, 1905), as quoted in Preobrazhenskii, 73-78, 85-91.

[40]*Varshavskii Dnevnik*, no. 86 (March 27, 1905), quoted in ibid., 119-121.

[41]*Novosti*, no. 78 (March 27, 1905), quoted in ibid., 108-110.

[42]*Den'*, no. 85 (March 27, 1905), quoted in ibid., 117-119.

[43]*Zaria*, no. 259 (March 31, 1905), quoted in ibid., 190-194.

[44]Witte's name in Russian is pronounced the same as that of the third-century Christian child martyr Vitus, fitting nicely into the expression for the nervous disorder chorea—St. Vitus' dance.

[45]*Novoe Vremia*, no. 10 (March 29, 1905), quoted in Palmieri, 4.

[46]*Russkoe Slovo*, no. 87 (March 31, 1905), quoted in Preobrazhenskii, 199-204.

[47]Ibid., 121-145, 148-198. In March 1905, Rozanov could not foresee that in the next two years many of the Thirty-Two would be demoted or defrocked for their efforts at reform and social change, or that just a little over a decade later most of the rest would give their lives for the church.

[48]Ibid., 228; Kuznetsov, 144; Malvy, 310-311.

CHAPTER IV

[1]*Moskovskii Listok*, no. 108 (1905), in G. M. Kalinin, *Reformy Vero-terpimosti na Poroge XX veka i Sostoianie gosudarstvennoi Tserkvi v Rossii* (Nizhni-Novgorod, 1905), 27-37; *VO 1905-1907*, 14-21, 123-153; Nikon, II, 279-280; Evlogii, 150-160; Vladimir Rozhkov, *Tserkovnye Voprosy v Gosudarstvennoi Dume* (Rome, 1975), 44-45.

[2]V. M. Skvortsov, "K Istorii Vozniknoveniia Patriarshago Voprosa," cited in I. V. Preobrazhenskii, *Tserkovnaia Reforma* (St. Petersburg, 1905), 324-325; Sergei Witte, *Vospominaniia* (Berlin, 1922), I, 319-336, 342-351, 358, 421; John S. Curtiss, *Church and State in Russia, 1900-1917* (New York, 1965), 227-231.

[3]Preobrazhenskii, 271-273.

[4]Ibid., 52-57, 285-286; F. V. Blagovidov, *O Tserkovnoi Reforme* (Kazan,

1905), 66-67; N. D. Kuznetsov, *Preobrazovaniia v Russkoi Tserkvi* (Moscow, 1906), 105.

[5]Antonii Khrapovitskii, "Pervaia Dokladnaia Zapiska Sviat. Prav. Sinodu," *Bogoslovskii Vestnik*, III, 12 (1905), 698-710; Alexander Bogolepov, *Church Reforms in Russia* (Bridgeport, 1966), 18-21; Kuznetsov, 72-75; G. I. Shavel'skii, *Vospominaniia Poslednago Protopresvitera Russkoi Armii i Flota* (New York, 1954), 163-167.

[6]Bishop Antonii noted that the oft-repeated quote from the Eastern Patriarchs in 1848 to Pope Pius IX was not to be taken as justification for the theory that bishops' decisions had to be ratified by the people. The people are conservers of the Orthodox faith, but it is the bishops who are responsible to God for it.

[7]*OEA*, I, 112-120; Skvortsov in Preobrazhenskii, 316-329.

[8]Kuznetsov, 103-124, 139-142.

[9]*Tserkovnyi Vestnik*, I, 14 (April 7, 1905), quoted in Preobrazhenskii, 295-302; and Kalinin, 37-47.

[10]S. Iu. Kamenev, "Vitte i Pobedonostsev," *Vestnik Evropy*, I, 2 (February 1909), 668-691; Kuznetsov, 150-152; Witte, I, 67.

[11]*OEA*, I, *oglavlenie*. The bishops' replies were first summarized in a *vvedenie* and then broken down diocese-by-diocese, with the bishop's responses given at length.

[12]Boris V. Titlinov, *Tserkov' vo Vremia Revoliutsii* (Petrograd, 1924), 7-15; A. R., *Istoricheskaia Perepiska o Sud'bakh Pravoslavnoi Tserkvi* (Moscow, 1912), 1-6; R. F. Byrnes, *Pobedonostsev* (Bloomington, Ind., 1969), 366-368.

[13]*OEA*, I, i-3, 33-34, 113-114, 124, 146; II, 262, 291, 504; III, 3-4, 345-346. Bishop Germogen would lose his position a few years later in a dispute with the Synod over the influence of Grigorii Rasputin in the church. He would be rehabilitated after the February Revolution in 1917, only to be martyred by the Bolsheviks in June 1918. Archbishop Agafangel would later be named successor to the Patriarch in 1922, but in 1927 would refuse to acknowledge submission of the church to the Soviet state. He died in prison, October 1928.

[14]*OEA*, vved. 1, 3, 7; II, 206-207, 507. Bishops Antonii Korzhavin and Germogen Dolganev, along with Metropolitan Antonii Vadkovskii, were all to try in vain to stop the rise of Grigorii Rasputin's influence, first in ecclesiastical government and later in political affairs. All would fail, with varying degrees of personal misfortune for having tried. Bishop Antonii Stadnitskii, one of three candidates for the patriarchate in 1917, would observe how the closeness between the laity and their clergy would temporarily stalemate Bolshevik efforts to destroy the church. Arsenii would be named one of the potential heirs to the patriarchal throne, but would be imprisoned and would die in exile in Tashkent in 1936, at the height of Stalin's purges.

[15]*OEA*, vved. 1, 3-6; I, 210-211, 424-426. For example, the letters of St. Cyprian of Carthage (mid-third century) revealed that he encouraged participation by both clergy and laymen (*laici stantes*) who had remained true to Orthodox belief. This was a practice acceptable to the church in Rome as well. In 264-265 A.D., about the same time that Cyprian's council met in Carthage, a council was called to deal with Paul of Samosata, bishop of Antioch, who had been teaching that Jesus was not truly divine. He was refuted by a presbyter of Antioch, Malchion, who convinced the council that

Paul's views were at variance with the traditions of the church and persuaded them to depose him and inform the bishops of Rome and Alexandria of the decision. Malchion even signed the letter. Nikon and Konstantin pointed out that Eusebius in his *Church History*—published sometime after 324—stated that both presbyters and deacons participated in the Council of Antioch. Earlier, at Bostra-in-Arabia, the famed polemicist Origen, at the time still a presbyter, had convicted the local bishop, Beryllus, of heresy and brought him back to traditional Orthodoxy.

In the West, at councils at Elvira and Arles (306 and 314), presbyters and deacons participated as full members in the debates, both as representatives of bishops who were not present and in their own right as authorities on various matters. Two of these experts, Sicilianus and Majorinus, were sent to the Council of Arles at the order of Emperor Constantine himself.

At the First Ecumenical Council at Nicaea (325), contemporary historians—Eusebius, Socrates and Sozomen—indicated that twenty-six presbyters participated in their own right, together with deacons and laymen. Athanasius of Alexandria, the man who turned the tide against the teachings of Arius at Nicaea, was only a deacon at the time. The only laymen present who did not actively participate in the deliberations of the council were the Emperor and his numerous civil servants.

Bishop Nikon went on with a detailed demonstration of active participation by presbyters and deacons in several other ecumenical councils. The Emperors or their deputies were regularly present, together with a fairly large number of civil servants and aristocrats, all of whom were lay persons. Konstantin concluded that there could be no serious opposition to the participation of clergy in the coming sobor.

[16]*OEA*, vved. 1, 6-7; I, 211; II, 464-489; III, 102-108. Sokolov and Evlogii noted that in the year 920, when the problem of a fourth marriage for Emperor Leo VI (the Wise) came up, the final communiqué of the council deliberating the matter stated that the hierarchy and clergy consulting together had decided it was impermissible. In September 1191, at a council in Constantinople to depose Patriarch Dositheus who had occupied the throne irregularly, the metropolitans spoke first, but the various clerks in the patriarchal bureaucracy also had the opportunity to express themselves. The final vote was a voice vote of all present.

In Russia, at a council held in 1503-1504, just before the death of Ivan III, laymen and priests had joined the bishops in anathematizing the Judaizer heretics and authorizing the church to hold vast properties. In 1551, under Ivan IV, the famous Stoglav Sobor had again included the participation of laymen and clergy along with the bishops. At the Sobor of Brest (1596), when the West Russian church had submitted to Rome, laymen had vehemently protested and had nullified the sobor by stirring up opposition and keeping an independent Orthodoxy alive until the 1640 Sobor of Kiev under Peter Mogila rejected Unia and reconstituted an Orthodox administration in the Ukraine. Archimandrites, abbots and archpriests had signed the minutes of the Moscow Sobor of 1656, which authorized Nikon's reforms, and at the Great Sobor of 1666-1667, which deposed Nikon, clergy, boyars and civil servants had participated in the deliberations. Therefore, it was clear that a tradition existed for lay and clerical participation at sobors.

[17]*OEA*, vved. 1, 7-16; I, 5-7, 99, 180-181, 211-212, 325-326, 426, 521; II, 66-71, 174-180, 207-208, 224-251, 258, 465; III, 4, 30-31, 102, 258, 276, 280, 319-321, 578.

[18]Besides Ioann, Sergei of Finland, Evlogii of Kholm and Antonii of St. Petersburg also made this distinction about the nature of the proposed sobor. *OEA*, vved. 1, 16-18; II, 289, 307, 465; III, 85, 195-196, 282-283.

The Olonets Diocesan Commission, chaired by Archimandrite Faddei Uspenskii, agreed that laymen and lower clergy could participate in decisions that did not involve dogmas or their interpretation. Faddei cited Professor Nikolai Zaozerskii's *O Tserkovnoi Vlasti* (Sergiev Posad, 1894) to show that laymen and lower clergy had made decisions of implementation, but not definition, of doctrine in sobors of the early church.

[19]Balta was a vicar bishopric of Podolia in the Ukraine. None of the three Patriarchs named would have been welcomed by the Russian government. Joachim was an active promoter of the lapsed authority of the patriarchate of Constantinople and, therefore, of Greek predominance in Orthodox administration. Photios had been eased out of the patriarchate of Jerusalem and transferred to Alexandria in 1899, largely due to Russian pressure. Damian had been elected to replace him, but in 1905 the Russian Foreign Ministry was working to get rid of him, too. The Ministry favored the Slavic and Arab populations in the patriarchates, hoping to enhance Russian prestige and influence. This was yet another example of the subordination of ecclesiastical needs to political purposes. See Adrian Fortescue, *The Orthodox Eastern Church* (New York, 1907), 273-290.

[20]*OEA*, vved. 1, 18-30; I, 7, 56, 99, 212, 349; II, 208, 225, 493; III, 31, 260-261, 289, 490.

[21]Paisii had reason to be a cantankerous old man. In 1905, he was sixty-eight years old and on the verge of retirement. His clerical career had not been a notable success. For nearly a quarter of a century he had been a white priest and had served in a parish and taught at the Vitebsk Seminary and later at the Vitebsk gymnasium. He took monastic tonsure upon the death of his wife in 1882 and then served as a rector of the Tiflis Diocesan Seminary until 1889. From 1891 until 1902 he was vicar bishop of Vladimir-in-Volhynia and also served for a few months in Krements, like his first see a vicarate of Volhynia. Then, instead of being elevated to the see of Volhynia itself, he was transferred to Turkestan—an appointment he hated—and remained there until he retired in January 1906. The see of Volhynia, meanwhile, was taken by Khrapovitskii, whom he especially disliked. Paisii died in December 1908 at the John the Baptist Monastery in Astrakhan. Altogether, his career was rather disappointing. See *VO 1908-1909*, 50-51.

[22]*OEA*, vved. 2, 1; I, 47-53. A flood of literature on metropolias came out in 1905-1906. Among the more influential works were Alexei P. Lebedev, *Dukhovenstvo drevnei Vselenskoi Tserkvi* (Moscow, 1905); P. V. Gidulianov, *Mitropolity v pervye tri veka Khristianstva* (Moscow, 1905); I. M. Pokrovskii, *Russkiia Eparkhii v XVI-XIX vekakh*, 2 vols. (Kazan, 1897); and Nikolai Zaozerskii, "Okruzhno-Mitropolich'e upravlenie," *Bogoslovskii Vestnik*, I, 1 (1906), 131-133.

[23]*OEA*, vved. 2, 1-2; II, 148-153. During his pastorate at Orenburg (1903-1909), Ioakim proved effective in reconciling Old Believers to Orthodoxy. Transferred to Nizhni-Novgorod in 1909, he was archbishop there till his assassination by the Bolsheviks in 1918. See Michel Polsky, *Les Nouveaux Martyrs Russes* (Montsurs, 1976), 38-40.

[24]*OEA*, vved. 2, 2-3; III, 381-398.

[25]Bishop Nikanor would be transferred to Olonets in 1908 and would catch the eye of Archbishop Tikhon Belavin, by that time in Iaroslavl. After

the 1917-1918 Sobor, when Tikhon was elected Patriarch, Nikanor rose in the patriarchal administration, becoming archbishop of Krutitsk, vicar of the Patriarch. He was arrested in 1922 and died in prison. See Polsky, 177-178.

[26]*OEA*, vved. 2, 3-9; I, 412-421, 520-595; II, 54-65, 338-345, 413-420. Bishops Nazarii and Konstantin would shortly observe first hand how government interference in the church—or indifference to its fate—would weaken it and leave it open to the scorching fury of the Bolsheviks. Nazarii would be put to death for appealing to the League of Nations to intervene to stop persecution. Konstantin got a close look at the workings of the government while he was archbishop of Mogilev (1911-1921), the site of the supreme military command from 1915-1918. He would observe the paralyzing influence of Rasputin on Tsar Nicholas II and learn from the head chaplain of the armed forces how thoroughly Rasputin had disrupted the Synod and the ministries of the government. Konstantin was arrested, imprisoned, and died at the hands of the Bolsheviks.

Pitirim Oknov's response, however, is interesting in the light of his subsequent activities. He managed to worm his way rapidly up the hierarchical ladder during the next several years, in part through the assistance of Rasputin, until he finally became metropolitan of St. Petersburg (1915-1917). He conducted himself in that role as if he already were Patriarch, disgracing the image of the church and demoralizing its administration through his activities. He protected and defended Rasputin before all, in spite of the overwhelming evidence of the latter's debauchery. Ejected from his see shortly after the 1917 Revolution, Pitirim was incarcerated in the Beshtai Monastery in the Caucasus. During the confusion of retreat and evacuation in 1920, he came on his knees to refugee bishops preparing to leave Russia and begged not to be left behind. They agreed to take him along, but he died just before the evacuation took place. His career stands as a reminder of the disgrace of the church and was one of the reasons public opinion was initially indifferent to the fate of the church when the Bolsheviks launched their persecution.

[27]*OEA*, vved. 2, 9-11; II, 66-122; III, 85-131, 257-271.

[28]*OEA*, vved. 2, 12-15; I, 120-122, 326-329; II, 1-53, 464-489.

[29]*OEA*, vved. 2, 14; III, 506-520.

[30]*OEA*, vved. 2, 16; I, 93-98.

[31]*OEA*, vved. 2, 17; II, 54-65.

[32]*OEA*, vved. 2, 17-18; I, 80-101; III, 1-18.

[33]*OEA*, vved. 2, 18-21; II, 145-174; III, 55-72.

[34]See Alexander Ivantsov-Platonov, *O Russkom Tserkovnom Upravlenii* (St. Petersburg, 1898).

[35]*OEA*, vved. 2, 21-24; I, 33-52, 208-259, 422-519; II, 1-53, 66-122, 145-174, 338-395; III, 86-87, 381-388. Vadkovskii grouped the dioceses as follows: Petersburg metropolitanate—Petersburg, Finland, Arkhangelsk, Olonets, Vologda, Novgorod, Pskov, Riga, Tver and Smolensk. Moscow metropolitanate—Moscow, Iaroslavl, Kostroma, Vladimir, Nizhni-Novgorod, Kaluga, Tula, Riazan, Penza, Orel and Tambov. Vilna metropolitanate—Lithuania, Volhynia, Kholm, Warsaw, Minsk, Mogilev and Polotsk. Kiev metropolitanate—Kiev, Podolia, Kishenev, Chernigov, Poltava, Ekaterinoslav, Kherson, Taurida, Kharkov and Kursk. Kazan metropolitanate—Kazan, Samara, Simbirsk, Saratov, Orenburg, Ufa, Ekaterinburg and Turkestan. Irkutsk metropolitanate—Siberia. Georgia metropolitanate—all of Georgia, Mingrelia,

Kutais, Tiflis and Gorii. Voronezh metropolitanate—Voronezh, the Don, Stavropol, Terek, Astrakhan and the Caucasus.

[36]*OEA*, vved. 2, 24-25; I, 530-536.

[37]*OEA*, vved. 2, 26-28; III, 60-63, 358-361.

[38]*OEA*, vved. 2, 28-32; I, 8, 96-97, 122, 218, 420, 530-531; II, 2, 58, 102, 227, 262, 318, 420, 492, 510, 534-536; III, 62, 178, 395.

[39]*OEA*, vved. 3, 1-2; II, 490-503.

[40]Lavrentii had been transferred to Kursk as bishop in 1898 and to Tula in 1904. He died in March 1908. *VO 1908-1909*, 47-48.

[41]*OEA*, vved. 3, 2-6; I, 50-51, 144-145, 418; II, 54, 103-105, 206, 389; III, 1-3, 59, 186-194, 253-255, 273, 281-289, 577.

[42]Antonii Khrapovitskii would be bypassed in 1912 for the Moscow metropolitanate and again in 1915 for the Kiev metropolitanate, gaining appointment to the latter only in 1918 when Vladimir Bogoiavlenskii was murdered by the Bolsheviks. Khrapovitskii was in exile soon thereafter, ironically spending some time under house arrest with Metropolitan Andrei Sheptyskii of Lvov, and then moved to Yugoslavia, where he broke with the Russian hierarchy—under the control of the Bolsheviks—and established a hierarchy in schism in Europe and America. His biography can be found in Nikon Rklitskii, *Zhizneopisanie Blazheneishago Antoniia*, 10 vols. (New York, 1953-1963). Evlogii was transferred from Kholm to Volhynia to replace Khrapovitskii in 1914. Later he shared Antonii's house arrest with Metropolitan Andrei, but became a bitter foe of Khrapovitskii after the latter broke with the Russian hierarchy. Evlogii became metropolitan of the Russian church in Western Europe and died in 1946, ten years after Antonii. See Evlogii's *Put' Moei Zhizni* (Paris, 1947). Arsenii Stadnitskii was to be one of the candidates for Patriarch when that office was restored in 1917 (along with Khrapovitskii and Tikhon Belavin) and served as *locum tenens* of the patriarchate when Patriarch Tikhon died in 1925. He was himself arrested in 1927 and died in exile in Tashkent in 1936. His life is well covered in John Curtiss, *The Russian Church and the Soviet State* (Boston, 1953). Tikhon Belavin of the Aleutians and North America became metropolitan of Moscow and was elected Patriarch of Moscow and All Russia in 1917. For his attempt to rally Orthodox against the Bolsheviks he was subjected to brutal harassment and imprisonment, leading to his death in 1925. The best monograph on Patriarch Tikhon was written by Peter Haskell in 1972 as a master's thesis at the University of Minnesota. See also Vasilii Vinogradov, *O Nekotorykh Vazhneishikh Momentakh poslednago perioda zhizni i deiatel'nosti Sv. Patriarkha Tikhona, 1923-1925 gg.* (Munich, 1959).

[43]*OEA*, vved. 3, 6-9; I, 55, 179, 530; II, 145, 186-194, 224, 446, 495; III, 108, 121-128, 505-506.

[44]*OEA*, vved. 3, 9-12; I, 350-354, 416-421; III, 515-518.

[45]*OEA*, vved. 3, 13-23; I, 29, 218, 521; II, 52, 148, 227, 253, 261, 466, 509; III, 85, 128, 260, 270. In 1943, when Russia was facing defeat in World War II, Stalin, who had been a student at Tiflis Seminary when Stefan Arkhangelskii was on the faculty, authorized the selection of a Patriarch to replace Tikhon Belavin. Sergei was elected and occupied the patriarchal throne for a year before he died. The revival of the church helped strengthen the war effort in its final months. See the Moscow patriarchate's publication *Patriarkh Sergii i ego Dukhovnoe Nasledstvo* (Moscow, 1947); also Wassilij Alexeev and Theofanis G. Stavrou, *The Great Revival: The Russian Church under German Occupation* (Minneapolis, 1976).

⁴⁶*OEA*, vved. 3, 24-26; III, 86, 129-130, 270, 357-358.
⁴⁷*OEA*, vved. 3, 27-32; II, 147-148, 466-467; III, 86, 129-131, 199-213, 256, 260-261, 268-271, 318, 359, 399.
⁴⁸*OEA*, vved. 3, 33-34; II, 60-61; III, 14-15, 181, 268.
⁴⁹*OEA*, vved. 3, 34-36; I, 79, 520-521; II, 57, 79, 230-231, 399; III, 5, 271, 290-292.
⁵⁰*OEA*, vved. 3, 36-38; I, 29, 98, 144, 198; II, 57; III, 15, 86, 200, 213-214, 271, 395-396.

CHAPTER V

¹A contemporary eyewitness account of the operations and frustrations of the bureaucracy can be found in Bernard Pares, *Russia and Reform* (London, 1907), in his chapter "Administration and Officials," 154-178.
²*OEA*, vved. 3, 41-70; I, 65, 77-79, 88, 124, 139, 157-158, 185, 219-220, 539; II, 2-3, 18, 54-57, 177, 217-224, 263, 318-321, 406-408, 512-514; III, 18, 38-43, 63-64, 236-237, 256, 260-261, 268, 270-271, 290-292, 315, 318, 324, 347-348, 382-386, 388, 406-407, 412-415, 472. Bishop Ioakim would become archbishop of Nizhni-Novgorod in 1910 and would serve there until his arrest by the Bolsheviks in 1918. Deposed from his see, he returned thereafter to his native Crimea to live with his family, only to be assassinated there by a local Bolshevik command.
³Fedor Dostoevskii, *Brat'ia Karamazovy* (Moscow, 1963), I, 102-103.
⁴See Robert F. Byrnes, "Preliberal Reformer," in *Pobedonostsev: His Life and Thought* (Bloomington, Ind., 1969), 44-73; Donald Mackenzie Wallace, *Russia* (New York, 1881), 536-555, 568-572; and A. P. Lopukhin, "Pravitel'stvennyia reformy v dukhovnom vedomstve" and "Dukhovenstvo i tserkovnoe upravlenie," in his *Istoriia Khristianskoi Tserkvi v XIX veke* (Petrograd, 1900-1901), 635-641 and 721-724, for a survey of the legal reforms in civil and church courts.
⁵*OEA*, vved. 4, 1-3; I, 2, 52-53, 292-295, 323-328, 357, 456-457, 465, 524; II, 12-17, 184, 276, 366-367, 469, 515-516; III, 387. Pitirim's main source for his remarks was canon lawyer Alexander Lavrov's *Predpolagaemaia Reforma tserkovnago suda*, 2 vols. (St. Petersburg, 1873-1874). Lavrov had been one of the major canon lawyers at Moscow Academy in the 1870s and 1880s. He was tonsured in 1878 with the name Alexei and became archbishop of Lithuania in 1885. He died in 1890. See *Russkii Biograficheskii Slovar'* (St. Petersburg, 1896-1918), II, 18-19. See also Samuel Kucherov, *Courts, Trials and Lawyers under the Last Three Tsars* (New York, 1953), for an account in English of some of the confusion in the legal system during those years, and Richard Pipes, *Russia Under the Old Regime* (New York, 1974), 281-296, for an overview of administrative deficiencies.
⁶*OEA*, vved. 4, 3-4; I, 294-299; II, 185-204. Again, it is painful to recall, Pitirim was one of the worst examples of ecclesiastical obfuscators and frustrators of efficient administration when he, as metropolitan of Petrograd, could have done much to reform and expedite administration.

[7]*OEA*, I, 465-480. The summary unfrocking of Fr. Georgii Gapon after Bloody Sunday, 1905, and of Fr. Fedor Tikhvinskii, a deputy in the Third Duma, for refusing to abandon the Trudovik Party, 1907, are but two clear examples of how priests had no opportunity to present their cases before their accusers in the ecclesiastical courts, on the one hand, or to resist predetermined government pressure on the other.

[8]The *Svod Zakonov* was a digest of the *Polnoe Sobranie Zakonov Rossiiskoi Imperii (Complete Collection of the Laws of the Russian Empire)* which reduced several tens of volumes to two.

The codex of canon law suggested by the Novgorod Diocesan Commission would conform to the practices of the ecumenical church in Roman and Byzantine times. It would be divided into several sections according to the type of transgression and the transgressor. The first part would define the types of crimes that properly belonged in the jurisdiction of the ecclesiastical courts.

The second section, subdivided into several subsections, would parallel the civil code and would define those violations of civil law which were also transgressions of a moral or religious nature. For example, clerical personnel who violated the civil code would normally be considered to have violated some provision of canon law as well. Robbery or public violence—or even murder—would be areas where both types of law were violated. There would also be a section dealing with persons who were not directly under the jurisdiction of the ecclesiastical courts but who nevertheless committed crimes which called for the intervention by the church authorities. Violating churches, disrupting monasteries or convents, destroying ecclesiastical properties or institutions would be such cases. The offender would not normally fall under church jurisdiction, but the nature of his crime would place him under ecclesiastical penalties. There would be a section detailing the types of punishment that would be dealt to persons of clerical rank or of lay status who violated church law. Persons of clerical rank would receive such punishments as unfrocking and incarceration in monasteries or convents for periods of three months to several years, depending on the seriousness of the transgression. Lesser transgressions would draw fines, plus the loss of the right to function as clergymen or church officials for a period of time.

Laymen who violated churches or ecclesiastical institutions or assaulted clergy or emissaries of the church would be deprived of the right to participate in the ceremonies and sacraments of the church for specific periods of time, required to do public penances and charitable works, or permanently excommunicated from the Orthodox church. The church would take pains to emphasize that whatever civil penalties might also be attached to such actions were not punishments of the church nor imposed at the instigation of the church. The church could also go a long way in those areas where criminal and canon law overlapped to mitigate the harshness of the former and to work towards the rehabilitation and restoration to society of the offender.

[9]*OEA*, vved. 4, 4-15; I, 35, 121-122, 151-152, 186, 287-290, 327-328, 356, 388, 457-487; II, 13, 76-81, 235-238, 296-297, 323, 365-368, 406, 494.

[10]*OEA*, vved. 4, 15-20; I, 141, 156-157, 358, 444-450; II, 15, 65, 85, 236-238, 242, 298, 517; III, 40, 70, 202-203, 238, 482, 580.

[11]*OEA*, vved. 4, 21-25; I, 29-31, 76-78, 89-92, 104-105, 222, 257-259, 291-293, 466, 468-471, 476-477, 525; II, 18, 239-241, 324, 407-409, 422-423, 428, 468, 539; III, 71, 90-95, 179-181, 316, 388, 476-477, 581. Had

Konstantin's foresight been put into effect, it is doubtful that he would have witnessed the deterioration of church administration to the degree it reached during World War I, the murder of many of his confreres, or that he would have experienced his own martyrdom after the Revolution.

[12]The *reglament* can be found in *PSZ*, 1st series, VI, no. 3718, 314-346; Alexander Muller, *The Spiritual Regulation of Peter the Great* (Seattle, 1972) is an English translation.

[13]*OEA*, vved. 4, 62-72; I, 102, 203, 515-518; II, 25-38, 65, 157; III, 65, 412-413, 436-437, 484, 591. On the Elena-Alexander controversy, see George Vernadsky, *Russia at the Dawn of the Modern Age* (New Haven, 1959), 86-89; and Sergei M. Soloviev, *Istoriia Rossii s drevneishikh vremen* (Moscow, 1959-1966), V, 104-111.

[14]The Synod chancellory estimated this defection at 250,000; *VO 1905-1907*. Byrnes estimated it at 300,000 (pp. 267-268).

[15]*OEA*, vved. 4, 72-80; I, 10, 35, 82, 139, 153-155, 202, 305-306, 371-372, 533; II, 34, 77, 83, 117-118, 186-187, 294-298, 323; III, 71-72, 170, 268, 384-388, 406-407.

[16]*OEA*, vved. 5, 1-2; III, 390-392.

[17]*OEA*, vved. 5, 2-4; I, 17-19, 42, 110-111, 160-161, 246; II, 372-373, 412-413; III, 309, 367-368, 503-504.

[18]*VO 1894-1895*, 318-364.

[19]*OEA*, vved. I, 133-134; III, 347- 348. Some of the bishops who cautioned against giving convocations of clergy too much influence in 1905 would be deposed by hostile convocations of clergy in 1917. Antonii Khrapovitskii was the most notable of these; eleven others were similarly dismissed.

[20]*OEA*, vved. 5, 5-19; I, 143, 162, 254, 316-318, 523, 529, 557; II, 5, 28, 98, 177, 229-230, 270, 282, 380-383, 404, 443, 444, 487; III, 184, 240, 349, 442; Ekaterinburg, 24-25.

[21]*OEA*, vved. 6, 1-3; I, 44-46, 76-77; II, 560-561.

[22]*OEA*, vved. 6, 3-7; I, 74-77; III, 171, 370.

[23]*PSZ*, 3rd series, X, pars. 496-509 and XII, pars. 423-451. Parts of these laws are reproduced in George Vernadsky, Ralph T. Fischer and Sergei Pushkarev, eds., *A Source Book for Russian History from Earliest Times to 1917* (New Haven, 1972), III, 688-690. Unfortunately, the sections referring to the Orthodox clergy are omitted.

[24]*OEA*, vved. 6, 7-8; I, 20-21, 110-112; III, 174-175.

[25]This privilege was granted on February 26, 1906. Antonii Khrapovitskii, Evlogii Georgievskii, Nikolai Ziorov, Dmitri Kovalnitskii (who nearly immediately retired), Arsenii Stadnitskii and Nikon Rozhdestvenskii were among those appointed.

[26]*OEA*, vved. 6, 8-16; I, 74-77, 111, 173, 320-322; II, 169-170, 203, 312-313, 449-451, 489; III, 26, 173-175, 436.

[27]*OEA*, vved. 6, 17-18; I, 44-46, 133, 145; II, 169-170, 560-561; III, 1-25, 42, 171-172, 370.

[28]*VO 1905-1907*, 107-177. Among the major problems that exercised the bishops was the impact of atheistic revolutionary propaganda on the peasant masses and the urban proletariate in the wake of the collapse of the Gapon organization in Petersburg and other clergy-led movements elsewhere. Atheist-socialist propaganda was taking on a new, more menacing aspect during the time that the bishops were compiling their responses.

[29]See *PSZ*, 3rd series, X, no. 1429 and XXVII, nos. 246 and 692, for regulations covering state control of immovable ecclesiastical properties. See

Anatole Leroy-Beaulieu, *The Empire of the Tsars and the Russians* (New York, 1902), I, 205-215, for a discussion of how the state managed those properties.

³⁰*OEA*, vved. 7, 1-5; I, 4-21, 80-101, 201-211; II, 205-220, 450-458, 478-485; III, 1-25, 85-131, 230-256, 420-430, 441-444. Vladimir had worked for such an arrangement for Orthodox properties in Japan also when he served in the Japanese mission in the early 1880s.

³¹Leonid's position is remarkable in that the parish in Georgia was precisely the place around which Georgian nationalists were rallying against Russian political control, on the one hand, and through which demands for granting autocephaly to the Georgian church were being orchestrated, on the other.

³²*OEA*, vved. 7, 5-6; II, 504-528.

³³*OEA*, vved. 7, 6-8; I,533-535; II, 6-8, 208-216; III, 260-269, 485-492. Bishop Evfimii (whose patronymic was Doremidorovich, presumably because his father had musical inclinations) had been a very effective parish priest in the Nizhni-Novgorod diocese from 1860 to 1893. Among his other achievements, he built three schools in his parish, served as *blagochinnik* for nearly twenty years and was well aware that, even with autonomy and legal status, the parish would remain dependent upon the civil bureaucracy in one form or another in order to be able to function effectively. See *VO 1913*, 101-102.

Arsenii of Pskov bitterly pointed out that Peter the Great's destruction of the Russian parish resulted in the destruction of the bulwark of Orthodox spirituality and Russian nationhood in the Pskov and Novgorod areas and left the population defenseless against Catholic and Polish propaganda. The bishops regularly referred to Alexander Papkov's brochure on reviving the parish: *Neobkhodimost' Obnovleniia Pravoslavnago Tserkovno-obshchestvennago stroia* (St. Petersburg, 1902).

³⁴*OEA*, vved. 7, 8-10; I, 126-135; II, 125-144, 261-271; III, 186-194, 269-271, 441-444.

³⁵*OEA*, vved. 7, 10-12; I, 22-32, 325-411; II, 240-248, 330-336, 400-412, 480-485, 498-503; III, 323-325.

³⁶*OEA*, II, 89-101.

³⁷*OEA*, vved. 7, 13-15; I, 102-111, 168-176; II, 125-144, 305-312; III, 265-271, 441-444, 577-588. Bishop Serafim had the unique experience of being rector of the Tiflis Seminary when Joseph Dzhugashvili-Stalin was a student there. Later, during the first phases of Stalin's terror, he was imprisoned in Rostov and shot by the GPU. *VO 1898*, 4; Michel Polsky, *Les Nouveaux Martyrs Russes* (Montsurs, 1976), 174, 265-268.

³⁸*OEA*, vved. 7, 15-17; I, 529-548; II, 218-223, 480-489; III, 290-313, 381-388.

³⁹Konstantin armed the monks of the Glinskii Monastery at one point to repel peasant bands. See L. I. Emeliakh, *Antiklerikal'noe Dvizhenie Krestian v period pervoi russkoi revoliutsii* (Moscow, 1965), 27-28, 36-37.

⁴⁰*OEA*, vved. 7, 17-19; I, 280-287; II, 261-271; III, 230-256, 265-271, 393-437.

⁴¹*OEA*, vved. 7, 19-20; II, 45-53.

⁴²In virtually every *VO* between 1888 and 1914 there was a long section on "drunkenness" and the church's unsuccessful efforts to curb it.

⁴³*OEA*, vved. 7, 21-32; I, 252-260; II, 239-243, 290-316; III, 120-133.

⁴⁴*OEA*, vved. 8, 1-2; I, 16-17, 132-133; II, 6-7, 440-441; III, 225-229, 494.

354   A VANQUISHED HOPE

[45]*OEA*, vved. 8, 2-5; I, 122, 163, 179, 192-193, 262-263, 314, 540-548; II, 122, 373, 440, 486, 555; III, 68-69, 443-444.

[46]*OEA*, vved. 8, 5-16; I, 17-18, 33, 80, 103; II, 8, 123, 201, 213, 284, 311-312; III, 98-99, 183-184.

[47]*OEA*, I, 20-21, 40-42; II, 140-144. Both Arsenii and Antonii had served in the Kazan archdiocese and had observed how counter-productive anti-Raskol legislation was and how it discouraged rapprochement with the state church.

[48]Old Catholics, led by deposed Archbishop Johann von Döllinger of Munich, held a series of seven conferences between 1871 and 1905 seeking union with the Orthodox and Anglicans—with no success. Döllinger died in 1890. See Josef L. Altholz, *The Churches in the Nineteenth Century* (Indianapolis, 1967), and Bernard O'Reilly, *Life of Pope Leo XIII* (New York, 1887), 462-465. O'Reilly was one of the main sources for a series of articles written by V. A. Sokolov for *Bogoslovskii Vestnik* in 1903 and 1904.

[49]Serafim also noted that there was some question as to whether the Synod had had the canonical right to excommunicate Count Leo Tolstoi in 1901. The sobor should review that excommunication and examine whether or not it could be lifted and the count welcomed back into the arms of Orthodoxy. *OEA*, I, 148-177.

[50]As a result of growing nationalism in Bulgaria, as well as Russian pressure, the Bulgarian clergy had agitated for a Slavonic liturgy and Bulgarian bishops instead of a Greek liturgy and Greek hierarchs under the control of the Greek patriarchate at Constantinople. After being denied these they finally established their own exarchate in 1870, but were excommunicated and anathematized by Constantinople. See Adrian Fortescue, *The Orthodox Eastern Church* (New York, 1907), 318-323, and L. S. Stavrianos, *The Balkans since 1453* (New York, 1961), 371-375.

[51]*OEA*, I, 33, 548; II, 120, 372-374, 485-487; III, 68-69, 130-131, 190-194, 442-444, 495-496.

[52]Evlogii, 165-166; Sergei Witte, *Vospominaniia* (Berlin, 1922), II, 50-51; Nikon, III, 120; *VO 1905-1907*, 69-70.

CHAPTER VI

[1]L. I. Emeliakh, *Antiklerikal'noe Dvizhenie Krestian* (Moscow, 1965), 1-10, 27, 60-65.

[2]Francis McCullagh, *The Bolshevik Persecution of Christianity* (London, 1924), 30-33; Evlogii, 104-107; Nikon, VI, 87-88. Antonin's dissatisfaction with reform in the state church was so deep-seated that eventually, after the Revolution, he became one of the founders of the schismatic Living Church.

[3]Evlogii, 161-167, 179-180; Sergei Witte, *Vospominaniia* (Berlin, 1922), I, 244-245; Howard D. Mehlinger and John M. Thompson, *Count Witte and the Tsarist Government in the 1905 Revolution* (Bloomington, Ind., 1972), 57-64; *VO 1905-1907*, 1-5. The peasant violence is covered thoroughly in Emeliakh; S. M. Dubrovskii, *Krestianskoe Dvizhenie v revoliutsii 1905-*

1907 g.g. (Moscow, 1956); Sidney Harcave, *First Blood* (New York, 1964); Richard Charques, *The Twilight of Imperial Russia* (London, 1965), in the chapter "The Hungry Village," 59-75; and Bernard Pares, *Russia and Reform* (London, 1907), 418-486.

[4]*ZhP*, I, i-ii; Vadkovskii, 94-97.

[5]*ZhP*, I, iii-vii. Nicolas Zernov, in *The Russian Religious Renaissance* (New York, 1963), erroneously implies that the vigor of the bishops' replies (*otzyvy*) caused Nicholas II to permit the issuing of the rescript in December, whereas the Tsar had committed himself already in February as a result of Witte's plea in the Committee of Ministers and Vadkovskii's leading a delegation of bishops to Tsarskoe Selo.

[6]*ZhP*, I, ix.

[7]Ibid., vii-xi.

[8]Ibid., xi-xii.

[9]Ibid., i-xiii.

[10]Dmitri had taught at the Kiev Academy from 1867 to 1895 as a layman. He took monastic vows only in 1895 and was named inspector of the academy. In 1898 he was made head of a Kiev monastery and vicar bishop of Chigirin in the Kiev archdiocese. In 1902 he became bishop of Tambov, then was made archbishop and transferred to Kazan in 1903 and to Odessa and Kherson in 1905. His was a classic example of the musical chairs bishops complained about. *VO 1913*, 97-99.

[11]P. V. Tikhomirov, "Kanonicheskoe dostoinstvo Petra Velikago po tserkovnomu upravleniiu," *Bogoslovskii Vestnik*, I, 1 (1904), 75-106; and I, 2, 217-247.

[12]*ZhP*, I, 1-14.

[13]In 1848, Pope Pius IX had written to the Orthodox Patriarchs suggesting that steps be taken towards reconciliation and ending the 800-year schism. The Patriarchs replied in the negative, stating, among other things, that they could not simply end the schism of their own volition. Hierarchs who would presume to end the schism would be rejected by their people, who were the true conservators of Orthodox belief. See Timothy Ware, *The Orthodox Church* (Hammondsworth, England, 1972), 211, 255.

[14]*ZhP*, I, 14-23. Glubokovskii cited a range of fathers from *PG* and *PL*, various scripture scholars, such as Constantine von Tischendorff, the works of Theodore Mommsen, Adolf Harnack and other western scholars, together with the works of Russian scholars like Alexei P. Lebedev's "Ob uchastii mirian na soborakh," *Dushepoleznoe Chtenie*, no. 3 (1906), 350-394. Lebedev was also a member of the Commission.

[15]At Antioch (267), Trullo (692), Alexandria (341), Arles (314), Elvira (306) and Toledo (633).

[16]*ZhP*, I, 23-33.

[17]Ibid., 33-36.

Voting for consultative voices were: Archpriest F. I. Titov, Professors N. S. Suvorov, V. F. Pevnitskii, S. T. Golubev, I. S. Berdnikov, N. I. Ivanovskii, N. A. Zaozerskii, N. N. Glubokovskii and I. I. Sokolov, Lieutenant-General A. A. Kireev and Dvorianin F. D. Samarin.

Voting for decisive voices were: Archpriest P. Ia. Svetlov, Fr. A. P. Rozhdestvenskii and Professors V. Z. Zavitnevich, V. I. Nesmelov, M. A. Mashanov, A. I. Brilliantov and N. P. Aksakov.

[18]Such authors as Sergei Bulgakov, Georges Florovsky and Nikolai Berdiaev, who two generations later helped shape the thought of men like

Jacques Maritain and Teilhard de Chardin in the West, were profoundly influenced by Zavitnevich.

[19]*ZhP*, I, 36-45, 64-67, 69.

[20]Under western pressure, the Turkish government had been forced to liberalize its administration in the years after Russia was defeated in the Crimean War. Since the Turks ruled their non-Moslem peoples through their religious administrations, liberalization meant changing the ecclesiastical administration of the Constantinople patriarchate. Among the changes was the introduction of laymen in the lower chamber of the bicameral administration. See L. S. Stavrianos, *The Balkans since 1453* (New York, 1961), especially the chapter "Reform and Revolution in the Ottoman Empire," 381-392; and Alexei P. Lebedev, *Istoriia Greko-vostochnoi Tserkvi pod vlastiiu Turok* (St. Petersburg, 1903).

[21]*ZhP*, I, 45-54, 64-67, 69; *OEA*, III, 85-90.

[22]*ZhP*, I, 54-58. Kireev and Aksakov were well aware of the dangers of a schism. The church was rent by two major schisms in the aftermath of the 1917-1919 Sobor during the Bolshevik persecution: the Living Church, led by Alexander Vvedenskii and for a time supported by Bishop Antonin Granovskii; and a schism led by Antonii Khrapovitskii in exile.

[23]Ibid., 58-64; II, 422-423; *Tserkovnyia Vedomosti*, no. 16 (1906), 859, 872.

Voting for an episcopal veto before the sobor were: Professors Ilia S. Berdnikov, Vasilii Pevnitskii, Nikolai Ivanovskii, Stefan Golubev, Nikolai Suvorov, Ioann Sokolov and Alexander Brilliantov, and Fedor Samarin.

Voting against a veto were: Archpriests Fedor Titov and Pavel Svetlov, Fr. Alexander Rozhdestvenskii, Professors Nikolai Aksakov, Mikhail Mashanov, Vladimir Zavitnevich, Nikolai Zaozerskii and Viktor Nesmelov, and General Alexander Kireev.

[24]*ZhP*, II, 410-434, 444-446, 467-469, 483-489, 581-589.

[25]N. P. Aksakov, "Vsetserkovnyi Sobor i vybornoe nachalo v Tserkvi. Ot gruppy Peterburgskikh Sviashchennikov," *Bogoslovskii Vestnik*, III, 12 (1905), 711-777.

[26]*ZhP*, I, 64-77, 87-93, 171-173; II, 471-483; *OEA*, III, 85-86.

[27]*ZhP*, I, 77-81; *Tserkovnyia Vedomosti*, no. 16 (1906), pribavlenie, 389b. The Spasskii cathedral, begun in 1815 and consecrated in 1881, was dynamited in 1932. A Palace of Soviets, surmounted by a gigantic statue of Lenin, was planned as a replacement, but the marshy ground would not support such a structure. Today the site holds the Moscow open-air swimming pool.

[28]*ZhP*, I, 81-87, 93-100. Ioann Sokolov's key area of competence was the Byzantine church. He had just published his *Konstantinopol'skaia Tserkov' v XIX veke* (St. Petersburg, 1904), adding pressure to restore Byzantine norms in Russia.

[29]*ZhP*, I, 100-102. Samarin's argument was repeated later by men such as Georges Florovsky, in the latter's article "Sobornost': The Catholicity of the Church," in *Bible, Church, Tradition* (Belmont, Mass., 1972), 37-55, printed originally in 1934. An example of the transmission of this line of thought to the West is Pierre Batiffol, *Le Catholicisme de St. Augustine*, 2 vols. (Paris, 1920); and Karl Adam, *Das Wesen des Katholizismus* (Tübingen, 1937). Abbé Roger Hasveldt, in *L'Église: Mystère Divin* (Paris, 1958), expresses this idea of *sobornost'* throughout his work without ever using the

term. His use of the French term "catholicité" exactly reproduces the meaning of *sobornost'*.

³⁰*ZbP*, I, 77-81, 100-115, 161-163, 212-222; *Tserkovnyia Vedomosti*, no. 17 (1906), 959-965. See V. Z. Zavitnevich, "O Vozstanovlenii Sobornosti v Russkoi Tserkvi," *Tserkovnyi Vestnik*, no. 14 (April 7, 1905), for a similarly argued case for decentralizing the church administration.

³¹Titov was wrong in his belief that cultural differences and administrative separateness did not affect the political fortunes of the empire. There was a vigorous independence movement in Georgia during those years, and it directly affected the church because Georgians also demanded restoration of autocephaly. Bishop Nikon Sofiiskii of Vladimir was transferred to Georgia in July 1906 to help stem this movemnt and was assassinated in his cathedral by Georgian nationalists (May 28, 1908). His successor, Innokentii Beliaev, who was transferred from Tambov, worked closely with Prince I. I. Vorontsov-Dashkov, governor-general of the Caucasus, to repress the nationalist agitation and pressure for autocephaly. Innokentii died in 1913.

Fr. Koialovich's area was the scene of intense rivalry between Uniates and Orthodox between World Wars I and II, when the region was part of Poland. To defuse some of the hostility the Polish government went to the extreme of demolishing some of the churches the two groups were fighting over. The cathedral at Lida was spared, but was closed. A long and bitter process known as "revindication" went on in the 1920s in which the Polish government transferred former Uniate and Latin churches back to those groups. The churches had been made Orthodox after the two suppressions of Unia and after the Kholm area was detached from Poland (1912). Both Metropolitan Sheptyskii of Lvov and the Latin hierarchy had protested, but to no avail. Much of the property attached to those churches and monasteries was taken over by the Polish government.

³²*ZbP*, I, 386-417, 424-428, 546-549; III, 15-17; Alexander Svitich, *Pravoslavnaia Tserkov' v Pol'she i ee Avtokefaliia* (Bucnos Aires, 1959), 1-7; E. E. Golubinskii, *O Reforme v byte Russkoi Tserkvi* (Moscow, 1913), 107-113; *VO 1908-1909*, 45-47; *1911-1912*, 88-93.

³³*ZbP*, I, 115-143. Kuznetsov referred to the late V. V. Bolotov's *Lektsii po Istorii Drevnei Tserkvi*, vol. 4; *V period vselenskikh soborov* (Petrograd, 1918), which at that time was circulating in manuscript form as copied by Bolotov's students from their lecture notes, and also to N. K. Sokolov's *Vvedenie v Tserkovnoe Pravo* (St. Petersburg, 1904), as he developed his argument.

³⁴*ZbP*, I, 143-152, 162-165, 190-217, 219-220, 286, 292, 295-297; Witte, I, 320.

³⁵*ZbP*, I, 152-162, 165-171, 215-216; II, 589.

³⁶*ZbP*, I, 177-189, 190-198, 200-201; II, 579-589.

³⁷*ZbP*, I, 220-254.

³⁸Ibid., 254-265, 285.

³⁹Ibid., 272-281.

⁴⁰Ibid., 292-295; II, 468-469, 590-618; III, 26-41; Nikon, III, 135-156, 187-198.

358

A VANQUISHED HOPE

CHAPTER VII

[1]ZhP, I, 295-308, 316-318. Berdnikov went into considerable detail describing how Bismarck, the German chancellor in 1871, had found himself in a situation where he believed the Catholic church had been placed in opposition to the state by events beyond his control. The defeat of Catholic France, on the one hand, and the proclamation of papal infallibility—with its attendant claim of total autonomy for the church—on the other, put the German state automatically in opposition to the church. Thus, the May Laws were passed and the *Kulturkampf* began. The church was suddenly visited with a persecution that decimated its hierarchy, clergy and lay supporters and threatened its very institutional existence. Because of the current situation in Russia, and particularly because of the hostility against the church in the Duma, the Russian church was itself standing on the brink of such a confrontation.

[2]Ibid., 308-316. Ostroumov cited Alexei P. Lebedev, *Sobranie Tserkovno-istoricheskikh Sochinenii* (Moscow, 1902), VII; Theodore Balsamon, *Syntagma*, V, *PG* 138; and a wide range of other sources. See George Vernadsky, "Die kirchlich-politische Lehre der Epanagoge und ihr Einfluss auf das russische Leben im XVII Jahrhundert," *Byzantinisch-neugriechische Jahrbücher*, VI (1928), 121-125.

[3]ZhP, I, 318-346. Kuznetsov ranged through the canons of the seven ecumenical councils for examples of caution with regard to the state. Among the sources he cited were Anatole France's *The Separation of Church and State* (Russian edition, Moscow, 1906), and his own *Preobrazovaniia v Russkoi Tserkvi* (Moscow, 1906).

[4]ZhP, I, 347-352. Titov argued that the Russian church was so closely bound up with the very identity of the Russian people that in the end the church would be safeguarded and would flourish whatever the outcome of the present political crisis. The Slavonic church historically was an outpouring of the native genius of the Slavic peoples, unlike the Western church, which was imposed from above upon heterogeneous and diverse peoples. Therefore, although the Western church found itself being rejected by various nations because it was cosmopolitan and alien, that could never happen in Russia.

[5]Ibid., 352-358; *Tserkovnyia Vedomosti*, no. 21 (1906), pribavlenie, 1392; no. 24, 1825, 1841. Glubokovskii also cited Ulrich Stutz, *Tserkovnoe Pravo v Russkim perevode* (Iaroslavl, 1905).

[6]ZhP, I, 359-373. The two key works cited repeatedly in the heated exchanges were F. A. Kurganov, *Ustroistvo Upravleniia v Tserkvi Korolevstva Grecheskago* (Kazan, 1871), which regarded the right of the Greek government—at that time—to interfere in ecclesiastical affairs as a good arrangement; and "Lex in Confirmatione Concilii," *PL* 84, where Visigothic kings in Spain made final confirmation of church council decisions but did not interfere in formulating the decisions.

[7]ZhP, I, 378-379.

[8]Ibid., 325, 366, 368, 373-378; V. M. Skvortsov, *Tserkovnyi Svet i Gosudarstvennyi Razum* (St. Petersburg, 1912-1913), I, 106-114; F. I. Mishchenko, "O sostave predstoiashchago Pomestnago Sobora Vserossiiskoi Tserkvi," *Trudy Kievskoi Dukhovnoi Akademii*, no. 1 (1906), 50-111.

⁹*ZhP*, I, 428-430.

¹⁰I. Berdnikov, "K Voprosu o Preobrazovanii Eparkhial'nago Upravleniia," *Pravoslavnyi Sobesednik*, I, 2 (1906), 20-35.

¹¹Nikandr cited Antonii Khrapovitskii's reply to the Synod's questionnaire on this matter. See *OEA*, I, 122-123.

¹²*ZhP*, 430-443, 463-479.

¹³Ibid., 443-445, 631. Not surprisingly, the Tolstoi issue came up in several contexts. A rather heated debate took place in Bishop Arsenii Stadnitskii's fifth sub-commission on education concerning Tolstoi's influence in the demoralization of religious schools. See *ZhP*, IV, 252-253.

¹⁴*ZhP*, I, 445-457, 505.

¹⁵Ibid., 462-463, 509-519.

¹⁶Ibid., 479-503, 549-554, 563.

¹⁷Alexander A. Papkov, *Neobkhodimost' Obnovleniia Pravoslavnago Tserkovno-obshchestvennago stroia* (St. Petersburg, 1902), as reviewed by Nikolai Zaozerskii in *Bogoslovskii Vestnik*, III, 10 (1902), 200-216.

¹⁸*ZhP*, I, 519-526.

¹⁹Ibid., 526-534.

²⁰Ibid., 534-546.

²¹*ZhP*, II, 1-31, 52-58, 60; III, 267-283, 297-302, 305-306, 332-341, 351-359, 363-364; I. V. Preobrazhenskii, *Tserkovnaia Reforma* (St. Petersburg, 1905), 283-285.

²²*ZhP*, II, 9-11, 409-410; III, 282-286, 307-318, 321, 351, 371.

²³Disorders in the seminaries are described in Antonii Khrapovitskii's "Vtoraia Dokladnaia Zapiska" in *OEA*, I, 129-136; Nikon, I, 100-108. L. I. Emeliakh, *Antiklerikal'noe Dvizhenie Krestian* (Moscow, 1965); P. S. Gustiatnikov, *Revoliutsionnoe Dvizhenie Studentov v Rossii, 1899-1906gg.* (Moscow, 1971); William H. E. Johnson, *Russia's Educational Heritage* (Pittsburgh, 1950), "The Beginning of the End," 172-205; and Patrick L. Alston, *Education and the State in Tsarist Russia* (Stanford, 1969), are just a few of the many works that describe the violence in schools of all types.

²⁴*ZhP*, II, 141-142, 500-502, 532; S. P. Sokolov, "Skorbnyi List Dukhovnykh Seminarii v 1906-1907 uchebnom godu," *Bogoslovskii Vestnik*, II, 5 (1907), 230-246.

²⁵*ZhP*, II, 69, 86-87, 628-630, 645-648; III, 211-216, 267, 283, 302-304, 346-347, 374-376; Nikon, II, 100-108.

²⁶*ZhP*, II, 118-119, 406-411, 491-510, 525-578; *Tserkovnyia Vedomosti*, no. 20 (1906), 1243; Nikon, III, 160-169. Later, after Mikhail formally converted to the Old Belief, Antonii would question his background.

²⁷D. V. Filosofov, *Neugasimaia Lampada* (Moscow, 1912), 16-31; G. M. Kalinin, *Reformy Veroterpimosti* (Nizhni-Novgorod, 1905), 12-13; Preobrazhenskii, 50-51; Nikon, III, 127-135; *Stenograficheskie Otchety Gosudarstvennoi Dumy, 1906 god, pervyi sozyv, sessiia pervaia*, II, 1949-2009.

²⁸S. Iu. Witte, *Vospominaniia* (Berlin, 1922), II, 311-320; Skvortsov, I, iv-ix.

Shirinskii-Shikhmatov was one of the founders of the yellow rightist weekly *Okrainy Rossii* (*Russian Frontiers*) in early 1906. The group associated with this journal later evolved into the Russian Frontier Society in 1908. Among Shirinskii-Shikhmatov's associates was the notorious Hundreder D. I. Pikhno of Kiev, one of the main antagonists of Witte and Vadkovskii in the Special Sessions of the Committee of Ministers.

[29]*ZhP*, I, 322-323, 343-344, 383, 497; II, 73, 310, 618-674; Mehlinger and Thompson, *Count Witte* (Bloomington, Ind., 1972), 307-308.

[30]Witte, I, 245-246, 303; II, 307-311, 320; *ZhP*, II, 437-478, 634; A. Ia. Averkh, *Stolypin i Tret'ia Duma* (Moscow, 1968), 22-30.

[31]Filosofov, 127-133.

[32]*ZhP*, III, i-iii; Filosofov, 127-133.

[33]*ZhP*, III, 1-26.

[34]Ibid., 45-77, 130.

[35]Ibid., 143-159. On the Hundreds, see Hans Rogger, "Was there a Russian Fascism?" *Journal of Modern History*, 36 (December 1964), 398-415; and Harrison Salisbury, *Black Night, White Snow* (New York, 1978), 160-171.

[36]*VO 1905-1907*, 36-66, gives a resumé of the recommendations of the sub-commissions and of the resolutions of the spring and autumn general sessions of the Pre-Sobor Commission, together with a list of all the participants.

CHAPTER VIII

[1]Nikon, II, 151-161; III, 242; *Stenograficheskie Otchety Gosudarstvennoi Dumy, 1907 god, vtoroi sozyv, sessiia vtoraia*, II, 1481-1610; Vitalii Maksimenko, *Motivy Moei Zhizni* (Jordanville, N.Y., 1955), 180-182.

[2]L. I. Emeliakh, *Antiklerikal'noe Dvizhenie Krestian* (Moscow, 1965), 60-64; Boris Titlinov, *Tserkov' vo Vremia Revoliutsii* (Petrograd, 1924), 22-23; *Tserkovnyia Vedomosti*, no. 32 (1906), 2420.

[3]Peter Scheibert, "Die Petersburger religiösphilosophischen Zusammen-künfte von 1902 und 1903," *Jahrbücher für Geschichte Osteuropas*, 11 (February 1965), 539-560; Evlogii, 202-203.

[4]G. M. Kalinin, *Reformy Veroterpimosti* (Nizhni-Novgorod, 1905), 13-14. Mikhail's lectures were published under the title *Svoboda Khristianstva* (Moscow, 1906). His contention that the economic and social aims of socialist parties could be reconciled with Christianity particularly outraged Khrapovitskii. See Nikon, II, 242-250.

[5]John S. Curtiss, *Church and State in Russia, 1900-1917* (New York, 1965), 204-205; Nikon, II, 151-161, 287-291; III, 242.

[6]Nikon, II, 180-186; A. Ia. Averkh, *Stolypin i Tret'ia Duma* (Moscow, 1968), 26-27.

[7]*Bogoslovskii Vestnik*, I, 3 (March 1908), 603-609.

[8]Ibid., 590-603; *Obzor Deiatel'nosti Komissii i Otdelov Gosudarstvennoi Dumy, 1907-1908gg., tretii sozyv, sessiia pervaia*, 67-100.

[9]Nikon, II, 216-227. Khrapovitskii held Bishop Platon Rozhdestvenskii, rector of the academy, responsible for the radicalization of the student body. He denounced Platon for being a confederate of Pavel Miliukov of Moscow University, the leader of the Constitutional Democratic (Cadet) Party. The fact that Platon identified with the Cadets when he himself was elected to the Duma was sufficient proof of the bishop's ideological and disciplinary

softness in Antonii's eyes. Khrapovitskii also traced Kiev's trouble to the appointment of A. Pesotskii, an advocate of administrative leniency, as secretary of the academy in 1904 in response to student unrest.

[10]Khrapovitskii felt that if the temporary regulations of 1906 had not been put into effect in the academies, then the authorities could have gotten rid of students and professors who advocated radical reforms—such as Alexander Popov, a Kiev student who later became editor of the journal *Vek*, which criticized the church, and Alexander Vvedenskii of Petersburg Academy.

[11]Nikon, II, 222-228; III, 96-110, 122; Evlogii, 171-172; *VO 1913*, 97-98. After serving in the short-lived second Duma, Platon was named archbishop of the Aleutians and North America, returning to Russia just before World War I (March 1914). During the war, he was active in raising supplies for soldiers and recruiting chaplains for the army. After the Revolution, he returned to the United States and headed the Russian church in America until his death in 1934.

[12]Evlogii, 195-196; *Stenograficheskaia Otchety Gosudarstvennoi Dumy, tretii sozyv, sessiia pervaia*, I, 1132-1161, 1378-1392; IV, 2447-2453; Vladimir Rozhkov, *Tserkovnye Voprosy v Gosudarstvennoi Dume* (Rome, 1975), 152-160.

[13]Nikon, III, 156-160.

[14]The literature on Rasputin is voluminous. Mikhail Rodzianko, *The Reign of Rasputin* (New York, 1927), shows how Rasputin paralyzed the government. René Fülop-Miller, *Rasputin, the Holy Devil* (New York, 1929), which was translated into many languages, is the most popular. Bernard Pares, *The Fall of the Russian Monarchy* (London, 1939), gives an even more graphic account of Rasputin's paralyzing effect on the government. Sergei D. Sozonov, *Fateful Years, 1909-1916* (London, 1928), is based on the author's own suffering at Rasputin's hands. A rather different picture, of course, is given in Maria Rasputin and Patte Barham, *Rasputin: The Man behind the Myth, a Personal Memoir* (Englewood Cliffs, N.J., 1977).

[15]Georgii Shavel'skii, *Vospominaniia* (New York, 1954), I, 50-59; II, 254-259; Fülop-Miller, 54-69; Sergei Trufanoff, *The Mad Monk of Russia: The Life, Memoires and Confessions of Illiodor* (New York, 1918), 87-97, 133 135, 229-245, Nikon, III, 10-14; IV, 55-56; *VO 1911-1912*, 55-56; Michel Polsky, *Les Nouveaux Martyrs* (Montsurs, 1976), 50-53.

[16]Nikon, II, 288-291; IV, 55-56; Evlogii, 197-199; Shavel'skii, I, 372-392.

[17]Evlogii, 189-242; Averkh, 44-153; Edward Chmielewski, *The Polish Question in the Russian State Duma* (Knoxville, 1970), 82-160; *VO 1913*, prilozhenie, 38-39; *1914*, 114-116.

CHAPTER IX

[1]Some more recent studies are Gerhard Simon, *Church, State and Opposition in the USSR* (Berkeley, 1974), particularly chapters 1 and 2; Wassilij Alexeev and Theofanis Stavrou, *The Great Revival* (Minneapolis,

1976); Eric Widmer, *The Russian Ecclesiastical Mission in Peking* (Cambridge, 1976); Robert Nichols and T. G. Stavrou, eds., *Russian Orthodoxy under the Old Regime* (Minneapolis, 1978); Paul R. Valliere, "Russian Orthodoxy and the Challenge of Modernity: The Case of Archimandrite Makary," *St. Vladimir's Theological Quarterly*, 22, 1 (1978), 3-15; and Boris Shragin and Albert Todd, eds., *Landmarks: A Collection of Essays on the Russian Intelligentsia—1909* (New York, 1977). Soon to be published are Peter Weisensel and T. G. Stavrou, eds., *Russian Travellers in the Orthodox East, 1169-1914: A Bibliographical Dictionary*; and a study of Archimandrite Mikhail Semenov by Paul R. Valliere.

Bibliography

A. REFERENCE WORKS

Blagovidov, F. V. *Ober-Prokurory Sv. Sinoda v XVIII i v pervoi polovine XIX stoletiia.* Kazan: Tsentral'naia Tipografiia, 1899, 1900.

Lavrov, A. F., ed. *Pravila Sv. Apostol, Sv. Soborov vselenskikh i pomestnykh, i Sv. Ottsov s tolkovaniami.* 10 vols. Moscow, 1875-1884..

Polnoe Sobranie Zakonov Rossiiskoi Imperii, s 1649 goda. 1st series (1649 to December 12, 1825), 45 vols.; 2nd series (December 12, 1825 to March 1, 1881), 55 vols.; 3rd series (March 1, 1881 to 1913), 33 vols. St. Petersburg, 1830-1916.

Pravoslavnaia Bogoslovskaia Entsiklopediia, ili bogoslovskii entsiklopedicheskii slovar'. 12 vols. St. Petersburg, 1900-1912.

Russkii Biograficheskii Slovar'. 25 vols. St. Petersburg, 1896-1918.

Sviateishii Pravitel'stvuiushchii Sinod. *Sostav Sv. Prav. Sinoda i rossiiskoi tserkovnoi ierarkhii na 1915g.* Petrograd, 1915.

_____. *Spiski Sluzhaishchikh po Vedomstvu Pravoslavnago Ispovedaniia za 1915g.* Petrograd, 1915.

Threskeftike kai Ethnike Egkyklopaideia. 12 vols. Athens, 1966.

Vernadsky, George, Ralph T. Fischer, and Sergei Pushkarev, eds. *A Source Book for Russian History from Earliest Times to 1917.* 3 vols. New Haven: Yale University Press, 1972.

Volkov, A. F., and Iu D. Filipov, eds. *Svod Zakonov Rossiiskoi Imperii.* 4th ed. 2 vols. St. Petersburg, 1904-1905.

B. GENERAL WORKS

Altholz, Josef, L. *The Churches in the Nineteenth Century.* Indianapolis: Bobbs-Merrill, 1967.

Bolotov, V. V. *Lektsii po Istorii Drevnei Tserkvi.* Petrograd, 1918.

Florinsky, Michael T. *Russia: A History and an Interpretation.* 2 vols. New York: Macmillan, 1966.

Fortescue, Adrian. *The Orthodox Eastern Church*. New York, 1907.
Lebedev, Alexei P. *Istoriia Greko-vostochnoi Tserkvi pod vlastiiu Turok. Ot padeniia Konstantinopolia (1453g.) do nastoiashchego vremeni*. 2nd ed. St. Petersburg, 1903.
_____. *Dukhovenstvo drevnei Vselenskoi Tserkvi*. Moscow 1905.
_____. *Vselenskie Sobory VI, VII, i VIII vekov*. St. Petersburg, 1904.
Leroy-Beaulieu, Anatole. *The Empire of the Tsars and the Russians*. Tr. Zenaida Ragozin. 3 vols. New York, 1902.
Makarii Bulgakov. *Istoriia Russkoi Tserkvi*. 11 vols. St. Petersburg, 1889-1903.
Maloney, George A. *A History of Orthodox Theology since 1453*. Belmont, Mass.: Nordland, 1976.
Miliukov, Pavel N. *Ocherki po Istorii Russkoi Kul'tury*. 10 vols. in 2. St. Petersburg, 1909, 1916.
Nichols, Robert L., and T. G. Stavrou, eds. *Russian Orthodoxy under the Old Regime*. Minneapolis: University of Minnesota Press, 1978.
Palmieri, Aurelio. *La Chiesa Russa, le sue odierne condizioni e il suo riformismo dottrinale*. Florence, 1908.
Pipes, Richard. *Russia Under the Old Regime*. New York: Charles Scribner's Sons, 1974.
Schmemann, Alexander. *The Historical Road of Eastern Orthodoxy*. New York: Holt, Rinehart and Winston, 1963.
Smolitsch, Igor. *Geschichte der Russischen Kirche, 1700-1917*. Leiden: E. J. Brill, 1964.
Stavrianos, Leften S. *The Balkans since 1453*. New York: Holt, Rinehart and Winston, 1961.
Vasiliev, A. A. *History of the Byzantine Empire*. 2 vols. Madison: University of Wisconsin Press, 1961.
Vernadsky, George. *A History of Russia*. 5 vols. New Haven: Yale University Press, 1943-1969.
Vlasovs'kii, Ivan. *Naris Istorii Ukrains'koi Pravoslavnoi Tserkvi*, 4 vols. New York: Ukr. Prav. Tserkva, 1955-1961.
Wallace, Donald Mackenzie. *Russia*. New York, 1881.

C. COLLECTIONS AND PUBLISHED DOCUMENTS

Antonii Khrapovitskii. *Otchet po Vysochaishe naznachenoi revizii Kievskoi Dukhovnoi Akademii v Marte i Aprele 1908 goda*. Pochaevo-Uspenskaia Lavra, 1909.
_____. *Polnoe Sobranie Sochinenii*. 4 vols. Pochaevo-Uspenskaia Lavra, 1906; Kazan, 1909.

Antonii Vadkovskii. *Rechi, Slova, i Poucheniia.* 3rd ed. St. Petersburg, 1912.

Berdiaev, Nikolai A. *Dukhovnyi Krizis intelligentsii. Stat'i po obshchestvennoi i religioznoi psikhologii, 1907-1909gg.* St. Petersburg, 1910.

Bonch-Bruevich, Vladimir D. *Iz Mira Sektantov. Sbornik Statei.* Moscow, 1922.

_____. *Materialy k Istorii i Izucheniiu religiozno-obshchestvennykh dvizhenii v Rossii.* Petrograd, 1908.

_____.. *Materialy k Istorii i Izucheniiu Russkago Sektanstva i Raskola.* St. Petersburg, 1909-1910.

Filosofov, D. V. *Neugasimaia Lampada. Stat'i po tserkovnym i religioznym voprosam.* 2 vols. Moscow, 1912.

Gosudarstvennaia Duma. *Prilozheniia k Stenograficheskim Otchetam.* Tretii sozyv, 18 vols.; chetvertyi sozyv, 21 vols. St. Petersburg, 1908-1916.

_____. *Stenograficheskie Otchety.* Pervyi-tretii sozyv, 17 vols.; chetvertyi sozyv, 13 vols. St. Petersburg, 1907-1917.

Grekulov, E. F., ed. *Religiia i tserkov' v istorii Rossii (Sovetskie Istoriki o pravoslavnoi tserkvi v Rossii).* Moscow, 1975.

Ianov, Vladimir. "Protokol Otdel'nago Korpusa Zhandarmov, Ianvaria 13-go, 1905gg." *Krasnaia Letopis',* I (1922), 311-322.

Iasevich-Borodaevskaia, Varvara I., ed. *Materialy k Vysochaishemu Ukazu 12 Dekabria 1904g.* St. Petersburg, n.d.

Ivantsov-Platonov, Alexander M. *O Russkom Tserkovnom Upravlenii. Dvadtsat' statei iz NN. 1-16 gazety "Rus'" 1882 toma.* St. Petersburg, 1898.

Kladovnikov, Semen. "Protokol Otdel'nago Korpusa Zhandarmov, 27 Ianvaria, 1905g." *Krasnaia Letopis',* I (1922), 322-325.

Komitet Ministrov. *Osoboe Soveshchanie o voprosakh o zhelatel'nykh preobrazovaniiakh v postanovke Pravoslavnoi Tserkvi.* St. Petersburg, 1905.

_____. *Zhurnaly Komiteta Ministrov po Ispolneniiu Ukaza 12 Dekabria 1904g.* St. Petersburg, 1908.

K Tserkovnomu Soboru: Sbornik gruppy Peterburgskikh Sviashchennikov. St. Petersburg, 1906.

Kuznetsov, Nikolai D. *Preobrazovaniia v Russkoi Tserkvi. Rassmotrenie Voprosa po Ofitsial'nym Dokumentam v sviazy s potrebnostiami zhizni.* Moscow, 1906.

Lavrov, A. F. *Predpolagaemaia Reforma tserkovnago suda.* 2 vols. St. Petersburg, 1873-1874.

Ministerstvo Vnutrennykh Del. "Doklad Direktora Departamenta Politsii Lopukhina Ministru Vnutrennykh Del o sobitiiakh 9-go Ianvaria, 1905g." *Krasnaia Letopis',* I (1922), 330.

_____. "Spravka Ministerstva Vnutrennykh Del." *Krasnaia Letopis',* I (1922), 297-298, 330-332.

——————. "Upravlenie Moskovskago General-Gubernatora Gospodinu Ministru Vnutrennykh Del." *Krasnaia Letopis'*, I (1922), 300-301.

Pobedonostsev, Konstantin P. *38 Pisem byvshago Ober-Prokurora Sviateishago Sinoda K. P. Pobedonostseva k vysokopreosviashchenneishemu Makariiu, Arkhiepiskopu Tomskomu,* Tomsk, 1910.

——————. *Questions religieuses, sociales, et politiques.* Paris, 1897.

——————. *Pis'ma i zapiski.* 2 vols. Moscow-Petrograd, 1923.

Preobrazhenskii, I. V. *Tserkovnaia Reforma. Sbornik statei dukhovnoi i svetskoi periodicheskoi pechati pro voprosu o reforme.* St. Petersburg, 1905.

Rozanov, Vasilii V. *Okolo Tserkovnykh Sten.* 2 vols. St. Petersburg, 1906.

Skvortsov, Vasilii M. *Tserkovnyi Svet i Gosudarstvennyi Razum. Opyt tserkovno-politicheskoi khrestomatii.* 2 vols. St. Petersburg, 1912-1913.

Stechkin-Stroev, Sergei. "Protokol Otdel'nago Korpusa Zhandarmov, 3-go Fevralia, 1905g." *Krasnaia Letopis'*, I (1922), 326-327.

Sviateishii Pravitel'stvuiushchii Sinod. *Otzyvy Eparkhial'nykh Arkhiereev po Voprosu o tserkovnoi reforme.* 3 vols. St. Petersburg, 1906.

——————. *Polnoe Sobranie postanovlenii i rasporiazhenii po Vedomstvu Pravoslavnago Ispovedaniia.* 10 vols. St. Petersburg, 1869-1916.

——————. *Predsobornoe Soveshchanie.* 5 vols. St. Petersburg, 1912-1916.

——————. *Vsepoddaneishii Otchet Ober-Prokurora Sviateishago Sinoda (K. Pobedonostsev) po Vedomstvu Pravoslavnago Ispovedaniia.* 17 vols. *(za 1888-1889gg.; za 1890-1891gg.; za 1892-1893gg.; za 1894-1895gg.; za 1896-1897gg.; za 1898g.; za 1899g.; za 1900g.; za 1901g.; za 1902g.; za 1903-1904gg.; za 1905-1907gg.; za 1908-1909gg.; za 1910g.; za 1911-1912gg.; za 1913g.; za 1914g.)* St. Petersburg, 1891-1916.

——————. *Zhurnaly i Protokoly Zasedanii Vysochaishe Uchrezhdennago Predsobornago Prisutstviia.* 4 vols. St. Petersburg, 1906-1907.

Vekhi: Sbornik Statei o russkoi intelligentsii. Moscow, 1909.

D. MEMOIRS OF CONTEMPORARIES

Bulgakov, Sergei N. *Avtobiograficheskiia Zametki.* Paris: YMCA Press, 1946.

Evlogii Georgievskii, *Put' Moei Zhizni. Vospominaniia Mitropolita Evlogiia, Izlozhennye po ego rasskazam T. Manukhinoi.* Paris: YMCA Press, 1947.

Gapon, Georgii. *Story of My Life.* New York, 1906.

_____. *Zapiski Georgiia Gapona: Ocherk rabochnago dvizheniia v Rossii 1900-1905kh godov.* Moscow, 1918.

Kizevetter, A. A. *Na Rubezhe Dvukh Stoletii (Vospominaniia 1881-1914).* Prague, 1929.

Moscow Patriarchate. *Patriarkh Sergii i ego Dukhovnoe Nasledstvo.* Moscow, 1947.

Nevison, Henry W. *The Dawn in Russia: Scenes in the Russian Revolution.* London, 1906.

Nikon Rklitskii. *Zhizneopisanie Blazheneishago Antoniia, Mitropolit Kievskago i Galitskago.* 10 vols. New York: Severo-Amerikanskaia i Kanadskaia Eparkhiia, 1953-1963.

Pares, Bernard. *Russia and Reform.* London, 1907.

Preobrazhenskii, I. V. K. P. *Pobedonostsev. Ego Lichnost' i deiatel'nost' v predstavlenii sovremennikov ego konchiny.* St. Petersburg, 1912.

Shavel'skii, Georgii I. *Vospominaniia Poslednago Protopresvitera Russkoi Armii i Flota.* New York: Izd. Chekova, 1954.

Vinogradov, Vasilii V. *O Nekotorykh Vazhneishikh Momentakh poslednago perioda zhizni i deiatel'nosti Sv. Patriarkha Tikhona, 1923-1925gg.* Munich, 1959.

Vitalii Maksimenko. *Motivy Moei Zhizni.* Jordanville, N.Y.: Holy Trinity Monastery, 1955.

Witte, Sergei Iu. *Vospominaniia: Tsarstvovanie Nikolaia II.* 2 vols. Berlin, 1922.

E. MONOGRAPHS

Anderson, Vladimir. *Staroobriadchestvo i Sektanstvo.* St. Petersburg, 1904.

Averkh, A. Ia. *Stolypin i Tret'ia Duma.* Moscow, 1968.

Barsov, Timofei V. *Sinodal'naia Uchrezhdeniia nastoiashchago vremeni.* St. Petersburg, 1899.

_____. *Sviateishii Sinod v ego proshlom.* St. Petersburg, 1895.

Blagovidov, F. V. *K Rabote obshchestvennoi Mysli po Voprosu o Tserkovnoi Reforme.* Kazan, 1905.

Bogolepov, Alexander A. *Church Reforms in Russia, 1905-1918.* Tr. A. E. Moorehouse. Bridgeport, Conn.: Russian Orthodox Church of America, 1966.

Bowlt, John E. *The Silver Age: Russian Art in the Early Twentieth*

Century and the "World of Art" Group. Newtonville, Mass.: Oriental Research Partners, 1979.

Byrnes, Robert F. *Pobedonostsev: His Life and Thought.* Bloomington: Indiana University Press, 1969.

Charques, Richard. *The Twilight of Imperial Russia.* London: Oxford Paperbacks, 1965.

Chetverikov, Sergei. *Opisanie Zhizni Optinskago Startsa Ieroskhimonakh Amvrosiia.* Kaluga, 1912.

Chmielewski, Edward. *The Polish Question in the Russian State Duma.* Knoxville: University of Tennessee Press, 1970.

Cracraft, James. *The Church Reform of Peter the Great.* Stanford, Calif.: University Press, 1971.

Crummey, Robert O. *The Old Believers and the World of Antichrist: The Vyg Community and the Russian State, 1649-1855.* Madison: University of Wisconsin Press, 1970.

Curtiss, John S. *Church and State in Russia, 1900-1917.* New York: Octagon Books, 1965.

Dunlop, John B. *Staretz Amvrosy: Model for Dostoevsky's Staretz Zossima.* Belmont, Mass.: Nordland, 1972.

Durasoff, S. *The Russian Protestants.* Rutherford, N.J.: Fairleigh Dickinson University Press, 1969.

Emeliakh, L. I. *Antiklerikal'noe Dvizhenie Krestian v period pervoi russkoi revoliutsii.* Moscow, 1965.

Fülop-Miller, René. *Rasputin, the Holy Devil.* New York: Viking, 1929.

Galai, Shmuel. *The Liberation Movement in Russia, 1900-1905.* Cambridge, England: University Press, 1973.

Gapon, Georgii. *Poslanie k Russkomu Krestianskomu i Rabochemu Narodu.* St. Petersburg, 1905.

Gidulianov, P. V. *Mitropolity v pervye tri Veka Khristianstva.* Moscow, 1905.

Golubinskii, E. E. *O Reforme v byte Russkoi Tserkvi.* Moscow, 1913.

Gussarova, A. *Mir Iskusstva.* Leningrad, 1972.

Haltzel, Michael. *Der Abbau der deutschen ständischen Selbstverwaltung in den Ostseeprovinzen Russlands: Ein Beitrag zur Geschichte der russischen Unifizierungspolitik 1855-1905.* Marburg/Lahn: J. G. Herder-Institut, 1977.

Harcave, Sidney. *First Blood: The Russian Revolution of 1905.* New York: Macmillan, 1964 .

Kalinin, G. M. *Reformy Veroterpimosti na Poroge XX veka i Sostoianie gosudarstvennoi Tserkvi v Rossii.* Nizhni-Novgorod, 1905.

Krachkovskii, Iulian F. *Piatidesiatletie Vossoedineniia zapadnorusskikh Uniatov s Pravoslavnoiu Tserkov'iu (1839-1889gg.).* Vilna, 1889.

Kurganov, F. A. *Ustroistvo Upravleniia v Tserkvi Korolevstva Grecheskago.* Kazan, 1871.

Medlin, William K. *Moscow and East Rome: A Political Study of the Relations of Church and State in Muscovite Russia.* Geneva: Librairie E. Droz, 1952.

Mehlinger, Howard D., and John M. Thompson. *Count Witte and the Tsarist Government in the 1905 Revolution.* Bloomington: Indiana University Press, 1972.

Mel'gunov, S. P. *Iz Istorii Religiozno-obshchestvennykh dvizhenii v Rossii XIX veka. Staroobriadchestvo. Religioznyia Goneniia.* Moscow, 1919.

_____. *Staroobriadchestvo i Osvoboditel'noe Dvizhenie.* Moscw, 1906.

Muller, Alexander V. *The Spiritual Regulation of Peter the Great.* Seattle: University of Washington Press, 1972.

Myshtsyn, Vasilii N. *Po Tserkovno-obshchestvennym Voprosam.* 2 vols. Sergiev Posad, 1905-1906.

Ognev, N. V. *Na Poroge Reforma Russkoi Tserkvi i Dukhovenstva.* St. Petersburg, 1907.

Papkov, Alexander A. *Neobkhodimost' Obnovleniia Pravoslavnago Tserkovno-obshchestvennago stroia.* St. Petersburg, 1902.

_____. *Tserkovno-obshchestvennye voprosy v epokhu Tsaria Osvoboditelia.* St. Petersburg, 1902.

Pares, Bernard. *The Fall of the Russian Monarchy.* London, 1939.

Pascale, Pierre. *Avvakum et les Débuts du Raskol.* Paris, 1938.

Pipes, Richard. *Social Democracy and the St. Petersburg Labor Movement, 1885-1897.* Cambridge: Harvard University Press, 1963.

_____. *Struve: Liberal on the Left.* Cambridge: Harvard University Press, 1970.

Pokrovskii, I. M. *Russkie eparkhii v XVI-XIX vekakh, ikh otkrytie, sostavi i predely. Opyt tserkovno-istoricheskogo statisticheskogo i geograficheskogo issledovaniia.* 2 vols. Kazan, 1897, 1913.

Polish Research Center. *The Orthodox Eastern Church in Poland.* London, 1942.

Polsky, Michel. *Les Nouveaux Martyrs Russes.* Montsurs: Editions Resiac, 1976.

Prokoptschuk, Gregor. *Metropolit Andreas Graf Scheptyskyj: Leben und Wirken des grossen Förderers der Kirchenunion.* Munich: Verlag Ukraine, 1967.

Prugavin, Alexander S. *Staroobriadchestvo vo Vtoroi Polovine XIX veka. Ocherki iz noveishii istoriia raskola.* Moscow, 1904.

Roberts, Spencer E., tr. *The Four Faces of Rozanov: Christianity, Sex, Jews, and the Russian Revolution.* New York: Philosophical Library, 1978.

Rozhkov, Vladimir, *Tserkovnye Voprosy v Gosudarstvennoi Dume,* Rome: Opere Religiose Russe, 1975.

Runciman, Stephan. *The Great Church in Captivity.* London: Cambridge University Press, 1968.

——————. *The Orthodox Churches and the Secular State*, Trentham, New Zealand: Auckland University Press, 1971.

Sablinsky, Walter. *The Road to Bloody Sunday: Father Gapon and the St. Petersburg Massacre of 1905*. Princeton: University Press, 1976.

Salisbury, Harrison. *Black Night, White Snow: Russia's Revolutions, 1905-1917*. Garden City, N.Y.: Doubleday, 1978.

Schneiderman, Jeremiah. *Sergei Zubatov and Revolutionary Marxism: The Struggle for the Working Class in Tsarist Russia*. Ithaca: Cornell University Press, 1976.

Schwartz, Solomon. *The Russian Revolution of 1905*. Chicago: University Press, 1969.

Semenov, Mikhail. *Svoboda Khristianstva*. Moscow, 1906.

Sokolov, Ioann. *Konstantinopol'skaia Tserkov' v XIX veke*. St. Petersburg, 1904.

Soloviev, Vladimir. *La Russie et l'Église Universelle*. Paris, 1889.

Stavrou, T. G., ed. *Russia under the Last Tsar*. Minneapolis: University of Minnesota Press, 1969.

Svitich, Alexander. *Pravoslavnaia Tserkov' v Pol'she i ee Avtokefaliia*. Buenos Aires: Nasha Strana, 1959.

Tikhomirov, Lev. A. *Monarkhicheskaia Gosudarstvennost'*. Buenos Aires: Russkoe Slovo, 1968.

Titlinov, Boris V. *Tserkov' vo Vremia Revoliutsii*. Petrograd, 1924.

Vvedenskii. A. I. *Tserkov' i Gosudarstvo. Ocherk vzaimootnoshenii Tserkvi i Gosudarstva v Rossii, 1918-1922*. Moscow, 1923.

Zaozerskii, Nikolai A. *O Tserkovnoi Vlasti*, Sergiev Posad, 1894.

——————. *O Nuzhdakh Tserkovnoi Zhizni Nastoiashchego Vremeni*. Sergiev Posad, 1909.

Zernov, Nicolas. *The Russian Religious Renaissance of the Twentieth Century*. New York: Harper and Row, 1963.

F. ARTICLES

Aksakov, Nikolai P. "Vsetserkovnyi Sobor i vybornoe nachalo v Tserkvi. Ot gruppy Peterburgskikh Sviashchennikov. Otvet na zapisku Antoniia, Ep. Volinskago." *Bogoslovskii Vestnik*, III, 12 (1905), 711-777.

Antonii Khrapovitskii. "Pervaia Dokladnaia zapiska Sviateishemu Pravitel'stvuiushchemu Sinodu." *Bogoslovskii Vestnik*, III, 12 (1905), 698-710.

Berdnikov, I. S. "K Voprosu o Preobrazovanii Eparkhial'nago Upravleniia." *Pravoslavnyi Sobesednik*, I, 2 (1906), 20-35.

Kamenev, S. Iu. "S. Iu. Vitte i K. P. Pobedonostsev o sovremennom polozhenii Pravoslavnoi Tserkvi." *Vestnik Evropy*, I, 2 (February 1909), 651-691.

Kireev, Alexander A. "Sovremennoe Polozhenie Starokatolicheskago Voprosa. Pis'ma russkoi S. Peterburgskoi Komissii—Komissii Starokatolicheskoi (Rotterdamskoi). Otvet Komissii uchrezhdennoi v Rotterdame i preobrazovanoi v Gaage, dlia vozsoedineniia Starokatolicheskoi i Russko-Pravoslavnoi Tserkvi—vysokochtimoi S. Peterburgskoi Komissii, 6 (19) Iulia 1907." *Bogoslovskii Vestnik*, III, 11 (1908), 423-454.

Korol'kov, I. "Pamiati Mitropolita Antoniia." *Trudy Kievskoi Dukhovnoi Akademii*, no. 4 (1916), 481-497.

Lebedev, Alexei P. "O proiskhozhdenii aktov Vselenskikh Soborov." *Bogoslovskii Vestnik*, II, 5 (1904), 46-74.

_____. "Ob uchastii mirian na soborakh." *Dushepoleznoe Chtenie*, no. 3 (1906), 350-394.

_____. "Zachem by nam nuzhen Patriarkh? Iz universitetskikh lektsii 1906g." *Bogoslovskii Vestnik*, I, 1 (1907), 1-59.

Malvy, Antoine. "La Reforme de l'Église Russe." *Études*, CVII (1906), 160-182, 306-329.

Mishchenko, F. I. "O Sostave predstoiashchago pomestnago sobora Vserossiiskoi Tserkvi." *Trudy Kievskoi Dukhovnoi Akademii* (1906), 50-111.

Pavlov, A. S. "Otnoshenie Tserkvi k gosudarstvu." *Bogoslovskii Vestnik*, I, 2 (1902), 213-240; I, 3, 436-457.

_____. "Otnoshenie Tserkvi k neprinadlezhashchim ei khristianskim obshchestvam." *Bogoslovskii Vestnik*, I, 4 (1902), 647-672.

Petrov, Nikolai. "Zapiski o Gapone." *Vsemirnyi Vestnik*, III (1907), 58-61.

Rogger, Hans. "Was there a Russian Fascism?" *Journal of Modern History*, 36 (December 1964), 398-415.

Simon, Gerhardt. "Antonij Vadkovskij, Metropolit von St. Petersburg (1846-1912)." *Kirche im Osten*, 12 (1969), 9-32.

Smolitsch, Igor. "Der Konzilsvorbereitungsausschuss des Jahres 1906. Zur vorbeschichte des Moskauer Landeskonzil von 1917-1918." *Kirche im Osten*, 7 (1964), 53-93.

Sokolov, S. P. "Skorbnyi List Dukhovnykh Seminarii v 1906-1907 uchebnom godu." *Bogoslovskii Vestnik*, II, 5 (1907), 230-246.

Svetlov, Pavel Ia. "O Novom Mnimom Prepiastvii k edineniiu Starokatolikov i Pravoslavnykh." *Bogoslovskii Vestnik*, II, 5 (1903), 134-150.

Tikhomirov, Lev. A. "Zaprosy Zhizni i Nashe Tserkovnoe Upravlenie." *Moskovskiia Vedomosti*, nos. 343-345 (December 13-15, 1902).

Tikhomirov, P. V. "Kanonicheskoe dostoinstvo reformy Petra Velikago po tserkovnomu upravleniiu. Neskol'ko istoriko-kanonicheskikh spavochki soobrazhenii v dopolnenie k stat'im L. A. Tikhomirova i N. A. Zaozerskago o tserkovnom upravlenii i tserkovnoi vlasti." *Bogoslovskii Vestnik*, I, 1 (1904), 75-106; I, 2, 217-247.

Valliere, Paul R. "The Problem of Liberal Orthodoxy in Russia, 1905." *St. Vladimir's Theological Quarterly*, 22, 3 (1976), 115-131.

Witte, Sergei Iu. "O Sovremennom Polozhenii Pravoslavnoi Tserkvi." *Slovo*, no. 108 (March 28, 1905).

──────. "Voprosy o Zhelatel'nykh Preobrazovaniiakh v postanovke u nas Pravoslavnoi Tserkvi." *Slovo*, no. 108 (March 28, 1905).

Zaozerskii, Nikolai A. "Chto est' Pravoslavnyi Prikhod, i chem on dolzhen byt'?" *Bogoslovskii Vestnik*, III, 11 (1911), 523-562; III, 12, 653-687.

──────. "Istoricheskoe obozrenie istochnikov prava Pravoslavnoi Tserkvi." *Kanonicheskie Istochniki*, I (1891).

──────. "Okruzhno-Mitropolich'e upravlenie." *Bogoslovskii Vestnik*, I, 1 (1906), 131-133.

──────. "Osnovanyia nachala zhelatel'nago dlia Russkoi Tserkvi uchrezhdeniia Patriarshestva." *Bogoslovskii Vestnik*, III, 12 (1905), 625-657.

──────. "Proekt organizatsii tserkovnago ustroistva na nachalakh patriarshe-sobornoi formy." *Bogoslovskii Vestnik*, I, 1 (1906), 124-144.

Zavitnevich, Vladimir. "O Vozstanovlenii Sobornosti v Russkoi Tserkvi." *Tserkovnyi Vestnik*, XIX (April 7, 1905).

Zubatov, Sergei. "Zubatovshchina." *Byloe*, no. 4 (1917), 170-172.

Index